Political Journalism in London, 1695–1720

Studies in the Eighteenth Century
2398–9904

This major series from Boydell & Brewer, published in association with the British Society for Eighteenth-Century Studies, aims to bring into fruitful dialogue the different disciplines involved in all aspects of the study of the long eighteenth century (c.1660–1820). It publishes innovative volumes, singly or co-authored, on any topic in history, science, music, literature and the visual arts in any area of the world in the long eighteenth century and particularly encourages proposals that explore links among the disciplines, and which aim to develop new cross-disciplinary fields of enquiry.

Series editors: Ros Ballaster, University of Oxford, UK; Matthew Grenby, Newcastle University, UK; Robert D. Hume, Penn State University, USA; Mark Knights, University of Warwick, UK; Renaud Morieux, University of Cambridge, UK

Previously published

Material Enlightenment: Women Writers and the Science of Mind, 1770–1830, Joanna Wharton, 2018

Celebrity Culture and the Myth of Oceania in Britain, 1770–1823, Ruth Scobie, 2019

British Sociability in the Long Eighteenth Century: Challenging the Anglo-French Connection, edited by Valérie Capdeville and Alain Kerhervé, 2019

Things that Didn't Happen: Writing, Politics and the Counterhistorical, 1678–1743, John McTague, 2019

Converting Britannia: Evangelicals and British Public Life, 1770–1840, Gareth Atkins, 2019

British Catholic Merchants in the Commercial Age, 1670–1714, Giada Pizzoni, 2020

Lessons of Travel in Eighteenth-Century France: From Grand Tour to School Trips, Gábor Gelléri, 2020

Political Journalism in London, 1695–1720: Defoe, Swift, Steele and their Contemporaries, Ashley Marshall, 2020

Fictions of Presence: Theatre and Novel in Eighteenth-Century Britain, Ros Ballaster, 2020

Ephemeral Print Culture in Early Modern England: Sociability, Politics and Collecting, Tim Somers, 2021

The Geographies of Enlightenment Edinburgh, Phil Dodds, 2022

Changing Pedagogies for Children in Eighteenth-Century England, Michèle Cohen, 2023

Political Journalism in London, 1695–1720

Defoe, Swift, Steele and their Contemporaries

Ashley Marshall

THE BOYDELL PRESS

Published in association with

© Ashley Marshall 2020

All Rights Reserved. Except as permitted under current legislation no part of this work may be photocopied, stored in a retrieval system, published, performed in public, adapted, broadcast, transmitted, recorded or reproduced in any form or by any means, without the prior permission of the copyright owner

The right of Ashley Marshall to be identified as the author of this work has been asserted in accordance with sections 77 and 78 of the Copyright, Designs and Patents Act 1988

First published 2020
The Boydell Press, Woodbridge
Paperback edition 2024

ISBN 978 1 78327 545 8 Hardback
ISBN 978 1 83765 129 0 Paperback

The Boydell Press is an imprint of Boydell & Brewer Ltd
PO Box 9, Woodbridge, Suffolk IP12 3DF, UK
and of Boydell & Brewer Inc.
668 Mt Hope Avenue, Rochester, NY 14620–2731, USA
website: www.boydellandbrewer.com

A CIP catalogue record for this book is available
from the British Library

The publisher has no responsibility for the continued existence or accuracy of URLs for external or third-party internet websites referred to in this book, and does not guarantee that any content on such websites is, or will remain, accurate or appropriate

*For Ron Paulson,
mentor, friend, confidant*

Contents

Acknowledgements ix

Works Frequently Cited xi

Introduction 1

Part I: Mapping Early Eighteenth-Century Political Journalism

1 The Culture of Political Journalism, 1695–1714 13
2 Early Hanoverian Political Journalism, 1714–1720 45

Part II: Defoe, Swift, Steele

3 Power and Politics in Defoe's Radical *Review* 81
4 Swift, Oldisworth, and St. John: The High Toryism of *The Examiner* 125
5 Steele's Party Journalism 157

Part III: Envisioning and Engaging Readers

6 The Journalists on Popular Politics and Public Engagement 199

Conclusion: Journalism and Authority 249
Appendix: London Political Newspapers and Periodicals, 1695–1720: A Tabular Representation 257

Bibliography 293
Index 309

Acknowledgements

This book was completed thanks to support from the University of Nevada, especially from the Department of English and the College of Liberal Arts. A generous Scholarly and Creative Activities Grant made travel to archives at the University of California-Berkeley, the University of Texas, and the British Library possible. A year-long sabbatical gave me the time to do the requisite archival research and to complete the manuscript. I am grateful to the guides and librarians who helped me find what I needed, and to the librarians at the University of Nevada for working so hard to obtain microfilms and for making other resources available. I am also grateful to my colleagues, and especially to my former Chair, Eric Rasmussen, for providing support letters and more general – and more important – encouragement. I want also to recognise my friends at the University of Nevada and beyond it, who make this such a wonderful place to work and to live.

My most faithful readers continue to be Rob Hume and Ron Paulson, both of whom are generous in their counsel and helpful in their perspective. Rob is as thoughtful, careful, and sharp a reader as one could ever have, and his admirable instincts and his meticulous attention to detail have done me a world of good as a scholar since my first semester of graduate school. Ron's perspective is almost always a bit different from my own, which means he helps me see what I usually haven't seen; his combination of intellectual rigor and methodological flexibility makes him as excellent a reader as he is a scholar. This book is dedicated to him, for his years of patience, advice, instruction, confidence-keeping, and friendship.

I continue in gratitude for the friends and colleagues in the field who have offered practical assistance, kindness, and support over the fifteen years of my publishing career. This includes Eve Bannett, Brian Cowan, Alan Downie, Brean Hammond, Gene Hammond, Ian Higgins, Kirsten Juhas, Jim May, Andreas Mueller, Alex Pettit, Hermann Real, Ric Reverend, Peter Sabor, Marcus Walsh, Howard Weinbrot, Cal Winton, and James Woolley. I would also add to that list the late Bill Speck, whose pioneering work on Swift's *The Examiner* was crucial to me as I launched this book and who was unfailingly generous and supportive in our conversations. One part of the Swift chapter was presented at the Seventh Münster Symposium on Jonathan Swift (June 2017), and I am grateful both to the principal organisers of that fabulous event (Kirsten Juhas and Hermann Real, as well as the vitally important Erika Real) and also to all of the attendees who made it such an extraordinary symposium. Many thanks to the anonymous readers of my manuscript for Boydell and Brewer, whose extensive, thoughtful, and constructive commentary genuinely made this a better book.

I want to thank my family for all the support and understanding along the way and for cheering me on no matter what from the beginning. And to Stephen, always, for keeping me in the game.

My biggest thanks go to my partner in all things, David Fenimore: for love and comfort and dinners and pep talks and perspective, and for all the life we've lived, and for all the more to come.

Works Frequently Cited

The Spectator	Addison, Joseph, and Richard Steele, *et al.*, *The Spectator*, ed. Donald F. Bond (5 vols., Oxford: Clarendon Press, 1965).
The Tatler	Addison, Joseph, and Richard Steele, *et al.*, *The Tatler*, ed. Donald F. Bond (3 vols., Oxford: Clarendon Press, 1987).
The Review	Defoe, Daniel, *Review of the Affairs of France* (1704–1713), ed. John McVeagh. 9 vols. in 18 books (London: Pickering & Chatto, 2003–2011).
The Englishman	Steele, Richard, *The Englishman: A Political Journal*, ed. Rae Blanchard (Oxford: Clarendon Press, 1955).
The Guardian	Steele, Richard, *The Guardian*, ed. John Calhoun Stephens (Lexington: University Press of Kentucky, 1982).
Steele's Periodical Journalism	Steele, Richard, *Steele's Periodical Journalism, 1714–1716*, ed. Rae Blanchard (Oxford: Clarendon Press, 1959).
Tracts and Pamphlets	Steele, Richard, *Tracts and Pamphlets by Richard Steele*, ed. Rae Blanchard (1944; Rpt. New York: Octagon Books, 1967).
English Political Writings	Swift, Jonathan, *English Political Writings 1711–1714: The Conduct of the Allies and Other Works*, ed. Bertrand A. Goldgar and Ian Gadd (Cambridge: Cambridge University Press, 2008).
The Examiner	Swift, Jonathan, *The Examiner* (wr. by Swift, 1710–1711), in *Swift vs. Mainwaring:* The Examiner *and* The Medley, ed. Frank H. Ellis (Oxford: Clarendon Press, 1985).

Introduction

> "'Tis the *Press* that has made 'um *Mad*, and the *Press* must set 'um *Right* again'
> – Roger L'Estrange, *Observator*, 13 April 1681

> 'Burke said there were Three Estates in Parliament; but, in the Reporters' Gallery yonder, there sat a Fourth Estate more important...'
> – Thomas Carlyle, *On heroes, hero-worship and the heroic in history* (1841)

The remarkable boom in political journalism and newspapers during Queen Anne's reign (1702–1714) is well known. Historians of the press and of late Stuart Britain have done excellent work on the 'why' of an emergent daily press, and on the causes and nature of the transformation after 1695. They highlight the lapse of the Licensing Act that year as a signal moment in the history of printing and of public politics. As W. A. Speck concludes, 'The most spectacular effect of the end of censorship was the rise of the newspaper'.[1] Remarkably little scholarship, however, has been devoted to the content and clashing, evolving ideologies of London's political papers – the focus of the present study.

The growth of political journalism was driven by and contributed to the bitter partisan controversy of the early eighteenth century: party considerations infused every aspect of English society, and the epithet often applied to these years ('the rage of party') is richly earned. The rise of a daily press not only 'greatly facilitated the political education of Londoners', but also 'contributed to an ideological polarisation of public opinion along party lines'.[2] The intensity of the conflict was sustained by Triennial elections: between 1679 and 1716, sixteen general elections occurred, an average of one every two and a half years. Add to these factors the passionate debates about the monarch's power versus parliamentary rights, about the expensive and seemingly endless War of the Spanish Succession, about the

---

[1] Speck, 'Political Propaganda in Augustan England', *Transactions of the Royal Historical Society*, 5th series 22 (1972), 17–32, at p. 20. See also Siebert's *Freedom of the Press in England 1476–1776: The Rise and Decline of Government Controls* (Urbana, 1952), pp. 306–18.
[2] Gary S. De Krey, *A Fractured Society: The Politics of London in the First Age of Party 1688–1715* (Oxford, 1985), p. 215.

succession to the English throne, and a whole host of other disputed topics – and the result is a staggering amount of printed polemic. Another clear consequence of this change is the politicisation of the people and the drastic expansion of public politics. Jürgen Habermas's conclusions in *The Structural Transformation of the Public Sphere* are admittedly problematic – but late Stuart and early Hanoverian commentators acknowledged that something important had shifted. The author of *The Commentator* (1720; Defoe?) eloquently describes the early eighteenth century, with the rise of a daily newspaper press, as 'the *Dawn* of *Politicks* among the Common People'.[3] 'Daily' signifies a wholly new concept of public politics: Richard Steele's description of newspapers as 'the Histories of every Day' underscores the diurnal reinterpretation of past and present events.[4]

The sheer scale of newspaper production in Anne's reign is impressive, and never mind the talent behind some of the papers – Jonathan Swift, Joseph Addison, Defoe, Steele, Arthur Mainwaring, John Oldmixon, to name only the most familiar of the pens. In 1704, roughly 44,000 copies of papers were printed weekly; by 1712, the total was closer to 70,000. In 1709, at least eighteen papers were published weekly or more frequently – 55 issues, *in toto*, per week.[5] Between 1712 and 1716, as many as 45 journals were launched. Small wonder contemporaries voiced concern about the sudden and prodigious proliferation of print matter. Defoe's reflection in *The Review* that there are 'above two Hundred Thousand single Papers publish'd every Week in this Nation' (vol. 7, p. 4) is obviously an exaggeration, but it does signal his sense of the news deluge. In 1703, one author cautioned, 'the Liberty of the Press will be the ruin of the Nation', and though his Tory conviction of the madness of 'appeal[ing] to the Collective Body of the People' is not surprising,[6] the Whigs were not without their own anxieties. The author of *An Essay on the Regulation of the Press* (1704; Defoe?) concludes, ''tis pitty the Press should come into a Party-strife' (12). Liberty of the press had its defenders, but no one could deny that the culture had changed: 'What Heaps of *Nonsense and Forgery!* What Reams of

---

[3] Daniel Defoe, *Religious and Didactic Writings of Daniel Defoe*, vol. 9: *The Commentator*, ed. P. N. Furbank (London, 2007), no. 2 (p. 24). P. N. Furbank and W. R. Owens list this work as a probable attribution (*A Critical Bibliography of Daniel Defoe* [London, 1998]).

[4] Steele, *The Englishman: A Political Journal*, ed. Rae Blanchard (Oxford, 1955), p. 392.

[5] These numbers show up, with slight variations, in a number of sources. See for example Andrew Pettegree, *The Invention of the News: How the World Came to Know about Itself* (New Haven, 2014), p. 245.

[6] *A Dialogue Between A Member of Parliament. . . and a Country Farmer* (London, 1703), p. 5.

Declarations, Manifesto's, Hymns, Ballads, and other merry Conceits! And what Loads of Weekly Journals!'[7] The daily deluge of printed material was a novel phenomenon, and with it came new questions about authority and authenticity.

Our own world of 'post-truth' political discourse is extreme – the degree to which fact and hard data fail to matter in partisan debate – but there was in these years an intimate relationship between news and falsification. Journalists wrote to confuse and deceive as well as to enlighten, and on both sides of the party divide propagandists spin elaborate conspiracy theories that evidently rang true to a significant part of their readership. Mark Knights contends that, 'It was integral to the polemical combat to claim that a rival was distorting the truth, telling lies, misrepresenting things to the public'; this is the '"fictional impulse" inherent in partisanship'.[8] The competing political visions and rival truth claims to be found in the journalism of this period 'exacerbated a state of epistemological uncertainty, in which readers, voters, writers and representatives were disoriented by their inability to take things at face value'. Literary scholars have appreciated that this uncertainty represents 'a causal factor in the emergence of the novel', but Knights was the first to relate it 'to the political culture around it or sufficiently related to the routine process of politics'.[9] St. John's 1709 observation that 'no man looks on things as they really are, but sees them through that glass which party holds up to him'[10] will seem painfully relevant to consumers of the modern political press. Partisanship creates and perhaps requires double vision.

Many features of this thriving culture of journalistic production have been studied. Knights's work on early modern conspiracy theories and on the problem of misrepresentation is exemplary. Scholars have studied the physical development of the newspapers;[11] circulation, especially in Lon-

---

[7] *The Commentator*, no. 3 (p. 25).
[8] Mark Knights, 'History and Literature in the Age of Defoe and Swift', *History Compass* 3 (2005), p. 11. See also his *Representation and Misrepresentation in Later Stuart Britain: Partisanship and Political Culture* (Oxford, 2005).
[9] Knights, 'History and Literature', 12.
[10] Quoted in Knights, 'History and Literature', 8; Knights cites *Camden Miscellany*, 26 ['Letters of Henry St. John', ed. H. T. Dickinson], Cam. Soc., 4th ser., vol. 14 (Cambridge, 1975), p. 147.
[11] In his study of *The English Newspaper: Some Account of the Physical Development of Journals Printed in London between 1622 and the Present Day* (Cambridge, 1932), Stanley Morison details format changes, variations in style and heading, font choices, and the use of decoration.

don;[12] the impact of the Stamp Act of 1712;[13] the sources of the foreign news reported in papers;[14] and Robert Harley's skillful use of journals to disseminate propaganda and counter-propaganda at the end of Anne's reign.[15] The provincial press has received some attention.[16] Jeremy Black has shown that the opposition press 'harmed British foreign policy by presenting a feature of a divided and disloyal nation'.[17] The role of the periodical in shaping attitudes toward femininity and masculinity has been carefully studied.[18] Literary critics have contributed thoughtful analyses of Addison and Steele's *Tatler* and *Spectator* – the two papers that have dwarfed all others in accounts of journalism in this period. Critics have, to a lesser extent, commented upon Steele's *Guardian*, Swift's *Examiner*, and Defoe's *Review*, but the emphasis has been on the 'literary' rather than on the 'political', and few accounts of the English newspaper seem interested in the 'news' dimension.

The relative lack of engagement with content has meant that surprisingly little has been done to identify the basic ideologies and shifting outlooks of even the most important periodicals. William Bragg Ewald's *The Newsmen of Queen Anne* (1956), a now dated introduction to its subject, includes a 'Descriptive List of Periodicals', but the descriptions convey little about the

---

[12] The seminal pieces are Sutherland, 'The Circulation of Newspapers and Literary Periodicals, 1700–1730', *The Library* 4th series 15 (1934),110–24; Henry Snyder, 'The Circulation of Newspapers in the Reign of Queen Anne', *The Library* 5th series 23 (1968), 206–35; and Snyder, 'A Further Note on the Circulation of Newspapers in the Reign of Queen Anne', *The Library* 5th series 31 (1976), 387–89. See also J. M. Price, 'A Note on the Circulation of the London Press, 1704–1714', *Bulletin of the Institute of Historical Research* 31 (1958), 215–24.

[13] J. A. Downie, 'The Growth of Government Tolerance of the Press', in Robin Myers and Michael Harris (eds.), *The Development of the English Book Trade, 1700–1899* (Oxford, 1981), pp. 36–65, esp. pp. 52–56; J. A. Downie, *Robert Harley and the Press: Propaganda and Public Opinion in the Age of Swift and Defoe* (Cambridge, 1979), Ch. 7.

[14] Black, 'The British Press and Europe in the Early Eighteenth Century', in Michael Harris and Alan Lee (eds.), *The Press in English Society from the Seventeenth to Nineteenth Centuries* (Rutherford, NJ, 1986), pp. 64–79.

[15] Downie, *Robert Harley*.

[16] G. A. Cranfield, *The Development of the Provincial Newspaper 1700–1760* (Oxford, 1962); C. Y. Ferdinand, *Benjamin Collins and the Provincial Newspaper Trade in the Eighteenth Century* (Oxford, 1997). For Ireland, see Robert Munter, *The History of the Irish Newspaper, 1685–1760* (Cambridge, 1967), Ch. 6.

[17] Black, 'The British Press and Europe', p. 77.

[18] Kathryn Shevelow, *Women and Print Culture: The Construction of Femininity in the Early Periodical* (London, 1989); Shawn Lisa Maurer, *Proposing Men: Dialectics of Gender and Class in the Eighteenth-Century English Periodical* (Stanford, 1998).

focuses or commitments of the papers. When journals other than the most celebrated are named, they tend to be labelled Whig or Tory – or government and opposition – but these categories rarely get us very far. Neither Whig nor Tory papers were consistent in their identities or objectives, and all were forced to adapt to evolving political circumstances.

The first section of the book is devoted to a cartographic survey of newspapers and periodicals. The point is partly to contextualise the major periodical writers of this period – Defoe, Swift, Steele, and to a lesser extent Addison – and partly to show the different ways in which newspapers signalled ideological commitment. Chapter 1 covers the period from 1695 to 1714; Chapter 2 explores the very different milieu of early Hanoverian London. One object of these surveys is to characterise some of the ideological positions of and topical battles we find in the papers; another is to highlight the ways in which particular journals were in (usually antagonistic) conversation with one another. Few scholars, for example, tend to consider Steele's high-minded, ethically instructive *Tatler* in relation to the overtly political, aggressively Tory *Examiner*, but their authors were responding to one another, directly and indirectly. The centrality of *The Examiner* to Steele's journalism has never been fully appreciated.

The middle part of the book is devoted to closer analysis of some the major journalistic ventures of this period. Chapter 3 focuses on the issues of continuity and change in Defoe's highly influential *The Review* (1704–1713); it challenges the persistent characterisations of that paper as a ministerial outlet, arguing instead that the relationship between Mr. Review and the successive ministries under which it appeared is more unstable and ambivalent than scholars tend to assume. Chapter 4 concerns *The Examiner*, arguably the most important Tory paper of the last four years of Anne's reign. What little attention *The Examiner* has enjoyed has gone to Swift's contributions in 1710–1711; I analyse the whole life of that paper, challenging the consensus about how Swift came to be involved and why he resigned his position. The fifth chapter covers Steele's journalistic career, and seeks particularly to disentangle the politics of *The Tatler* and *The Spectator* from the agendas in his later Stuart and Hanoverian periodicals. Steele was a remarkably versatile journalist, and his succession of papers – many of which lasted only a matter of months – represent a multifaceted critique of Tory ideology and its spokesmen. Steele is as committed as any contemporary to exploring issues of political and journalistic authority; he fosters public discourse even among the 'low', and he relentlessly seeks to undermine the authority claimed by Tory propagandists.

The final chapter is devoted to the ways in which rhetorical choices reflect journalists' ideological commitments. Chapter 6 studies how periodical writers imagined and addressed 'the public', and the nature of their judgments of 'street politicks'. The point is neither to support nor to refute Habermasian notions of the 'public sphere'; the historical reality of political participation by citizens is not my concern. I am more interested in rhetorical constructions of the public. Swift, Defoe, Addison, Steele and others deliberately write about subjects and citizens in particular ways: Tory papers often use third-person and the language of subjection, tending toward homily; Whig writers address their readers (commonly 'citizens' rather than 'subjects') more directly. Most conclusions about early eighteenth-century periodicals treat them as a monolithic corpus without attending to distinguishing characteristics – including the nature of their personae (if any) and how they engaged with their envisioned audiences. Chapter 6 highlights important distinctions in terms of the manner in which journalists talk about and imagine popular politics, while also exploring the relationship between rhetorical strategies and journalistic ethos. There I also consider the marked change that occurs in the way Whigs and Tories relate to 'the people' after the Hanoverian succession, and, finally, the ways periodical writers respond to each other and read each other publicly, whether by means of animadversion, stylistic critique, or character assassination. When journalists read each other for the benefit of readers, they are trying to shape reception – and to change how readers read is to change how they participate in public politics. This chapter might be considered a complement to Rebecca Bullard and Rachel Carnell's wide-ranging and illuminating collection, *The Secret History in Literature, 1660–1820*, concerned with issues of the blurred boundaries between fact and opinion, with the problems of misrepresentation, with the limits of readerly discernment, and – most relevant for my purposes – the question of how political 'secret history trained its readers in new forms of textual engagement'.[19]

What we find reflected in early eighteenth-century journalism is a major transition: the emergence of an intensely, consistently politicised public. The surge in newspaper production both reveals and fosters an unprecedented degree of public participation in the political process. Tim Harris and other historians are surely right to warn against overemphasising the role of the press in politicising the people, and downplaying the importance of other socio-cultural processes. That said, my premise is that we need a

---

[19] Rebecca Bullard, Introduction to Bullard and Rachel Carnell (eds.), *The Secret History in Literature, 1660–1820* (Cambridge, 2017), p. 10.

clearer sense of how journalists conditioned (or tried to condition) their readers to engage in the political events of the moment.[20] The daily production and consumption of news helped politicise the people. Whig writers such as Steele and Defoe quarrel fiercely with Tories like Swift and Leslie, but they fight over more than the issues. Whether a writer addresses 'fellow citizens' or docile subjects signals an important premise about the role of journalism: was it meant to help cultivate a rational populace, or merely to convey the official message to be consumed by obedient subjects? At least in Anne's reign, Tory journalists often register discomfort with the notion that mere citizens could reflect upon the government's doings; they contest not only the ideology of their rivals but also the rhetorical relationships found in Whig papers. The culture of political journalism in these years is dynamic, and some of that energy comes from the fact that the job of journalism is itself being debated. Mr. Examiner sees his function as representing the state to the subjects, whereas Steele – sometimes quite aggressively – dins into readers their duty to be critically engaged. The notion of public politics substantially expands in the early eighteenth century, and the emergent paradigm of state accountability does not go uncontested. The daily press certainly politicised readers (or auditors) of the news; it also offered a site for debates about such politicisation.

Newspapers and periodicals positioned themselves, vis-à-vis authorities and the people, in very different ways. The Whiggism or Toryism of any particular paper is not necessarily crucial to our understanding of the culture, but mapping the range of rhetorical stances and ideologies is essential, and that is one object of this book. Chapters 1 and 2 represent breadth surveys, complemented by more detailed engagement with *The Review*, *The Examiner*, and Steele's varyingly political periodicals. These papers reflect different ways of imagining the relationship between journalism and politics. Both *The Review* and *The Examiner* have complex affiliations with the governments they serve, and throughout Steele's journalistic corpus we see him adapting to new circumstances and to his own shifting position within the evolving political milieu. One aim of the present study is to explore some of the ways in which journalists envisioned their political function: do they convey state information to the populace, or do they contribute to a culture of governmental accountability? Are they informing readers or provoking them? Are they educating subjects or trying to win party votes?

---

[20] See, for example, Tim Harris, 'Understanding popular politics in Restoration Britain', in Alan Houston and Steve Pincus (eds.), *A Nation Transformed: England after the Restoration* (Cambridge, 2001), pp. 125–53.

A discussion of partisan journalism in these years almost inevitably becomes a discussion of authority. The very technology of the daily press led to a (permanent?) crisis in authority, as Knights and others have observed: the proliferation of texts meant a proliferation of competing narratives. The battle for authority was not always made explicit, but it does almost immediately become an inextricable feature of political controversy. The journalists advance disparate notions about political authority, using the medium to make their cases on at least a weekly basis. They argue either for the sanctity of royal (or ministerial) power or for the prerogatives of parliament and the people (and after 1714, the parties awkwardly reverse their positions on this issue). Crucially, they seek to undermine the authority of their opponents, sometimes through issue-based refutation and sometimes by challenging an antagonist's right to speak. Most journalists in the early eighteenth century directly or indirectly defend the legitimacy of their intervention in the public realm. Steele and other contemporaries impugned Mr. Examiner not only for his content but also for his claim to speak for the government. Journalists vied for authority, and they frequently sought to demonstrate that they – and the party for which they spoke – truly represented the nation.

The dynamism of early eighteenth-century partisan periodical culture comes not least from the fact that the nature of public politics had not yet been settled. Journalists either encourage or seek to inhibit the increasing politicisation of the public; they raise questions about whether a particular government is fairly representing its people; they preach obedience and loyalty or active, sceptical citizenship. In a variety of ways, journalists tell people what to think, while also promoting a more constant consciousness of the nature and limits and sources of authority.

Journalism is about power. Partisan periodicals and newspapers comment (to varying degrees) upon the nature and basis and limits of power, and about subjects' rights to demand representation. Historians have done good work on governments' strategic management of the press as a way of preserving and strengthening their authority.[21] A theme of much early eighteenth-century journalism is power: state power, citizens' power, and the power of the media to mediate between them. The existence of a (relatively) unregulated daily press changes the power dynamic between the state and the people. Not only does such daily politicisation create a culture of constant surveillance and an expectation of accountability; it also enfranchises subjects by inculcating political literacy and offering a model of public commentary on matters that had previously been handled with

---

[21] The best study remains Downie, *Robert Harley*.

less scrutiny. In *The Commentator*, Defoe (?) succinctly captures this new mindset: the free press is 'a *natural Appendix* to a just Government, as it gives every Man a Right to speak to it' (22). The press was not merely a mechanism through which citizens learned of events, but also an active influence upon events, a vehicle that could shape policy by galvanising public opinion in one direction or another. The present study represents, among other things, an attempt to understand the ways in which journalists tried to matter – and sometimes did.

PART I

Mapping Early Eighteenth-Century Political Journalism

Chapter 1
The Culture of Political Journalism, 1695–1714

What follows is an attempt to provide an overview of the development and the kinds of political journalism from the lapsing of the Licensing Act in 1695 through the end of the reign of Queen Anne. This survey is representative rather than exhaustive, an attempt to characterise some of the kinds of journalistic enterprises we find in this period, and to contextualise the works of the major authors covered in the middle part of this book: Defoe, Swift, and Steele. The ideological outlooks and apparent aims of major and minor journals – including ephemeral papers, where the extant issues are sufficient – are detailed in the tabular appendix to this book. That table indicates the range and diversity of the canon of political journalism during these years. This chapter does not treat Swift's, Defoe's, and Steele's major party periodicals at length, but does place those enterprises within the milieu of late seventeenth- and early-eighteenth century journalism. A key argument of this chapter is that the distinction between 'news' and 'expression of ideology' is problematic. This chapter answers three questions. First, what kinds of venture do we see in this period? Second, how did newswriters manage, varyingly indirectly, to take sides in partisan and ideological battles? And third, what exactly is the relationship between (particular) newspapers and (particular) advocacy journals?

Context

The year 1695 was doubly important: the Licensing Act expired, and the first election was held under the new Triennial Act. Both changes contributed to fervent partisan rivalry, though the press would reflect that increased controversy more after *c*. 1700 than in the closing years of the seventeenth century. Queen Mary had died at the end of 1694; some contemporaries felt that William was less legitimate as sole monarch than he had been ruling alongside James's daughter. Country Whigs – like their successors under Anne – advocated parliamentary sovereignty and checks on monarchical power; Country Tories queried the legitimacy of standing armies and voiced opposition to the expensive continental wars that lasted throughout William's and most of Anne's reigns. The two wars of our period involving England were the Nine Years' War or King William's War (1689–1697) with France and the War of the Spanish Succession (1702–1713). Most newspapers and advocacy journals respond in some way to these conflicts.

In the late seventeenth century, England became a recognisable fiscal-military state. The implementation of a standing army after 1688 was accompanied by a vast expansion in the operations of the English navy. Under William, the central government grew. The upsurge in fiscal bureaucracy was transformative, and it generated increasing anxieties about administrative corruption, venality, and the problematic implications of patronage.[1] The press served both to provide some sense of public scrutiny and to breed discontent and doubt. The constant warfare meant unprecedentedly high taxes and – for the first time – national debt in England. The need to mobilise national financial resources led to the foundation of the Bank of England in 1694. The development of the fiscal-military state put acute pressure on the landed interest, unhappy about the fact that new mechanisms for the production of wealth undermined their role at the head of society. Hence one major cause for the split between the Whig merchant classes, advocates of trade and money-making industry, and the Tories, committed to traditional hierarchies. That the English papers reflect and increase the polarisation between the parties, at least by Anne's reign, is not astonishing.

The Revolution of 1688 had redefined English monarchy, and in the generation that followed partisans debate the nature and validity of that redefinition. The events of 1688–1689, W. A. Speck concludes, 'inaugurated not merely a new reign but a new kind of kingship'.[2] Under William, the balance of power shifted decisively in favour of Parliament. Tory writers have little to say about parliaments; their Whig rivals repeatedly emphasise that the monarch is in executive terms secondary to the people's representatives. The fundamentals of political power were contested,

---

[1] See John Brewer, *The Sinews of Power: War, Money and the English State, 1688–1783* (New York, 1988).
[2] W. A. Speck, *Reluctant Revolutionaries: Englishmen and the Revolution of 1688* (Oxford, 1989), p. 20.

and that contest looms large in early eighteenth-century periodicals: Mr. Review and Mr. Examiner promulgate radically different ideas about sovereignty, about the legitimacy of resistance (Defoe) versus the need for passive obedience and submission (Swift). In these years, in other words, party writers stake out positions not only on specific issues and events but also on the most basic and vital questions about power.

Domestic politics were dominated, in Anne's reign, by debates about the succession – as Joseph Hone has shown – and by religious controversy.[3] In 1702, Tories hailed the new Queen as the matriarch of the Church of England, and many dissenters were initially uneasy about what her rule would mean for them. But in her parliamentary address of 25 May 1702, Anne vowed to 'be very careful to preserve and maintain the Act of Toleration',[4] a promise of which Defoe frequently reminds both the queen and her public. Whatever potential balance Anne hoped to achieve between the High Church and the Protestant dissenters was never realised. Late in 1702, the Tories introduced a bill against the practice of occasional conformity, meant to prevent dissenters from taking occasional communion in order to become eligible for public office. The bill was defeated by a Whig majority in the House of Lords, but in 1704 the high-flyers 'tacked' it on to a land tax measure in an effort to guarantee its passage. The Tack failed, and the Whig outcry against the high Tories' dirty politics was considerable. The early volumes of Defoe's *Review* target the high-flying Tackers and work to create distance between them and more moderate Tories. Dissenters feared not only policy against themselves but also more violent acts of retribution.

Anglicans also felt besieged. In the previous reign, churchmen had been alarmed by the transformation of the episcopacy away from traditional High Church principles. As Steve Pincus observes, there was under William 'a revolution in the ideological and religious commitments of the episcopate', a change brought about by the installation of new bishops committed to Low Church notions of comprehension and toleration.[5] High Churchmen warmly welcomed Anne, anticipating a renewed

---

[3] Joseph Hone's *Literature and Party Politics at the Accession of Queen Anne* (Oxford, 2017) is a compelling account of cultural responses to the accession of Queen Anne and the politics of that moment; he argues that the best 'way of conceptualizing party politics is through contemporary arguments about dynasty, allegiance, and royal legitimacy' (p. 10). Though Hone claims a wide generic basis for his study – pamphlets, plays, newspapers, sermons, and so on – in practice he engages directly with very few periodicals.

[4] Anne's speech is quoted in *The London Gazette* (28 May 1702); see also Boyer, *History of the Reign of Queen Anne* (1703), 42.

[5] Steve Pincus, *1688: The First Modern Revolution* (New Haven, 2009), p. 402.

commitment to their ideals and a guarantee of their continued centrality to English politics. One famous battle cry of Anne's reign was 'the Church in danger', issued loudly by Anglicans either convinced or trying to convince the Queen that Whig values threatened their establishment. Whig journalists explicitly mock High Church paranoia, maintaining that 'the Church in danger' is a disingenuous slogan meant to justify the marginalisation of dissenters. Addison and Steele, among lesser-known contemporaries, also disclaim the Church's exclusive claim on moral guardianship, offering as an alternative Whig notions of politeness and civility and self-regulation.

The multi-year news event of Anne's reign was the War of the Spanish Succession, and partisans fought about when and on what terms to treat for peace. The conflict arose from the death of the childless Charles II, the last of the Spanish Habsburgs, which left the Spanish throne in dispute. The details are complex; the crux is that Louis XIV wanted to install his grandson, Philip of Anjou, as the Bourbon king of Spain. Fearing a Catholic empire, England joined the Grand Alliance (along with Holland, Prussia, Hanover and other German states, and Austria, among others), determined to establish the Austrian Archduke (Charles) as king of Spain. Those were the contenders for the Spanish crown until the sudden death (April 1711) of Charles's older brother, the Austrian Emperor Joseph I. This death made Charles emperor of Austria, which meant – as Defoe and others insisted – that he should not be allowed to take possession of the Spanish throne as well. To give Charles both Austria and Spain would be as destructive to the balance of power in Europe as a Franco–Spanish union; earlier advocates of Charles's accession began instead to support a partition. The Treaty of Utrecht (1713) that ended the war for all allies but Austria – achieved via clandestine negotiations between England and France – stipulated that Philip should, after all, inherit the Spanish crown, but only on the condition that France and Spain never be united. In England, the other significant slogan of Anne's reign – 'no peace without Spain' – captured the convictions of the Whigs, who wanted to continue the war against France until Louis XIV accepted a treaty barring his grandson's rule of Spain. The other major proviso was that Louis acknowledge the Hanoverian succession and evict the Old Pretender – whom he had declared to be King James III after James's death in 1701 – from France. By 1710–1711, Allied victory in Spain looked increasingly impracticable, and that was the major problem with which Anne's last ministry had to deal. Debates about war and peace dominate Defoe's *Review*, and are also crucial to Swift's and Steele's journalistic missions.

Among the most divisive moves Anne made during her rule was the ministerial change of summer 1710. Swift's primary job in *The Examiner* was to cultivate support for that change. In retrospect, that alteration appears all but inevitable. In the 1709 Barrier Treaty, Britain had offered huge concessions to the widely distrusted Dutch, and the Getruydenberg peace proceedings of early 1710 had failed because of unreasonable Allied demands of the French. The duumvirate of the Earl of Godolphin and the Duke of Marlborough was determined to continue fighting, but the English populace were weary of an expensive, seemingly interminable war. Ever more oppressive taxes, the bloodbath of Malplaquet, and the bill for naturalisation of foreign Protestants all intensified anti-Whig sentiment. By the late spring of 1710, popular discontent with the Whigs had erupted into a furore, and Anne had lost faith in her counsellors. Godolphin fell in August; by September the dismissal of his ministry was complete; and the Tories routed the Whigs in the October general election. Thus commenced Robert Harley's tenure as 'prime minister', lord treasurer, and leader of what he hoped would be a moderate, non-partisan cohort. His chief objectives were simple: restore financial stability and end England's involvement in the war. Through a process of secret and separate negotiations with France, the Harley ministry finally achieved peace (spring 1713), but the nature of that peace would prove extremely controversial in 1713–1714 and would lead to charges of treason against Harley *et al.* in George I's reign. The Treaty of Utrecht guaranteed Philip's renunciation of the French – rather than the Spanish – throne, a highly unsatisfactory compromise for English subjects justly suspicious of the House of Bourbon. Other concessions made to France further outraged the Whigs (though in fact Harley's treaty was advantageous to England).

The last year of Anne's reign – and of Stuart rule in England – was tumultuous. The peace had been hard-earned. In addition to creating unrest among the Whigs at home, the ministry had drawn the enduring hostility of Hanover, which had unequivocally expressed its desire to have the war continue until better terms could be secured. Harley and St. John, as well as the Duke of Ormonde and servants of the ministry such as Matthew Prior and Swift, would be in hot water under the Hanoverian regime as of the winter of 1714–1715. As of 1712–1713, moreover, Harley and St. John were pulling in different directions. Harley favoured moderation and a coalition of moderate Whigs and Tories, while St. John supported a High Church administration. On 27 July 1714, Anne dismissed Harley from his post as lord treasurer; St. John was finally in charge, but only for a few days. The Tory party had fragmented, and when Anne died on 1 August, it was left hopelessly divided. The party's political marginality under George

I and George II was by no means unavoidable at that point, but – to the immense frustration of Swift and fellow travellers – the Tories could not regroup and become a meaningful oppositional force.

The newspapers and advocacy journals of this period, especially those from 1702 to 1714, reflect tremendous political disagreement. The treatment of dissenters, the basis of political power, England's relationship to France and to the Dutch and her other allies, the assessment of public credit and the value of trade, the Queen's right to change her ministry without apparent cause – all of these issues are fervently debated, along with a host of other policies and occurrences. A fundamental question underlies all of these debates among journalists – to wit, how they should be relating to the people and to the state, and what the nature of their mediation between those two forces should be. To that issue, we will return in Chapter 6, but the emergence of a sustained corpus of political journalism clearly meant that the journalists were daily politicising English subjects in an unprecedented and enduringly metamorphic way.

The culture of journalism under William III

The termination of the Licensing Act inevitably had a transformative effect on the political press. The day after the act expired (3 May), Richard Baldwin recommenced his *Historical Account of the Publick Transactions in Christendom*, and three days later *The Flying Post* was launched, one of the three major triweeklies to appear in 1695 and last beyond Anne's reign (the others were *The Post Boy* and *The Post Man*). Between March 1696 and the king's death in 1702, more than a dozen new papers emerged, only three of which continued for any significant length of time: *Dawks's News-Letter*, *The London Post*, and *The Protestant Mercury*.[6] Scholars have justly concluded the Williamite press to be dramatically less interesting and dynamic than what we find in Anne's reign. R. B. Walker describes the newspapers under William as 'reticent', light on editorial commentary and devoted mostly 'to safe areas such as criticism of Louis XIV and the Jacobites'.[7] Partisan remarks were unacceptable. Extant issues of John Dunton's *Pegasus* (1696) exhibit virulent anti-Jacobitism; he himself highlights the unusual nature of focused polemical journalism: 'This Paper being written in a different Method from all other News Papers. . .' (no. 19). His 'news'

---

[6] R. B. Walker, 'The Newspaper Press in the Reign of William III', in *The Historical Journal* 17 (1974), 691–709, at p. 701.
[7] Walker, 'The Newspaper Press', p. 708.

is supplemented by 'Observations' on current events, making *Pegasus* an early precursor to the editorial style of *The Tatler* and *The Spectator*. But Dunton's partisan outlet represents an exception to the rule in the nineties. In general, as C. John Sommerville suggests, only after 1700 would 'papers... speak more directly' and '*tell* readers what they thought'.[8] Before then, readers were left to assemble the news for themselves, using limited resources – namely, the *Gazette* and *Votes of the House of Commons*, in addition to pamphlets, newsletters, and the foreign broadsheets found in coffeehouses and taverns.

The early 1690s were dominated by literary periodicals that might now seem apolitical but which did foster popular engagement with the press and with the (broadly defined) culture of the day. Works like J. de la Crose's *History of Learning* (1691) and *Memoirs for the Ingenious* (1693), collecting individual creative submissions, helped create a virtual public. Among the most successful ventures of the 1690s was Dunton's *Athenian Mercury* (1691–1697), a wide-ranging question-and-answer style journal treating subjects religious, historical, literary, social, and so on. The late seventeenth century was a rich time for these intellectual journals. Although these and like ventures do not engage in party politics, they are by no means apolitical. One need look only to Swift's *Tale of a Tub* to see conservative anxiety about the challenge posed to ancient authority by modern Whig innovation. These ventures encouraged English readers to speak for themselves, with having given them a sense of their own imagination; they helped create an engaged readership even if they could not fully anticipate the political implications of such engagement.

The major triweeklies and other news ventures launched in the 1690s lasted into Anne's reign, and others lived and died under William. What is the nature of these new enterprises, papers like Benjamin Harris's *Intelligence Domestick and Foreign*, Ichabod Dawks's *Protestant Mercury* (1696–1700) and his *Dawks's News-Letter*, and Anne Baldwin's *New Observator* (launched in 1701)? They tend to be overwhelmingly foreign in their coverage, offering reports from abroad, mostly relating to sieges and other military happenings. They malign safe targets such as Jacobites, the Pretender, France, and the Catholic Church. Even where editorialising is light, these writers do betray their (conventional) Protestant bias, expressing sympathy with persecuted continental Protestants and promoting the war with France. These papers, along with the weekly *Historical Account of the Publick Transactions in Christendom* (Aug 1694–1695?), are conspicuously

---

[8] C. John Sommerville, *The News Revolution in England: Cultural Dynamics of Daily Information* (Oxford, 1996), p. 14.

reticent on domestic matters, no doubt a response to William's desire to monitor the press. Between October 1689 and April 1695, seventeen trials were held for unlicensed printing.[9]

The bottom line on late seventeenth-century journalism is that it was not intended to shape political controversy. Under William, journalism mostly unifies rather than divides. What Englishmen would take for granted by the end of Anne's reign, in other words, was essentially unheard of under William. The papers of the nineties were less partisan than those of the Exclusion Crisis had been, and drastically less polemical than what follows in the next decade.

Content and outlook, 1702–1714: the newspapers

Little has been said about the content of early eighteenth-century newspapers. Scholars routinely note the predominance of foreign news in these papers: 'Local news', says William Bragg Ewald, 'was comparatively sparse'.[10] Andrew Pettegree has affirmed this notion of early eighteenth-century newspapers: they 'continued to eschew overt editorialising', sticking to foreign reportage and maintaining an 'extremely circumspect' treatment of domestic politics.[11] This is not untrue, though the tendency has been to treat these papers as *either* focused upon the continent *or* disseminating ideology. Plenty of papers do both, albeit with different degrees of directness. The precise nature of advocacy in journalism – the editorialising presence – has been significantly underexplored. One of the most prolific students of eighteenth-century newspapers, Jeremy Black, offers this characterisation: 'The contents of the newspapers [over the eighteenth century] were similar.... [T]he age was a deeply conservative one, eager to support God and the king, despite the actions of prelates and monarchs'.[12] Such a summation does not do justice to do the more radical journals (e.g., *The Observator*), and it blurs important distinctions among the whole corpus of politicised papers. I offer only brief characterisations of a few major examples here; the point is to illustrate the different ways in which writers of straight news signal their ideological commitments, and the development of specialist enterprises that focus on particular aspects of the political milieu.

---

[9] Lois Schwoerer, 'Liberty of the Press and Public Opinion: 1660–1695', in J. R. Jones (ed.), *Liberty Secured? Britain Before and After 1688* (Stanford, 1992), p. 229.
[10] William Bragg Ewald, Jr., *The Newsmen of Queen Anne* (Oxford, 1956), p. 2.
[11] Andrew Pettegree, *The Invention of the News: How the World Came to Know about Itself* (New Haven, 2014), p. 247.
[12] Jeremy Black, *The English Press in the Eighteenth Century* (Philadelphia, 1987), p. 26.

In Ewald's taxonomy of journalistic enterprises, he regards the major triweeklies – *The Post Man, The Post Boy,* and *The Flying Post* – as 'newspapers' in the strictest sense, heavy on foreign reports and light on domestic commentary.[13] To the list of newspapers can be added the long-running official government organ, *The London Gazette,* as well as *The Daily Courant* (the only daily paper until *The Spectator*). In the first years of Anne's reign, *The London Post* (1699–June 1705) probably belongs in this group, as does *The English Post* (1700 to at least October 1709). *The Weekly Packet* (1712–1721) likewise purported to offer 'news without any pronounced bias'; its focus was general, including discussions of arts and sciences as well as the state and trade.[14] As in the 1690s, the majority of the content comes in the form of reports from abroad or précis of continental affairs compiled from ship accounts, dispatches, and other papers: most foreign news was plagiarised from continental and English publications. Editors had much to choose from, and so the selection of what to include or leave out reflects necessary abridgement well as partisanship.[15] Many papers are essentially xenophobic,[16] though Whig editors often express support of foreign Protestants. In the contentious climate of the early eighteenth century, no sensible editor could appear tolerant of France, and indeed even the zealously anti-Catholic Defoe fell under suspicion when he admitted '*French* Greatness' and '*French* Grandeur' in opening numbers of *The Review*.[17] This is not to say that journalistic treatments of France's government or military are consistent; on the contrary, how papers present the enemy turns out to be helpful in distinguishing their agendas.

The least polemical of the partisan news outlets is *The London Gazette,* founded in 1665 and still in existence. The *Gazette*, a precursor to *The Daily Gazetteer* (1735–1746), remained throughout Anne's reign an 'official' venue, an organ of the government ostensibly meant to be above politics.[18] Between its inception and 1678, the biweekly *Gazette* was the only source for English printed political news, and when Anne took power in 1702 it was the sole government paper. As Rachael Scarborough King reminds us, the creators of the *Gazette* 'saw it not as radically new but as extending the

---

[13] Ewald, *Newsmen of Queen Anne*, p. 2.
[14] Henry Snyder, 'The Circulation of Newspapers in the Reign of Queen Anne', *The Library* 5th series 23 (1968), 206–35, p. 212.
[15] Black, 'The British Press and Europe', 66–67.
[16] Black, 'The British Press and Europe', 73.
[17] Defoe, *Review*, vol. 1, p. 22.
[18] For a discussion of pre-*Gazette* 'official' outlets, see Peter Fraser, *The Intelligence of the Secretaries of State & Their Monopoly of Licensed News 1660–1688* (Cambridge, 1956).

form and function of an existing news genre: the manuscript newsletter'.[19] In Anne's reign, the *Gazette*'s pro-government slant revealed itself in small ways, such as the report of Ned Ward's arrest for publications 'Reflecting upon Her Majesty' (no. 4280); the presumption of Anne's pre-eminence (even over Marlborough, by the summer of 1710) in leading a successful war (4702); and the claim that the Church is *not* in danger (4287). The ministry tried to use the *Gazette* for partisan ends, but even the mild editorialising of the Huguenot Charles Delafaye as editor gave offence. In May 1707, Steele was offered the post and charged with improving the paper's accuracy; he obliged, but was frustrated. In his *Apology* (1714), he recalled that as Gazetteer, 'he worked faithfully... without ever erring against the Rule observed by all Ministries, to keep that Paper very innocent and very insipid'.[20] After the ministerial change of 1710 ushered in a Tory government, the Whig Steele was clearly no longer an appropriate keeper of the official outlet.[21] Clerks handled the editing until late 1711, when Swift secured the post for his fellow poet and High Churchman, William King, a sort of protégé.[22] King served through June 1712, to be followed by another of Swift's friends, Charles Ford, who maintained the paper until Anne's death. Despite the talent behind the *Gazette*, however, in Anne's reign it was regarded as colourless or worse. Defoe regularly criticised its confused continental reportage and stylistic shortcomings, and Marlborough was sufficiently incensed by its inaccurate military accounts that he insisted reports from own headquarters be sent to *The Post Man*. The two last editors of Anne's reign were both high Tories, but the paper's Toryism must have struck contemporaries as tame alongside not only *The Examiner* and *The Post Boy*.

Like the *Gazette*, *The Daily Courant* (March 1702–June 1735) tried to be a neutral outlet, though its orientation was increasingly clearly Whig.[23] The *Courant* commenced on the fourth day of Anne's reign, appeared Monday through Saturday, and ran to some 4,800 copies per week; it was to be the only daily paper in London until *The Spectator* commenced in the spring of 1711. Its initial editor, Samuel Buckley, had access to the Secretary of State office's news sources; the paper gained a reputation for accuracy, and

---

[19] Rachael Scarborough King, 'The Manuscript Newsletter and the Rise of the Newspaper, 1665–1715'. *Huntington Library Quarterly* 79 (2016), 411–37, p. 412.

[20] Steele, *Tracts and Pamphlets*, 339.

[21] Steele might have been dismissed because of his thinly veiled attack on Harley in *The Tatler* of 4 July 1710.

[22] David Woolley (ed.), *The Correspondence of Jonathan Swift, D. D.* (4 vols., Frankfurt am Main, 1999–2007), vol. 1, p. 411.

[23] *The Daily Courant* was the only source of daily news until *The Daily Post* (1719–1746) and *The Daily Journal* (1721–1737).

Buckley worked scrupulously to appear to present unfiltered news. Under the Harley ministry, the *Courant* served Whig interests in a variety of ways, including two well-timed leaks in 1711. While the Tory ministry was secretly negotiating with France, the Allies and the Whigs were calling for unity. In late summer 1711, England's dealings with France were (partially) discovered, forcing the ministry to announce some of the preliminary peace terms; they withheld those terms that were particularly favourable to England, which made the treaty look more lopsided in France's favour than was in fact the case. In October, the *Courant* published these preliminaries, sparking considerable controversy. In December, it followed with Hanover's memorial of protest against the treaty. By the end of its life, the *Courant* would be a subsidised organ of the Whig government, but its Whiggish leanings were apparent early on.

Most newspapers that started with no editorial voice eventually, in the contentious political milieu of Anne's reign, developed one, and even those that stick exclusively to news manage to communicate ideology. Benjamin Harris's *London Post, With Intelligence Foreign and Domestick* (1699–1705) becomes in its last two years trenchant in its criticism of High Church bigotry, occasional conformity, and particular figures like Sacheverell and Benjamin Hoadly. *The Evening Post* (1706; 1709–1732) reports on the war with a special emphasis on French difficulties and French deception. Several issues in 1710–1711 make note of widespread desertions among French troops, as well as that army's 'Want of Water' (no. 124), the country's want of money, and the whole population's want of food. The anti-French sentiment alone does not reveal *The Evening Post*'s partisan commitments; what signals its Whiggishness is its attitude toward England's obligation to the Allies. After *The Daily Courant* published the shocking preliminaries in October, it also printed (6 December) the Hanoverian adviser Baron von Bothmer's unequivocal protest of those terms. *The Evening Post* need not take sides explicitly; just to print Bothmer's impassioned plea for the continuation of war is enough to communicate Whig sympathies. The *Post* does not enter into ideological warfare, neither drawing conclusions about political power nor using allegories to insinuate the wisdom of resistance or non-resistance. At least until the end of Anne's reign, only on the subject of the war does the editor seem to align himself with one side over the other. After the accession of George I, the *Post* becomes – as one would expect – more strongly Whig.

The predominant concern of *The English Post, with News Foreign and Domestick* (October 1700 through at least fall 1709), edited by Nathaniel Crouch, is religion, specifically Protestant freedom from persecution. The paper is even more intensely anti-French than *The Evening Post*, and especially between its inception and 1702, it routinely objects to the maltreatment of French Protestants. Like his fellow Whig Defoe, Crouch not only welcomes foreign Protestants but also maintains – in the face of Tory xenophobia – that they represent an economic boon. *The English Post* mocks French power, but reminds English readers of France's assurances of victory (see no. 1292) – a good tactic if one is trying to keep a war-weary populace willing to fight. Much is said in *The English Post* against the French enemy, but – unlike in some other papers – the need to punish them *as Catholics* is always essential.

The Post Man and the Historical Account (Oct 1695–Feb 1730) is, to a degree unlike any other contemporary paper, obsessively focused on the war. The anti-Catholicism is manifest and unsurprising: the paper was penned by the French Protestant John De Fonvive. But its objectives have everything to do with continuing and winning the war – that is, with thumping the French. The majority of the issues publicise war-related polemics, including technical, focused accounts, 'true plans of attacks', panegyrics on major and minor European military figures, *The History of Flanders*, *The Seat of War in Bavaria*, *The History of the Siege of Thoulon*, and so on. Many English newspapers privilege paeans on Marlborough or calls for patriotism, but *The Post Man* is – significantly – puffing more detailed and predominantly continental works, more European than exclusively English. *The Post Man*'s detailed coverage of the war, and support of continuing it vigorously, explains why Marlborough demanded that his reports be published in this paper rather than in the *Gazette*. Defoe commended De Fonvive's paper for its coherence, concluding it to be 'Wrote ... most to the Purpose, and most worth Reading of any Paper yet Extant'.[24]

Two of the most polemically significant newspapers of this period are *The Flying Post* (May 1695 to at least 1733) and *The Post Boy* (May 1695–Sept 1728), and they provide illustrative case studies in how newswriters communicated partisan commitments. Respectively, they promulgate Whig and Tory ideology; the latter paper was launched to counter the former. In the middle of Anne's reign, while under the control of the French Huguenot Abel Boyer, *The Post Boy* functioned less as a party paper, but after 1709 it was a tool of the High Tory St. John. *The Flying Post* of Anne's reign has rightly been described as 'the flagship of Whig propaganda', and its editor, the Scot George Ridpath, was a thorn in Tory sides throughout this period.[25] He also produced *The Observator* late in Anne's reign. Upon the

---

[24] Defoe, *Review*, vol. 2, p. 118.
[25] P. B. J. Hyland, 'Liberty and Libel: Government and the Press during the Succession Crisis in Britain, 1712–1716', *The English Historical Review* 101 (1986), 863–88, p. 868.

death of William III, Ridpath not only offers warm eulogies but emphasises the need for continuity, implicitly urging Anne to carry on the war against France and to preserve the religious liberties of her Protestant subjects (nos. 1067–68). This Whig triweekly features news from abroad with definite slant. On 2 January 1705, Ridpath prints a lengthy manifesto from the Hungarians, and its political idiom is thoroughly Whiggish. The manifesto traces the 'Origine and Constitution of some of our principal Liberties', including 'the power of chusing our Kings . . . our Crown being Elective and not Hereditary'. The application to English debates about the basis of power is clear. On 1 July 1712, Ridpath publishes an address from the Count de Zinzendorf, suggesting among other things that 'the Alliance ought to be renew'd which has for its End the Recovery of the Spanish Monarchy to the House of Austria' – again using a foreign dignitary to publicise the Whig position. This kind of manoeuvre represents engagement in domestic politics, carried out in the guise of continental reportage.

The Flying Post unsurprisingly becomes more polemical after the 1710 ministerial change. Ridpath's paper is anti-French and anti-Catholic, and under the Harley ministry he doggedly maintains the association between the Tory government and the Pretender. *The Flying Post* has *The Examiner* always in view, challenging that paper's positions and its interpretation of Marlborough's war (see no. 3234). *The Flying Post* contests the fundamental outlook of Tory mouthpieces:

> They whose Principle it had heretofore been that Parliaments had a Right to enquire into Leagues and Alliances, and to be consulted in Matters which had relation to War and Peace, came presently to give up that essential Policy, and to have nothing in their Mouths but the Prerogative. (no. 3434)

Ridpath raises the spectre of tyranny, the arbitrary rule brought on by those who would trade parliamentary right for the royal prerogative. After George's accession, *The Flying Post* predictably depicts Anne's last ministry as rabble-rousing breakers of the peace and disloyal friends of France – and violators of the constitution who sought to reintroduce the high-flying doctrine of 'Hereditary and Indefeasible Right' (no. 3640).

In the *Journal to Stella*, Swift complains: 'These devils of Grubstreet rogues, that write the *Flying-Post* and *Medley* . . . will not be quiet. They are always mauling lord treasurer, lord Bolingbroke, and me' (p. 455). See Abigail Williams (ed.), *Journal to Stella* (Cambridge, 2013).

The Post Boy, on the Tory side, likewise combined European news with partisan advocacy, oblique and overt. Abel Roper launched the paper in 1695 as a counter to Ridpath's Whig venture; at some point early in Anne's reign, Abel Boyer took Roper's place in writing much of the copy, moderating its Toryism. In fall of 1709, Boyer and Roper had a falling out and Boyer took control of the newspaper.[26] Under him, the paper was High Tory.

The Post Boy prints news from abroad, but Boyer prefaces that news with addresses of allegiance – collected from hither and yon, on behalf of cities, towns, and counties, by aldermen and justices of the peace and clergymen – to the Queen, and the pamphlets and poems he advertises are almost entirely Tory. The memorials to the Queen uniformly assert loyalty,[27] disparage the oppositional faction, and, most important, affirm the hereditary basis of Anne's rule. The addresses denounce the idea of political resistance and call for a speedily concluded, enduring peace. Throughout this period, Roper advertises partisan works, including *The Voice of the People, no Voice of God*, *The Examiner*, and the later Mr. Examiner William Oldisworth's hypercritical response to Steele, *Annotations on the Tatler* (1710).

The connections between *The Post Boy* and *The Examiner* are considerable. On 5 August, two days after the inaugural *Examiner* appeared, Roper reports, 'They talk of a great Change in our Ministry'. He indicates his favour by criticising the current Whig government. The next issue implies that such a transformation of the political landscape could make Anne 'the happy Instrument of healing all our Breaches'. On 19 August, Boyer includes a memorial promising 'a cheerful Acquiescence' in Anne's 'Wisdom in all the Parts of [her] Administration' – a not very subtle exhortation for others to accept the new state of affairs. This aligns closely with the message of the early *Examiner* essays. Swift and Roper were allies in the Tory cause: Swift contributed to *The Post Boy*, and in the *Journal to Stella* announced gleefully, 'Roper is my humble Slave'.[28] After *The Examiner* commenced, and the Oxford ministry fully installed, *The Post Boy* prints fewer memorials, and mostly ceases to defend the change. That was left to Mr. Examiner to do.

The tone is more neutral, the partisanship more indirect, than in *The Examiner*, but the slant remains High Church Tory. Roper persists in branding the Whigs a lying faction; he waxes triumphal about the election of a 'Loyal Churchman' (2457); he supports Sacheverell and scorns those

---

[26] G. C. Gibbs, *ODNB* entry for Abel Boyer.
[27] This is not a new phenomenon. As Sommerville points out, such addresses had appeared in the 1650s (*News Revolution*, p. 71) and had functioned similarly.
[28] Swift, *Journal to Stella*, p. 412. Later he reports, 'I have been drawi[n]g up a Paragraph for t[h]e Post boy, to be out to morrow, and as malicious as possible, and very proper for Abel Roper th[e] Printer of it' (p. 460).

who use him badly. Throughout spring 1714 Roper wrangles with both *The Flying Post* and Steele's *Englishman*. Two weeks later, he takes issue with Steele's 'seditious' arguments about the demolition of Dunkirk, ironically incredulous that 'a Brother of the Quill' could be capable of 'put[ting] Forgeries of [such] Magnitude upon our Readers'. Roper mocks Whig fears of the Pretender, celebrates the Queen, and, like Mr. Examiner, values obedience and authority.

In accounts of early eighteenth-century news reportage, the implication has been that coverage of continental affairs is somehow separate from a periodical's domestic political commitments, which is of course not true. All of these papers convey an attitude, though they are much less explicitly polemical than the 'advocacy' journalism of Swift, Defoe, Steele, Mainwaring, and others. To the advocacy journals we need now turn.

Content and outlook, 1702–1714: advocacy journals

The corpus of these papers is extensive and more miscellaneous than that of newspapers. Swift, Steele, Defoe, Leslie, Mainwaring, and Oldmixon are some of the big names, but a host of minor pens and anonymous partisans contribute to the post-1695 boom in advocacy journalism. These papers are frequently antagonistic in nature, the writers sparring with each other and criticising pamphleteers, preachers, mobs, and ministers. They tend to include some degree of news reportage, invariably with noticeable editorial viewpoint.

Responses to The Examiner

The Examiner inspired more responses than any other paper of Anne's reign. The most prominent of its critics is Steele, an outspoken opponent of the major Tory paper and the ministry it served. Steele's party journalism will be the subject of Chapter 5, which demonstrates among other things the extent of his fixation upon Mr. Examiner. From the beginning, the Whigs recognised that such a paper – aggressively High Church and obnoxiously 'authoritative' – could not go unanswered. In Oldmixon's telling, 'The old Ministry [Godolphin's] saw it was absolutely necessary to set up a Paper in Opposition to the *Examiner*, to dispel the Mists it cast before the Peoples Eyes'.[29] To that end, Arthur Mainwaring recruited Joseph Addison for *The Whig-Examiner*, which began on 14 September

---

[29] Oldmixon, *Memoirs of the Press* (1742), p. 8.

1710 and lasted only five numbers. Scholars have highlighted its brevity and ineffectuality; partisan battle was not Addison's forte. The opening issue offers the obligatory statement of purpose, which is 'to censure the Writings of others, and to give all Persons a rehearing, who have suffer'd under any unjust Sentence of the *Examiner*'. Most of the first issue is a counter to *Examiner* no. 6, which commented unfavourably upon Samuel Garth's *Dispensary* and more generally grumbled about the Whig pretence 'to make a Monopoly of our Sense'. Addison is keen to respond to the *Examiner* in literary-critical terms. In no. 2, he explains that, 'Having done with the Author's Party and Principles, we now shall consider his Performance, under the three Heads of Wit, Language, and Argument'. He quibbles with language and style, mocking Mr. Examiner's 'High Nonsense', which 'stalks upon hard Words, and rattles thro Polysyllables' (no. 4).[30]

The Whig-Examiner does not ignore his opponent's politics. In no. 2, he accuses the author of *A Letter to the Examiner* (St. John) of being too complimentary of the French king and the Duke of Anjou. No. 4, likely co-authored by Addison and Mainwaring,[31] continues the attack on the *Letter*, whose author is misguided in his arguments about Spain; ungrateful for Marlborough's astonishing military victories; and unfair to the previous Whig ministry. The final (and most interesting) number, probably also collaborative, is overtly ideological, though it retains the characteristic focus on language. Addison and Mainwaring warn that '*Passive-Obedience*' and '*Non-Resistance*' both sound 'mild, gentle, and meek-spirited', and are thus 'apt to fill the Mind with no other Ideas but those of Peace, Tranquility, and Resignation' (no. 5). *The Whig-Examiner*'s task, then, is to 'shew this Doctrine in [its] black and odious Colours', to ensure that 'these smooth ensnaring Terms' are 'rightly explain'd to the People'. What consistency *The Whig-Examiner* has comes from its sensitivity to language, to the politics of culture, and to the pernicious effects of false connotations on the popular reception of loaded political terms.

The Whig-Examiner was supplanted by the much more effective *Medley*, produced by Mainwaring with some assistance from Oldmixon and Steele. The first two numbers overlap with the last two *Whig-Examiner*s; the inaugural issue (5 October 1710) takes the form of 'A Letter to the *Whig-Examiner*'. Mainwaring clearly wanted his journal to appear as an ally to Addison's paper, perhaps to give the impression of a cohort of Whig critics

---

[30] In *The Reader* of 26 April 1714, Steele quotes these passages from *The Whig-Examiner* in his own critical response to *The Examiner*. *The Reader* is printed in Rae Blanchard (ed.), *Steele's Periodical Journalism, 1714–1716* (Oxford, 1959).

[31] Ellis, Introduction, *Examiner*, p. liii.

of the Tory *Examiner*. The opening number is a rejoinder to Defoe's *Essay upon Publick Credit* (1710), in which Defoe implicitly defends the ministerial change; not very subtly *The Medley* challenges that change. When Mainwaring targets Mr. Examiner and his 'Fellow-Labourers in the new most glorious *Scheme*', the scheme to which he refers is the Tory takeover (no. 1). In no. 5, he questions 'whether we are much the better for our late Changes', leaving little doubt about his answer. No. 7 concludes an allegorical tale about French politics, meant to demonstrate 'the ill Consequences of removing Able and Successful Ministers' (33).

Mainwaring fashioned *The Medley* an antidote to Tory poison, and his paper is as antagonistic to the High Church party as *The Examiner* is to the routed Whigs. He repudiates the dogma of 'the *Hereditary*, &c.', a 'dangerous Tendency' that 'was quietly laid to sleep at the *Revolution*' but has been renewed by the Tories (no. 3). *The Medley* counters *The Examiner*'s views about the basis of political power, as well as its more negative interpretation of the value and implications of 1688–1689. *The Examiner* warns that the Revolution gave some people foolish notions about the legitimacy of resistance, complaining about incursions on royal power from below. *The Medley* upholds the Revolution, disparages promulgators of non-resistance, and uses classical parallels to raise alarm about 'bad Emperors' (109). The Tories, in Mainwaring's telling, are against notions of liberty and property; he prophesies their ruin, maintaining that they 'will have nothing else to blame but themselves and their own Principles, which have the misfortune to be inconsistent not only with Reason or Truth, but with the Revolution too, on which the present Government is founded' (425). Mainwaring is by turns defensive and offensive vis-à-vis *The Examiner*, but he is always assertive, uncompromising, and bold. His masterful use of irony – including playful self-mockery and a pretence of friendship to and admiration for his rival – represents an effective complement to his hard-hitting polemic.

Other Whigs participate in the attack, one which continues into George I's reign. *The Protestant Post-Boy* (1711–1712) challenges both *The Post Boy* and *The Examiner*.[32] *The Patriot* (1714–1715) shares much with the Whig advocacy journals of Anne's reign, voicing hostility to the Pretender and to the false doctrines of passive obedience and non-resistance, and – now belatedly – to *The Examiner*. The author, John Harris, is adamant about 'The Villany of the *Examiner*, the *Post-Boy*, and other Hirelings' in propagating

---

[32] In October 1711, Swift reports, 'A rogue that writes a news-paper called *The Protestant Post-boy*, has reflected on me . . . but the secretary has taken him up, and he shall have a squeeze extraordinary' (*Journal to Stella*, p. 297).

non-resistance (30). He joins his Whig allies in calling for vengeance against the former ministry, and against its pens, including Oldisworth and Swift, among other 'Tools to the last Four years Managers' (84). *The Patriot* combines the Addisonian preachment of benevolence with the partisan zeal of Steele; in fact, when he signs his name to the final number, Harris makes a point of noting that many readers have taken Steele to be the author of the paper. *The English Examiner* of 1715, like many early Hanoverian Whig papers, repeats the litany of charges against the Harley ministry and its pens. The title insinuates the un-patriotism of Swift's and Oldisworth's paper, a rhetorical reinforcement of the arguments against the Tories. *The English Examiner*, predictably, celebrates the Dutch and reviles the French; it insists upon the necessity of impeaching Harley *et al.*, who 'Sold and Betrayed' England 'to a foreign Prince' (2), reiterating allegations of Jacobitism. These positions are not surprising, but the fact that the paper appropriates the title of Swift and Oldisworth's periodical reveals the perception of the original *Examiner*'s prominence in disseminating Tory ideals and defending Anne's last ministry.

Radical journalism: The Observator and The Rehearsal

Though *The Observator* – a radical Whig journal – did not instigate the same number of responders as *The Examiner*, it did help provoke one of the best-known High Church papers, *The Rehearsal*. Both reflect extreme positions, respectively country Whig and high-flying Tory, and both helped shape debate in Anne's reign.

John Tutchin's *Observator* launched on 1 April 1702, a few weeks after William's death. Tutchin had since the mid-1680s been a fearless Whig propagandist. His poems against the accession of James II earned him a sentence of jail time, a fine, and regular public whippings; he requested to be hanged instead, but after considerable public uproar he was released. His xenophobic *The Foreigners* (1700) inspired Defoe's celebrated response, *The True-Born Englishman*. Tutchin borrows his title from Roger L'Estrange's *Observator*, a Tory venue of the 1680s. Tutchin found himself in trouble on more than one occasion for his paper's outspoken criticism of the government; in 1704 he was arrested for commenting upon the navy administration. Though the precise cause of his death (September 1707) is unknown, one plausible account is that his enemies exercised their vengeance, beating him fatally. After his death, several contributors kept *The Observator* alive, and George Ridpath (editor of *The Flying Post*) ran it from *circa* 1710 until he was forced into exile in 1713.

Like L'Estrange, Tutchin uses the dialogue form, framing most issues (beginning with no. 19) as a conversation between the Observator and a Countryman. Like his rival Leslie, Tutchin might well be looking back to Marvell's polemical *Rehearsal Transpros'd* (1672–1673), written against episcopal tyranny and religious persecution. Marvell turns his adversary – Samuel Parker – into the character 'Bayes', animadverting by way of an ongoing dialogue in which he gets to control both sides. Though Leslie and Tutchin use dialogue form, they both revise the relationship between the two speakers on display in Marvell's tract. Nicholas Phillipson suggests that in *The Rehearsal* Mr. Observator's 'Whiggery was systematically demolished by the relentless ... iconoclasm of a companion who had been conspicuously passive in Tutchin's dialogue'.[33] I disagree. As I will argue in Chapter 6, Tutchin's Countryman is not as submissive as Leslie's. Mr. Observator treats his conversationalist with affection and takes his opinions seriously; his Countryman is a reader of newspapers and pamphlets, and he is willing (and encouraged) to offer opinions and pass judgments. Leslie's Countryman is not a friend but a pupil, one who shares Mr. Rehearsal's conviction that commoners lack sufficient reasoning capacities to interpret events correctly on their own. *The Observator* models a different rhetorical relationship, one in keeping with its ideological commitments.

Throughout its lifespan (1702–1712), *The Observator* is ardently Whig in its orientation, but the focuses and arguments shift over the decade. In 1703, the first volume of collected *Observators* appeared with an argumentative preface establishing the ideology of the papers in no uncertain terms. Tutchin announces his '*Veneration* for the *Power* of *Parliaments* (which are our Constitution)'. Characteristically historical in his claims, here he looks back to the 'Infancy of Government', contesting the notion of hereditary right and asserting Whig dogma: government was instituted 'for the Good of the People'. Given that 'the People have a Natural Power Inherent in them to chuse their own Governours, and to settle 'em in Succession', then subjects may also 'alter [succession] when it proves prejudicial to the publick Tranquility'. Hereditary succession 'is the greatest Bar to Liberty that possibly can be'.

Tutchin's conclusion is one of radical – not middle-of-the-road – Whiggery: the 'true Power of Princes does Terminate, and is Controulable by the Peoples Laws' (no. 1). Cowan has observed that Defoe's attitudes about

---

[33] Nicholas Phillipson, 'Politeness and Politics in the Reigns of Anne and the Early Hanoverians', in J. G. A. Pocock (ed. with assistance from Gordon J. Schochet and Lois G. Schwoerer), *The Varieties of British Political Thought, 1500–1800* (Cambridge, 1993), 211–45, p. 219.

resistance – that it was legitimate in 1688 and 'could be used again' – distinguished him from most Whigs, who tended 'to define the Glorious Revolution as an exceptional, almost unique and unprecedented event'.[34] Tutchin is if anything a louder proponent of resistance. Most Whigs suggest that resistance is justifiable in extreme circumstances, but Tutchin adds no such qualifier; he is reticent about the destabilising implications of resistance. History affirms, for Tutchin, that the 'best Kings and Queens ... have always had a tender regard to the *Honour* and *Dignity* of Parliaments, they have heark'ned to their *Advice*, and have *Govern'd* by their *Councils*' (no. 2).

Tutchin's *Observator* papers are passionately anti-Catholic and anti-French, and, naturally, hostile to High Church Tories. In his anticlericalism, Tutchin is aggressive, brusque, forthright, relentless. He has, for example, no patience with or respect for the solemnities associated with 30 January: only 'the *Jacks* do make a Confounded Noise' about that day. 'The *Tantivy Priesthood* can wrest the Scriptures to any meaning', he complains, and 'There are *High-Flyers* in Government as well as in Religion, and these teach Princes that they must make no Concessions to their People' (vol. 3, pp. 94, 78). Unlike other Whig outlets, Tutchin's paper is predominantly concerned to make an argument about political power. It is distinguished not only by its radical Whig positions, but also by its belligerence and its tenacity, its biweekly assault on high-flyers and their tyranny-fostering credenda.

In 1708–1710 (post-Tutchin) the paper broadens its focus. The war looms larger, the contributors objecting to Tory land-focused military strategy (vol. 6, no. 89) and to the human cost of the battles (vol. 7, no. 2). Unsurprisingly, the Whig *Observator* worries about the success of the Union with Scotland and raises alarm about Jacobite rebellions. In the spring of 1708, the contributors begin to play up the importance of Protestant unity. Tutchin's old animosity toward 'the Pretender's Church-Faction' continues in the post-Tutchin *Observator* (vol. 9, no. 23), especially around the time of Sacheverell's trial. Exactly when Ridpath took control of *The Observator* is unclear, but he is the principal pen behind the paper during the Harley ministry, and the partisan heat of 1702–1708 returns.

In its last two years (1710–1712), *The Observator* sounds much like it had under Tutchin. The advent of a Tory ministry provokes a renewal of the attack on the 'slavish Doctrine of Unlimited Non-Resistance and Hereditary Right' (vol. 9, no. 85). The paper, again recalling Tutchin, deplores the Church party and disparages those who '*would set Princes above Laws*' (73). The contributor(s) spotlight the pernicious practices and false loyalty

---

[34] Brian Cowan, 'Daniel Defoe's *Review* and the Transformations of the English Periodical', *Huntington Library Quarterly* 77 (2014), 79–110, p. 87.

of high-flyers, explicitly with an eye toward the upcoming election, about which Mr. Observator is full of advice.

What Ridpath has that Tutchin did not is a clearly defined target: as of the fall of 1710, *The Observator* devotes itself to answering – attempting to discredit – the new Tory outlet, *The Examiner*. Like most Whig respondents to *The Examiner*, including Mainwaring, Oldmixon, and Steele, Ridpath takes furious exception to its criticisms of Marlborough, which represents 'not only a Breach of Good Manners, but a Failure in point of Loyalty' (vol. 9, no. 91). He calls into question Mr. Examiner's sense of allegiance and his honesty, and, like *The Medley*, mocking his self-importance by means of ironic praise: he is 'taller by Head and Shoulders than all the *little smattering Whig-Remarkers about Town*'. Mr. Examiner – at this time, Swift – is 'a Monarchical Author' who yet banters his Queen and teaches 'his Mob to speak to their Sovereigns' in a too-familiar, impudent style (96).

Under Ridpath, *The Observator* has two major (and related) objectives, both of which have to do with refuting *The Examiner*. One is to expose – à la Tutchin – the malicious motives of high-flying advocates of hereditary right and unlimited passive obedience. The other, a new concern, is to affirm the equally dangerous folly of leaving Spain to the house of Bourbon. Ridpath contends that both the Allies and Queen Anne were resolved to win Spain entirely, not to settle for partition, and that Mr. Examiner, Mr. Review, and the ministry are therefore advocating a resolution contra to the queen's wishes. In the closing numbers of *The Observator*, Ridpath asserts that '*the Political Question propounded in*' Swift's *Conduct of the Allies* amounts to '*Treason*', implies that the constitution has been under attack by the Tories, and argues '*we are in greater Danger by the* French *than by the* Dutch' (vol. 11, nos. 35, 53). After a brief middle period, under a Whig ministry, when *The Observator* was less defensive and pugnacious, the ferocity of the Tutchin phase is revived in 1710–1712. *The Observator* was arguably the most radical of the Whig journals under Anne. The Tories could not, of course, let it go unanswered.

The principal critic of *The Observator* is the Anglican nonjuror and Jacobite incendiary Charles Leslie, whose *Rehearsal* was founded partly to counter Tutchin. A Jacobite agent, Leslie served the Pretender and even joined him for a while in Italy in the wake of the failed rebellion of 1715. Leslie's venture, also in dialogue form, 'was far more jocular and mimicked the *Observator* in a way that drew attention to Tutchin's angry tone'.[35] As Mainwaring had tried to make his Whig readers 'merry' with Mr. Examiner, so Leslie seeks to expose and ridicule the bluster of his ever-incensed

---

[35] Sommerville, *News Revolution*, p. 125.

adversary. He explains his enterprise as an effort to respond not to Whig pamphleteers but to their news-writing fellows, since 'the greatest Part of the *People* do not Read *Books*', but instead 'Gather together about one that can *Read*, and Listen to an *Observator* or *Review* (as I have seen them in the Streets) where all the *Principles* of *Rebellion* are Instill'd into them'.[36]

The Rehearsal is primarily concerned to promote the sanctified and unassailable authority of the Church and monarchy: '*Kings* are *Civil Bishops* and *Bishops* are *Spiritual Kings*' (vol. 2, no. 27), an acknowledgement of the Tory twin pillars. Leslie highlights the Church's scriptural authority (vol. 3, no. 1), and frequently insists upon the separation of dissenters from that Church. On 15 October 1707, he challenges the dissenters' argument 'that *Bishop* and *Presbyter* are the same', and that '*Episcopacy* Crept in [to the Church] by *Degrees*', maintaining that the Church was from its origins episcopal in nature. Leslie takes issue with *The Observator*'s support of Scottish Presbyterians against Scottish Episcopalians, obviously keen to defend the latter. Toward the dissenters, Leslie has nothing but contempt: they who do not partake in communion are 'not only throwing themselves out of the *Church*, but even forsaking *Christ* himself' (vol. 2, no. 6). Leslie defines his Anglican priesthood as the representatives of the true spiritual code, asserting that to scorn the bishops is to scorn religion (vol. 2, no. 28).

The Rehearsal promulgates an extremely conservative view of political power: not for nothing does Mr. Review brand Leslie 'the known Advocate of Tyrants' (vol. 5, no. 18). Though '*Kings* and *Bishops* may have more or less Power . . . as People are Dispos'd to *Obedience* or *Rebellion*', the '*Right*' of those leaders is always 'Deriv'd by *Succession*' (vol. 2, no. 16). Leslie's antagonism toward populism is manifest: 'Our *Constitution* is not upon the Foot of the *People*. No *Law* to this Day allows of Taking *Arms* against the *Government*, on any *Pretence* Whatsoever' (vol. 3, no. 15). He blames both Defoe and Benjamin Hoadly for '*Infect*[ing] . . . the *People*' and spreading false notions about the right to resist (vol. 3, no. 19), complaining crisply that for Defoe 'all *Rebellion* is the *Inspiration* of *God*' (18). Contra rabble-rousing Whigs, Leslie insists that, 'All *Civil* Power is *Deriv'd* from the *Crown*', and that the people 'ever were, and must be in *Subjection*' (vol. 3, no. 28). *The Rehearsal* seeks to expose rebellion as something other than a principled defence of natural rights: rebellion is always 'for *Power*', and 'Other things, as *Religion*, *Liberty*, &c. are made the *Pretence*, to stir up the

---

[36] Leslie, *The Rehearsal*, preface to vol. 1; quoted from J. A. Downie, 'Stating Facts Right About Defoe's *Review*', in Downie and Thomas N. Corns (eds.), *Telling People What To Think: Early Eighteenth-Century Periodicals from* The Review *to* The Rambler (London, 1993), 8–22, p. 17.

People' (vol. 2, no. 13). *The Rehearsal* and *The Examiner* are the two most authoritarian partisan papers of Anne's reign, and both argue from a nostalgic, conservative position against the more populist, liberty-endorsing politics of Tutchin and Defoe.

The Tatler *and* The Spectator

Few scholars of periodical literature, as Downie has wryly observed, have wished 'to taint' Addison and Steele's 'deathless prose ... with the dirty world of the politics of Queen Anne's reign'.[37] Their major papers have tended not to be discussed alongside other advocacy journals of this period. Most studies of eighteenth-century journalism have eschewed the grubby particulars of partisan warfare and lionised the exalted, high literary moralising of Addison and Steele, rather than the other way around – but in any case, the impression has been that never the twain should meet. Downie was among the first seriously to acknowledge and reckon with the 'flagrantly partisan' aspects of *The Spectator*, and other modern scholars have followed suit, but the general consensus has been that *The Spectator* and *The Tatler* belong in a special category. This is not incorrect, but that the two are so frequently linked is misleading. What, then, is the position of *The Tatler* and of *The Spectator* vis-à-vis contemporary papers?

Addison's and Steele's most celebrated papers are usually described as principally about providing instruction and diversion, but with a secondary, broadly ideological, political stance. Charles A. Knight describes *The Spectator* as having 'replaced propaganda with ideology as a mode of political discourse', carrying 'on a political discourse without appearing to do so'.[38] As Calhoun Winton has noted, a significant part of this stance is 'the sympathetic representation of those "trading interests" which did ... represent a large part of the Whig strength'.[39] *The Spectator* project, Cowan concludes, was a 'response to the crisis of Whig political fortunes in the later years of Queen Anne's reign', a reaction to Tory resurgence. Addison and Steele, continues Cowan, imply that 'a truly reformed coffeehouse might stand out as a respectable alternative to the Sacheverellite Tory claim that only the Church of England can offer a solid foundation

---

[37] Downie, 'Periodicals and Politics in the Reign of Queen Anne', in Robin Myers and Michael Harris (eds.), *Serials and their Readers 1620–1914* (New Castle, 1993), 46–61, p. 51. Subsequent quotation at p. 53.

[38] Charles A. Knight, '*The Spectator*'s Generalizing Discourse', in J. A. Downie and Thomas N. Corns (eds.), *Telling People What To Think: Early Eighteenth-Century Periodicals from* The Review *to* The Rambler (London, 1993), 44–57, pp. 54–55, 44.

[39] Calhoun Winton, *Captain Steele: The Early Career of Richard Steele* (Baltimore, 1964), 140.

for the moral revitalization of society'.[40] Precisely how legible this nuanced argument was to contemporaries is perhaps debatable, but that Addison and Steele wanted to contest the notion that the church had an exclusive claim on morality seems likely.[41]

Both *The Tatler* and *The Spectator* affected political neutrality, but through innuendo and gentle conditioning their authors 'demonstrate[d] quietly that Whiggism was the natural consequence of the public values and attitudes that they articulated'.[42] They sought, says Ophelia Field, 'to make Whiggery synonymous with Englishness'.[43] Ronald Paulson concludes that Addison in particular 'can be said to have created in his 'Pleasures [of the Imagination]' an epistemology based on liberty, as a reaction to Jacobite and Roman Catholic tyranny'.[44] Downie has also pointed specifically to the early issues of *The Spectator*, which call attention to a potential credit crisis faced by Anne's new Tory ministry. Downie hypothesises that the timing of the launch of *The Spectator* might suggest Addison's intentions 'to perpetuate the period of political instability which the change of government had precipitated'. If *The Spectator* had ended after a dozen numbers, Downie reasons, scholars would be much less likely to characterise it as apolitical.[45]

Addison's scepticism about satire – which Steele does not entirely share – is also politically charged. Though he encourages mirth and laughter, in Addison's lexicon satire involves humour coupled with something other than benevolence. In *Spectator* no. 47, he quotes Hobbes admiringly: 'The Passion of Laughter is nothing else but sudden Glory arising from some . . . Conception of some Eminency in our selves, by Comparison with the Infirmity of others' (vol. 1, p. 200). Though Steele grants the possibility of good-natured satire, Addison insists, 'Our Satyr is nothing but Ribaldry, and *Billingsgate*'. This 'cruel Practice tends to the utter Subversion of all Truth and Humanity among us', and should be denounced by 'all who have either the Love of their Country, the Honour of their Religion, at Heart' (4:88). Laughter at others is proud and unsocial, an aesthetic as well as a public problem, and both

---

[40] Brian Cowan, 'Mr. Spectator and the Coffeehouse Public Sphere', *Eighteenth-Century Studies* 37 (2004), 345–66, pp. 347, 349.

[41] Lawrence E. Klein, 'Joseph Addison's Whiggism', in David Womersley (ed., with assistance from Paddy Bullard and Abigail Williams), *'Cultures of Whiggism': New Essays on English Literature and Culture in the Long Eighteenth Century* (Newark, 2005), 108–26, p. 110.

[42] Abigail Williams, *Poetry and the Creation of a Whig Literary Culture, 1681–1714* (Oxford, 2005), p. 160.

[43] Ophelia Field, *The Kit-Cat Club* (London and New York, 2009), p. 257.

[44] Ronald Paulson, *The Beautiful, Novel, and Strange: Aesthetics and Heterodoxy* (Baltimore, 1996), p. 50.

[45] Downie, 'Periodicals and Politics', pp. 54, 56.

producers and consumers of satire are guilty of un-patriotism. The key, for our purposes, is that Addison's critique of satire represents a form of anti-Tory satire. He defines satire as almost inevitably Juvenalian, an expression of superiority and deprecation, and in doing so he values Horatian (Whig) *sermones* over Tory diatribe. Throughout his paper, Mr. Spectator satirises his Tory rivals as 'incompetent, simple-minded old men who have lived beyond their usefulness',[46] but he legitimates his satiric characterisation by distancing his mode from ignoble Tory mockery. Paulson's conclusion is compelling: Addison 'isolat[es] ridicule as a Tory eccentricity', and by 'claiming not to write satire', he creates 'as rhetorically effective a satire as can be imagined'.[47]

Eighteenth-century scholars often treat *The Tatler* as part of the '*Spectator* project', and while that may be true, *The Tatler* (Apr 1709–Jan 1711) predates *The Spectator* (Mar 1711–Dec 1712, and Jun–Dec 1714). Let us, though, take them in reverse order, beginning with *The Spectator*, since most conclusions about the pair of papers are better suited to it than to *The Tatler*. Beyond favourable depictions of the trading interest, what is the nature of *The Spectator*'s politics? One key is the portraits of Sir Roger de Coverly and Will Honeycombe, members of the landed gentry who are (gently) caricatured in *The Spectator*; they stand in for nostalgic Tories unable to adapt to a post-Revolution world, but they are presented as moderate, and Sir Roger's interaction with the Whig Sir Andrew Freeport takes the form of 'an agreeable Raillery' (vol. 2. p. 3). Throughout, Addison is keen to minimise party distinctions, dismissive of the 'Whig' and 'Tory' labels. As he concludes in no. 125, 'we should not any longer regard our Fellow-Subjects as Whigs or Tories, but should make the Man of Merit our Friend, and the Villain our Enemy' (vol. 1, p. 512). Given that the political landscape was at this time dominated by the Tories, Addison's desire to play down the partisan divide makes sense, and he clearly enjoyed affecting to occupy the *via media*: 'the honest Men of all Parties should enter into a Kind of Association for the Defence of one another and the Confusion of their common Enemies' (vol. 2, p. 1).

The enemy in *The Spectator* is France, and Addison focuses on the continent, disparaging the Catholic power and the Sun King, but without commenting on Jacobitism at home. The Pretender is not a presence in *The Spectator*. Anticipating peace, Addison expresses his concern that English

---

[46] Ronald Paulson, *The Fictions of Satire* (Baltimore, 1967), p. 216.
[47] Paulson, *Beautiful, Novel, and Strange*, p. 73; Paulson, *Fictions of Satire*, p. 218. I deal with this issue in 'Thinking about Satire', in Paddy Bullard (ed.), *A Handbook of Eighteenth-Century Satire* (Oxford, 2019), 475–91.

manners will suffer from the war's end; he voices his 'wish that there was an Act of Parliament for Prohibiting the Important of *French* Fopperies' (vol. 1, p. 192). He derides Louis for 'Ostentation of Riches, the Vanity of Equipage, Shame of Poverty, and Ignorance of Modesty', and so on (vol. 2, p. 48). There are other topical allusions, to Marlborough, for example, and to the occasional conformity bill passed by the Tories, which Roger cheerfully reports on 8 January 1712. But on the whole Addison steers clear of partisan conflict. An anomalous essay is no. 287, an extended paean on liberty and a discourse on the dangers of 'a Despotical Government', along with a correspondent use of history to warn against tyranny (vol. 3, p. 19). The issue is dated 29 January, the day before the anniversary of King Charles the Martyr; as Bond suggests, Addison's caution against absolutism is effective coming as it does on the eve of the day when 'Tory divines were likely to rhapsodize over the "divinely" monarchical form of government' (vol. 3, p. 21n1).

One dimension of *The Spectator*'s engagement with party affairs is its apparent discouragement of popular politics. Cowan posits that Addison and Steele 'were not . . . enthusiastic about the potential for public politics', and a key part of the *Spectator* 'project was to close off and restrain, rather than to open up, venues for public debate . . . especially . . . on matters of political concern'.[48] One finds this tendency, famously, in their derision of newsmongers. On 30 June 1711, Addison frowns upon the 'State-Pedant [who] is wrapt up in News, and lost in Politicks', highlighting such a figure's superficial knowledge: 'If you mention either of the Kings of *Spain* or *Poland*, he talks very notably, but if you go out of the *Gazette* you drop him' (vol. 1, p. 438). Almost a year later, he holds forth on the manufacture of paper, countless sheets of which 'are stained with News or Politicks' and 'fly thro' the Town in *Post-Men, Post-Boys, Daily-Courants, Reviews, Medleys* and *Examiners*. Men, Women and Children contend who shall be the first Bearers of them, and get their daily Sustenance by spreading them' (vol. 3, p. 380).

The Tatler's attitude toward popular involvement is more complicated, its political commentary more extensive. Steele's criticism of state pedants is sharper than Addison's: he condemns 'Volunteers in Politicks, that undergo all the Pain, Watchfulness, and Disquiet of a First Minister, without turning it to the Advantage either of themselves or their Country'. They represent a 'numerous . . . Species', and an active one: 'There is nothing more frequent than to find a Taylor breaking his Rest on the Affairs of *Europe*, and to see a Cluster of Porters sitting upon the Ministry. Our Streets swarm with

---

[48] Cowan, 'Mr. Spectator and the Coffeehouse Public Sphere', p. 346.

Politicians, and there is scarce a Shop which is not held by a Statesman' (vol. 2, p. 394). Significantly, Steele's most acerbic comments on this subject date from the Godolphin ministry's time in power – a happy period for Steele, who maintained in April 1709 that that 'the Island was never in greater Prosperity, or the Administration in so good Hands' (vol. 1, pp. 42–43). He presents Godolphin as a 'Master of Great Abilities', 'industrious and restless for the Preservation of the Liberties of the People', and so on (44). That he objected to sceptical public engagement in the spring of 1710, with the Godolphin ministry under pressure during and after the Sacheverell trial, is unsurprising. As Nicola Parsons has rightly noted, the doctor's trial affected the paper: 'While the *Tatler*'s bias against the public's use of news was evident from its very first number, it was reinvigorated by the trial, particularly by the role the press played in engaging the general reading public with the serious issues under debate, and the manner in which this public engagement was manifest'.[49] In a time of too-influential Tory mobs, Steele's disapprobation of a public 'Turn to Politicks' makes sense (vol. 3, p. 202). In his not-much-later journalism, however, Steele is a good deal more comfortable with the notion of a critical public. I have already quoted his declaration, in *The Englishman* for 14 November 1713, that a dutiful subject 'may, nay he ought to have a jealous Eye upon the Officers and Servants of his Prince' and work 'to alarm his Fellow-Subjects' when necessary (75).

At no point during the life of *The Tatler* is Steele shy about alluding to public events, which itself suggests his greater inclination to politicise the people. Most scholars have downplayed the role of the news in the paper, but Steele wanted his periodical to be a source of information and for political instruction.[50] During the period of overlap between his control of *The Gazette* and the life of *The Tatler*, he double-dipped, printing the information to which he was privy in the former capacity in the new paper as well.[51] In the inaugural *Tatler*, he explains that what follows '*should be principally intended for the Use of Politick Persons, who are so publick-spirited as to neglect their own Affairs to look into Transactions of State*' (vol. 1, p. 15). The principal focus of *The Tatler*'s news is the war, and the bottom line tends to be that 'the Allies ... will not admit of a Treaty, except *France* offers what

---

[49] Nicola Parsons, *Reading Gossip in Early Eighteenth-Century England* (Basingstoke, 2009), p.106.
[50] The presence of news changes over the life of the paper: 'After the hundredth issue in late November the news is only included on a further six occasions', Parsons observes, but this difference does not mark 'the paper's renunciation of politics'. Instead, it 'merely signalled that the paper's political engagement had changed its form' (Parsons, *Reading Gossip*, p.103).
[51] Parsons, *Reading Gossip*, p. 103.

is more suitable to her present [beleaguered] Condition', and that France is seeking 'to break the good Understanding of the Allies' (vol. 1, pp. 21, 28). The crucial Protestant-vs-Papist division we find in many Whig papers is on display in *The Tatler*, which endorses the naturalisation of foreign Protestants (vol. 1, p. 82) and generally highlights the perfidy of France and of the Catholic Church (e.g., pp. 60–61).

In the summer and fall of 1710, Steele finds himself under fire for *The Tatler*'s engagement with politics. The Tory *Moderator* of 3 July queries his favourable comparison of Marlborough to Hannibal (20 June), and as Bond points out, 'As late as October 1713 this . . . allusion was still rankling in the minds of the Tory party-writers' (vol. 3, p. 17n11), as witnessed by Oldisworth's *Examiner* of 12 October. *Tatler* no. 187, in which the portrait occurs, is Steele's first clear counter to Tory propaganda against the Whigs' hero-general. Rightly or not, contemporaries regarded Steele's unflattering portrait of the 'Cunning' Polypragmon (no. 191) as a comment on Harley. On 8 July, a month before the ministerial change was complete, Steele prints a letter complaining that he has 'turn[ed] Politician in the present unhappy Dissentions'. The letter-writer hopes that Steele will not be swayed by 'the Staggering Party' (Whigs) and will avoid 'offend[ing] the very better Half of the Nation' (the Tories). Steele responds by downplaying his political engagement, though not before registering his disagreement 'about the Words Staggering and Better Part' (pp. 50–51).

The Tatler is not as polemical as Steele's subsequent journals, but he cannot resist engaging in partisan battles. He counters Tory propaganda, and in August he controversially recounts Stanhope's victory in Catalonia. The account given in no. 210 matches, verbatim, that printed in *The Daily Courant* and *The Gazette* (of which Steele was still in charge), and *Examiner* no. 5 disapprovingly notes Steele's panegyric. On 3 October, Steele mocks the news-hungry Upholsterer, whose predilections are clearly Tory: he reads and admires *The Post Man, The Moderator, The Post Boy*, and *The Examiner*, all (from Steele's perspective) rabble-rousing disseminators of misinformation (vol. 3, p. 201). In the closing issue of *The Tatler*, Steele acknowledges that his paper 'touched upon Matters which concern both the Church and State', but insists that 'the Points I alluded to are such as concerned every Christian and Freeholder in *England*' (364). Whether or not Steele is sincere in regretting his political engagement is difficult to say. Subsequently, he would waver between the indirect (*The Guardian*) and the virulent (*The Englishman*). In any case, *The Tatler* is more patently politicised than *The Spectator*; Steele's papers are more attuned to continental affairs. Despite his anxiety about hoodwinked Tory mobs, provoked by their reading of Tory propaganda, Steele seems unable to avoid appealing to some readers to be invested in current events and in the battle between Protestant and Papist.

The aims of political journalism, 1695–1714

> 'The Observator' is best to *towel* the Jacks, &c.; 'The Review' is best to promote peace; 'The Flying-Post' is best for the Scotch News; 'The Post-Boy' is best for the English and Spanish News; 'The Daily Courant' is the best Critick; 'The English Post' is the best Collector; 'The London Gazette' has the best authority; and 'The Post-Man' is the best for every thing.
>
> (*The Life and Errors of John Dunton* [1706], vol. 2, p. 438)

Dunton's list of superlatives is partisan and not very reflective of the content of the works he names, but his comment illustrates the contemporary appreciation that not all Whig or Tory papers were meant to perform the same work. This is an elementary point, and one with which no one would quibble, but to date the distinctions among these papers have scarcely been noted. One purpose of the preceding survey was to highlight some of these distinctions, in audience, purpose, and tone. Dividing the vast corpus of political papers in this period into 'news' and more opinionated 'advocacy journals' is important, but it does not fully illuminate the range of types of papers or their objectives. What sorts of missions are journalists trying to accomplish? To what uses were political papers being put?

One primary agenda is simply to disseminate information, to report on current events, to offer trade data, to catalogue births and deaths, promotions, royal movements, and so on. Most characterisations of early eighteenth-century political journalism underestimate the degree to which the newspapers offer domestic commentary; dispatches from the continent and tales of foreign leaders often represent indirect allusions to local debates. The content of what is being reported is also important: do English subjects have the right only to news about the war and local 'public' affairs, or should they also (as Boyer's *The Political State of Great Britain* [1703–1729] suggests) be privy to parliamentary debates?

Most political journalists are promulgating ideology, either by means of indirect conditioning (à la *Tatler* and *Spectator*) or explicitly. *The Examiner* and especially *The Rehearsal* are anti-populist, defensive of the royal prerogative, commending obedience and deference. Some Whig writers are committed to challenging the slavish Tory creed of passive obedience and non-resistance, though to different degrees. Defoe, Tutchin, and Ridpath are extreme in their ideas about the legitimacy of resistance; unlike more moderate Whigs, they offer no caveats suggesting that only extreme circumstances can justify rebellion. Tutchin's matter-of-fact declaration that the 'true Power of Princes does Terminate, and is Controulable by the Peoples Laws' is offered without qualification: the radical implication is that monarch serves at the people's pleasure.[52] Examining ideological commitments helps us appreciate the problem of labelling a periodical merely 'Whig' or 'Tory'. Steele's *Englishman* and Mainwaring's *Medley* are both Whig outlets furiously unhappy with the Harley ministry and determined to answer *The Examiner* – but Steele, unlike Mainwaring and many other Whig journalists, argues not only against hereditary right but also *for* a populist basis of power. His position needs to be distinguished from Addisonian Whiggery, in which moralism and moderation appear to take precedence over partisanship, a predominantly cultural commitment with political implications. Steele and Addison have almost invariably been conceived of as allies with essentially similar ideological profiles: they support Revolution principles, a balanced government, the growth of commerce, and religious toleration.[53] But Steele's non-collaborative papers in particular reflect more radical populism than Addison would ever endorse. A different kind of ideological argumentation is to be found (to take a later example) in Trenchard and Gordon's fiercely anticlerical *Independent Whig* (1720), which laments the decline of the Reformation spirit within the Church, criticising high-flyers for their dependence upon ceremony and for presuming to mediate between individuals and God.

A number of papers are devoted to topical propaganda. Defoe's 1713–1714 *Mercator* is ostensibly 'about' defending the ministry's Treaty of Commerce, though he has broader objectives as well, and *The British Merchant* was launched to counter *Mercator*. Steele and Addison scuffle over the Peerage Bill of 1719, establishing their short-lived *Plebeian* (Steele) and *Old Whig* (Addison) to participate in the controversy. Most newspapers and journals are to some extent about policy, about interpreting events of the war, about responding to crises such as the Sacheverell trial or the ministerial change, and about telling people what to think on the events of the day. That topical commentary, however, is inseparable from more ideological agendas. Often the discussions of policy, events, or elections are presented in the form of advice: journalists in this period frequently presume to counsel not only the people but also the ministry, parliament, and even the monarch.

Political journalists often write to antagonise and debunk (e.g., Steele's 1714 *Lover* or Mainwaring's 1710–1712 *Medley*), but they are frequently

---

[52] *Vindication* prefaced to vol. I of the *Observator* (p. 2).
[53] Charles A. Knight, *A Political Biography of Richard Steele* (London, 2009), p. 2.

motivated by more positive aims, by the desire to defend or uphold values. We see this especially among High Church papers, expressing anxiety about change, appealing to tradition, and seeking to remind readers that Anglicanism is the lifeblood of the English constitution. Samuel Parker's monthly *Censura Temporum* (1708–1710) is single-minded in its purpose: commend publications that support the Church of England and its ideals, denounce those that do not. Swift's final *Examiner* papers and Oldisworth's later contributions are about, among other things, cultivating Tory unity. Many writers profess bipartisanship, disingenuously claiming, like Steele, to stand neuter, but a tiny number of papers actually seem bent on neutralising conflict. Yet another category is moralistic preachment, whether in the Addisonian manner (gently Horatian and decidedly Whig) or in the grumpier, more heavy-handed style of the Tory *Hermit* (1711–1712).

Journalists in this period wrote for a variety of reasons and to distinct audiences, and even among Whig and Tory papers one finds a wide range of interests, tones, and emphases. *The Hermit*, for example, is rigorously ideological, promulgating obedience above all things; the Tory *Plain Dealer* of the same year is singularly uninterested in the church or in dictating morality. Its author is exclusively concerned to support the Swiftian arguments against continuing the war. *The Examiner* of Swift and Oldisworth offers both ideological strictures and specific topical arguments. What one finds, in other words, is a noticeable degree of specialisation among Whig and Tory journals, and on both sides one gets the impression of multi-faceted attacks on the opposite party. A major purpose, one shared by more journalists than not, has to do with the question of political authority and representation. Periodical writers in particular raise questions, implicitly or explicitly, about who does or should have a political voice. Which side speaks for the nation? How should the government's actions and policies be interpreted, and who is entitled to weigh the merits of official decisions? How Whigs and Tories address these questions varies at any given moment, but broadly speaking something fundamental shifts after Anne's death. George's accession and the changes it wrought meant a radically different political landscape, and with that transformation came a marked change in the culture of partisan journalism.

Chapter 2
Early Hanoverian Political Journalism, 1714–1720

Political journalism in the half dozen years after Anne's death (1 August 1714) has received little extended commentary from scholars, who have usually been more interested in the transformative 1695–1714 period or in the period of anti-Walpole opposition and *The Craftsman* (1726–1752). Most critics observe that the rage of party so pronounced in late Stuart England quieted down after 1715: 'The party struggle of Anne's reign was over. The issues which had divided the political nation had disappeared or were subsiding'.[1] The Tories ceased to exert meaningful influence on the state, and the new king had little patience for opposition. In the tumultuous years following George's accession, 'the opposition periodic press was faced with an unprecedented campaign of official suppression'.[2] Tory and Jacobite periodicals were frequently squelched by the authorities within a year of their commencement; the disaffected had less freedom to voice their disaffection. More generally, so the story goes, the political landscape was calmer. The replacement of the Triennial Act with the Septennial Act (1716) meant fewer elections and therefore 'reduced political activity, and lessened popular participation'.[3] Kathleen Wilson's treatment of popular politics in this period is an exception: *The Sense of the People* (1995) acknowledges the continued role of the press in politicising the people, though it is broader based and necessarily less detailed in its discussion of newspapers.

This chapter seeks to answer a basic question: how does political journalism function between the summer of 1714 and *circa* 1720, before the

---

[1] Glyn Williams and John Ramsden, *Ruling Britannia: A Political History of Britain 1688–1988* (New York and London, 1990), p. 55. See also Downie, 'The Development of the Political Press', in Clyve Jones (ed.), *Britain in the First Age of Party 1680–1750: Essays Presented to Geoffrey Holmes* (London, 1987), 111–27, p. 119.

[2] P. B. J. Hyland, 'Liberty and Libel: Government and the Press during the Succession Crisis in Britain, 1712–1716'. *The English Historical Review* 101 (1986), 863–88, p. 884.

[3] Williams and Ramsden, *Ruling Britannia*, 56.

bursting of the South Sea Bubble and the start of a new phase in English politics? Though historians have highlighted both acute Whig paranoia and strong Tory opposition to the new regime, literary critics have made little attempt to read the cultural production of this period in those terms. The assumption has been that Tory papers were suppressed and ineffectual, and that Whig papers reflect triumphalism – that, in other words, there was no meaningful opposition press and that the Whigs could contentedly endorse and disseminate George's policies. This is not the case. What we find, on the contrary, is a succession of short-lived but quickly replaced Jacobite papers that taken together do represent a significant form of opposition, often fairly radical in its aims and evidently widely enjoyed. Whig journalists are not comfortable but anxious about the strength of popular Toryism and eager to contest it. Addison and his Whig allies labour, in these years, not only to encourage unity but to establish what turns out to be a myth: a notion of popular Hanoverianism. On both sides, there is considerable concern with the proper nature and limits of public politics. Tory journalists – like the Whigs of Anne's reign – find themselves defending the liberties of the people against perceived tyranny. The Whigs tend to encourage loyalty, and Addison in particular affirms the legitimacy of the new government's unpopular policies. Whig journalists attempt not so much to reflect a loyal populace but to create one.

What follows begins with brief contextual background about the transition from Stuart to Hanoverian rule. I then discuss Tory (section two) and Whig (section three) responses to the regime change as reflected in the periodical culture; the Whig reaction is complicated by the Whig split of *circa* 1717. The chapter concludes with a section devoted to Daniel Defoe. Though his canon of periodical writing remains somewhat uncertain, he clearly contributed both to loyalist and opposition propaganda; his career illustrates the limits of assuming rapport between George I's government and the Whigs supposed to have flourished under it. Some of the papers with which Defoe was involved typify the partisan struggle of these years; others (especially weeklies such as *Applebee's*) are outliers, and should be understood as representing one direction in which English journalism would go in the 1720s and beyond. The chapter's bottom line is simple: we tend to underestimate the complexity and uncertainty of the political reality of 1714–1720, as well as the role Whig and Tory journalism played in this contentious transitional moment.

Contexts: regime change and early Hanoverian politics

The narrative of transition from Stuart to Hanoverian rule now seems inevitable, but for many contemporaries events unfolded uncertainly.[4] At the time of Anne's death, English subjects did not know some important things: would there be a Jacobite attempt on the throne, and if so would it work? What kind of government would George I establish? That George's regime would be exclusively Whig was not a given, likely though that seems in retrospect. Anne's demise left the Tories hopelessly divided, and how the party would fare under the new regime depended upon unity. Opinions about the Tory future differed, and even St. John wavered between pessimism and determination. To Francis Atterbury he waxed gloomy, but he wrote to Swift that 'misfortunes may perhaps to some degree unite us. [T]he Torys seem to resolve not to be crush'd, and that is enough to prevent 'em from being so'.[5] The immediate future of party politics was not yet definite in the fall of 1714. St. John, Swift and others understood that their old plans had been 'broke[n] to shatters',[6] but they nevertheless tried to imagine ways of adapting to and surviving in the new world.

The events of early 1715 were quickly to eradicate whatever confidence the Tories had in George's broad-mindedness, and to demonstrate the ruthlessness of the Whigs in power. The year began with the anonymous publication of Atterbury's *English Advice to the Freeholders of England*, a scorching pamphlet calling upon the Tories to recognise the dangers of a single-party regime and to band together in opposition to the Whig government. The authorities were not amused; a reward was offered for the discovery of the author; and by March the period of Whig retribution had begun with a vengeance. Prominent members of Anne's last ministry were in the hot seat: Matthew Prior's papers were seized, and he was arrested and interrogated at length; St. John's papers were requested, at which point he fled. Swift was warned by Erasmus Lewis to destroy any incriminating evidence so that it did not 'fall into the hands of [his] Enemy's'.[7]

Literary critics continue to underestimate the degree of popular Toryism in early Hanoverian England, despite the work of historians. The Whig ascendance neither happened abruptly nor reflected the pro-Hanoverian

---

[4] I discuss Swift's experience of the regime change in '"*fuimus Torys*": Swift and Regime Change, 1714–1718', *Studies in Philology* 112 (2015), pp. 537–74.

[5] Printed in Macpherson, *Original Papers* (1775), vol. 2, p. 651; David Woolley (ed.), *The Correspondence of Jonathan Swift, D. D.* (4 vols., Frankfurt am Main, 1999–2007), vol. 2, p. 47.

[6] Swift, *Correspondence*, vol. 2, p. 63.

[7] Swift, *Correspondence*, vol. 2, p. 112.

will of 'the people'. In 1978, Nicholas Rogers pointed out that 'One of the most remarkable features of early Hanoverian politics was the persistent and deep-rooted hostility of Londoners to the new regime.'[8] Rogers offers many specific instances of anti-ministerial demonstrations and of sometimes violent 'Tory militancy'.[9] During the proceedings against Harley, St. John, and Ormonde, mobs rallied behind those ministers, defying the government to punish them. Tory ideologues were not the only ones contributing to the unrest; tradesmen suffered in the early years of Hanoverian rule, and the Whigs had failed to cultivate support among commoners. Much of the disaffection, then, was among plebeians, not ideologically driven Jacobites, but the government's brutal response to popular protest drove many moderates toward more radical positions.

Despite their success at the polls, the Whigs hardly enjoyed a comfortable ascendance, and the government resorted to violent measures carried out in the name of public security. In 1715, the authorities redefined riot laws so that most demonstrations had to be ruled not misdemeanours but acts of treason. The other change involved accountability: if rioters were injured or killed in the process of being incapacitated, magistrates would no longer be penalised.[10] In his diary of 1715, Dudley Ryder – though steadfast in his support of Hanover – privately admits uncertainty about the wisdom of this policy: 'I said what I could to justify the Act (which would have had to have been only temporary and not as it is perpetual) but I did not sufficiently answer their objections and I think they were in the right of it.'[11]

The government increased not only the severity but also the visibility of the punishment; executions and the mutilation of the resulting corpses were public spectacles. In February 1716, Ryder describes the execution of two traitors, warmly commending the king for his 'resolution':

> I think he has given in this a greater proof than ever of his fitness to govern this nation, and I am persuaded it will have a good effect at home to make the Tories partly despair and partly come over to the King. (*Diary*, 188)

---

[8] Nicholas Rogers, 'Popular Protest in Early Hanoverian London', *Past & Present* 79 (1978), 70–100, p. 83.
[9] Rogers, 'Popular Protest', 72, 71. Linda Colley attempts to show that 'the tory parliamentary party retained ideological identity, a capacity for concerted political action, and considerable political power' under George I and George II; *In Defiance of Oligarchy: The Tory Party 1714–1760* (Cambridge, 1982), p. 7.
[10] Rogers, 'Popular Protest', pp. 73–75.
[11] William Matthews (ed.), *The Diary of Dudley Ryder, 1715–1716* (London, 1939), p. 94.

The public punishments were supplemented by Whig vigilantism, widely practiced and implicitly encouraged. The standing army was doubled. What followed was essentially a witch-hunt for Jacobites. In July, the government suspended habeas corpus, ostensibly to provide security against conspiracy and insurgence. This got Swift's attention from Dublin: 'The suspending the Habeas Corpus Act has frightened our Friends in Engl^{d}'.[12]

The Whigs' violent proceedings, despite Ryder's optimism, increased disloyalty and dissent. The effect of such oppressive measures, and of the redefinition of popular protest as treason, was to drive less radical Tories (says St. John) 'into the arms of the Pretender'.[13] The ferocity and persistence of Jacobite unhappiness in this period warrants consideration, however disordered and ultimately ineffectual the mission. The rebellion of 1715 was a flop, and the alliance with France (after Louis XIV's death in 1715) enervated the Jacobite cause. The general election of 1715 resulted in a Whig landslide, though the Tories fared better than the Whigs had in either 1710 or 1713.[14] The numbers were bad, in other words, but not disastrous: the problem was the Tory failure to consolidate power as an oppositional force. The only remaining minister with Tory credentials, the second Earl of Nottingham, was removed from office in February 1716, a dismissal confirming the party's marginality. The Whig split of 1717 changed the relationship between the court and the opposition, though it did not mitigate Tory irrelevance. The church party lacked the organisation to re-establish its potency, and by 1723 – in the wake of the failed invasion scheme and the Atterbury plot of 1721–1722 – the Whig ministry had a secure majority.

George's conflict with the Whigs started early in the new regime and it principally concerned Britain's role in the Great Northern War (1700–1721) between Russia and Sweden. In 1717, George officially entered his new kingdom into the affair, offering naval help to Russia and its allies (Denmark-Norway, Saxony-Poland, Prussia). He had aligned Hanover with Sweden's enemies in 1715, and his decision to have Britain join the fight manifestly furthered Hanoverian interests. His promise of support in the form of the British navy directly violated the Act of Settlement,

---

[12] Swift, *Correspondence*, vol. 2, p. 141.
[13] Henry St. John, *Letter to Sir William Wyndham* (1717); in *The Works of Lord Bolingbroke* (4 vols., 1844; Rpt. London, 1967), vol. 1, p. 129.
[14] In 1715, the Whigs won 316 seats to the Tories' 197; in 1710, the Whigs had won 181 seats and in 1713 only 150. The Whig majority was significantly slimmer in 1715 than the Tory majority had been in the last years of Anne's reign, when the Whigs had managed to function as an effective oppositional force; W. A. Speck, *Tory & Whig: The Struggle in the Constituencies, 1701–1715* (London, 1970), p. 123.

according to which England was not – without parliamentary consent – to be involved in any war to defend territories not under English dominion. George needed to convince parliament to support his anti-Swedish policy, and he used the 'Gyllenborg Plot' to help do so. In January 1717, the Swedish envoy Count Carl Gyllenborg had been arrested on suspicion of Jacobitism; his papers were seized from the embassy, a move that violated diplomatic immunity. Rumors spread that Charles XII of Sweden was involved in planning a Jacobite coup, and the king wished to use such rumors to persuade the House of Commons to pay for military measures against Sweden.[15]

As of 1716, prominent Whig leaders were competing (viciously) for control, but the events of 1717 brought the situation to a crisis: Stanhope and Sunderland supported His Majesty, and Walpole and Townshend did not. The latter pair worked to raise opposition in the Commons, and the Prince of Wales was sympathetic to their position. They laboured to create tension between the king and his son, urging the prince to resent his father for giving him so little power as regent. Townshend was dismissed in the spring of 1717, and Walpole resigned; by the summer, they were uncomfortably allied with Tories, looking to swell opposition numbers, to revive a Country party to counter Court Whigs. More independent Whigs were appalled, and the conflict initiated a struggle among government and opposition Whigs over what the true principles of the party were. Despite the manifest Whig ascendancy in these years, then, there was anything but party solidarity.

What of religious controversy? High Churchmen were unhappy about the directions in which English politics seemed to be moving. Many English clergymen, perhaps even a majority, W. A. Speck reminds us, 'responded sympathetically to the rallying cry 'the church in danger' in the parliamentary elections held only a few weeks after George was crowned'. The king controlled ecclesiastical promotions, establishing 'a virtual whig monopoly of episcopal preferment'. In December 1714, he issued a proclamation forbidding clergymen to preach political sermons, and in 1717 'the high churchmen lost their national sounding board when convocation was suppressed' – essentially for the duration of the century.[16] The silencing of convocation occurred in the wake of the lower house's denunciation of Benjamin Hoadly, Bishop of Bangor, for his insistence upon the state's authority over the Church. In the Bangorian controversy, the king sided with the bishop, keen to marginalise the High Church and limit its power.

---

[15] Paul S. Fritz, *The English Ministers and Jacobitism between the Rebellions of 1715 and 1745* (Toronto, 1975), p. 28.
[16] W. A. Speck, *Stability and Strife: England 1714–1760* (London, 1977), pp. 91, 93.

'The practical consequence of the controversy', Justin Champion concludes, 'was the silencing of the Church as a constitutional institution'.[17] Writers like Toland, Steele, Trenchard and Gordon contributed significantly to the prominent anticlerical campaign of these years. The high Tories who had expected so much under Anne were disappointed under the new regime; the role of the Church in the English polity had changed utterly. The Church ceased to exert its old influence, while its dissenting enemies enjoyed fewer restrictions and more privileges.[18] By the 1720s, England was an essentially pluralist society – witness the spread of Socinianism, deism, even atheism – but the events and official attitudes of 1714–1720 made more prominent heterodoxy possible, and committed Anglicans were understandably discomfited by the new reality.

The rage of party that marked Anne's reign might well have been somewhat stilled in a time of Whig hegemony, but there was much uncertainty and violence. The government's measures were extreme; the king's motives were unclear; both parties struggled to retain their identity; and factions within each sought to show that their principles were most in line with traditional party values. After 1717, the Whigs were divided – albeit not fundamentally – and throughout George's reign, and beyond, the Tories had little coherence. What do Whig and Tory political journalists seem to be trying to accomplish in these unsettled years?

Tory resistance and the Jacobite press

> What might lawfully be printed in Queen *Anne*'s Reign is become Treason now.
> –*Robin's Last Shift*, 31 March 1716

Scholars have mostly presumed the Tory press of these years to be enervated, occasionally impassioned but reflecting little sense of coherent effort; the exception, again, is Wilson, whose discussion of popular politics is sound and helpful. The government tried (and managed) to suppress some of outspoken enemies through the threat of persecution. George I employed unofficial informers to identify clandestine libellers; in the case of print publication, warrants would be issued for the arrest of authors and

---

[17] Justin Champion, '"To govern is to make subjects believe": Anticlericalism, Politics and Power, *c.* 1680–1717', in Eliane Glaser (ed.), *Religious Tolerance in the Atlantic World: Early Modern and Contemporary Perspectives* (London, 2014), 41–72, p. 45.
[18] H. T. Dickinson, *The Politics of the People in Eighteenth-Century Britain* (London, 1995), p. 5.

printers. On several occasions, printers had their tools and materials seized and held. And of course, there were fines and legal fees associated with being arrested, even if the arrest did not lead to prison time or worse.[19] Important Tory outlets like *The Examiner* and *The Monitor* did not survive the regime change, though the former revived briefly in November 1714. Between Anne's death and the end of 1716, more than twenty opposition papers were published in London; according to Hyland, 'at least sixteen were investigated (usually more than once) by the government. Only three of the sixteen survived into 1717'.[20] Mist's *Weekly Journal* managed to persist until 1737, despite constant government interference, each instance of which apparently served to make his paper more popular; in 1728, when Mist crossed a line and was forced into exile, *Mist's* became *Fog's*. The paper began as a relatively tame anti-government outlet, becoming more outspoken in the 1720s. The Tory newspaper *The Post Boy* lasted until 1728, but Jacobite and High Church advocacy papers rarely survived more than a few months. Given the potency of the threat of seditious libel, there was, then, little opportunity for Tories to cultivate a sustained opposition press. But what tendencies and positions do we find represented in what was printed? What are the aims of early Hanoverian Tory journalists?

In the first few months of Hanoverian rule, some Tories were still jockeying for position in the new government – testimony to the fact that what now seems inevitable did not appear so to contemporaries. The revived *Examiner* (Nov 1714–Mar 1716) is a good example: Mr. Examiner (Joseph Browne?) writes much as he had before Anne's death, arguing that Whig irreverence toward the Church is part and parcel with their disrespect for state authority: 'what the *Church* loses, the *Crown* loses' (5). The Tories sanctify hierarchy, and the '*Conscience* and *Religion*' they defend are 'essential to Government', representing 'the greatest Inducements to *Obedience* and *Loyalty*' (10). The upshot is simple: the king would be well advised to put his new government in Tory rather than in Whig hands. By January, such a position would no doubt seem naïve, but the paper ended in the fall. As Hyland notes, this paper also cost threepence a copy, pricier than most other journals of the day; this perhaps reflects awareness of the government's commitment to quashing cheaper opposition outlets.[21] On 8 October 1714, the short-lived *Controller* – a 'Sequel to the EXAMINER' – debuted, a sharply anti-Whig paper explicitly committed to uniting and inspiring

---

[19] Laurence Hanson, *Government and the Press 1695–1763* (1936; Rpt. Oxford, 1967), pp. 39, 46, 50.
[20] Hyland, 'Liberty and Libel', p. 884.
[21] Hyland, 'Liberty and Libel', pp. 874–75.

to action the downtrodden Church party. The author addresses himself to 'Gentlemen Freeholders', urging them on in minatory terms: 'NOW's the Time. NOW 'tis in your Power'. Before you have 'given the Power out of your Hands', he continues, consider '*which* [party] may give you *cause* to *Rejoice*, and *which* to *Repent*. 'Tis a *happy thing*, when *one's* Welfare *depends* upon *one's own* Choice'. The Whigs have turned the world upside down before, and if the Tories 'are Cheated by the Whigs again', he concludes, 'it is your own Fault, and . . . you *certainly will* smart for it'. Exactly what course the Controller recommends is difficult to say, but his message to his church party allies is clear: do not go gently into that oligarchical Whig night. *The Controller* was quickly suppressed.[22]

However ephemeral most Tory papers tended to be in early Hanoverian London, the government had its hands full in monitoring and squelching them. Two significant instances are Robert Mawson's popular *Weekly Journal* and George Dormer's handwritten *Newsletter*, both attacked by loyalists.[23] In *The Flying Post* of 20 October 1715, the *Weekly Journal* is described as being 'writ on Purpose to poison the Mob with Prejudices against the Government', and all of its 'Seditious Reflections' are 'carefully dispers'd thro' Alehouses &c. . . . and sold cheap, on Purpose to give them a Currency among the Rabble'. In October 1715, when Mawson printed the Pretender's Scottish manifesto, 'the ministry seized its first good opportunity to bring the publisher to order'. Within the next month, *The Weekly Journal* was no more, but Mawson wasted little time: he promptly shifted his subscribers to another weekly, *The News Letter* (appearing in January 1716). That paper tracks the ongoing efforts and movements of the Jacobites, portrayed as a potent force with the potential to succeed, perhaps to encourage like-minded readers to maintain their revolutionary spirits.

Some Tory writers responded to government proscription with still more vehement criticism and overt, unapologetic Jacobitism. The most significant case is that of *Robin's Last Shift* (1716) and its sequels. These periodicals are anti-Hanoverian, pro-Church, and audacious in their allegiance to the hereditary basis of power. Hyland describes them as representing 'the natural outcome of the government's attempt to suppress all criticism'; their authors assume that they will not be long tolerated by the Whigs, so they 'promote with as much emotional appeal as possible . . . every common prejudice held against the Whigs in general, and Walpole and Townshend in particular'.[24]

---

[22] Hyland, 'Liberty and Libel', p. 874.
[23] Hyland, 'Liberty and Libel', p. 876. See also James Sutherland, *The Restoration Newspaper and its Development* (Cambridge, 1986), pp. 34–35.
[24] Hyland, 'Liberty and Libel', pp. 878–79.

Wilson explains that, 'The extensive reporting on the combative activities of troops and the harassment of citizens throughout the country helped set the stage for a more aggressive discussion of the subject's liberties, which Jacobite newspapers and weeklies took up with relish'.[25] *Robin's Last Shift* and the two related enterprises typify this phenomenon.

Robin's Last Shift, the work of George Flint, appeared on 18 February; like the sequels it is avowedly Jacobite. As Wilson suggests, Flint's Jacobitism, 'in the context of Whig repression and judicial terror, held out the promise of deliverance in the form of James III, who would bring liberty and justice to his people'.[26] On 3 March 1716, Flint unambiguously commits himself to divine right, insisting that 'Englishmen can have no Pretence whatsoever to rise up against their *lawful King*' – and there is no question which king he means. What follows, an affirmation of subjects' duty to their rightful monarch and of the hereditary basis of kingship, amounts to a denial of the legitimacy of 1688–1689. The ideology promulgated here is dangerous, as is Flint's deliberate attempt to provoke like-minded readers toward violent resistance: 'Blood will have Blood; Mischief will have Mischief; and the Barbarous and Cruel sooner or later perish' (3 March). Flint carefully distinguishes the king's wishes from the ruthless acts of his government, but he repeatedly maintains the tyranny of those 'unpopular' and 'cruel' policies sponsored by the Whigs. He reflects upon the innocent patriot – like himself – who 'If he ventures upon a poignant Truth or two . . . must perish for it in a Prison' (10 Mar). For its anti-government censure and its blatant Jacobitism, *Robin's Last Shift* was promptly shut down. Flint and his allies responded by launching a new paper, with identical formatting including the same elaborate headpiece, every bit as politically toxic as the first.

The Shift Shifted, launched in early May 1716, relentlessly – treasonously? – defends English Catholics: 'in conversing with the Papists, we find them to be . . . a well-bred, inoffensive, just and charitable People. How we can Account for our Hatred to these People, our Brethren, our own Flesh and Blood, and for our Affection to their Reverse, the ugly *French* Hugonots, I profess I don't know' (no. 3). Throughout, he maintains that the papists have done no harm to the English constitution, but that the Presbyterians 'have destroyed *BOTH*' Church and State, and will 'do't again' (no. 3). As in *Robin's Last Shift*, here the legality of 1688 is called into question: the message of no. 11 is that the people are *not* 'the Original of Power', and that

---

[25] Kathleen Wilson, *The Sense of the People: Politics, Culture and Imperialism in England, 1715–1785* (Cambridge, 1995), p. 113.
[26] Wilson, *Sense of the People*, p. 113.

those who rebelled against the rightful king 'fight against God himself'. The events of the 1640s are invoked on multiple occasions, again with the lesson that the Whigs demonstrated their desire 'to subvert and destroy the Church and State', whereas the Tories have always been loyal – at least to a monarch lawfully entitled to the throne. A theme of *The Shift Shifted*, as of its predecessor, is the ruthlessness of the current administration: 'These Severities beget Disaffection, and Disaffection recruits Severities: And thus ... They will beget one another to the End of the Chapter, unless Severities cease' (9).

The *Mercurius Politicus* for August 1716 offers an illuminating comment upon the conflict between Flint and the government. The author, perhaps Defoe, reports that the authorities have been 'extraordinarily employ'd ... in searching after the Authors, Printers, and Dispersers of' opposition writings, including Flint's. He recalls the recent prosecution of those involved in *The Shift Shifted*, but explains that such punishment had failed to be immediately effective:

> as they [Flint *et al.*] found the People eager to see the Paper, even so eager that they gave Six-pence a piece for a Paper of Three Half-pence, so they continued ... to Print it, sometimes at one Printing-house, sometimes at another, and at last a private Press was set up ... in a House ... and the Paper continued to be dispers'd into private Hands, and carried about by private Persons; but as it is utterly impossible to cause a Paper to spread for a constancy where every one that sells it is liable to Prosecution, so the Government found means to trace it in every part. (p. 195)

This account makes clear not only the government's intolerance of criticism but also the lengths to which Jacobite writers would go to maintain some semblance of an opposition press. The passage also represents powerful testimony to the popular demand for Flint's style of resistance.

Scholars have emphasised the ineffectuality of the resistance in these years, but few have engaged with the radical nature of what these papers were doing or with the strength of popular Toryism. *The Shift Shifted* calls for the active political engagement of fellow revolutionaries. Throughout, one finds an unusual number of questions posed to the audience; the rhetorical device is effective, encouraging readers to question the government, to be sceptical, to demand answers (e.g., no. 3: 'What can be the Cause of that?'). The author's idiom is also more vernacular ('they had more need be willing to kiss their Backsides, were it possible thereby to appease them', no. 10), more populist in its appeal. *The Shift Shifted* represents a twofold warning:

if English Christians (i.e., Anglicans and Papists) do not unite against Presbyterianism, moral topsy-turvydom will ensue; and, secondly, that the persecution of righteousness ends badly for tyrants. Remarking upon reports from Poland, the author ominously foretells, 'There seems to be a fatal Day coming upon Oppressors, in more Places than one' (10). *Robin's Last Shift* and *The Shift Shifted* were followed by *Shift's Last Shift* (1717). The government spent considerable energy prosecuting those involved, arresting and questioning 'perhaps as many as one hundred people' associated with the trilogy.[27] Flint ultimately escaped from prison and fled to France, where like Bolingbroke he took refuge in the service of the Pretender.[28] The case of *Robin's Last Shift* and its sequels illustrates both institutional anxiety about popular Jacobitism and the audacious resolve of some Tories to maintain an opposition voice.

Committed Tories were unable to institute many long-running anti-establishment papers, but their suppression cannot be the only story we tell.[29] Tory journalism suffered under the new Whig regime, but what opposition press there was continued to put pressure on their rivals and to contest the legitimacy of George's policies. That opposition also had considerable popular support. Wilson's conclusion is right: by 1715, 'an overtly Jacobite critique of Whig and Hanoverian power . . . took equally material forms in protest, armed insurrection – and the press'. Political journalism 'took a leading role in disseminating Jacobite opinion, circulating new agendas, hardening resistance to the new regime and keeping Tory and Stuart hopes alive'.[30] Wilson is less interested in the role of the newspapers than in the broader ways in which the opposition continued to function despite Whig efforts, but she does make clear that the periodical press played an important part in cultivating popular unrest. The Whigs responded to the discontent – in the streets and in the press – through both policy and polemic, urging loyalty, obedience, and popular disengagement.

---

[27] Hyland, 'Liberty and Libel', p. 879.
[28] Hanson, *Government and the Press*, p. 64.
[29] *The Scourge*, a weekly launched in February 1717, is for example a kind of successor to *The Rehearsal*, angrier and more defensive in the context of the Whig ascendancy under George, determined not to accept a new Whig hegemony.
[30] Wilson, *Sense of the People*, pp. 108–09.

Whig journalists and the myth of popular Hanoverianism

Several new papers were launched in the early years of George I's reign, most of them – unsurprisingly – loyally Whig in orientation. After the regime change, the government promoted and subsidised Whig journalists and papers, and their rivals were rigorously restrained, harassed, and silenced. The old flagship of Whig propaganda under Anne, Ridpath's *Flying Post*, 'reemerg[ed] triumphant . . . in the new regime', and it was 'only one of some thirty-five Whig papers and periodicals that flourished by 1716'.[31] 'Flourished' is an overstatement: many of the Whig outlets that commenced in this period did not enjoy long runs. *The Daily Benefactor* and *The Patriot* lasted only a few months, *The Free-Thinker* just about a year; Addison's *Freeholder* and Steele's *Englishman* (second series) each ran roughly half a year. *The English Examiner* and *The Grumbler* appear to have been ephemeral, as was the sham *Flying-Post* to which Defoe contributed. Thomas Burnet reports that both his *Grumbler* and *The Free-Thinker* were started at the request of the government,[32] but evidently only for a temporary purpose. *The London Gazette* was taken from the Tory Charles Ford, and the Whig Samuel Buckley installed in his place; that paper is still in existence. The Whig *Post Man* ran until c. 1730, *The Daily Courant* until 1735; the Tory *Post Boy* survived until 1728. Boyer's *Political State of Great Britain*, a Whig parliamentary history, lasted until 1729; both *The St. James's Evening Post* (1715–c. 1760) and *The White-hall Evening Post* (1718–1801) had long runs. The loyalist *Read's* weekly survived (changing titles from *The Weekly Journal* to *Read's Weekly Journal*) from 1715 to 1761.

There was no dearth of Whig papers, then, but many of them appear to have been relatively short-lived, whether because they had specific agendas, lost government support, or did not find a lasting readership. The authorities did, however, effectively disseminate loyal propaganda beyond London. G. A. Cranfield's *Hand-List of English Provincial Newspapers and Periodicals* (1961) shows that at least twenty-six provincial papers were launched in the decade following George's accession, half of those commencing between 1714 and 1718. Pro-Hanoverian periodicals, like sermons and broadsides and pamphlets, were energetically hawked throughout England, and especially between 1714 and 1716 the polarising message was clear. As Addison

---

[31] Wilson, *Sense of the People*, p. 88.
[32] On 6 April 1718, Burnet reports that 'The Government have sett the Author upon' *The Free-Thinker*; in David Nichol Smith (ed.), *The Letters of Thomas Burnet to George Duckett, 1712–1722* (Oxford, 1914), p. 148. In July 1715, he had reported that he had 'at the desire of a very considerable Man laid down' *The Grumbler*, 'though it brought in some specie' (92).

concluded in *Freeholder* no. 13, 'the Contest is not in Reality between *Whigs* and *Tories*, but between *Loyalists* and *Rebels*' (98). That essential divide must have seemed to many contemporaries an accurate representation of reality. Wilson highlights the fact that the Whig leadership and their pens sought 'to mobilise and foster loyalty' – in other words, to create rather than to represent acceptance of and support for the new government.[33] They aimed to promote (not to describe) the successful entrenchment of the new Whig dynasty. The distinction is crucial.

Reading Whig journalism of this period with historical hindsight, one might be tempted to interpret it as the comfortable assertion of new dominance. That was not the case. Popular Toryism was a force in London and the provinces, and Hanoverian rule was far from widely celebrated. The Whigs were anxious and alarmed, the political situation tense and uncertain. The authorities' desire to punish Anne's last ministers was unpopular; the mobs were militant during the proceedings against those prominent Tory lords. What we find in the Whig press is, among other things, the cultivation of a myth of Hanoverian popularity, a fiction of majority loyalism, and an attempt to persuade the authorities – against considerable resistance – to give Harley *et al.* their due comeuppance. In July 1716, Ryder reported a version of this phenomenon, the concerted Whig effort to bolster support for the king's party. He described emergent Whig mug-houses, meant 'to encourage the friends to King George and keep up the spirit of loyalty . . . among them'. In addition to drinking the healths of the royal family, 'the company sing a song that is composed against the Tories and Jacobites'. Ryder approves of these important institutions: 'I am persuaded these mug-houses are of service to the Government to keep up the public spirit and animate its friends, and I believe in time it will gain over the populace and *make King George become popular*'.[34] One job of the Whig periodical press in early Hanoverian England was similar – not to reflect the triumph of the new regime but to help enact that triumph.

The successful establishment of secure Hanoverian rule, from the Whig perspective, required not only the myth of populism but also the reality of retribution. In *The Wisdom of Looking Backward* (1715), White Kennett issued a sharp warning to his fellow Whigs: do not content yourselves to look forward to a brighter future without punishing the ministers of the last four years. He urges his fellow travelers to reflect thus: '*How near our Danger, how wonderful our Escape, how unpardonable, if we still catch at a Yoke that is cast off, and again entangle our selves in a broken Snare*' (ii).

---

[33] Wilson, *Sense of the People*, p. 86.
[34] *Diary of Dudley Ryder*, pp. 279–80; emphasis added.

The Whig journalists of 1714 and 1715 needed little prodding: their papers thump the previous ministry, call for the impeachment of Harley, St. John, and Ormonde, and malign the principles and practices of the Tories. The Whig press in these years is generally concerned with vengeance, including against popular protesters. The political reality was that the government initially felt unable to give rioters their just deserts, and even after redefining riot laws they had not succeeded in silencing popular antagonism to the new regime. Journalists make a point of detailing the capture and prosecution of insurgents, fostering an image of government strength. The Whig press also, crucially, affirms the new regime's equation of public demonstration with treason.

Whig writers call for impeachment proceedings against Anne's ministers, repeat allegations of Jacobitism, and in general champion strong measures. The best-known of these political journals is the second series of Steele's *Englishman* (1715), discussed at length in Chapter 5. Steele had an ally in the author of *The English Examiner* (1715), who repeats the litany of charges against the Harley ministry and its pens, and of *The Observator. Being a Sequel to the Englishman* (launched February 1715), who exhorts George to 'perfect what is already begun, crush the Enemies of God and *Israel*'. The re-interpretation of 1710–1714, and the characterisation of George's accession as a change to be widely celebrated, is a theme throughout much of the Whig press. *The Annals of King George* recounts in considerable detail the transition to Hanoverian rule, accentuating and exaggerating the positive responses (at home and abroad) to George's accession. Like Addison, this author offers a vision of popular Hanoverianism more hopeful than realistic. As late as 1718, almost two years after the failed uprising, some Whig journalists are tub-thumping in the manner of 1713–1715, clearly under pressure to maintain the polarities between the loyal party and the unpatriotic, peace-disturbing high-flyers.

Defining Whig principles: the call for loyalty

Among the most important Whig papers of early Hanoverian England is Addison's *Freeholder* (Dec 1715–Jun 1716). This biweekly shares with other Whig papers the hostility to Tory doctrines of passive obedience, though in the wake of the Jacobite revolt, he found himself emphasising 'a distinction between lawful resistance and conspiratorial revolt'.[35] His stress on the duty of subjects (e.g., p. 114) is in these terms. Addison's overarching concern

---

[35] Edward A. Bloom and Lillian D. Bloom, *Joseph Addison's Sociable Animal: In the Market Place, on the Hustings, in the Pulpit* (Providence, 1971), p. 139.

is with loyalty to the present regime, and *The Freeholder* was meant partly 'to mobilise patriotic emotions', to affirm that 'loyalty to Hanover and the Whigs was dictated by love of country'.[36] His title suggests that he speaks for something like the average voter, and contests the notion – promulgated by Swift and others – that Tories were 'the party of the small landowner'.[37] Addison upholds George as a constant ruler, a stranger to the language but not to the 'Laws and Religion' of England (76). He reframes the partisan landscape: 'Our Country is not now divided into two Parties, who propose the same End by different Means; but into such as would preserve, and such as would destroy it' (98). Much less heatedly polemical than Steele's *Englishman* of the same moment, *The Freeholder* represents Addison's Horatian attempt 'to free the People's Minds from those Prejudices conveyed into them by the Enemies of the present Establishment' (273), 'to reconcile Men to their own Happiness' (107). Addison carried on his journal after the passage of the Septennial Act the paper was meant to defend (May 1716), testimony to the ongoing unrest among the populace.

Addison's tone is measured, calm, self-assured. The choice is strategic, corresponding with his argument that the disaffected form a small and powerless minority, 'too inconsiderable to put' the king in any meaningful danger (45). Addison nonchalantly reminds readers of those demographics who 'are in the Interest of the present Government' (52). The 'Schemes' of alienated Tories, like the 'Means by which they are promoted', are 'contradictory to common Sense'. Addison suggests that popular authority is on the side of Hanover, not the Jacobites: what one finds among 'our . . . Fellow-Subjects' is 'Chearfulness . . . to oppose the Designs of the Pretender' (103). There is so little cause for real concern that Addison can maintain 'Party-fictions' to be 'the proper Subjects of Mirth and Laughter'. The fiction of a popular anti-Hanoverianism is meant only 'to give a Spirit to a desperate Cause' (71).

The Freeholder defends the King's extreme measures. The inaugural issue praises 'His present Majesty' for his unwillingness 'to have a single Slave in his Dominions' (41), and the following number boasts that the king 'hath too much Goodness to wish for any Power' beyond what is needed to protect his subjects' welfare (43). Later, Addison directly confronts those Tories who think:

---

[36] Williams, *Sense of the People*, p. 94.
[37] James Leheny, Introduction to Joseph Addison, *The Freeholder*, ed. Leheny (Oxford, 1979), p. 2.

that nothing but unlimited Mercy, or unlimited Punishment, are the Methods that can be made use of in our present Treatment of the Rebels: That he has omitted the middle Way of Proceeding between these two Extreams: That this middle Way is the Method in which His Majesty, like all other wise and good Kings, has chosen to proceed. (179).

Addison disagrees with those critics who 'insinuate . . . that there should be no Impressions of Awe upon the Mind of a Subject, and that a Government shou'd not create Terror in those who are disposed to do ill' (180). He also insists upon George's 'undoubted title', maintaining flatly that, 'if every *Briton*, instead of aspiring after private Wealth or Power, would sincerely desire to make his Country happy, His present Majesty would not have a single Malecontent in his whole Dominions' (60).

Addison rhetorically affirms the logic of the 1715 Riot Act: there is no legitimate, rational basis for popular protest. Addison's cool confidence jars against the paranoia, the vigilantism, the apprehensions and acts of violence on both sides. His optimism is perhaps strategic, an attempt to persuade moderate freeholders and others with Tory sympathies that the king 'will daily make all Opposition fall before him' and unite his people (44). His self-appointed role is a didactic one: 'I shall . . . endeavor to open the Eyes of my Countrymen to their own Interests' (42). The need for such coaxing – the need to 'undeceive' (70) – does suggest, however, limits to Addison's assurance, and awareness that he is not representing but trying to create a political reality of majority loyalty and minority disaffection. Steele occasionally labours along similar lines in his 1714–1716 journalism, as in *Town-Talk* no. 8, where he imagines that 'the *English* Genius . . . awakes; They resent, with Indignation, the Imposition of a Pretender to their Sovereign's Throne', and so on (243).

Addison is not alone in his promotion of loyalty. *The St. James's Evening Post* (Jun 1715–c. 1760) reports news from abroad, but during the summer and fall of 1715 its pages are dominated by memorials commending the king and damning dissent. The primary audience seems to have been Anglicans, the object to urge that demographic to serve the new regime. James Read's *The Weekly Journal, or, British Gazetteer* (1716–1720) is even more focused in its loyalist preachment. On 7 Jan 1716, Read describes 'a true English Subject' thus: 'HE is one that quietly and contentedly moves in his own Sphere, without intermeddling in nice and secret Matters of State, that are out of his Reach, and inconsistent with his Duty. That heartily obeys the King in all his Commands'. *The Weekly Journal* reports the comings and goings of the Pretender, the trials of rebels, the arrests of suspected Jacobites; Read highlights George's clemency, concluding that many who 'deserv'd Death' were pardoned (29 June 1717). He refutes and lambastes high Tory weeklies, especially *Mist's*. A defender of the government, he castigates the 'scandalous' Defoe, employed by Mist to 'take the liberty at all times insipidly to ridicule and insult his Majesty's friends and allies with foolish comparisons and dull reflections'.[38] The relentless calls for loyalty reflect Whig defensiveness as much as does the mythologising about Hanoverian popularity.

The 'tradition of Spectatorial Whiggery' continued into George's reign, carried on by papers marked by apparent non-partisanship and by 'jibes against the impolite pretensions of the high church clergy'.[39] Brian Cowan instances *The Lay Monk* (1713–1714), *The Censor* (1717), and *Pasquin* (1722–1724), though the likeness is imperfect. *The Censor* is Addisonian in many respects: he initially poses as one withdrawn 'from the World' (no. 1); he vows 'to be as true an Attendant upon Virtue, as a Spy upon Vice' (3); he moralises, imagining himself as a guardian of English manners; he is full of principled wisdom, aphoristically delivered ('Acquisitions of *Knowledge* are much more estimable than those of *Fortune*' (18)). He speaks the language of Whiggery, stressing politeness, liberty, slavery; he challenges bigotry and relies upon a conspicuously biblical idiom. As Cowan has argued of Addison's *Spectator* project, so this author implicitly repudiates the High Church's exclusive claim on morality. But *The Censor* is decidedly un-Addisonian in one important respect. On 26 February 1717, he turns abruptly to politics on 26 February 1717:

> an INDIFFERENCE in a Day of common Danger to our *Country* is of all others the most stupid and not-to-be-forgiven Crime. . . . [W]hen the Difference lyes between the Faithful Subject and the Actual REBEL, the firm *Patriot* and the profes'd *Foe* to his Country; in short, between a *Popish* and a *Protestant* Line, then to be Indifferent is to be justly suspected to be *Guilty*. (25)

He offers no apology for leaving aside his initial plan of settling the 'Philosophical, Moral, and Polite Part of the World'. This smacks of Steele, not Addison, not the gentle Horace but the provoked and judgmental Juvenal.

---

[38] Quoted in Hanson, *Government and the Press*, p. 104.
[39] Cowan, 'Mr. Spectator and the Coffeehouse Public Sphere', p. 360.

The Whig split

'Whig' becomes a much more complicated and less helpful descriptor during the schism of 1717–1720. After the Whig split, some Tories awkwardly cooperated with disaffected Whigs, leading to a re-emergence of a Country vs. Court conflict. As W. A. Speck has observed, the 'Whig' and 'Tory' labels so essential to characterising late Stuart papers become decreasingly helpful over George I's and then George II's reign; 'government' and 'opposition' are more useful.[40]

Whigs were ascendant in the first half dozen years of George's reign, but they were also divided. A major debate in the spring of 1719 concerned the Peerage Bill, which 'provided that not more than six beyond the existing number of 178 English peers could ever be created, the King's peer-creating prerogative to be limited to the filling of vacancies caused by extinct peerages'. Rae Blanchard explains that 'The underlying purpose . . . was to provide further for the Whig supremacy by ensuring a permanent Whig majority in the Lords.'[41] During summer 1717, while Walpole and Townshend joined forces with opposition Tories, Stanhope and Sunderland pursued several controversial measures, which were not well received by moderates who thought of themselves as 'old Whigs', as country rather than court. The Peerage Bill was the most contentious. The specific details of this controversy are not necessary for our purposes, which are merely to characterise the nature of two conflicting journalistic responses produced by erstwhile allies, Steele and Addison, who had joined Sunderland as the two secretaries of state in Stanhope's ministry.

The first issue of Steele's *The Plebeian* (14 March 1719) details the problems with the Bill, which 'carries with it so great an Alteration of the Constitution', 'implies . . . a Breach of the Union' with Scotland, and 'encroaches so much upon the Prerogative of the Crown' (460). Steele concedes that 'WHIGGISM . . . is a Desire of Liberty, and a Spirit of Opposition to all Exorbitant Power', parliamentary or regal, but he maintains that 'the *Prerogative* of the Crown is reduc'd so low' by various restrictions from 1689 (462). Steele's apparent defence of royal sovereignty is a prudent cover for his actual concern – the role of the House of Commons. On 19 March, Addison (anonymously) countered Steele with *The Old Whig*. In no. 1, Addison reiterates the importance of curtailing the prerogative as a way of preventing an excess of power among the Lords. He cites the divisive

---

[40] W. A. Speck, 'Politics and the Press', in Michael Harris and Alan Lee (eds.), *The Press in English Society from the Seventeenth to Nineteenth Centuries* (Rutherford, NJ, 1986), 47–63, pp. 48–49.

[41] Steele, *Tracts and Pamphlets*, p. 453.

incident of December 1711 – Anne's constitutionally dubious manoeuvre of creating twelve new peers to guarantee the passage of the peace treaty – and argues that the Bill will prevent such egregiousness from happening again. *The Old Whig* lasted only two issues, *The Plebeian* only four; Steele's second and third numbers were published before Addison could respond with its second, leaving the latter open to mockery ('one of the *Infirmities of Age*' is '*Slowness*'[42]).

The short-lived paper war deteriorated into personal barbs and name-calling; Steele knew who was responsible for *The Old Whig*, and was prepared to do characteristically fierce battle with his former friend. What was at stake was a fundamental dispute about the division of powers, Steele keen to defend the status quo and Addison convinced 'that it was a defect of the constitution as at present established that the King might control two of the three organs of the state'.[43] In the second number of *The Plebeian*, Steele accuses Addison of being 'so *old a Whig*, that he has quite *forgot his Principles*'[44]; Addison retaliates, dubbing his rival a Grub Street hack and sell-out. As Calhoun Winton observes, the erstwhile collaborators had drifted apart after Steele's expulsion from parliament in 1714; they almost split in 1716 over the proposed Septennial Bill, avoiding open conflict only because Steele changed his mind. The wrangle over the Peerage Bill represented the first public quarrel between them. Addison had re-emerged from retirement in order to answer Steele's paper; Steele must have been wounded by that re-entry into the political arena.[45] Addison was no doubt equally pained to be on the receiving end of his old friend's aggressive polemic. In any case, they did not reconcile; Addison died in June.

The Tories obviously did not have exclusive claim on anti-ministerial sentiments or publications. Even one of the most outspoken champions of the Protestant interest, Defoe, had cause to feel critical of the George's government. To his early Hanoverian journalism, we need now turn – a canon both typical of the partisan periodical culture of these years and anticipatory of new directions in English journalism.

---

[42] Steele, *Tracts and Pamphlets*, p. 487.
[43] Peter Smithers, *The Life of Joseph Addison* (1954; 2nd edn. Oxford, 1968), pp. 448–49.
[44] Steele, *Tracts and Pamphlets*, p. 470.
[45] Calhoun Winton, *Sir Richard Steele, M.P. The Later Career* (Baltimore, 1970), pp. 161–62.

Defoe's early Hanoverian journalism

Defoe's situation at the time of Anne's death cannot have been wholly comfortable, and his case represents a potent reminder of the confused and complex nature of political allegiances in the early years of Hanoverian rule. Though a Whig regime would suit his temperament and his convictions much better than a Tory one, his association with Harley left him 'the butt of endless attacks as a turncoat and hireling of the disgraced Tories'.[46] He was not exclusively a political writer, as Furbank and Owens remind us; at the time of the transition he was working on what turned out to be the very successful *Family Instructor* (1715). But he was involved with several journals at the end of Anne's reign and the early years of George's rule, and the nature of his involvement is problematic enough to warrant consideration here. For one thing, the attribution of a considerable number of contributions to Defoe has been contested, and no consensus has emerged. For another, Defoe appears to have been working both sides of the party divide, raising what are now familiar questions about his loyalty and his honesty.[47]

At the time of Anne's death, Defoe had to some extent been serving the Harley ministry – but he had also just begun to write for the sham *Flying-Post and Medley*, a paper devoted to criticising that ministry.[48] This *Flying-Post* – not the same enterprise as the original *Flying Post*, with which it overlapped – was launched on 27 July 1714, the day of Harley's dismissal. Defoe's early writing after the collapse of the Tory party, then, was a trenchantly Whig paper written against Queen Anne's last ministry. The paper stops short of attacking Harley personally – perhaps because of Defoe's residual allegiance to him – but nevertheless renders harsh judgment of Anne's last government. In its 19 August 1714 issue, *The Flying-Post and Medley* hinted that the Earl of Anglesey had Jacobite leanings; the Earl was furious, and made sure that Defoe, the editor, and the publisher were arrested. Defoe came to trial in June 1715, managing through sheer luck not to be severely punished.

---

[46] P. N. Furbank and W. R. Owens, *A Political Biography of Daniel Defoe* (London, 2006), p. 137. John Richetti's *The Life of Daniel Defoe* (Malden, MA, 2005) includes a chapter on 'Queen Anne to the Hanoverians', in which he covers pamphlets but not Defoe's post-*Review* journalism.

[47] What follows is indebted to Furbank and Owens's discussion (*Political Biography*, Ch. 7).

[48] P. N. Furbank and W. R. Owens, 'Defoe and the Sham *Flying-Post*', *Publishing History* 43 (1998), pp. 5–15.

In the midst of the trouble over this episode, Defoe appealed to Harley in terms that now seem both confusing and disingenuous. He tells Harley that he needs to 'Lay before your Ldpp a brief hystory of Fact on a Broil which I have just Now upon my hands', and proceeds to explain his involvement with *The Flying-Post* as a covert attempt to undermine that journal. 'It has been long That I have been Endeavouring to Take off the Virulence and Rage of the [original] Flying Post', he says, and at last 'an Occasion Offred me which I Thought might be Improv'd Effectually to Overthrow it'. Defoe recounts the quarrel that led to the formation of the sham *Post*, and explains that he hoped the success of the new *Flying-Post* would help destroy the original. He also maintains that he contributed 'paragraphs of forreign [sic] News but Declin'd Medling with home Matters'.[49] In short, he has been an innocent contributor unwilling to participate in domestic politics, but now stands wrongfully accused. The whole episode smacks of dishonesty – and of desperation. Furbank and Owens note, moreover, that this letter is not anomalous. It sounds a lot like the ones Defoe sent to Charles Delafaye, Undersecretary of State, in 1718, attempting to account for his awkward involvement in *Mist's Journal* and *Mercurius Politicus*.

Defoe's position vis-à-vis the Whig government between 1715 and 1718 is complicated. The Anglesey affair had ended badly for him; he was at one point worried that he would be forced into exile. In Defoe's telling, he decided to appeal to Chief Justice Parker, who not only put a stop to the proceedings against him but also recommended him to Townshend. In his 26 April 1718 letter to Delafaye, he explains his and Townshend's strategy for making the best use of his services: 'It was proposed . . . That I should still appear as if I were as before under the Displeasure of the Governmt; and Seperated From the Whiggs; and That I might be more Servicable in a kind of Disguise, Than If I appeard openly'. To that end, he began writing 'a Monthly Book called Mercurius Politicus', and also took 'a share in' another Tory venture, *Dyer's Newsletter*. Both *Mercurius Politicus* and the *Newsletter*, he continues, had 'To Pass as Tory Papers, and yet be Dissabled and Ennervated, So as to do no Mischief . . . to the Governmt'.[50] In December 1716, Townshend was dismissed, and Defoe's employment with him was at an end. By January 1717, with the Whig split becoming apparent, Defoe mocked both sides, and in the spring he (probably) published *The Old Whig and Modern Whig Revived*, 'a tract caustic both towards the Government

---

[49] George Harris Healey (ed.), *The Letters of Daniel Defoe* (Oxford, 1955), p. 446.
[50] Defoe, *Letters*, pp. 451–53.

and the Walpolite Opposition'.[51] Defoe scorns the division of the Whig party into 'old' and 'new', which as he complains throughout *The Review* only helps the Tories.

Defoe's assurance that he wrote against the government only to prevent more severe criticism is, naturally, suspect. Whatever his intentions, the reality is that in 1716–1717, while in Townshend's employ, he was producing what functioned as (Low-Church) Tory propaganda. *Mercurius Politicus* (with which he claimed to be involved)[52] appeared in May 1716 as a rival to Boyer's long-running Whig monthly, *Political State of Great Britain*. Defoe's introduction to the first instalment highlighted the paper's corrective role, obliquely challenging Boyer: '*The Writers, who till now have supply'd this needful Work . . . do little more than make Collections out of Coffee-house Politicks*', and '*are so deficient in Fact, and so Partial in relation, that we should promise our Readers nothing, if we did not assure them to give a more Genuine . . . account of Things*'. In 1717, John Toland complained that *Mercurius Politicus* 'frequently reflects upon the proceedings of the Government, under pretence of telling what people say *pro* and *con* upon whatever passes, to the makeing [sic] of malicious and sometimes very dangerous insinuations'.[53] Toland's characterisation is accurate.

The monthly relies heavily on other authors and texts to communicate its ideology; it quotes extensively from pamphlets, memorials, and speeches that are varyingly critical of the government, while claiming to be impartial. Throughout 1716–1717, the paper indirectly advocates treating the Scottish rebels and other disaffected parties with mercy. In the inaugural issue, Defoe maintains, 'It is not the Business of these Collections to enter into the Debate, neither does it consist with the Impartiality profess'd in the Introduction' (p. 68) – but he then prints a long memorial calling for royal clemency. The author describes rebels compelled into rebellion rather than choosing it for themselves, including women and children, insisting that 'universal Forfaulture of Estates will produce nothing material to the Publick' (73). In this case, the memorial is particularly eloquent and forceful, and printing it represents *de facto* endorsement of its position. In July 1716, Defoe includes fervent Tory speeches against the Septennial Act, including one calling for an active defence of the English liberties threatened by this unconstitutional bill. The criticism of the government ended abruptly in late 1718, about the time Defoe elsewhere suggests a return to the Whig

---

[51] Furbank and Owens; *Political Biography*, pp. 152–56; the quotation is p. 156. *The Old Whig and Modern Whig Revived* is considered a probable attribution.

[52] P. N. Furbank and W. R. Owens, *A Critical Bibliography of Daniel Defoe* (London, 1998), pp. xxii–xxiii.

[53] John Toland, *Second Part of the State Anatomy* (London, 1717), p. 29.

fold.[54] But in 1716–1717 he was involved in opposition propaganda, whether for financial reasons or out of real frustration with particular policies of the administration (e.g., its policy toward Spain). A common theme involves the 'Prosecutions and Executions which have been ordered and carried on against the Persons and Estates of the Enemies of the present Administration' (Jan 1717, p. 1), and like many opposition writers Defoe seems determined, albeit obliquely, to legitimate some degree of dissent. But as an opposition paper, *Mercurius Politicus* is rather tame, which is probably why it survived. Whether Defoe was genuinely trying to subvert it from within must remain a matter of speculation.

By the summer of 1717, Defoe had started working for Nathaniel Mist's high-flying (even Jacobite) *Weekly Journal, or, Saturday's Post* (launched in late 1716).[55] James Sutherland points out that, before the *Craftsman* commenced in 1726, Mist's 'carried the biggest guns of the Tory press', and its readers 'had come to expect strong meat'.[56] The government was extremely unhappy with Mist's popular paper, and Mist was much tormented for his trouble – though as the administration was painfully aware, prosecuting him only increased the appeal of his journal: the authorities 'worried about the evident popularity of [Mist's] wares which they found hard to counter. A government memorandum of 1722 complained that "There never was a Mist or any other Person taken up or tryed but double the number of papers were sold upon it". . . . In 1741 the *Daily Gazetteer* recollected that "Mist's treasonable Papers were sold sometimes for Half a Guinea a-piece", such was the demand for them'.[57]

Defoe was quickly outed, in both *Read's Weekly* and *The St. James's Weekly*. Despite his insistence that he had infiltrated the Tory paper only to weaken it, the evidence suggests otherwise. Furbank and Owens demonstrate, persuasively, that Defoe was deceiving not Mist but Delafaye and Delafaye's superiors.[58] In any case, his contributions were incisive, provocatively anti-government, and they brought more punishment upon Mist. On 1 February 1718, Defoe wrote a letter for the journal, signed by 'Sir Andrew Politick' and encouraging the editor to inquire into the Whig government's

---

[54] Furbank and Owens, *Political Biography*, p. 173.
[55] The Tory author of *Heraclitus Ridens*, 'himself unsparing in criticism of the government, eulogized Mist as a fellow worker in the cause' (Hanson, *Government and the Press*, p. 104). The paper became *Mist's Weekly Journal* in spring 1725; Mist fled to France in 1728, and his successor Charles Molloy resumed publication under the title *Fog's Weekly Journal*.
[56] James R. Sutherland, *Defoe* (Philadelphia, 1938), p. 221.
[57] This quotation comes from Paul Chapman's *ODNB* entry for Mist.
[58] Furbank and Owens, *Political Biography*, p. 165.

apparent desire to embroil England in a costly war it had no business fighting.⁵⁹ On 25 October 1718 appears an even more incendiary missive from Sir Andrew, raising devastating queries about the imminent war with Spain. The authorities called the letter treason; when questioned, Mist named Defoe as the author. Maximillian E. Novak takes Defoe's account (as offered to Delafaye) as honest, crediting Defoe with having 'succeeding in muting criticism of the government' – a somewhat naïve interpretation of the evidence.⁶⁰

Writing in April 1718, Defoe told Delafaye that Townshend had enlisted him to be a government spy, but Furbank and Owens make an excellent case for not believing that account. Their conclusion about Defoe's journalistic production in 1716–1718 is worth quoting at length:

> If Defoe was the founder of *Mercurius Politicus*, which it seems fairly clear he was, it must have been because it was something he wanted to do, and the journal said things he wanted said. Its outlook is perfectly consonant with the one conveyed in 'Sir Andrew Politick's' letters, which there is strong evidence that he wrote. The two taken together provide a clear picture of his political affiliations [at the time]. But that their purpose was to advance the interests of the Whig administration ... is a proposition that brute logic forbids one to swallow.⁶¹

Defoe's *Review* had promulgated radically Whig ideals, and his early Hanoverian periodical publication is every bit as radical – not so much in its ideology, but certainly in the fierceness of its opposition.

Defoe's next journalistic venture was the triweekly *White-hall Evening Post*, launched in September 1718. Furbank and Owens read Defoe's 29 November letter to the editor as his 'publicly announcing his return to his old allegiance, i.e. to the Whigs and to the Government side'.⁶² This paper begins at more or less the same time that *Mercurius Politicus* abandons its criticism of the government, and Furbank and Owens speculate that Defoe could have been pressured by the authorities to make nice in the wake of 'Sir Andrew's' sedition. In any case, *The White-hall Evening Post* represents a major shift from *Mist's*, especially in its attitude toward the war with Spain. In no. 21, as elsewhere, the author (probably Defoe) reports a

---

⁵⁹ Furbank and Owens, *Political Biography*, p. 161. They print the 25 October 1718 letter in appendix B (pp. 194–98).
⁶⁰ Maximillian E. Novak, 'Defoe's political and religious journalism', in John Richetti (ed.), *The Cambridge Companion to Daniel Defoe* (Cambridge, 2008), 25–44, p. 38.
⁶¹ Furbank and Owens, *Political Biography*, p. 171.
⁶² Furbank and Owens, *Political Biography*, p. 173.

warrant 'against N. Mist, Printer of the weekly Journal or Saturday's Post, for some Reflections in his Paper of Saturday sevenight last, on the Conduct of the Government in Relation to the *just and necessary* Measures taken against the Spaniards' (emphasis added). The authorities, he continues, found among Mist's things 'Copies of a seditious Libel, reflecting on his Majesty and Government in a most notorious Manner'.

If Defoe were responsible for this issue, then it amounts to a considerable *volte face*, from Mist's man and anti-war opposition gadfly to loyalist defender of the government's righteous aims. In no. 32, the author praises the king and his cause, mocking 'a certain Minister' who boasted that the parliament would not support George's desire to go to war with Spain. That minister, in so proclaiming, 'shew'd that he understood very little, either of the Interest King George has on good Foundation fixt in the Hearts of his People, and of the mutual and entire Confidence which reigns there, or of the Experience which the King has now for four Years had of the Zeal, the Loyalty, and Affection of the present House of Commons'. His majesty comes in for commendation elsewhere, too, for having 'always conducted by a Spirit of Reconciliation and Peace' (no. 50); throughout the paper sides with the authorities, highlighting the progress under the Hanoverian regime (including better treatment of dissenters [no. 45]).

Something must be said here of another paper with which Defoe was long assumed to have been connected, John Applebee's *Original Weekly Journal*. This journal represents a kind of enterprise prominent in George's reign: the weekly, comprising *Tatler*-esque essays, foreign and domestic news, local gossip, and advertisements, alongside poems, criminal biographies, and editorials.[63] Applebee launched his paper in October 1714 as a rival to *Mist's* and *Read's*; it ran until 1737 (as *Applebee's Weekly Journal* after 1720). The first to associate Defoe with *Applebee's* was William Lee, whose *Daniel Defoe* (1869) added 300,000 words to the dubious Defoe canon. In Lee's telling, Defoe began writing for the weekly in June 1720 and continued to do so until March 1726. Furbank and Owens object that the attribution is based exclusively on stylistic evidence, expressing their surprise that no contemporary allusion to Defoe's involvement with the paper has been found. Defoe was a popular target for Whigs and Tories alike, and his connection with *Mist's* and other outlets hardly went unnoticed, so the absence of any complaint about him as Applebee's man is indeed peculiar. In a counterblast to Furbank and Owens's de-attribution, Novak calls for a reintegration of at least some of *Applebee's* into the Defoe canon, again

---

[63] Aaron Hill connects these weeklies to *The Tatler* and *Spectator* in 1730; *The Plain Dealer*, vol. 1, p. v.

largely based on internal evidence.⁶⁴ My object is not to settle the matter of Defoe's involvement (or not), though I tend to agree with Furbank and Owens that caution is in order. What I wish to point out here is that the arguments made about his authorship have been to date the only meaningful critical commentary on Applebee's entire venture and thus figure prominently in any attempt to characterise it.

Defoe scholars disagree about the nature of *Applebee's*, and in particular about how thoughtful and significant a paper it is – at least in the early 1720s, the only period of the journal's life to which critics have paid much attention. Furbank and Owens conclude that 'much of the material is a kind of sub-*Spectator* whimsical foolery', a characterisation meant to support their argument that the work does not sound like Defoe.⁶⁵ Novak contests this description, highlighting the fact that the author(s) reflect(s) on 'such serious subjects as atheism, the plague, contemporary morality, marriage problems, and mortality', as well as on the specific religious controversies of George I's reign.⁶⁶ In the early 1720s, *Applebee's* fixates on the South Sea Bubble and other schemes and projects, missing few opportunities to pass judgment on the blind pursuit of wealth.

Novak is correct that *Applebee's* paper touches upon a variety of important issues, though the commentary and reportage are nowhere near as momentous c. 1720–1721 as they had been in 1715–1717. In its earliest years, the *Original Weekly Journal* featured quite a lot of news, mostly concerning continental battles, the movement of the Pretender, and the Jacobite rebellion. In early 1718, Applebee began to include correspondence from a variety of types of readers, male and female, moralising and bantering. These epistles include everything from matrimonial advice to musings on the nature of the press to portraits of European leaders (e.g., Charles XII of Sweden). The tone of the letters is often – not always – lightweight. Though Novak is right that the paper treats serious subjects, it does not seem meant to shape political controversy.

Applebee's was 'a much more cautious affair than *Mist's Journal*, often ... accused of sitting on the fence'.⁶⁷ *Mist's* was a radically Tory outlet, and Applebee was almost without exception careful not to reveal his own radical Toryism. His ability to give no offence, to preach and practice moderation, contributed to the paper's long life. Like several other Anglican

---

⁶⁴ Maximillian E. Novak, 'Daniel Defoe and *Applebee's Original Weekly Journal:* An Attempt at Re-Attribution', *Eighteenth-Century Studies* 45 (2012), pp. 585–608.
⁶⁵ P. N. Furbank and W. R. Owens, 'The Myth of Defoe as "Applebee's Man"', *The Review of English Studies* n.s. 48 (1997), 198–204, p. 202.
⁶⁶ Novak, 'Daniel Defoe and *Applebee's Original Weekly Journal*', p. 586.
⁶⁷ Furbank and Owens, 'The Myth of Defoe as "Applebee's Man"', p. 200.

journalists working under George I, Applebee disseminates the myth of George as protector of the Church. On 2 March 1717, Applebee prints an address from the House of Convocation to his majesty, reproaching the members of 'a restless and implacable Party' for their designs against the government and affirming that, 'Our Safety is bound up in Yours, While You sit Secure upon Your Throne, the Church of England can never want a Powerful... Defender'. The 11 July 1719 issue insists that the king 'hath the Welfare of the Church by Law Established under his... Care'. Throughout 1715, *Applebee's* passes judgment on the Jacobites. Applebee, though rumoured to be a high-flyer,[68] clearly wants to stay in the government's good graces. He advocates loyalty to the new regime in 1715, taking pains to note crimes committed by papists.

Applebee's is not an overtly ideological paper, for the most part, and what (moderately Tory) partisan commentary it offers is heavily diluted by gossip and socio-moral advice. But by the early 1720s, one does find the journal expressing higher Tory sentiments, particularly in the letters-to-the-editor that Defoe was long assumed to have written. In other words, as Furbank and Owens point out, the contributions Lee associated with Defoe contain strikingly un-Defovian commitments:

> Can we really suppose the author of *Jure Divino* composing (1 December 1722) a straight high-Tory defence of 'passive obedience to monarchs?... [W]ould Defoe have described the execution of Charles I as 'the most unnatural Murder that ever was committed since the Crucifixion of our Blessed Saviour'... or have spoken such bitter words about 'Sectaries and Dissenters', blaming them for the spread of the 'infamous' Arian heresy....[69]

These High Church missives, whether or not Defoe penned them, represent a feature of *Applebee's* not present in the journal's earlier years.

What kind of venture, then, was *Applebee's Original Weekly Journal*? The paper's identity is Anglican and anti-Jacobite, but otherwise rather a mixed bag. The advertisements are predominantly for goods or books related to health and medicine; religio-political pamphlets are rarely puffed. The events abroad, including those of the Northern Wars, get a lot of ink, but so many perspectives are offered – reports from different countries and letters from British subjects of all stripes – that the

---

[68] Furbank and Owens, 'The Myth of Defoe as "Applebee's Man"', p. 200.
[69] Furbank and Owens, 'The Myth of Defoe as "Applebee's Man"', p. 201.

authorial position is difficult to discern. If Applebee looked to promulgate ideology, he bungled the job.

One feature of the paper is a high degree of self-consciousness about readership, and conceivably Applebee was simply trying to produce a journal that would appeal to various demographics. *Applebee's* is, after all, somewhat chaotic, in content and in form. Reports from the continent adhere to no single style or length; they are intermixed with reprints from domestic and foreign sources and with gossip and advice columns. Some issues are heavy on amorous tales or letters from unfortunate wives and the editor's empathetic responses (2 Jan 1720); others consist entirely of military news, including several narrating the particulars of the defeat of the Turks at Belgrade (late summer 1717). Many issues after early 1718 begin with a letter introductory, but in several numbers that letter appears in the middle, before and after other kinds of coverage. These notes from readers offer Applebee a chance to reflect on the competing expectations of his audience, and suggest a kind of identity crisis. The 23 July 1720 issue, for example, commences with a communiqué from a concerned citizen urging Applebee to focus on 'Solid and Weighty Subjects' that 'will bring Reputation to [his] Paper'. In the next issue, Applebee prints a note offering the opposite advice: 'I Find you are prompted . . . to enter upon Grave and Sober Things', but readers want 'something to make [them] Laugh'. Applebee's response is predictable: one cannot please everyone. His construction of this mixed readership reveals competing visions of what the periodical press should and should not try to do. These competing perspectives reveal Applebee's uncertainty about what kind of content is appropriate for that medium.

Applebee likes to report crime and violence, and from early 1716 he routinely includes dying speeches and extended accounts of trials as well as other 'materials about the lives of the citizens of the London underworld'. Applebee, Michael Shugrue notes, had a friend in the Ordinary of Newgate Prison, who after 1720 supplied him with news and confessions from inmates.[70] Applebee's interest in crime is well-known: he published lives of criminals hanged at Tyburn, and *Applebee's* (especially in the 1720s) includes several brief but vivid criminal narratives. Novak associates this tendency with Defoe, with whose *Moll Flanders* and *Colonel Jack* (both 1722) there are obvious connections.[71] Whether Applebee's interests drove

---

[70] Michael Shugrue, 'Applebee's Original Weekly Journal: An Index to Eighteenth-Century Taste', *The Newberry Library Bulletin* 6 (1964), 108–21, pp. 111–12.

[71] Maximillian E. Novak, *Daniel Defoe, Master of Fictions: His Life and Ideas* (Oxford, 2001), p. 599. *Colonel Jack* is a relatively safe attribution, *Moll Flanders* much less

Defoe's, or Defoe's drove Applebee's, or the two had little to do with one another, is at this point difficult to say. In any case, *Applebee's* represents a journalistic venture different in kind from anything we find in Anne's reign. The miscellaneous nature of the contents is not all that unusual – see Dunton, or even *The Spectator* and *The Tatler*, as well as their imitators. But the way Applebee and his contributors engage with readers, and the quasi-novelistic moments within the paper, do seem to suggest a new notion of entertainment.[72] If Defoe's more obviously partisan contributions exemplify the complex political allegiances of early Hanoverian England, the weeklies with which he was (probably) involved represent a more innovative kind of journalism, unpractised in late Stuart London but increasingly culturally prominent in the 1720s and 1730s.

Conclusion: the opposition press and the government, from Anne to George

That the corpus of partisan journalism under Queen Anne differs drastically from that produced in the early years of George I's reign is well known. Scholars tend to explain the difference in terms of a political cooling off: the Tories were marginalised, elections were less frequent, and the 'rage of party' all but disappeared. Some of this is accurate. The long-running battle between individual writers we find between 1702 and 1713–1714 (à la Swift versus Mainwaring and Steele) is not replicated under George I. The polarising rhetoric of 'Whig vs. Tory' subsides considerably. The personalised antagonism of late Stuart papers, with their relentless naming of names, is to some extent muted after 1715. That said, the notion that partisan journalism reflects the abating of political heat is misleading. The early years of George's reign were violent and vengeful. The Whig 'fears' of Jacobite rebellion were no doubt exaggerated: that party gained real political capital by keeping the threat alive. But the hyperbolic rhetoric about the 'implacable' and 'outrageous' church party signals bloodthirstiness: the author of the 1718 *Observator* flatly maintains the need 'to Suppress [the Tories], and

---

so; Ashley Marshall, 'Beyond Furbank and Owens: A New Consideration of the Evidence for the "Defoe" Canon', *Studies in Bibliography* 59 (2015), 131–90, p. 146.

[72] In 'The Growth of Government Tolerance of the Press to 1790', J. A. Downie connects 'the desire for reading-matter' after 1715 with 'the rise of the novel, or, more strictly, an increased market for prose fiction' (p. 56); in Robin Myers and Michael Harris (eds.), *The Development of the English Book Trade, 1700–1789* (Oxford, 1981), pp. 36–65.

even Extirpate them effectually *as a Party*: The Common Wealth cannot otherwise exist; the Government must be under constant Alarms'. Whig journalist after Whig journalist used loyalty to justify the call for a settling of the scores, and the authorities were prepared to enact draconian measures against dissidents. As Atterbury warned his fellow Tories in *English Advice to the Freeholders of England*, 'the Whigs have prepared ... Evils for us, which are not to be oppos'd by the King' (25). Tories were right to feel that Whig paranoia meant blocking the expression of legitimate opposition.

We should not be under the impression, however, that the opposition press was comfortably tolerated in late Stuart England. The lapse of the Licensing Act in 1695 brought about an information revolution, to be sure, but as John Feather has bluntly concluded, 'it is nonsense to suppose that England suddenly acquired a free press in anything like the sense in which the concept was to be understood in the liberal democracies of the nineteenth and twentieth centuries'.[73] Between 1695 and the passing of the Stamp Act in 1712, at least fifteen bills were proposed to regulate the press; though they failed, the frequency of the attempts is telling.[74] After 1710, St. John took pains to prosecute booksellers, printers, and publishers in an effort to weaken the anti-ministerial attacks. As Downie reminds us, 'contemporaries were quick to point out ... [that] there was a certain irony in Bolingbroke suddenly emerging as a champion of press freedom in *The Craftsman*', given his earlier role as regulator.[75] When the ministry finally passed the Stamp Act, the intentions were to silence the opposition, though those intentions were not fully realised. In September 1712, Swift reports to Stella that 'Grubstreet is dead and gone last Week', but he acknowledges that Whig papers were not the only victims: 'The Observator is fallen, the Medleys are jumbled togeth[e]r with the Flying-post', but the Tory *Examiner*, he adds, is 'deadly sick' as well. The 'Spectator keeps up', he continues, 'and doubles its price' (442).[76] In the *History of the Four Last Years of the Queen*, which Swift was drafting at the time, he reflects at greater length on the failure of the Stamp Act to achieve the results hoped for by the government:

---

[73] John Feather, 'The English Book Trade and the Law 1695–1799', *Publishing History* 12 (1982), 51–75, p. 52.

[74] J. A. Downie, 'How useful to eighteenth-century English studies is the paradigm of the "bourgeois public sphere"?' *Literature Compass* 1 (2003), 1–19, p. 7.

[75] Downie, 'How useful', p. 15.

[76] In *Spectator* no. 445, Addison reports, 'This is the Day on which many eminent Authors will probably Publish their Last Words.... [F]ew of our Weekly Historians ... will be able to subsist under the Weight of a Stamp, and an approaching Peace' (vol. 4, pp. 62–63).

> For the Adverse Party, full of Rage and Leisure since their Fall . . . employ a sett of Writers by Subscription, who are well Versed in all the topics of Defamation, and have a Style and Genius levelled to the Generality of Readers; while those who would draw their Pens on the Side of their Prince and Country, are discouraged by This tax. (*PW*, vol. 7. p. 24)

Whig organisation, among other things, helped the opposition press survive and flourish despite the ministry's desire to suppress it.

The relative inefficacy of governmental controls, though, does not change the fact of ministerial anxieties about anti-establishment press. As Downie has shown, Harley believed 'in the use of selective proscription as a weapon to be wielded side by side with the dissemination of government propaganda', but the hotter-headed St. John was inclined toward wholesale measures. Downie compellingly speculates that St. John 'envisaged a more repressive set of controls' than even the Stamp Act provided. He would have preferred 'the registration of printing-presses, and the implementation of a system of compulsory imprints, in order to maintain close control over the press'.[77] He did not manage to enact such laws, but like Swift he showed little patience for the 'fourth estate', and at least while in power he wished the news network only to do the government's bidding.

Whig unhappiness about the opposition press under George I, then, was in some ways familiar. The methods St. John hoped and tried to use were adopted under the new regime. The difference was that they were 'continued with more application and with rather more success', partly because the 'prerogative of the Secretaries to issue warrants was exercised freely'.[78] In the name of public safety and stability, Wilson explains, the authorities licenced 'Whig loyalists' to resort to whatever violence necessary to suppress dissenters; the effort to 'stamp out disaffection' is reflected likewise in the government's pursuits of its journalistic critics and their printers.[79] The most egregious case – admittedly somewhat anomalous – involved the arrest and eventual execution (1719) of John Matthews for printing a treasonous libel. In response to Matthews's arrest and death, some disaffected Tories naturally registered their disappointment. Elizabeth Powell, the widow of the Jacobite printer Edmund Powell, sympathetically depicted Matthews, thus joining 'the underground popular political protest already

---

[77] J. A. Downie, *Robert Harley and the Press: Propaganda and Public Opinion in the Age of Swift and Defoe* (Cambridge, 1979), pp. 154, 153.
[78] Hanson, *Government and the Press*, p. 64.
[79] Wilson, *Sense of the People*, p. 98.

under way, which ... made ... Matthews a favourite in-house martyr of the ... London press'.[80] Powell's husband had been forced into hiding in 1715 and died the following year; she launched two Jacobite papers, *The Orphan* and *The Charitable Mercury*, both immediately put down. The opposition press was not simply obliterated, despite government efforts and the fragmentation of the Tory party.

Tory journalism in early Hanoverian England tends toward the High Church and Jacobitism. Only the tamest of the Tory outlets could survive for long in such an environment, but the fiercest critics of the Whig regime were prepared to risk persecution and doggedly determined to create new outlets to make their voices heard. The conservative party, in Anne's reign associated with anti-populist politics, is after 1714 forced to champion 'a version of popular libertarianism'. Flint's tactics in *Robin's Last Shift* and its sequels 'first signaled the renewed attention to the liberties of the subject that had been the stock-in-trade of the so-called "Whiggish Jacobites" of the 1690s'. Jacobitism in the early years of George's rule, says Wilson, 'paradoxically combined a conservative agenda of a unified and monolithic church, a hereditary monarch and a homogenous polity with the championing of "the people's" liberties and rights against the claims and actions of the state'.[81]

The first years of George I's reign were tumultuous, and that the Whigs would manage to establish dominance was by no means a given. The fragmented and beleaguered Tories continued to put pressure on the new government, and to use the press – along with other means – to galvanise the opposition. The Whigs were pushed into the awkward position of having to promote anti-populism of the sort Swift and other Tories had subscribed to under the previous regime. The identity crisis must have felt acute to some. The attempts to consolidate power in 1714–1716 were followed by a Whig split that the party only survived because of Tory impotence. Partisans on both sides were on the defensive, the Tories trying desperately to pre-empt the formation of a single-party government and the Whigs labouring to marginalise the Tories despite widespread discontent with the new regime. The struggle for power gave urgency to political journalism, through which writers appealed – daily – to the populace, urging them either to rise up against or submit to the unpopular government, either to recommit to an

---

[80] Paula McDowell, *The Women of Grub Street: Press, Politics, and Gender in the London Literary Marketplace 1678–1730* (Oxford, 1998), p. 77. Powell's portrayal of Matthews appeared in her *Orphan Reviv'd* (1719–1720).
[81] Wilson, *Sense of the People*, pp. 113, 114, 116.

embattled Church or to redefine its civic importance, either to defend what Anne's last ministry had built or to condemn that ministry.

At the outset of George's reign, the Whigs seem to be talking up – trying to persuade the king and the Whig leadership to criminalise dissent – and the Tories often talk down, capitalising on and advancing popular discontent. One job of the political press was to mediate between the state and the people, and in 1714 the dynamic shifts. That change happens precisely because the nature of what Swift bitterly dubbed 'the new world' remained unsettled, and under George I – as under Anne – journalists offer competing visions of the polity in an effort to write those visions into reality.

I

PART II

Defoe, Swift, Steele

Chapter 3

Power and Politics in Defoe's Radical *Review*

Between February 1704 and June 1713, Daniel Defoe wrote some four million words as Mr. Review, the moralising commentator on the state of the English nation and on the balance of power in Europe. Over the course of these nine years, *The Review* unceasingly championed 'PARTY-PEACE' at home,[1] the Protestant Succession in England, toleration of dissent, and the Protestant interest in Europe. Equally consistent are Defoe's encouragement of trade, impatience with the landed gentry's insularity, and pontifical sponsorship of the 'Reformation of Manners'. What is not stable is the paper's essential political outlook: it begins as moderate Tory, and until 1708 preaches against party warfare, scarcely mentioning 'Whigs' and 'Tories'; between 1708 and 1710, Mr. Review is aggressively anti-Tory and anti-High Church; after 1710, according to the standard account, Defoe writes as an apologist for his benefactor Robert Harley, which means recommending Tory policies out of sync with his own values.

Scholars have explained these changes in straightforward ways. The best work on *The Review* is that of J. A. Downie, whose characterisation of the journal still represents the general consensus: Defoe 'consistently propounded the government line, however obliquely', even when that meant endorsing views other than his own.[2] Defoe, in other words, was always writing a pro-government journal, but he had to change his emphasis as the makeup of Anne's administration shifted from moderate to Whig to Tory. Before 1710, ministerial advocacy posed little problem for Defoe, who had merely to promote first moderation (until 1708) and then his actual, aggressively Whig views. After 1710, however, as Harley's ministry became more and more Tory, Defoe found himself awkwardly situated,

---

[1] Defoe uses this phrase frequently (e.g., *Review*, vol. 2, p. 2).
[2] J. A. Downie, *Robert Harley and the Press: Propaganda and Public Opinion in the Age of Swift and Defoe* (Cambridge, 1979), p. 64.

a spokesman for causes that in his heart of hearts he opposed: 'he had burnt his boats to embark with Harley', James Sutherland concludes, 'and he must stick to him now whatever course the minister might steer'.[3]

This last period of *The Review*, the problematic Harleyite phase of 1710–1713, is my principal concern here. Downie describes *The Review* as a ministerial organ under Harley, addressed to a Whig audience and therefore complementing the Tory-oriented *Examiner* of which Jonathan Swift was in charge from November 1710 to June 1711. In Downie's telling, *The Review* was sponsored and often supervised by Harley: it 'was the embodiment of Harley's desire for a periodical that would disperse Government propaganda'.[4] Defoe was, Maximillian E. Novak says, 'led gradually to defend all of the government's actions', and thus 'lost every principle except defending what must have seemed to him the indefensible actions of his government'.[5] For Downie, Novak, and others – including John McVeagh, editor of the only scholarly edition of *The Review* – Defoe was Harley's man, and his journal was chiefly devoted to supporting Harley's ministry. This consensus has been politely questioned in recent review essays by Nicholas Seager and Brian Cowan,[6] and I wish to extend their challenge. A fresh look at Defoe's *Review* suggests that it is a good deal more ambivalent toward Queen Anne's last ministry than scholarly characterisations of it have suggested.

What follows begins with a précis of some of the early changes we find in Mr. Review's attitudes and tendencies, and an account – much indebted to Downie – of the paper between its inauguration and Harley's return to power. Subsequent sections focus on the major events and debates of 1710–1713, from the ministerial change and General Election of 1710 through the (clandestine and controversial) peace negotiations to end the War of the Spanish Succession. In their discussions of war and peace, contemporary journalists had to take a stand on the Harley

---

[3] James R. Sutherland, *Defoe* (Philadelphia, 1938), p. 188.
[4] Downie, 'Daniel Defoe's *Review* and Other Political Writings in the Reign of Queen Anne' (M.Litt thesis, University of Newcastle upon Tyne, 1973), p. 52; I am grateful to Downie for generously loaning me a copy of his thesis.
[5] Maximillian E. Novak, *Daniel Defoe, Master of Fictions: His Life and Ideas* (Oxford, 2001), p. 395.
[6] Nicholas Seager, '"He reviews without Fear, and acts without fainting": Defoe's *Review*', *Eighteenth-Century Studies* 46 (2012), pp. 131–54; Brian Cowan, 'Daniel Defoe's *Review* and the Transformations of the English Periodical', *Huntington Library Quarterly* 77 (2014), pp. 79–110. Seager's conclusion is right: 'A fresh look complicates the still-prevalent view that Robert Harley simply dictated what Defoe wrote after the then Speaker brokered his release from prison in late 1703' (p. 132).

ministry, and Defoe's oblique reflections are important to how we assess his relationship to that ministry. By way of conclusion, I will situate Defoe's *Review* alongside Swift's *Examiner*; both papers were, according to the critical consensus, ministerial mouthpieces, but reading them side-by-side illuminates their considerable ideological differences. Mr. Examiner serves as a useful foil to Mr. Review, whose position vis-à-vis the incumbent ministry seems more complex, shifting, and ambivalent. My overarching concern is with the radicalness of Mr. Review's Whig ideology, a radicalness obscured by predominant treatments of this major periodical as essentially pro-government.

Some shifts in tone and focus

The Review is neither uniform in its focus nor entirely consistent in its tone, though its commitment to Whig notions about power, toleration, trade, and other key subjects never wavers. In 1704, Defoe's primary concern is with French history and the emergence of French power. From 1705 on, the perspective is less historical than present-centred, and coverage is predominantly domestic. In 1705, Mr. Review commences his cry for peace at home; his constant targets are the high-flying Tackers who destroy tranquillity at home and threaten the constitution. The following year, Defoe mostly addresses himself to questions of trade and credit and debt, dealing specifically with what should be demanded from and offered to bankrupt citizens. In 1707, of course, he has become fixated on the Union, labouring to cultivate support for Scotland and for England's official association with the Protestant northern nation. By 1708–1709, in the wake of the ministerial change and of the abortive Jacobite attempt, Mr. Review has returned to the subject of 1705, renewing his assault on traitorous Jacobites masquerading as mere high Anglicans. 1708 is another election year, and Defoe devotes himself to trying to convince readers 'that our *High-Flying* Gentlemen would be fatal to the Nation' (vol. 5, p. 141). The 1708–1709 *Review* also has much to say about the need for peace at home but for a continued war abroad. The following year, writing from Scotland, Defoe obsesses over Jacobitism; defends the naturalisation of foreign Protestants; and pits himself against those who believe in toleration for Scottish Episcopalians. In 1710–1711, Defoe holds forth on the Sacheverell trial and on the ministerial change. I will return to his assessment of the change in due course; here I wish only to note that as the Tories return to power, Defoe savages that party as not only corrupt but indubitably bound to the Jacobites. *The Review* of 1711–1713 is multiply focused: war and peace, trade, public credit, Sweden and Muscovy, the threat posed by the high Tory October Club, the need for partition, the alliance with the Dutch, the Episcopalians in Scotland, and the fate of the Protestant succession are all extensively treated.

Mr. Review is not a static figure; his tone and rhetoric shift across the life of his paper. In its first year, *The Review* does indeed seem to adopt Harleyite moderation. Defoe is calm, restrained, non-aggressive, non-polarising. In no. 13, he assures us that his paper is 'of neither Party', and 'shall Embroil no Parties, nor Commence Disputes' (vol. 1, pp. 85, 87), and for the most part he seems to try to keep his hand light. In the early months of the paper, Defoe adopts a pose of forbearance: 'I Confess 'tis not proper to Expose Men for every Miscarriage' (vol. 1, p. 138). Even where one might expect him to be tetchy, he stays cool. Addressing charges that *The Review* supports Jacobitism, Defoe responds without defensiveness, issuing a confident statement that 'the very Book it self shall live to be an Answer to' his critics (vol. 1, p. 123). He urges patience and remains unruffled. Mr. Review does occasionally critique English behaviour, but *sans* the holier-than-thou preachment of later volumes: 'I have always been of the Opinion, That our slighting, or not rightly understanding the Greatness ... of our Enemies, has been one of the most Fatal Errors of our Age' (vol. 1, p. 220). Throughout the spring and summer, and most of the fall, of 1704, Defoe not only eschews direct judgment of his countrymen; he is also optimistic about English greatness. The high emotion introduced in 1705 has much to do with a shift in focus, from French history and French power to more present-centred, emphatically domestic politics. As McVeagh notes, what we find in 1705 amounts to 'a re-definition of the periodical's character and purpose' (vol. 2, p. viii).

Defoe never fully returns to the academic, dispassionate voice of the first volume, though the display of high emotion varies. He is at his most vehement in the wake of the Tack; in 1707–1708; and in 1710–1711. His intensity is almost always directed at the duplicitous high-flyers, particularly those 'Ambo-Dexters' (vol. 6, p. 585) who take oaths to a government that they secretly conspire against. The polarising rhetoric emerges in 1705, and it never disappears for long. If the Tackers are voted in, Mr. Review warns during the 1705 election season, '*England* is Undone; farewell *Toleration*, farewell *Protestant Succession*, farewell Queen, farewell Religion, farewell Nation, for no Honest Man ought to stay in it' (vol. 2, p. 179). The election, naturally, provokes him toward such dichotomous formulations: on one side, 'the *Papists*, the *Atheists*, the *Drunken, Swearing*, and most *Vicious* of the people', on the other the solid citizens and good Protestants (191). At this point, Defoe is mostly willing to distinguish between the Tackers and the moderate Tories; by 1707–1708, there is little sign of that distinction.

Defoe's manner of speaking to and of 'the people' also shifts over the life of *The Review*, a subject to which we return more fully in Chapter 6. In the early volumes, though he emphasises his need to school and guide electors, he adopts an optimistic 'everyone is capable of judging fairly' stance. By 1707–1708, Mr. Review is less confident that the people are able to discern good from evil, fact from fiction. An increasingly prominent theme is popular credulity and high-flying deceptiveness: 'I confess, we are a Nation willing to be deluded, willing to be imposed upon, and nothing is so absurd, but we are pleased with it, rather than not have some News; and this encourages the Wretches that do it to the last Degree' (vol. 4, p. 696). In the beginning years of *The Review*, such critique tended to occur more indirectly, often in the Scandal Club sessions, where Defoe's 'Society' details the errors and deceptions of rival papers. In the Scandal Club segment of no. 46, the Society concludes, "tis a sufficient Authority for making Folks Fools, that they are willing to be made so' (vol. 1, p. 298). These insinuations are soon replaced by increasingly common Juvenalian outbursts on 'the Stupidity, Blindness and Madness' of the English (vol. 5, p. 101).

In one other important realm, Mr. Review shifts from the mostly indirect to the direct, from analogy to straight polemic. *The Review* is always committed to Whig ideology, and (as we shall see) to radically Whig conceptions of contract theory. In the initial numbers, written under the auspices of a moderate Tory government, Defoe is scrupulously careful to avoid direct endorsement of such ideals. In no. 9, he maintains that questions of power are not his concern in *The Review*: "Tis not my present Work, to Discourse of the Nature and Reasons of Governments, of Compacts between King and People; of Original Right by Propriety of time; of Native Freedom, Submission, &c'. (vol. 1, p. 61). The first several months of the paper are devoted to a study of the rise and sustenance of absolutism, but Defoe goes out of his way *not* to talk about English politics in these issues. He limits himself to an extensive discussion of 'The Arbitrary Government of the *French*' (vol. 1, p. 67). Defoe contrasts this model of government with that of England, whose 'Constitution . . . is so fenc'd and secur'd by the Laws and Popular Right, that the Liberties of the Nation are in a manner Impregnable' (73). His judgment is unequivocal: 'Despotick Absolute Power, makes great Names [e.g., Louis], but Legal Power makes great Nations' (74).

In 1704, Mr. Review uses his protracted discourse on French absolutism to disseminate his pro-resistance values. The message of his journal in its early months clearly amounts to a warning against a 'servile Temper', against overmuch submissiveness. In no.18, Defoe tells an anecdote of unjust punishment to which a French gentleman too readily assented, concluding thus:

> I don't design this for a Satyr upon the Temper of our own Country, yet I Question whether there is an *English* Man shall read this Paper, that will venture to say for himself, he could do the same – This I take to be the Effect of the Absolute Submission, that is paid to the [French] King's Command, and that Obedience without reserve; which, *as God be thank'd, they are all more obligd to than we are.* (vol. 1, p. 119)

At first, then, Defoe treats the question of obedience versus resistance in a continental context.[7] In his repeated insistence that such issues are irrelevant to England, he might be said to protest too much. In any case, he comes to be more explicit. By October 1710, he mourns the fact that:

> Our Poor unhappy People under the present Possession, are running upon all the fatal Precipices of Absolute Submission – Subjection to Tyranny, Obedience to Arbitrary Commands, giving up Constitution Priviledges, falling with Violence into the Gulph Persecution, and *with these*, into the entire Subversion of National Liberty (vol. 7, p. 427)

'If such Submission to the Absolute Will of the Prince is our Duty', he continues, 'Pray, Gentlemen, why do you Choose Representatives? Of what use is a Parliament?' (428). In the last half of *The Review*, Defoe does more prominent and persistent battle with the high-flying Charles Leslie's *Rehearsal*. From the time of *Jure Divino* (1706), Defoe is no longer able to avoid questions about the basis of power. What changes is not the ideology informing *The Review* but the way the ideology is conveyed.

The Review is a wide-ranging opinion paper carried on during a time of unsettled political circumstances; there are more shifts in tone and focus than can be described here. My concern in the present chapter is as much with what does not change as with what does, especially in terms of Defoe's relationship to the successive ministries under which he wrote.

---

[7] See also vol. 1, pp. 296–97.

Mr. Review and the ministries, 1704–1710

The Review would not have started were it not for Robert Harley. On 9 August 1702, Harley – then Speaker of the House of Commons – wrote to Lord Treasurer Godolphin, suggesting the wisdom of 'hav[ing] some discreet writer of the Government['s] side, if it were only to state facts right; for the Generality err for want to [*sic*] knowledg[e], & being impos[e]d upon by the storys rais[e]d by ill designing men'.[8] Four months later, Defoe would publish his inflammatory pamphlet *The Shortest-Way with the Dissenters*, sufficiently toxic as to land him in the jug. In April 1703, Defoe appealed to William Paterson, a politically connected London merchant: 'If you Should Find Room for my Name in your Conversation with the Gentleman I Mention'd, I Suppose I Need Not Name him, If you Find him Enclin'd to have Compassion for One who Offended him Onely because he Did Not kno' him, Venture in My Name in the Humblest Terms to Ask his Pardon', and so on.[9] The 'Gentleman' is Harley, who – very happily for the destitute author of the ill-advised *Shortest Way* – intervened. The 'ambitious' Speaker, as P. N. Furbank and W. R. Owens explain, 'had realised the potential usefulness of such a skilled writer and, with the assistance of ... Godolphin, he secured his release from Newgate and engaged him as an unofficial agent and adviser'. One component of the deal they struck 'was that Defoe should launch a political journal' – and thus the *Review* was born.[10]

Downie has pointed out, however, that the 'discreet writer' Harley had in mind in 1702 was probably not Defoe but his acquaintance William Paterson. Not until the following year did 'Harley finally manage ... to convince a reluctant Godolphin that Defoe should be employed by the government', and even then the role Harley envisioned for Defoe was that of intelligence agent, not writer.[11] At some point, Harley changed his mind, and when Mr. Review commences his journal on 19 February 1704, he intimates that he is beholden to those above:

> This Paper is the Foundation of a very large and useful Design, which, if it meet with suitable Encouragement, *Permissu Superiorum*, may

---

[8] Quoted in J. A. Downie, 'Stating Facts Right About Defoe's *Review*', in Downie and Thomas N. Corns (eds.), *Telling People What To Think: Early Eighteenth-Century Periodicals from* The Review *to* The Rambler (London, 1993), 8–22, p. 8. Downie's source is British Library Add. MS 28055, f. 3.
[9] George Harris Healey (ed.), *The Letters of Daniel Defoe* (Oxford, 1955), p. 6.
[10] P. N. Furbank and W. R. Owens, *A Political Biography of Daniel Defoe* (London, 2006), pp. 24, 25.
[11] Downie, 'Stating Facts Right', p. 8.

contribute to Setting the Affairs of *Europe* in a Clearer Light, and to prevent the various uncertain Accounts, and the Partial Reflections of our Street-Scriblers, who Daily and Monthly Amuse Mankind with . . . a Multitude of Unaccountable and Inconsistent Stories, which have at least this Effect, That People are possest with wrong Notions of Things, and Nations Wheedled to believe Nonsense and Contradiction. (vol. 1, p. 6)

Defoe's career as a journalist, then, began at Harley's behest and no doubt represented payback for Defoe's liberation. Upon his release from Newgate, Defoe had addressed himself gratefully to Harley, beseeching his benefactor to make use of him: 'It Remains for me to Conclude my Present Application with This Humble Petition that if Possible I may By Some Meanes or Other know what I am capable of Doeing'.[12] In May 1704, three months into his time as Mr. Review, Defoe would still be expressing his desire that Harley either 'find this Neglected fellow Servicable, or at least Make him So'.[13]

The nature and degree of ministerial subsidisation of the *Review* remain vague. Downie posits that, 'It seems virtually indisputable that Harley and Godolphin subsidised the *Review* through four successive ministries, if only indirectly in that they supplied money by which Defoe was able to placate his creditors'.[14] Though other scholars have concurred that Harley 'must have' provided funds to launch and maintain the *Review*, no extant documentation substantiates this (admittedly likely) conjecture.[15] Seager has echoed the consensus that the ministry was 'funding the *Review*; or at least it was funding Defoe, enabling him to keep his creditors at bay'.[16] That we lack specific information about the funds he received is unfortunate.

---

[12] Defoe, *Letters*, p. 10.
[13] Defoe, *Letters*, p. 14.
[14] Downie, 'Defoe's *Review*', p. 52. Elsewhere Downie discusses the 'extensive secret service payments . . . made to Defoe in return for his efforts in espionage', speculating – plausibly – that 'It would be reasonable to assume that Defoe was paid regularly throughout the period 1710 to 1714'; 'Secret Service Payments to Daniel Defoe, 1710–1714', *The Review of English Studies* n.s. 30 (1979), 437–41, pp. 437, 441.
[15] Despite the fact that some of Defoe's epistolary requests for funds were ignored, 'he seems to have found some encouraging signs, for he kept up the *Review* without a break'; David Harrison Stevens, *Party Politics and English Journalism 1702–1742* (1916; Rpt. New York, 1967), p. 49. Stevens's account, however, presents Defoe – convincingly – as financially strapped and importunate, appealing to Harley for assistance that either did not come or amounted to too little (pp. 49-50).
[16] Seager, '"He reviews without Fear"', p.134.

The paper we now think of simply as *The Review* first appeared under the title *A Weekly Review of the Affairs of France*,[17] and it was, initially, 'a tory organ', designed 'to cajole the moderate tories into maintaining their support for the government's war-effort', partly by 'build[ing] up an 'official' picture of the might of France'.[18] Defoe's emphasis on '*French* Greatness' and '*French* Grandeur' was intended to prove the necessity of defeating this 'Terrour of *Europe*', but readers were alarmed by what seemed like adulation of the enemy (vol. 1, p. 22).[19] As Godolphin wrote to Harley in June 1704, the author of *The Review* had to be punished: 'this magnifying of France is a thing so odious in England, that I can't think any jury would acquit this man if discovered'.[20] *The Review* for 4 July makes clear that Harley had communicated these anxieties to Defoe; in this apologia, Mr. Review insists that were his paper complete, no one would be able to 'say I was in the *French* Interest, or *Magnify'd the Enemy too much*' (vol. 1, p. 220). In a 7 July letter to Harley, Defoe conveys his eagerness to hear 'from your Self, that I had Explain'd the Review to your Satisfaction'.[21] Defoe was duly sanctioned, and 'Harley had acquired a propagandist and a paper that . . . would effectively spearhead the government's election campaign in 1705'.[22]

The major issue of the 1704–1705 parliamentary session was a new occasional conformity bill, which the high Tories wished to 'tack' onto a money bill so as to prevent otherwise certain rejection in the House of Lords. Harley enlisted moderate Tories to join with Whigs against this manoeuvre, and throughout the election campaign of 1705, Defoe championed Harley's cause, attempting to alienate moderate Tories from the high-Tory Tackers. Defoe was fiercely opposed to occasional conformity, a ploy he called '*playing-Bopeep* with God Almighty',[23] and as Mr. Review he gleefully denounced the Tackers, whose 'Vile' stratagem was 'a most Contemptible, Blind, Ridiculous Project' (vol. 2, p. 175). He encouraged the electorate 'not [to] Choose *a Tacker*, unless you will *Destroy* our peace,

[17] Defoe dropped 'Weekly' after seven issues. In February 1705, the name changed to a *Review of the Affairs of France, with Observations upon Transactions at Home*; in 1707, it became *A Review of the State of the British Nation*.
[18] Downie, *Robert Harley*, p. 65.
[19] As Defoe explained, not without reason, in no. 4, 'Methinks having the true Picture of our Adversary should be useful to instruct us in our needful Preparations' (vol. 1, p. 30).
[20] Quoted by Downie in *Robert Harley*, p. 66.
[21] Defoe, *Letters*, p. 26.
[22] Downie, *Robert Harley*, p. 66.
[23] Defoe, *A Collection of the Writings of the Author of the True-Born English-Man* (London, 1703), p. 146.

Divide our Strength, *Pull Down* the Church, *let in* the *French*, and *Depose* the Queen' (147).[24] Whenever the ministry benefited from the castigation of high-flyers, Defoe could oblige with no crisis of conscience.

In 1706, 'Defoe was disseminating Harleyite views' that were not (Downie observes) 'shared by his fellow ministers', and a break with those ministers was imminent. Though Downie considerably overstates Defoe's expressed eagerness for 'a speedy settlement' of the war – on which more later – he is correct in pointing out that Defoe follows Harley in amplifying the fact 'that the war had been undertaken only to reduce "the exorbitant power of France", not France itself'.[25] While Defoe was promulgating (some of) Harley's ideas in 1706–1708, he was also serving as an intelligence agent in Scotland, and finding his employer frustratingly non-communicative. Seager's conclusion seems accurate: 'Defoe, not Harley, dictated the content of the *Review* in volumes three and four [1706–1707], even if he had an eye on ministerial developments and wrote with these in mind. As much as enemies liked to depict Defoe as the government's tool, very little guidance was forthcoming from Harley'.[26] In January 1707, Defoe asks his boss to command him 'when to Leave this place or how to Govern my Self'; the next month he worries that he has been 'Dropt'; in late March he repeats his desire to know 'what Course I shall steer next'; in early April, he crossly declares, 'I shall no more Afflict you with Sollicitations for your Ordrs. I proceed by my Own Undirected judgemt, Giveing you a Constant Account, and Am forced to take your Long Silence for a Tacit professing your Satisfaction'. In May, however, he continues his complaint, and on 19 July he dolefully calls himself 'One Entirely forgott'.[27] Harley's only instructions had come on 12 June: Defoe was to 'write a Letter to Ld Treasurer [Godolphin] (inclose it to me) proposing Your own Service & where You can be most usefull'.[28] Downie ventures that 'Godolphin had deprived Harley of his personal propagandist more out of spite, than out of an urgent desire to employ him on his own behalf', but whatever the motivation, 'For the time being, the relationship between Harley and Defoe was over'.[29] So, for a

---

[24] See also in the same volume pp. 140, 155, 162, 186, and 403. In the *Review* for April 17 1705, he 'penned what amounted to Harley's election manifesto', figuring 'the General Election as a struggle between the Tackers and the rest' (Downie, 'Defoe's *Review*', p. 90).

[25] Downie, *Robert Harley*, p. 75.

[26] Seager, '"He reviews without Fear"', p. 138.

[27] Defoe, *Letters*, pp. 190, 202, 212, 213, 231. The comments in May are at pp. 225–26.

[28] Defoe, *Letters*, p. 228.

[29] Downie, *Robert Harley*, p. 78.

while, was Harley's government service; having fallen out with Godolphin and Marlborough, he resigned in February 1708.

With Harley gone, Defoe continued to write as a ministerial agent, but now the ministry was Whig all the way, and Mr. Review could be so too. This phase of *The Review* lasted until Godolphin's fall in August 1710. The new party politics of *The Review* are clear, as Downie has shown, if one compares Defoe's election propaganda in 1708 to that of 1705.[30] In the previous election, he had distinguished between moderate Tories and extremist Tackers, looking to deprecate the high-flyers while still appealing to their more reasonable counterparts. Even earlier, in 1706, Defoe casually aligns '*Tackers* and *Tories*' (vol. 3, p. 1). By 1708, under the aegis of the Whig junto, he vilifies the entire Tory party *sans* qualification, branding all Tories to be peace-destroying, union-breaking, credit-ruining, queen-insulting, church-threatening, nation-spoiling, tyranny-championing, would-be Jacobitical rogues. On 22 May 1708, Mr. Review ironically instructs his gentlemen readers to vote 'these honest Sort of Folk into this Parliament', and:

> you shall soon come to the Perfection of your Endeavours; a *Tory* Parliament, a *Tory* Ministry, a *Tory* Administration, a *Tory* Peace, a *Tory* Successor, and *Hey Boys up go we*; the Revolution, the Succession, the Union, the Toleration, shall all receive their due Regulations, and this Nation shall arrive to its immediate State of Bliss THE SHORTEST WAY. (vol. 5, p. 130)

Unlike before 1708 and after summer 1710, here the distance between Mr. Review and Daniel Defoe is largely non-existent: the government's man is free both to inveigh against the church party, and also to cast aspersions on the notions of a Tory peace while extolling 'the Thing we call Glory in this War' (vol. 5, p. 119). To '*Act Legally*', Mr. Review matter-of-factly declares, 'is to *Act Whiggishly*' (vol. 7, p. 388).

With Harley's return to power in August 1710, scholars conclude, Defoe was compelled to 'make his final and most decisive volte-face of Queen Anne's reign'.[31] The change in the political landscape necessitated another transformation of the political persona of Mr. Review.

---

[30] Downie, 'Defoe's *Review*', pp. 177–78.
[31] Downie, 'Defoe's *Review*', p. 210.

Harley's return: Mr. Review on the ministerial change

By the late spring of 1710, the Whig ministry had become so unpopular as to make a change inevitable. The duumvirate of Marlborough and Godolphin was determined to continue fighting, but oppressive taxes and the bloodbath at Malplaquet left a war-weary populace even more fatigued. The bill for the naturalisation of foreign Protestants had increased anti-Whig sentiment, and the Queen had lost faith in her counsellors. Godolphin fell in August; by September the dismissal of his ministry was complete; and the Tories routed the Whigs in the October general election. Thus commenced Harley's tenure as 'prime minister', lord treasurer, and leader of what he hoped would be a moderate, non-partisan cohort. In July 1710, obviously anticipating some kind of alteration in the political landscape, Defoe appealed to Harley. He insists upon the need for moderation – 'Now is The Time to find Out and Improve Those blessed Mediums of This Nations happyness, which lye between The wild Extremes of all Partyes' – and hails Harley as the man who can 'bring ... Exasperated Parties and the Respective Mad-Men to Their Politick Sences', and heal 'the Breaches on both Sides'. He vows to 'be Usefull' in this moderating project if he can, a resolution he would repeat in September.[32] At this point, most scholars have asserted, *The Review* ceased to be the Whig paper it had been from 1708 to 1710, and its author committed himself to Harley's cause. Furbank and Owens describe the Defoe of fall 1710 as 'a would-be Whig and praiser of the old ministry' who found himself 'serving the Tories and being swept along with them', occupying a position that was 'hopelessly false'.[33] Between 1710 and 1713, as since the beginning of *The Review*, Downie concludes, 'Defoe defended and justified the conduct of the government at all times'.[34] My contention is that Mr. Review's politics under the Queen's last ministry are more complicated than these characterisations suggest.

About the ministerial change itself, Mr. Review is ambivalent. What Defoe thought is impossible fully to know. He gave his support to Harley in letters, but when Sunderland was dismissed as secretary of state in June 1710, he was very unhappy indeed about the removal of a man 'with the most unblemish'd Character that ever I read of any Statesman in the World' (vol. 7, p. 181). On that occasion, Mr. Review voiced his anxiety about further dismissals, and in July he professed *'the Sense of the Nation'* to be against a ministerial change (233). Days before promising his support to

---

[32] Defoe, *Letters*, pp. 270–71.
[33] Furbank and Owens, *Political Biography*, p. 124.
[34] Downie, *Robert Harley*, p. 133.

Harley, in other words, Defoe – in his capacity as Mr. Review – was raising alarm about the impending alteration of the political situation. Soon after Godolphin's fall, Mr. Review seems uneasy but not despairing: 'The Government has made Alterations, the Queen is Changing Hands for the Administration, some go out, some come in – We say, we are sure Honest Men go out – It is our Business to hope, *and Time must Answer*, for those that come in' (293). He confesses himself 'as much concern'd at Change, as any Body', but says that nothing is to be done, and he 'shall therefore say nothing to these Changes, on one side nor on the other' (294), except to encourage his readers not to assume the worst and to continue to support credit. Mr. Review could not, realistically, simply throw his lot in immediately with the incoming ministry; to do so would be thoroughly to alienate his Whig readers. We cannot, perhaps, conclude much from his unenthusiastic response to the ministerial alteration.

The nature of *The Review* after that change is more suggestive. Under the Whig junto, Defoe was able to write as an anti-church Whig, deeply suspicious of and hostile to Tories of all stripes – something that he was, significantly, slow to abandon after Harley's reinstatement. As Cowan has noted, 'Harley and Defoe were perhaps never so far apart as they were immediately after Harley's triumphant return to power in the wake of the ministerial revolution and the resounding Tory victory at the polls of the general election in 1710.' Harley was 'head of the newly ascendant Tory coalition', which meant, among other things, that he 'had to embrace the Church of England (and hence distance himself from an overly lenient policy toward Protestant dissent)'.[35] As the Tory party took power under Harley, Mr. Review is still warning his readership about the dangers of Toryism: a week after Godolphin's dismissal, Defoe tellingly reflects, 'I should be very sorry, to see a Tory Administration; I should think it a Melancholy View of Things to see the old Game of Persecution, reviv'd among us' (vol. 7, p. 298). Defoe's Protestant zeal is a crucial component of the ideology of *The Review*, and his interpretation of the new regime was clearly influenced by his concerns about toleration of dissent. A few days later, he addresses the ministerial change, announcing his expectations from '*the New Ministry*'. They will be, he avers, '*of the Queen's Party*': 'The Nature of Things is such, the Constitution and setled Stream of our Government is such, they shall all be *Whiggs* in the Management' (305).[36]

---

[35] Cowan, 'Daniel Defoe's *Review*', p. 85.
[36] In August 1710, Defoe insists that England must and will play 'the Old Whiggish Game still' (vol. 7, p. 309) to keep the Pretender out. 'The Revolution is a *Whig* Settlement, the Confederacy is a *Whig* Alliance, the Government is a *Whig* Government', he asserts, and the management must also be Whig (p. 319).

This is a theme for Defoe in fall 1710, and his reminders that a just ministry will necessarily be a Whig one often read like advice for Harley and his incoming administration. He also wishes, presumably, to assuage fears about the incoming ministry, whether to please Harley or in the name of fostering peace at home.

What Defoe does not do, in the fall of 1710, is leave off vilifying the Tories. Downie describes his 1710 election propaganda as 'decidedly neutralist': he 'attacked bribery and corruption, lecturing on the abuse of electoral practices in general, rather than spreading the propaganda of one side [or] the other. His stance was Harleyite, as Harley's scheme necessitated only a marginal election result between the numbers of the two parties'. Mr. Review, he suggests, could not 'openly attack the Tories'.[37] But in the run-up to and aftermath of the election, Defoe seems anything but neutral. His first direct reference to the elections is on 5 October (vol. 7, p. 390), and he does appear to be decrying widespread corruption. But what might look non-partisan in an issue here or there reads quite differently in context: Mr. Review is unrelenting, in August and September, in his condemnation of the Tories. On 16 September, taking no pains to discriminate between moderates and high-flyers, he defines the opposition thus: 'A *Tory* is a Plunderer of his Country, a Persecutor for Religion, a Bloody Destroyer without Law, a Betrayer of Liberties, and one that will give us his Nation to *Popery* and *Arbitrary Power*, under the pretence of Passive Obedience and Non Resistance' (vol. 7, p. 360).

Throughout September, Defoe spills a lot of ink – with fewer digressions than usual on trade and credit – denouncing the clergy and the 'Tory' principles of hereditary succession and passive obedience. And in early to mid-October, Mr. Review's pre-election harangues on bribery and corruption have a distinctly partisan slant, as for example when he expresses his hopes that the Whigs never practice 'the abhorr'd Method of the Degenerate *Tory*' (408). When Defoe sneers at those 'on the Devil's Side' (407), he need not name the party he has in mind: no reader of *The Review* could be in any doubt. In the same issue, he flatly proclaims, 'The *Tories* stick at nothing; they Bribe, Feast, make Drunk, and Debauch the People', and 'they regard no Justice, no Truth of Fact' (409). Three days later, he appears to backtrack, condemning both 'a Tory, High-flying Parliament' and 'a Hot Whig' one (412), but this quasi-moderate issue is not typical of the *Review* in the fall of 1710. As late as the end of November, Defoe could still declare, decisively, that 'the natural tendency of Toryism' is 'to St. *Germains*' (486). While Harley is building a Tory – a moderate

---

[37] Downie, 'Defoe's *Review*', p. 230.

Tory, perhaps, but still a Tory – administration, Mr. Review is routinely affirming that only the Whigs are defenders of 1688,[38] and the Tories are enemies to the Revolution and thus to the English constitution.

Downie identifies Defoe's *Review* and Swift's *Examiner* as two periodicals 'preaching moderation' in the service of Harley's 'non-party' scheme.[39] To the question of Mr. Examiner's moderation, I will return in Chapter 4. For now, I wish simply to point out that to call *The Review* of the fall 1710 'moderate' is misleading. Defoe's 'moderation' under the Whig junto was immoderate Whiggism, and that did not disappear immediately upon Harley's triumphant return. Throughout the last years of *The Review*, 1710–1713, as we shall see in due course, Defoe continues to promulgate key Whig notions about power and politics. Where he appears to move more and more in Harley's direction is on the question of war and peace – but just how unambiguously supportive of ministerial goals was Mr. Review on this subject?

Mr. Review on war and peace

The War of the Spanish Succession (1701–1713), and the controversial treaty that ended it, are of enormous import to *The Review*'s position on state affairs: the war dominated English politics from the beginning of Defoe's journal to the very end. Downie has described the 'purpose' of *The Review* in these terms: it was meant 'to influence English public opinion on the question of the War. . . . As there were differing views both on the war's military objectives, and on how those objectives might best be achieved, it was crucial that . . . the nation should present a unified front to the threat posed by France. *The Review*'s task, then, was to support the government line on the war without revealing it to be such'.[40] More than half a century ago, Lawrence Poston III attempted to offer a more nuanced discussion of Defoe's take on Harley's peace campaign, though his analysis has been mostly ignored by later scholars.[41] What exactly does Mr. Review have to

---

[38] See for example *Review*, vol. 7, pp. 306 and 458.
[39] Downie, *Robert Harley*, p. 129.
[40] Downie, 'Stating Facts Right', pp. 12–13.
[41] Lawrence Poston, III, 'Defoe and the Peace Campaign, 1710–1713: A Reconsideration', *Huntington Library Quarterly* 27 (1963), pp. 1–20. Poston is interested in showing Defoe's consistency about the balance of power in Europe and about Austrian power in particular. He does, however, quietly question the degree of Defoe's sycophancy

say about the war – and eventually, the peace – and to what extent do his arguments support Harley's objectives?

When Defoe took up his pen as Mr. Review in February 1704, England was three years into the War of the Spanish Succession, which began after the death of Charles II of Spain. Charles named as his successor the French prince Philip of Anjou, grandson of Louis XIV, and Louis proclaimed Philip king, vowing that France and Spain would be united. Fearing a virtually unbeatable Catholic empire, England joined the Grand Alliance with Holland, Prussia, and Austria, all determined to install the Austrian archduke (Charles) as king of Spain. That state of affairs continued until the sudden death, in April 1711, of Austrian Emperor Joseph I, Charles's older brother. Charles succeeded Joseph as Emperor, which meant for many Europeans (including Defoe) that he should not be allowed also to occupy the Spanish throne. To give Charles both Austria and Spain would – many thought – be as destructive to the balance of power in Europe as a Franco-Spanish union; earlier advocates of Charles's accession began instead to clamour for a partition. The Treaty of Utrecht (1713) that ended the war for all allies but Austria – achieved via clandestine negotiations between England and France – stipulated that Philip should, after all, inherit the Spanish crown, but only on the condition that France and Spain never be united.

My principal focus concerns the period after Harley's return to power in summer 1710, but some characterisation of Mr. Review's position on the war before then is useful contextualisation. By the time Defoe commenced the *Review*, England was feeling the effects of the costly conflict, and one of the key aims of the journal at the outset was to remind readers of the dangers of French power in an attempt to renew commitment to the war. Especially in 1704–1705, Defoe is in rallying mode, emphasising the 'mighty Victories' that 'have Crown'd our Armies' (vol. 1, p. 697) and highlighting the need to diminish French power. The prevailing theme of *the Review*, in its first half-dozen years, is peace at home *now* and peace abroad no sooner than it can be safely and honourably achieved.[42] France, Mr. Review repeatedly warns his readers, will not be 'soon Conquer'd' or 'Easily beaten': the '*French* will not fly any faster than they are driven; they will collect all their Strength to make a Stand, they will defend their Frontiers, lose their Ground by Inches' (vol. 2, p. 284, vol. 3, p. 446). Defoe maintains that the object of the war is not to depose 'the Government of *France*, as a Kingdom' (vol. 3, p. 496), but he absolutely supports beating France roundly. Though he never suggests

---

to Harley: Defoe would come to 'hint that the war might have been better conducted by Harley's predecessors' (p. 4).

[42] *Review*, vol. 2, p. 109.

that the Allies might lose the war, he does caution his readers not to be too confident: 'Security in War is the most certain Fore-runner of Disaster', and so on (vol. 4, p. 48). The Allies have been successful, and their conquests must continue: 'FRANCE is to be reduc'd by nothing but by Blows' (424). The Allies were defeated at Almansa in April 1707 and at Toulon in August, in response to which Mr. Review tries to revive English spirits.[43] 'The thing is plain', he insists, 'have we lost our Men, we must raise more, what should we do? Have we lost our Ships, we must build more? Have we spent the last Years Funds, we must find new Ones? – The present War is a just Necessity' (650). On the need for 'the vigorous Prosecution of this War' Defoe is emphatic (693).

Like most of his contemporaries, Defoe wanted a good peace, but he insists that peace must not come too quickly, and he glorifies the war in no uncertain terms. To 'ruin *France*', he decrees, 'you must push at him by Land' (vol. 4, p. 749). In the run up to the 1708 elections, Mr. Review speaks ironically of 'the wonderful Advantages of a *Tory* . . . Parliament', which 'would put a Speedy End to this cruel War', insinuating that the peace secured by the high-flying party would be far from honourable (vol. 5, pp. 116–1717). Elect Tories, only 'IF you would make a Peace with *France*, *Higle de Pigle de*, as they call it, on *French* Terms' (139). Throughout the 1708–1710 period, Defoe continues his war-mongering, assuring readers that God 'smiles upon the Design' of the war, and that the favour of Providence 'should encourage us to go on with it' (465). The war has been bloody, destructive of life and trade, but 'after all our Thirst of Peace, let me put in one Caution' – namely, that the peace must be both safe and honourable (687). In June 1709, Mr. Review summarises his position: 'we may still carve for our selves' advantageous terms, 'And if we cannot do it by a Treaty, we may do it by the Sword – And we must do it by the Sword' (vol. 6, p. 142).

Such is Defoe's stance on the war on the eve of Harley's return to power. Downie has contended that as Mr. Review 'Defoe urged a speedy settlement' of the war: 'The answer was peace. "The honest end is peace, and the best reward of victory is peace", he advised, "an honourable, safe, and lasting peace, which I believe every honest man will join with me in a petition for"'.[44] To believe that the war should end in a good peace is hardly distinctly Harleyite: on 29 November 1710, the radically Whig *Observator*, after insisting that the Queen herself 'recommends the carrying on the War in all its parts', would also say that vigorous prosecution of that war was the way 'to procure a safe and honourable Peace'. Defoe called for eventual

---

[43] *Review*, vol. 4, pp. 473, 492, 497–99, 525.
[44] Downie, *Robert Harley*, p. 75.

peace, but Downie's quotations are misleading out of context. In the *Review* for 27 January 1711 Defoe is adamant:

> you must not be discourag'd, the War must not be given over – We are in the War as if it were but just now begun, we must not give it over in its beginning, let the People that manage it do as they will, the War must be carried on, the Quarrel must be pursu'd, the Enemy must be push'd to the last Gasp; no Arms can be laid down, no Agreement can be made without Honourable Conditions, and the Time of the Enemies Advantages, is not a Time to expect those Conditions. (vol. 7, p. 590)

This does not sound like urging a speedy settlement.

The pamphlet that does push for a quick end to the war is *Reasons why this Nation Ought to put a Speedy End to this Expensive War*, which appeared on 6 October 1711 and which no contemporaries associated with *The Review*. Furbank and Owens regard it as 'probably' by Defoe. Abel Boyer thought it to be Swift's work, and Maynwaring refused to believe 'the author to be a pensioner to the ministry, "notwithstanding all those airs he is pleas'd to give himself of a familiar Correspondence with them"'.[45] Despite some resemblances to *The Review*,[46] in terms of fundamental arguments there are significant differences. The author opens with an emotional plea, a vivid evocation of the 'Sufferings and Distresses of [our] Native Land'. Any lover of the country must feel how desperately peace is needed, and must lament how 'we [have] above Twenty Years groan'd under a Long and Bloody War' (3). Such an 'incisive and grim' picture of 'the plight of the nation after nine years of war' is poignant,[47] and unmatched in *The Review*. Mr. Review consistently downplays the horrors of war, repeatedly reminding his readers that the price has been utterly necessary to pay. The 'Bloody *War*, Heavy *War*, Chargeable *War*, Dangerous *War*' of *Reasons* is hardly the glorious, worthwhile cause of the *Review* (4). If this pamphlet is Defoe's work, then nowhere else does he so dwell upon the human cost of war, the 'Many Thousands . . . kill'd and wounded', or upon the 'Millions of Treasure expended' (13). Missing in *Reasons*, moreover, is the patriotic swagger of *The Review*. Here, the land wars are described as 'trifling Exploits', which 'please' the Allies when they win 'a few Inches of the Enemies Ground, bought too

---

[45] Furbank and Owens, *Political Biography*, p. 122.
[46] P. N. Furbank and W. R. Owens detail these in *A Critical Bibliography of Daniel Defoe* (London, 1998), pp. 116–17; this pamphlet is no. 128(P).
[47] Furbank and Owens, *Political Biography*, p. 121.

dear'. Even some of the 'Victories' celebrated by Mr. Review are described in *Reasons* as 'ruin[ing] us' (6). In *The Review*, Defoe is often in rallying mode; here, England's forces are depicted as cowardly, so 'intimidated' by 'the apprehensions of another Autumn Siege . . . that the Desertion is as great as ever' (8). Though Defoe is cautionary in his journal, reminding readers of France's might, he never suggests that the Allies *cannot* carry the day; in *Reasons*, subjects are chastised for having 'all along deceiv'd our selves with Hopes from the weakness of the *French*' and for 'entirely overlook[ing] [our own] Decay' (14).

Downie describes *Reasons* as complementary to *The Review* in terms of making a case for peace.[48] But in *Reasons* as in *The Review*, the argument for peace is qualified; its author affirms that to say that the war should end is not to encourage England to sue France for peace. Neither does it mean that the Allies should 'take such Conditions as [France] shall impose upon us'. Instead, the attempt to conclude the war should merely involve 'listening to a Treaty with a sincere Desire and Resolution' (10). If France does not offer decent terms, then peace will have to wait. Another key stipulation is the partition: 'the Author of this believ[es]', he says, 'that every one will grant a Partition of the *Spanish* Monarchy, appears much more reasonable than ever it did before' (43).

My own sense is that *Reasons*, if it is Defoe's work, does in fact complement the agenda of some of *The Review*, though not necessarily in fighting the ministerial fight. Defoe's primary agenda seems to have more to do with persuading his readership of the wisdom – indeed, the necessity – of the partition of Spain. That readership is diverse, and his different personae could conceivably have less to do with Harley than with a desire to convince Whig and Tory audiences alike of the prudence of partitioning Spain. If *Reasons* were written not for the Whiggish audience of *The Review* but for Tories even more keen for peace, that would explain the discrepancies between the pamphlet and the journal. Nowhere else does Defoe belabour the suffering of a war-torn England; nowhere else does he sneer at those who behave as if '*Britain* was under the Tutelage of the *Dutch*', as if Holland's 'Politicks were the Standard, by which every Step we took was to be tryed' (37). Novak describes *Reasons* as 'intended to give the impression of a national opinion on the side of Harley's decision to end the war at all costs'.[49] I disagree. In *Reasons*, he seems likelier to be preaching to a choir with whom he does not necessarily agree: he presses for a quick peace as

---

[48] Downie, *Robert Harley*, p. 141.
[49] Novak, *Daniel Defoe*, p. 397.

a way of courting readers who want to hear that, in order to make them receptive to what he has to say about the nature of the settlement terms.

In *The Review*, Defoe does not go as far; he does not suggest that peace should be secured sooner rather than later. The cumulative effect of the journal, at least until the publication of peace preliminaries, is to suggest that there is glory in war, and that France is not yet in a position to offer terms sufficiently advantageous to the Allies. In January 1711, Defoe explains that, 'God forbid, tho' I do not applaud the Method, I should attempt to Discourage the War in General' (vol. 7, p. 592). On 8 February, he declares simply, 'Taxes are absolutely Necessary to be rais'd; the carrying on the War makes that Necessity plain', and two days later he insists that he 'could easily Convince the World, that this Nation is far from being Exhausted of Funds upon which to raise large Summs of Money' to support the efforts abroad (609, 613). Throughout the winter, he continues to urge English subjects to take care of national credit, and he clearly links this advocacy with support of the war, reminding his readers of the high stakes involved: 'Money is the Sinews of the War; Credit is Money – Money is the Life and Soul of all our Opposition to *Popery*, of all our Alliance against *France*' (626). Mr. Review's state politics are often driven by his church politics, and he manifestly read the war as an utterly necessary battle of Protestant good against Catholic evil.

On the subject of the war in general, then, Mr. Review does not exactly do a complete *volte-face*; the same cannot be said about his position on Spain. The Whigs were committed to 'no peace without Spain' – no treaty that allowed Philip of Anjou to retain his right to the Spanish throne – and until 1711 Defoe endorses that proviso unequivocally. In late November 1707, he insists that 'it would be intollerable . . . to leave *Spain* in the Hands of the *French*, it must not be, cost what it will, and hazard what we will, we must make no Peace till that be settled' (vol. 4, p. 652). On 26 July 1709, he is definitive: '*Spain* is the only Thing we fight for' (vol. 6, p. 255). What is consistent from the beginning of *The Review* to the end is Defoe's commitment to the balance of power in Europe, and his demand about the utter necessity of controlling the Spanish succession has everything to do with the fear of France's disproportionate influence. On 1 September 1711, Mr. Review mocks those who, 'Clamouring at the Expence of the War', propose that the Allies 'give up *Spain*, as a Thing not worth the Blood and Treasure we expend for it'. To give up '*Spain* to the House of *Bourbon*, is a Thing so absurd, so ridiculous, you ought as soon to think of giving up *Ireland* to them' (vol. 8, pp. 325–26).

By fall 1711, however, Mr. Review has changed his mind, arguing not 'no peace without Spain' but 'no peace without partition' – a shift brought on by the death of the Austrian emperor. In October, he asserts that 'Providence

... will not permit any other End of this War to be ever made in the World, but that of a PARTITION' (vol. 8, p. 414). Whereas he had earlier, like most Whigs, unwaveringly demanded that Philip of Anjou be blocked from the Spanish throne, now he argues that '*If any of the* Spanish *Monarchy should be given to King* Philip, it should be such Parts, as most interfere with the Interest of *France*, and serve to make those two Monarchies uneasie to one another' (455). Defoe had shifted his position drastically, and the opposition noticed: 'they say [he grumbles] the *French* and I argue for the same Thing; the Tory Interest is wrapt up in my Argument' (468). Instead of the old admonitions about French exorbitance, Defoe begins to sound the alarm about Austria, keen to 'prov[e] the Danger of giving the *Spanish* Monarchy to the [Austrian] Emperor' (472). What has changed his mind, Mr. Review reminds his readers, is that Joseph died. In his 28 April 1711 issue, he reflects on the problems introduced by Joseph's death. Charles's claim to Spain is legitimate, but 'if he Enjoys [that] Crown ... and is made Emperor at the same Time, Then that Exorbitant Power' Austria previously enjoyed – a power that 'cost *Europe* so much Blood and Treasure to pull down' – will be 'at once Erected again' (85). To take Spain from Charles is to 'wrong him', but to give Spain to him and also allow him to be Emperor, 'you Endanger *Europe*', and Defoe's solution is clear: 'If ... you decline all manner of Partition, you resolve never to make Peace, not knowing for certain, that you can always make War' (86). Defoe's advocacy of this strategy is not, in one sense, surprising: the First Partition Treaty of 1698, dividing the Spanish empire, was the (temporary) achievement of Defoe's hero-king, William III.

If Defoe's concern was European balance of power, then his explanation was perhaps honest: circumstances had changed abroad, and the political calculus was altered by that transformation. Defoe was not alone in ceasing to wish to win Spain for Austria in the wake of Joseph's unexpected demise. As Charles W. Ingrao has shown, the death of the Emperor 'confront[ed] the monarchy's allies with the resurrection of the European empire of Charles V. Faced with this alternative to a Bourbon succession in Spain, most of its allies lost their enthusiasm for the Habsburg cause in the peninsula'. Even Charles, the Allies' initial choice to succeed in Spain, recognised upon his brother's death that Spain was lost to him.[50] Mr. Review's conversion might well be a matter of his (characteristic) adaptation of his arguments to what looked like reality. Throughout *The Review*, Defoe strikes the 'what's done is done' note, and such pragmatic resignation could conceivably be behind

---

[50] Charles Ingrao, *In Quest and Crisis: Emperor Joseph I and the Habsburg Monarchy* (West Lafayette, IN, 1979), p. 218.

his reversal on Spain. Mark Kishlansky points out that, by 1711, 'war fever had run its course in England', and 'the military situation in Spain continued to deteriorate'. The Whigs had wanted 'no peace without Spain', but – he continues – 'they could not achieve it either by arms or by diplomacy'.[51]

Mr. Review's conversion is usually explained, however, not in terms of a genuine reassessment of European affairs or of accepting an unsatisfactory new reality, but in terms of Defoe's commitment to advocating Harley's preferred policies. Defoe's response matched the ministry's, at least that of the more moderate figures within it: after Joseph's death, the Queen called an emergency meeting, and the administration 'saw an immediate argument for concluding peace without further trying to obtain Spain for the future Emperor'.[52] Joseph's demise was, in some ways, a stroke of good luck for Anne's ministers, who were by the spring of 1711 in secret negotiations with France and increasingly aware that Spain was not to be had for the Allies: 'To gather popular support for the eventual abandonment of Spain, the Tory press ... made maximum use of the threat to the balance of power that would be posed by Charles's succession to both the Spanish and Danubian monarchies'.[53] When Mr. Review underscores the imminent danger of an Austrian superpower, is he acting as Harley's man against his own better judgment? Perhaps. Or maybe his recognition of the new reality allowed him more comfortably to alter his position, to support the government line without perjuring his immortal soul.

Eventually, a change closer to home no doubt also influenced Mr. Review's stance on European affairs. Late in 1711, Defoe was given more reason not to join with the Whigs and endorse their increasingly untenable desire for Spain. In December, says McVeagh, 'when the Whigs betrayed the Dissenters over occasional conformity', Defoe 'moved further away from them and their immovable policy of no peace without Spain' (vol. 8, p. xviii). *The Review* for 20 December, arguing for a peace that does not turn Austria into a superpower, begins – tellingly – with a rant about occasional conformity, and Defoe associates the persecutors with those who want to continue the war (530). But Defoe had become pro-partition months earlier, after Joseph's death, and he did not waver from that position. On 6 September 1712, he asserted 'That no Treaty can be carried on, or Peace made by the Parties now in War . . . but on the Foot of *a Partition of the Spanish Monarchy*' (vol. 9, p. 43). He reached the same conclusion in *Reasons why*

---

[51] Mark Kishlansky, *A Monarchy Transformed: Britain 1603–1714* (London and New York, 1996), p. 332.
[52] Brian W. Hill, *Robert Harley: Speaker, Secretary of State and Premier Minister* (New Haven, 1988), p. 151.
[53] Ingrao, *In Quest and Crisis*, p. 219.

this Nation Ought to put a Speedy End to this Expensive War (43). Furbank and Owens suggest that Defoe's 'attitude had never been the extreme Whiggish one of demanding total victory for the Archduke Charles', and that 'he had consistently argued' that the war 'must inevitably end in a partition'.[54] But this seems to understate the degree to which Mr. Review's outlook shifted in the wake of Joseph's death. He was never gung-ho about Charles, just as he never waxes enthusiastic about the partition or about the treaty that finally ended the war for England. Mr. Review is, about the war and the peace at least, eventually more sensitive to what is necessary than he is futilely clamouring for ideals.

Before continuing with changes in the arguments of *The Review*, something needs to be said about *An Essay At a Plain Exposition of that Difficult Phrase A Good Peace* (1711). This *Essay* is attributed to 'the *Author of the Review*' on its title page, and its arguments are mostly in line with those of Defoe's periodical. Unlike *Reasons why this Nation*, it corresponds with Defoe's known analyses of the war and the prospects for peace. As in *The Review*, here the author warns that 'if *France* does not come up to reasonable Things' in future peace discussions, then 'we are where we were. The War goes on, nothing is abated of the Vigour of our Armies' (pp. 37–38). The confidence of *The Review* is on display: 'The *French* are not so considerable an Enemy, that we should be afraid to Engage with them any farther in the War' (39). The *Essay* is about neither defending the ministry nor promoting a speedy peace; it champions the partition treaty first made under William III. Whether or not Defoe was responsible for this pamphlet, it includes some passages that are unlikely to have helped Harley's cause in 1711. Given the secret negotiations with France, and the need therefore to downplay the French threat to England, Harley could not have been eager to see anti-French biases inflamed in government propaganda. The author of this piece reminds readers that 'The New War began purely on the *French* side, who made himself Aggressor' and acted 'to break [the] Peace' by 'Seizing and Taking Possession of the whole *Spanish* Monarchy' (14, 15). Neither would Harley have been pleased by the author's defining the 'Foundation for . . . *a Good Peace*' as a commitment to acting in complete concert with *all* Allies (18). As the pamphleteer insists, 'it is not in the Power of any of the Confederates, legally to make Peace, or treat of Peace, without common Consent' of the other Allies (19). At the time this piece was penned, the ministry was carrying out precisely these secret dealings; either the author is not trying to downplay the dangers of clandestine dealings or he is not in the know. What is clear is that the author of the *Essay* is not doing Harley's

---

[54] Furbank and Owens, *Political Biography*, p. 117.

bidding, except in maintaining that 'a Peace may be Honourable, tho' some part of the *Spanish* Monarchy should remain to the House of *Bourbon*' (24).

One of Defoe's new arguments, in 1712, does seem to represent a surprising change, and cannot really be explained except in terms of ministerial advocacy and/or his acute resentment (in the wake of December 1711) of the Whigs. Throughout the life of *The Review*, and especially as rumors of a separate peace began to circulate, Defoe defended the Allies and insisted that British and Dutch interests had to remain 'fast together'. The Dutch, he maintained in April 1709, 'have given manifest Proof of their Fidelity to the grand Alliance', and will 'continue so' (vol. 6, p. 62). By February 1712, however, he sounds a lot like Swift had in *The Conduct of the Allies*, declaring, 'It is high Time that we either put an End to the War, or that all the Allies oblige themselves to carry it on with us on a more equal Foot' (vol. 8, p. 622). Defoe matches Swift's authoritative incredulity: 'Whoever he is that would have us carry on the War upon any other Foot than this, I confess I cannot Understand him, and would be glad of some of [*sic*] our Wise Politicians, who daily Encourage us to carry on the War, would prescribe some Way how it shall be Rational for us to carry it on, without these Things' (624).

Some background on what prompted Swift's and Defoe's criticism of the Allies is in order. Harley and the equally moderate Duke of Shrewsbury, along with the Jacobite Earl of Jersey, spent the winter and spring of 1710–1711 in preliminary peace discussions with the French minister Jean-Baptiste Colbert, marquis de Torcy. Though St. John was long seen as a principal engineer of secret peace, he was kept in the dark for some time, chiefly because Harley wanted Dutch cooperation and knew that his hot-headed rival would be disinclined to placate any of the Allies.[55] In April 1711, after five months of clandestine conversations, the ministry communicated 'a skeleton agreement' to the Dutch,[56] including only selected details. Harley's plan was to 'present the Dutch with a *fait accompli*', and that their internal difficulties meant he could ignore them throughout the summer of 1711 was a happy convenience. Meanwhile, Matthew Prior was in Paris proposing peace terms; in mid-August he arrived back in London along with the French diplomat, inciting angry suspicions and outcry at home and abroad. Harley met the crisis with composure and characteristic evasion, offering 'a guarded and incomplete account' of the proceedings in the hopes that he might 'stave off enquiries until the preliminaries

---

[55] See Geoffrey Holmes, *Politics, Religion and Society, 1679–1742* (London, 1986), pp. 146–47.
[56] Keith Feiling, *A History of the Tory Party 1640–1714* (1924; Rpt. Oxford, 1970), p. 440.

were signed.'[57] Only those preliminary terms that related to *all* Allies were revealed: the particular benefits to England were left undisclosed, which made the treaty look less advantageous than in fact it was. The Allies were outraged. On 13 October, the Austrian envoy Count de Gallas published the preliminaries in the (Whiggish) *Daily Courant*, which predictably incited much activity from opposition pens. The ministry was roundly abused for its dirty dealings and betrayal of the Allies, and though Harley remained cool, some of his colleagues were justifiably anxious about the fate of their peace. In November, the situation became more tense, when the Hanoverian adviser published the Elector's unequivocal protest against the peace preliminaries.

Swift's *Conduct* appeared in November 1711, in the wake of the Hanoverian memorial against the preliminaries, and his 'major task ... was to depict the Allies' demands in an unfavourable light'.[58] Defoe never joins Swift in blaming the previous ministry (of Godolphin and Marlborough) for mismanagement, but *The Review* in the fall of 1711 – along with *Reasons why this Nation Ought to put a Speedy End to this Expensive War* – does reaffirm a number of important points made in *Conduct*. Both men accuse the Austrian emperor of selfishly preventing the peace: 'the Emperor', says Defoe, 'not the Queen, breaks the Alliance', selfishly refusing to treat 'unless he obtains all the *Spanish* Monarchy' (vol. 8, p. 519). Charles, he continues later, '*will part with nothing*, and we must fight on till we get him all' (527).[59] Like Mr. Review, Swift insists that those 'who are against any Peace without *Spain*' have simply not considered or in partisan spirit refuse to acknowledge 'that the Face of Affairs in *Christendom*, since the Emperor's Death, hath been very much changed'. Both Swift and Defoe contend that winning Spain for Austria has become utterly '*impracticable*'.[60]

But there are important differences between Swift's arguments and Mr. Review's. Downie suggests that Swift's influential pamphlet 'stimulated a lengthy controversy ... which was carried on for the government chiefly by Defoe', who not only 'prepared the way for the publication of the *Conduct*' but also 'cleared up the mess afterwards'.[61] I am not entirely persuaded that Defoe was paving the way for Swift's anti-Dutch polemic: three days before

---

[57] Hill, *Robert Harley*, pp. 163–65.
[58] Introduction to Swift's *English Political Writings 1711–1714*, ed. Goldgar and Gadd, p. 4.
[59] Swift is much less interested in blaming Austria than Defoe, and more focused on the Dutch. For his comments on Austria, see *Conduct* (in *English Political Writings*), 76–77.
[60] Swift, *Conduct*, pp. 93, 48.
[61] Downie, *Robert Harley*, p. 147.

the appearance of *Conduct*, Defoe repeated his conviction that, 'No Breach has ever been made in the Friendship and good Understanding between the *English* and the *Dutch*, but it has been a Judgment upon the Protestant Interest in general, a Wounding both Sides, and a Rejoycing to the *Popish* Interest of *Europe*' (vol. 8, p. 481). Defoe's (very occasional) kvetching about the Dutch is swamped by his repetition of their crucial significance to England and to Europe. On 21 February 1712, he refers to 'this New Discovery of the Mis-behaviour of our Allies', but in the next paragraph he emphasises that 'on a good Understanding between *Britain* and *Holland*, depends the Safety of the Protestant Interest in *Europe*' (643). In June, after mentioning the 'great variety of Notions fluttering in the Heads of our People, about the *Dutch*', he resolves 'that it is our Undisputed Interest to maintain a constant, steady Union' with them (831). Defoe spends much of the summer warning about a break with the Dutch, and about the prospect of war with them, which he feels would be catastrophic.[62] Perhaps with *Conduct* in mind, he concludes that those are not 'much the wiser, who have spent so much of their Time, and vented so much of their Spleen' on the subject: 'their Arguments hav[e] principally serv'd only to exasperate and provoke one Side against another; widen that Breach which these Things have made, in the Peace and good Neighbourhood of our People at Home, one Side against another, and to raising Feuds, Heats, and Animosities among us' (845). Swift has no use for the Dutch; Defoe highlights the necessity of an alliance with Holland but eventually disparages Austria.

A key disparity between *Conduct* and the relevant issues of *The Review* has to do with Defoe's multiplicity of interests. Swift is calling for peace, and attacking the previous ministry for not achieving it and the allies for not footing more of the bill. He complains that England 'engaged in this War as Principals, when we ought to have acted only as Auxiliaries,'[63] something Defoe – convinced that England must safeguard the Protestant interest in Europe – would never do. Where Swift laments that England has 'been squandring away [its] Mony upon the Continent', Defoe never doubts that the funds were well spent, however high the sum. Swift spills a lot of ink on Dutch failures to contribute money and men to the war cause, zealously detailing 'that whole Chain of Encroachments made upon us by the *Dutch*'. Defoe makes the point (quoted above) that the Allies need to do their part, but that charge never becomes a dominant theme in *The Review*, and when he does target the Allies he does so without singling out Holland. When Swift censures the Dutch, moreover, he does so to point out the necessity

---

[62] See for example *Review* vol. 8, pp. 873–75, 880–82, 884, 898–99, and 905–07.
[63] Swift, *Conduct*, p. 57. Subsequent quotations are at pp. 64 and 83.

of peace; Mr. Review, on the contrary, says that *either* England must 'put an End to the War' *or* the Allies have to increase their support (vol. 8, p. 622).

Defoe repeatedly asserts that to refuse to give Spain to Austria does not mean giving it to France, which would be every bit as 'Ruinous and Destructive' (vol. 8, p. 435). His bottom line is that the Allies are under no 'Necessity . . . to give the whole *Spanish* Monarchy either to one or other of the two Competitors' (493). Swift says little about France or about the danger of French power. What he does suggest, blandly, is that 'To have a Prince of the *Austrian* Family on the Throne of *Spain*, is undoubtedly more desirable than one of the House of *Bourbon*' – not Mr. Review's position by any means.[64] The forceful final pages of *Conduct* are devoted to disproving the arguments made by the 'no peace without Spain' Whigs: Swift is principally concerned to show that England should have peace, period, and that winning Spain for Austria is simply impossible. Defoe's mission is quite different: he contends, at length, that 'no peace without Spain' cannot mean relinquishing another throne to the Emperor, and the dominant theme of the *Review* in these months is the need to prevent an indomitable Austrian empire. Defoe advocates either acceptable partitioning *now* or the continuation of the war until such is possible – a continuation that would appal the author of *Conduct*.

Mr. Review's criticism of the Allies, then, seems almost incidental in context, and though he does argue that England should listen to France's peace terms, he reminds readers that to hear France out is not to accept her terms. On 1 January 1712, he remarks, 'Those who think every Man that Argues for a Treaty, Argues for a Peace; and every Man that argues for a Peace, Argues to give *Spain* and the *Indies* to King *Philip*, are meer Mad-Men' (vol. 8, p. 552). Defoe concedes that the Allies should treat with France, in other words, but never without also observing that treating is a process, and to treat is not to make a truce. To describe *Conduct* and *The Review* as serving the same cause is misleading. As Downie observes, moreover, Defoe sometimes 'deliberately wrote *against* the government, especially after the appearance of the *Conduct of the Allies*',[65] a fact which should give us pause if we are trying to read Mr. Review as mere ministerial mouthpiece.

Defoe's response to the Treaty of Utrecht is also revealing. Triumph there is none, which is surprising, if we understand him as one who 'pleaded for peace with the air of an enthusiast'.[66] He is resigned, perhaps

---

[64] Swift, *Conduct*, p. 93.
[65] Downie, *Robert Harley*, p. 133.
[66] Downie, 'Defoe's *Review*', p. 195.

relieved, but more clearly regretful, and revealingly noncommittal: 'I do not say in all this, that I approve or disapprove of the Peace, and tho' it be not to the purpose, I am very free to say, I wish the Scheme of Peace could have been made on better Terms, yet am glad it is not made upon worse' (vol. 8, p. 888). In March 1713, he avows that he 'aim'd at a another kind of Peace than either *is made,* or ever *was a making*', and that last phrase seems important (vol. 9, p. 279).[67] In *An Appeal to Honour and Justice*, his *apologia pro vita sua* published in 1715, he reflected in similar terms:

> No Man can say that ever I once said in my Life, that I approv'd of the Peace. ... I did not like the Peace, neither that which was made, nor that which was before a making; That I thought the Protestant Interest was not taken care of in either ... [T]he Peace I was for, was such as should neither have given the *Spanish* Monarchy to the House of *Bourbon*, or the House of *Austria*. (23)

Novak concludes that, though 'Defoe was eventually to write anti-war propaganda for Harley ... he was certainly not convinced of its wisdom'.[68] This is true, and we can go further: Mr. Review seems committed to the war effort until late in the game, and never comfortable with or hopeful about the peace toward which the Queen's last ministry was working.[69]

Throughout the clandestine peace negotiations and during the public proceedings, both Mr. Review and Mr. Examiner address the charges against the ministry, accusations of abandoning England's allies, conceding too much to France, and being in league with the Pretender. Swift is in defence mode, contemptuously mocking the Whig notion that the new ministers are 'Jacobites *and* High-flyers, *who are selling us to* France, *and bringing over the* Pretender?' He brands the rumors about 'the present Ministry' to be 'rude Invectives', partisan and patently false, and he

---

[67] Defoe would repeat the point often: 'I wish the Peace had been of another kind' (vol. 9, p. 336).

[68] Novak, *Daniel Defoe*, p. 372.

[69] *Mercator* (launched May 1713) was meant to defend the ministry's commerce treaty; it began in the immediate wake of Defoe's controversial publication of three pamphlets relating to the succession: *Reasons against the Succession of the House of Hanover*; *And what if the Pretender should come?*; and *An Answer to a Question that No Body Thinks of, viz., But what if the Queen should die?* Two of the three were completely ironic, but Defoe was nevertheless arrested. Harley arranged for Defoe's release on bail; he was arrested again a week later; and then he was released for good after a public apology. Defoe had good reason to want to support the government in late spring 1713.

affirms Harley's 'Flourishing Ministry' to be 'belov'd by the People' as well as approved by the Queen.[70] Swift is unyielding in his abuse of the Whigs, and he ridicules all accusations against the current administration as entirely baseless, even preposterous.

Mr. Review's responses to anti-ministerial objections are of another sort. He never definitively denies allegations about clandestine dealings, for example: 'Were there any visible appearance of a such a Treaty on Foot; Were we in any danger of taking this Scandalous Step', he opines, 'I might enter a little into the Dishonourable part of it, and shew how nothing but Treachery to the Government, and a visible Partiality to *France*, could bring us to any such Thing' (vol. 8, p. 186). Here as elsewhere, Defoe might well be exhorting the ministers themselves, warning them of how perfidious such secrecy would be. In any case, the effect of this kind of statement is not to suggest ministerial innocence but to highlight the dishonor involved. He later maintains, still provisionally, that 'if the present Ministry, together with Her present Majesty, are unfeignedly in the Interest of the Protestant Succession, and should go on to make it clear . . . past the Cavils of the Town, that they are so, as I own I always believ'd they would', then the government's opponents will have to admit their error (vol. 9, p. 329).

On 5 January 1712, Mr. Review is at his most defensive: 'This Clamour *of a Separate Treaty with France*, is Calculated to answer abundance of Ends among the common People'. What follows, though, is a rather feeble claim that there could not be '*Separate Engagements* of any kind' because the Queen promised there had not been (vol. 8, p. 560). When, later, he once more denies secret negotiations, he repeats that Anne had given her word, defending monarch, not ministry. He uses questions, not statements: 'Will you believe . . . that your Queen can *Lye unto God*?' and – in the next issue – 'Do you imagin[e] she believes there is a God, a Sovereign Judge, to whom Kings and Queens must Account?' (576, 581). Again, Mr. Review sounds not so much like he is vindicating Anne but like he is putting her and her ministers on notice: to enter into closet dealings with France is to betray England and the Almighty Himself. Another line of defence is equally non-compelling, and also reads like admonition: 'One of the Reasons why I cannot be afraid of the Terrible Ideas some People have form'd to themselves, that this Treaty shall Issue in a betraying us to *France*, is this; I do not see the Advantage any Ministry can propose by Concessions to *France*, when they may have Peace without them' (569). What Mr. Review does not do, on any occasion, is proclaim the ministry to be faithful guardians of the Protestant Succession protecting the Allied cause.

---

[70] Swift, *Examiner*, pp. 165, 185, 211.

Defoe cannot, of course, make any allegiance to the present ministry too clear, and he never writes against Harley or lends credence to imputations of mismanagement or treason. In late May 1712, moreover, Mr. Review nominally defends the ministry in the wake of a particularly controversial manoeuvre, one which bothered even the government's defenders. Convinced that a peace agreement was imminent, St. John (probably along with Harley) had issued the so-called 'restraining orders', directing the Duke of Ormonde – Marlborough's successor – to refuse to engage in offensive combat against the French army. The orders were, in Edward Gregg's phrasing, 'tantamount to a British desertion of the allies in the field'.[71] The cumulative result was a French victory at Denain that effectively ended Dutch resistance to the Tory peace. Defoe is characteristically cautious in his report:

> *...as it is said*, our General has positive Orders not to Fight – Or, as it was better expressed in the Parliament-House, *not to act offensively*.... For my part, this is a Thing *I shall meddle little with it, at least yet*.... You say the Peace is made, you are satisfied it has been Sign'd a great while ago, *and the like* – Well, and supposing that to be true, Would you have had the Queen then have Murther'd Ten Thousand Men in a Battle?' (vol. 8, p. 828)

This is a defence of sorts, though a cagey and qualified one; '*at least yet*' is a tell-tale addition. Given his audience, Defoe cannot go as far as Swift in warmly absolving the ministry of all wrongdoing – but the tepidity of his defences does need to be acknowledged.

When Mr. Review addresses the disturbing rumors about Harley's administration, the effect of his remarks is never to diminish suspicions. He instead tends to catalogue the charges in a way that calls them back to mind, an apophatic move. Though he nominally rejects the accusations, his rejection is usually tentative, and the memorable part of his discussion is not denial but the description of what he is putatively denying. Take this short example, from the last volume of the *Review*: 'I do confess I do not see the Danger of *French* Tyranny, *French* Management, and a *French* Pretender in the present Peace; – I do not say it may not be so, *but I do not see it*' (vol. 9, p. 195). What Defoe actually thought is another matter. As Seager has argued, Defoe could perform 'incredulity' about the Tory ministry's Jacobite leanings that he did not actually feel: 'he evidently had his doubts about Anne's intentions', and even 'urged Harley to request the

---

[71] Edward Gregg, *Queen Anne* (1980; 2nd edn. New Haven, 2001), p. 357.

queen to discourage the Jacobites' publicly. Defoe not only worried about their position vis-à-vis the Jacobites, but he also felt 'eager to push his political masters, including the queen, to more explicit positions'.[72]

In these last years of *The Review*, Defoe often adopts a 'what do I know' pose incongruous with the swagger he displays elsewhere. In January 1712, he reflects, not cheerfully, 'The Treaty is now begun, what the Terms shall be, I shall no longer Debate' (vol. 8, p. 598); in June, he writes, 'it is not for me, or any in my Station, to meddle with the Articles' of peace (842). At the end of the summer, he continues his show of humble un-examining: 'I do not enquire why we have drawn out of the War, or whether we have done well or ill in it: *I thank God that is none of my Province*' (vol. 9, p. 17). The impression one gets from these passages is that Defoe feels comfortable neither defending nor attacking the peace terms, and this reluctance to swing one way or the other is odd. Either he felt that – again because of audience – he could not indulge in too much vindication, or he was constrained by his position vis-à-vis the government from expressing overmuch dissatisfaction.

What does all of this suggest about Mr. Review's position on war and peace? Though Defoe repeats the cliché that the end of war is peace, he does not waver from the position that the war should be carried on – with allied assistance – until suitable terms can be secured. When the treaty is finally signed, his response is a combination of muted disapprobation and telling disengagement. At no point does he target the ministry. His gratitude toward Harley and his desire for any government subsidy he could get likely prevented him from voicing serious reservations even when he felt them. But one has to wonder, given the qualifications and the omissions, whether Defoe was not playing a very characteristic double game. Could he conceivably have been saying what he could in favour of the ministry while also communicating the (not unreasonable) charges against them? Or paying lip service to the need for peace while urging England to fight on? Seager describes the author of *The Review* as 'ingenious but dependent', which strikes me as exactly right.[73] His *volte-face* on the Allies and his fear-mongering about Austria led the opposition to brand him a turncoat, and those changes have encouraged scholars to regard Mr. Review as an unprincipled ministerial pen.[74] What I wish to suggest is that, though Defoe probably did serve Harley's cause when

---

[72] Nicholas Seager, '"She Will Not Be That Tyrant They Desire": Daniel Defoe and Queen Anne', in Cedric D. Reverand (ed.), *Queen Anne and the Arts* (Lewisburg, PA, 2015), 41–55, pp. 48, 49.

[73] Seager, '"He reviews without Fear"', p. 135.

[74] 'Undervalued or not, Defoe served Harley's cause faithfully in the *Review*' of 1711–1712 (McVeagh, *Review*, vol. 8, p. x).

he could do so without totally abandoning his principal commitments, he was not simply a grovelling hack dutifully endorsing the government line.

Swift vs. Defoe: the ideology of *The Review*

The differences between Swift and Defoe are a good deal more obvious than their similarities. Defoe, among the most outspoken Whigs and dissenters, was a family man, a champion of William III, repeatedly bankrupt, and a defender of the Scottish presbytery who wrote vehemently against toleration of Scottish Episcopalians. Swift, the Tory churchman, denounced dissenters of all stripes, maintaining that the Presbyterians and other non-Anglican Protestants were more dangerous to England than even the Catholics; his attitude toward William was lukewarm at best; he was probably never married and did not reproduce; he prided himself on being able to save money and accrued considerable wealth. In personal, temperamental, partisan, ideological, and authorial terms, the two are radically unalike. Only at the end of Anne's reign are they ever described as (uncomfortable) bedfellows, both agents of Harley: Mr. Examiner and Mr. Review, Downie and others have suggested, were spokesmen for the ministry, addressing distinct audiences in complementary ways. In 1/15, the Whig historian John Oldmixon would reflect that '*Foe* and *Swift* [were] fellow Labourers, in the Service of the *White-Staff*,[75] a conclusion following his account of France, Austria, and the Spanish crown. Swift's *Examiner* and *The Review* overlapped between early November 1710 and June 1711. *The Examiner* will be the subject of the next chapter, but some characterisation of it is necessary here in order to answer a simple question: what is the relationship between these two 'ministerial' papers?

Writing as Mr. Examiner in the wake of the ministerial change, Swift made no secret of his country Tory allegiances and appealed without exception to the landed gentry. At this time, Mr. Review is supposedly in his most Tory guise, attempting to make Harley's case on war, peace, and debt to an unreceptive Whig audience. Defoe was, in the run up to the 1710 general election, sounding alarms about the dread prospect of Tory dominance, and complaining bitterly about the days of '*Slavery* and *Subjection* to these *Men of Land*' (vol. 8, p. 100). Swift was triumphantly branding the Whigs 'the declining Party', 'Peevish' because utterly 'ruin'd'.[76] While Mr. Review is assuring his readers that the ministry will 'act...as *Whigs*', and mocking Tory

---

[75] [Oldmixon], *The Life and Posthumous Works of Arthur Maynwaring* (London, 1715), p. 276.
[76] Swift, *Examiner*, pp. 1, 3.

attacks on the Whigs, Mr. Examiner is drubbing all Whigs, and particularly those who claim to be moderates.[77] Swift's principal aim was to defend the new ministry and denounce the old Whig one led by Godolphin. A significant part of his role is to vindicate the ways of Anne to Whigs – 'they charge upon the Qu[een], for changing Her Ministry in the Heighth [sic] of a War' (377) – by depicting Harley's regime as protective of monarch and subjects and country. Reading *The Examiner* for these months alongside *The Review* makes conspicuous how reticent Defoe is on the virtues of the new guard. On 1 February 1711, Mr. Examiner boasts about 'a Flourishing Ministry, in full Credit with the Q[uee]n, and belov'd by the People', who act 'with no sinister Ends or dangerous Designs, but pursue with Steddiness and Resolution the true Interests of both' (211). Such unequivocal affirmation is characteristic of the paper, and – partly because Defoe had to appease a more Whig audience – entirely absent from *The Review*.

What similarities there are between *The Review* and Swift's *Examiner* have been overstated. Nominally, Swift and Defoe do Harley's work of 'moderation' – though Swift only in a decidedly limited and short-lived way. Even where they seem to marginalise extremes on both sides of the party divide, neither man strikes one as middle of the road. Both depict Anne in a favourable light, but Defoe's insistence to his readers that she is 'a Revolution Queen', committed to protecting the constitution, sounds as much like a warning to her as it does warm reassurance to her people (vol. 7, p. 551). Defoe agrees with Swift in endorsing 'the general Notion, that standing Armies in Time of Peace, are dangerous to the Liberties of the Country' – but unlike Mr. Examiner, he accepts that England needs to maintain some 'Regular Forces', or risk being 'quite naked to the Insults of our Enemies'. Swift would never subscribe to the notion that 'SOME FORCE – is as necessary to secure a Kingdoms Property, as too much is dangerous to its Liberty' (vol. 5, p. 11). Mr. Examiner and the Mr. Review of spring 1711 concur that Spain is no longer winnable for the Allies, though Swift has less to say against Austrian power than does Defoe. Swift is also eager to end the war at any cost, whereas Defoe is prepared to fight until optimal terms can be achieved.

On several issues, Mr. Examiner and Mr. Review directly (and unsurprisingly) clash.[78] Defoe tirelessly makes his case for the naturalisation of foreign Protestants, maintaining that 'the Opening the Nations Doors to

---

[77] *Review*, vol. 7, p. 449; *Examiner*, p. 22.
[78] C. John Sommerville describes the *Examiner* as designed 'to answer Defoe's *Review*', as well as the *Observator*; *The News Revolution in England: Cultural Dynamics of Daily Information* (Oxford, 1996), p. 128.

Foreigners has been the most direct and immediate Reason of our Wealth and Increase' (vol. 5, p. 669). 'Are there', he asks, 'no Protestants in the World but of the Church of *England*?' (703). Defoe always argued that 'the Encrease of Hands in a Nation is [its] Wealth and Strength' (vol. 6, p. 198). Swift mocks this view, noting the folly of those who 'take it into their Imagination, that Trade can never flourish unless the Country becomes a common Receptacle for all Nations, Religions and Languages' (*Examiner*, pp. 129–30). Swift takes pains to distinguish between the Old Whigs and their corrupt 'new' counterparts, a differentiation to which Defoe takes furious exception: 'this is to make an irreconcilable Breach among the *Whigs* as [the Tories] call them, upon a new Notion of *Old Whig* and *New Whig*' (vol. 6, p. 504). His complaint represents a suggestive context for Swift's efforts in *The Examiner* to separate the good Old Whigs from the villainous new ones.

A distressing event occurred on 8 March 1711, and the differences in Mr. Examiner's and Mr. Review's reports on it are noteworthy. During a Privy Council meeting on that day, the French refugee the Marquis de Guiscard – there to be interrogated on suspicion of treason – stabbed Harley with a penknife. Swift recounted the event of the '*Assassin*' at great length on 15 March, in hyperbolic fashion declaring it 'not to be parallel'd by any of the like kind we meet with in History', including the murder of Caesar (298). Problematically, Swift added that Guiscard had 'confessed in *Newgate*, that his chief Design was against Mr. *Secretary St. John*' – a lie, the source of which was almost certainly St. John himself, emerging as a rival to the lord treasurer and resentful of his celebrity in the wake of the stabbing.[79] Swift's naïve falsehood has puzzled scholars, who tend to imagine Mr. Examiner more devoted to the moderate Harley than the hot-headed high Tory St. John. Defoe was certainly more on Harley's side, and though he almost never mentions St. John by name, he does attack the October Club, of which St. John was a prominent member. The October men were Harley's High Church enemies, hostile to his moderation and keen to bring him down. On 14 April 1711, Defoe rebuked the 'Gentlemen of *October*', and branded 'Count *Guiscard* . . . an *October Man*'. As Guiscard stabbed Harley, 'so these would stab . . . the whole Nation' (vol. 8, pp. 57, 59). In the immediate wake of the near-murder, Mr. Review had also associated '*French* Assassinators' with '*French-October Men*', linking the attack on Harley with 'an Attempt upon the Queen, and an Insult upon the whole Nation' (vol. 7, p. 664). The Whig Defoe, in other words, capitalises on the stabbing to continue

---

[79] Swift's quotation is *Examiner*, p. 303. See Ellis's notes to ll. 110 and 113–24 on St. John's fabrications about this episode.

his assault on the high-flyers. Conceivably, Swift was tempted to identify St. John as the intended victim as a way of responding to such anti-Tory interpretations of the crisis.

More interesting than Swift's and Defoe's disagreements about specific issues is the more fundamental difference in the political ideologies of *The Review* and *The Examiner*. Seager has described Defoe as having 'had run-ins with the *Examiner*',[80] but 'run-ins' does not do justice to the ideological conflict between them. Mr. Examiner is emphatically Tory and authoritarian; his paper defends the royal prerogative against incursions from below. Throughout the *Examiner*, as elsewhere in his pre-1714 canon, Swift places a premium on obedience; he takes for granted that subjects should obey except in the most extreme cases, and he underscores, dramatically, 'the dismal Consequences of Resistance' (404). Mr. Examiner, in short, scorns civil liberties, preaches the dangers of popular encroachments on the royal prerogative, celebrates obedience, and insinuates the wisdom of the maxim that the king can do no wrong.

Defoe, of course, was appalled by all of these notions. *The Review* promulgates a political vision that is always firmly Whig in its essentials: the Queen is admired as long as she operates within the bounds of the constitution, parliamentary prerogative is invoked repeatedly, and passive obedience is deplored as blasphemous, a '*Cheat with which* [Tories] *have mock'd God and ... King*'. Defoe ridiculed the Tories for their 'abject Slavish Principles', their 'Non-Resisting Banter', their 'Passive Subjecting the Laws to the Will and Lust of a Tyrant', and so on (vol. 7, p. 618). Defoe's belief that '*It is the Undoubted Right of the Parliament of Great Britain, to Limit the Succession of the Crown*' is not surprising (vol. 9, p. 55). What is worth noting is how often he feels the need to remind his readers of this truth, and just how keen he is to protect parliamentary prerogative. In this respect, he resembles Mr. Examiner not a whit. Taking exactly opposite the view of the *Examiner*, he declares 'it Criminal for any Man to assert, *The Illegality of Resistance on any Pretence whatever*' (vol. 6, p. 593). Over and over again, Defoe expresses his incredulity that an 'Age should be doz'd with the Witchcraft of a Party, to deny the Lawfulness of Resistance in Cases of Tyranny and Oppression' (605). He impugns the 'High-Flying Party', who so zealously preach '*the Doctrine of Resistance ... that nothing but Resisting them, will Answer them*' (vol. 7, p. 137).

Defoe's notions about resistance were not middle-of-the-road but radical. Cowan's conclusion is spot-on:

---

[80] Seager, "'He reviews without Fear'", p. 141.

Defoe's fervent defense of resistance theory in his journalism, especially during the excited debates on the topic during the Sacheverell crisis of 1709–1710, has not received as much attention from historians of political thought as one would expect. Nor is it compatible with a picture of Defoe as a political 'moderate': his views of resistance and revolution were much more radical than those of many Whigs.

Cowan explains that Defoe believed not only that the 'resistance shown in 1688 was legitimate', but also that 'it could be used again', whereas even a good Whig like Robert Walpole tended 'to define the Glorious Revolution as an exceptional, almost unique and unprecedented event'.[81] Swift became much more negative about the Revolution and its effects after the Hanoverian accession – but his comments on 1688–1689 are almost invariably unenthusiastic or ambivalent.[82] In *The Examiner*, he is characteristically tepid about the results of the Revolution: 'when the Crown was new settled' in 1688–1689, 'it was hoped at least that the rest of the Constitution would be restored. But this Affair took a very different turn' (358). Swift's grudging commentary on the Revolution runs directly counter to Defoe's take, which his contemporaries found – says Cowan – 'one of the most shocking and salient aspects of his writing'.[83] In July 1706, Mr. Review matter-of-factly grants the legitimacy of rebellion, safely situating a hypothetical coup across the Channel: 'as to dethroning [the French king] for Tyranny, *that is the proper Business of his own People*' (vol. 3, p. 447).

In ideological terms, *The Review* shares nothing with *The Examiner* beyond those commonplace convictions that all of Defoe's contemporaries accepted. No one would suggest that Defoe's and Swift's politics are similar. But the tendency has been to connect the political missions of *The Review* and *The Examiner*, and doing so obscures the drastic discrepancies between the outlooks they reflect. The characterisation of Swift as an old Whig who 'accepted that the "people" had the right to resist tyrants, and professed to believe in the contractual theory of monarchy' has to

---

[81] Cowan, 'Daniel Defoe's *Review*', p. 87.
[82] Ashley Marshall, *Swift and History: Politics and the English Past* (Cambridge, 2015), pp. 162–72.
[83] Cowan continues: 'The notions of popular sovereignty and the legitimacy of revolutionary resistance to tyranny advanced . . . in the *Review* were highly controversial when they appeared'. Sacheverell's lawyers 'were able to score major points in the doctor's defense by claiming that his infamous sermon . . . was not aimed against dissenters and the Whig ministry but against such scandalous writers as Defoe in the *Review*', and several 'objectionable passages . . . were read aloud to the audience at the trial in order to drive home the point' ('Defoe's *Review*', p. 88).

some extent enabled scholars to read these two papers as complementary components of Harley's impressive propaganda machine.[84] So has the usual description of Mr. Review as Harley's pen, a sell-out who after 1710 abandoned his principles to help his benefactor's cause. What reading *The Review* alongside *The Examiner* demonstrates, among other things, is that though Defoe does occasionally do the ministry's work, he does so rather by the way, while also promulgating theories of power that are radically Whig. Another conclusion to be drawn: Harley was apparently counting on his propagandists to champion specific issues of policy, not to disseminate ideology.

Reading *The Examiner* alongside *The Review* brings another important quality of the latter into sharp relief: the consistent centrality of religion to its mission. Mr. Review sees himself as a guardian of toleration (for Protestant dissenters only) at home and of the Protestant interest abroad, both of which he apparently perceived as threatened under the Oxford regime. Cowan highlights Defoe's and Harley's 'differences on religious policy', and Defoe's sense of betrayal over the Occasional Conformity Act, passed under Harley in November 1711.[85] Defoe had further cause to feel disaffected from the Harley ministry after the Tories succeeded in repealing the bill for the naturalisation of foreign Protestants (1711). England's attitude toward Protestantism was of the utmost importance to Defoe, and these changes in policy under his patron surely rankled; from Defoe's point of view, such changes were dangerous, weakening the Protestant cause in Europe and strengthening the Catholic one. Add to this Defoe's obvious anxieties about Harley's peace settlement, and all it left to France, and the view of *The Review* as unproblematic government mouthpiece looks less and less plausible.

Defoe and Harley's ministry

What, then, was Defoe's role vis-à-vis Harley's ministry? Exactly what he was *trying* to accomplish throughout these nine, ever changing, politically fluctuating years is difficult to say. Results are easier to characterise than intentions. The cumulative effect of *The Review* after 1710, I have tried to

---

[84] J. A. Downie, 'Swift's Politics', in Hermann J. Real and Heinz J. Vienken (eds.), *Proceedings of The First Münster Symposium on Jonathan Swift* (München, 1985), 47–58, p. 51.

[85] Cowan, 'Daniel Defoe's *Review*', p. 85.

demonstrate, is *not* resoundingly defensive of the ministerial cause. To some extent, as Downie reminds us, Defoe could not afford too obviously to promote Harley's cause without discrediting himself and rendering him propagandistically useless. But the assumption that Defoe was simply trying, subtly and covertly, to win the Whigs over to Harley's cause is not as compelling, finally, as the conclusion that he was making concessions to that cause while also working to achieve his own polemical ends. The passage of the occasional conformity bill in 1711; Defoe's veneration for the old ministry supplanted by Harley's new one; and his oft-repeated desire to give France such a thumping as to guarantee good terms for the Allies – all of these make his total, unwavering support of Harley highly unlikely. He was no doubt sincerely grateful to the Great Trickster, and naturally he would have been delighted to continue to take payments for his efforts, but Defoe did not share Harley's politics, especially *circa* 1710–1711.[86] To call *The Review* oppositional would be wrong, but neither is it a clear-cut ministerial organ. Mr. Review is much cagier than one would guess from reading most discussions of his paper during its last phase.

Defoe's liking and admiration for Harley has been sometimes overstated. Novak takes issue with the 'odd notion' that 'Harley and Defoe got along well because they were very much alike', and rightly so. Defoe, he continues, 'probably felt grateful for Harley's decision to free him from prison, but he could not have been entirely happy with his subservient position and with having to beg Harley for his secret service money. Their relationship always had a certain edge to it'. Novak describes Defoe as 'play[ing] the card of sincerity' with Harley, a reading that entirely corresponds with what we know about this slippery, zealous, skillful prevaricator, the man whom nineteenth-century biographer William Minto styled, with reason, 'perhaps the greatest liar that ever lived'.[87]

Defoe's public and private writings do not reflect a uniformly positive attitude toward Harley's ministry. I have already discussed his doubts about Anne's intentions – vis-à-vis the Pretender – and about the administration. In a 20 September 1712 letter to Harley, Defoe expressed his alarm at the Whigs' rumors against the government:

---

[86] Manuel Schonhorn concludes that 'Defoe had chosen to form a deep allegiance and began a lifetime of loyalty with a statesman with whose political ideas he could not have been more compatible'; *Defoe's Politics: Parliament, Power, Kingship, and Robinson Crusoe* (Cambridge, 1991), p. 101. I disagree about both the depth of Defoe's allegiance and the compatibility of his politics with Harley's.

[87] Novak, *Daniel Defoe*, pp. 196, 197, 447; William Minto, *Daniel Defoe* (New York, 1879), p. 165.

> What Strange Things they are Made to believ[e], what wild Inconsistent Notions they have Infused into the Minds of One Another . . . is Incredible, and but for the Novelty of Them Are not worth Repeating. Such as, That The queen is For The Pretender, The Ministry Under The Protection of France, That Popery is to be Tollerated, That as Soon as a Peace is Declared The War with the Dutch will be proclaimed, That The French are to keep their Trade to the South Seas, That the people will be brought to address the Queen Not to Interrupt the Heredetary Right of The Royall Line Since The Heir is willing to Abjure popery, and The like. (*Letters*, 386)

On 3 October, he repeats his frustration with the 'Inumerable Storys Spread... in Prejudice of the Queen and of the present Mannagemt as to the Peace', and complains that the Jacobites have 'Terrefye[d] the poor people with the Apprehensions of the pretender'. Although everyone should 'See That the queen and the Ministry are the Onely Security they have left against the Jacobite Faction, yet the Other party . . . perswade Them, that The Queen and The Ministry are Their Enemies' (388). Despite Defoe's incredulous pose, as Furbank and Owens' discerningly note, 'One seems to detect, in his alarmist tones, the hint of a challenge to Harley: *it had better none of it be true*'.[88] Several of his letters from 1711 through early 1713 implicitly or explicitly invite Harley to mend the breaches between the parties, and, perhaps more significantly, to convince Defoe that the fearsome rumors are merely that. Defoe seems in some instances (says McVeagh) clearly to be 'asking Harley to clarify where he stood'.[89] Harley's agent was manifestly not convinced of the government's innocence in this regard.

Defoe's implicit request that Harley explain (or vindicate) himself corresponds with the broader advisory role Mr. Review clearly wanted to play. I discussed earlier his comments about the ministerial change in 1710, where he appears to be warning his incoming masters to behave Whiggishly. Defoe frequently reminds Harley that he feels well within his rights offering honest council, even to his boss: 'The Freedome you Allwayes gave me . . . Oblidges me to Talk to you, in Terms Too Course for the Distance between your Character, your Person, your Merit, *and Me*'.[90] But Defoe did more than whisper in his employer's ear: he used to *The Review* not only to reflect on policies but also, as Seager says, to attempt 'to shape the

---

[88] Furbank and Owens, *Political Biography*, p. 123. See also Defoe, *Letters*, p. 353.
[89] *Review*, vol. 8, p. xi.
[90] Defoe, *Letters*, p. 65.

direction of policy'.[91] Mr. Review is far more than Harley's mouthpiece; he sometimes seems to imagine himself as Harley's watchman. He almost certainly, moreover, wanted to take advantage of the fact that he had access to one of the country's most important leaders. Defoe tried in *The Review* not only to render government policy acceptable to a Whig audience but also – especially after 1710 – to sway an increasingly Tory ministry toward satisfactorily Whiggish courses of action.

Defoe's warmest defences of Harley tend to be responses to the October Club, made up of high Tory MPs, and they reflect his approval of Harley's relative moderation over Bolingbrokean extremism. In his attacks on the October Club, Defoe represents Harley as 'a true moderate', as compared to the 'militant Tory right wing' of St. John *et al.*[92] The '*October-Men* Revile [Harley] with *acting* upon damn'd *Whiggish Principles*', Defoe complains, 'and then themselves fall in with the *Whigs* to reduce him' (vol. 8, p. 557). To find Defoe criticising the Whigs might seem surprising, but the Whigs in power had sold out the dissenters on the occasional conformity issue in late 1711, and in any case in joining with the high-flyers Defoe despised had (from his point of view) abandoned their Whiggish principles completely. The October Clubbers, Mr. Review reports, want to depose Harley primarily for 'acting upon Principles less Violent than they expected' (559). At this time, Swift – particularly in his unpublished *History of the Four Last Years of the Queen* – is trying to build Tory unity, fabricating an image of the rivals Harley and St. John working together toward the same ends. Defoe, crucially, is doing the opposite. Though he never mentions St. John by name, he does highlight the fundamental conflict between the October Men and the prime minister, accentuating the breach that was to ruin the Tory party. In the *Secret History of the White-Staff* (1714), Defoe would provide a 'lucid and accurate picture of the power struggle between Oxford and Bolingbroke', trying among other things to persuade the new Whig regime that Harley had been lenient toward them and moderate in his politics.[93]

However keen Defoe was to attack Harley's opponents, he offered his own challenges to his employer. In *The Review*, he can be conspicuously lukewarm in his remarks on the ministry, and within and outside that paper – as Seager reminds us – 'Defoe wrote against Harley's policies'. Seager cites Defoe's polemical skirmishing with *The Examiner*; his 'apparent

---

[91] Seager, '"He reviews without Fear"', p. 135.
[92] Novak, *Daniel Defoe*, p. 392. Defoe was probably responsible for *The Secret History of the October Club* (1711), which defended Harley's moderation while also denouncing 'the hot High Flying hair Brain'd Tories' with whom the non-partisan lord treasurer felt compelled to cooperate when he took power in 1710 (p. 45).
[93] Downie, *Robert Harley*, p. 186.

disagreements over the Treaty of Commerce and the establishment of the South Sea Company'; and his 'imprudent . . . libel[ling of] Chief Justice Parker'. Throughout *The Review*, Seager concludes, Defoe was 'prone to "going rogue"'.[94] Furbank and Owens describe 'a curious episode', one 'very revealing as to Defoe's relations with his employer', from the winter after Harley's return to power.[95] On 26 December 1710, Defoe wrote his employer, unhappy about 'Two Vile Ill Natur'd Pamphlets', still in manuscript, which 'have fallen into My hands'. One ('Calld the Scots atalantis') is 'full of Invectives Against the Queen and Governmt'. The other pamphlet (*Atalantis Major*) 'is a Bitter Invective against the D of Argyle, the E of Mar, and the Election of the Peers'. Defoe boasts that he has ensured that 'it will be Impossible for them' to be printed, promises Harley a copy of the second, and hopes his actions will be well regarded. A week later, Defoe reported that he had 'with Some Difficulty . . . prevented [*Atalantis Major*] goeing to the press'.[96] Despite these assurances, *Atalantis Major* did appear in print, and it might even have been the work of Defoe himself. George Harris Healey justly brands Defoe's tale one of 'outrageous equivocations'.[97] We have no evidence that Harley ever discovered Defoe's deception, but that late in 1710 Defoe could publish an attack on the government that *The Review* was nominally devoted to defending is important. This episode does not prove that Defoe was, as Mr. Review, as subversive or disloyal as I have suggested – but it does suggest that Defoe was comfortable double-dealing with a benefactor to whom he had reason to be grateful and of whose moderation he basically approved.

The Secret History of the White-Staff, though ostensibly a defence of Harley, is hardly glowing in its account. John Richetti's characterisation is accurate: 'Strategic cunning rather than moral or political integrity is what Defoe credits the Tory Ministry with. . . . One wonders what his ministerial masters made of this defence, since Defoe's satiric narrative reduces political life to a riotous game, and the ministry is no better than their opponents, just smarter'.[98] Part I of the *Secret History* appeared in September 1714, part II a month later, and it describes Queen Anne's last lord treasurer as moderate but cunning, outmanoeuvring his enemies and enlisting the unwitting Jacobites and high Tories to serve his own ends. Whatever Defoe's intentions were, Harley was 'embarrassed by the *Secret History*', which 'contains a good deal of clever invention'. Aware of Harley's discomfiture, the

---

[94] Seager, '"He reviews without Fear"', pp. 141, 135.
[95] Furbank and Owens, *Political Biography*, p. 112.
[96] Defoe, *Letters*, pp. 306–07.
[97] Defoe, *Letters*, p. 307n1.
[98] Richetti, *Life of Daniel Defoe*, p. 133.

story goes, Defoe published a third part, *The Secret History of the Secret History* (January 1715), where he 'argues that the *Secret History* was a baseless fabrication, with no real relation to fact and no political purpose'.[99] The *Secret History of the Secret History* is puzzling. Did Defoe intend seriously to negate his earlier 'defence', to appease Harley's unhappiness? Was he for some reason trying simply to confuse the issue, to muddy the waters of judgment in the wake of Harley's fall? Was this trilogy a genuine attempt to clear his old master's name as the new Whig regime increased the violence of its behaviour toward Anne's erstwhile servants and the Tories? Was Defoe hoping that by demonstrating Harley's innocence he would effectively exculpate himself as well?

In his retrospective accounts of Queen Anne's last ministry, Defoe was compelled to be cautious, to defend himself without too warmly defending the men George I regarded as traitors. In his 1715 *Appeal to Honour and Justice*, Defoe does acknowledge that he felt himself to be 'Obligated' to the Queen and to Harley (38), which left him 'at least obliged not to act against them even in those things which I might not approve' (17). His denial that he worked for Harley is disingenuous, but his insinuated disapproval of some of the ministry's doings is sincere enough.[100] His verdict on the ministry, though, is as equivocal as some of his comments in *The Review*:

> It is none of my Work to enter into the Conduct of the Queen or of the Ministry in this Case, the Question is not what *they have done*, but what *I have done*? And tho' I am very far from thinking of them as some other People think, yet for the sake of the present Argument, I am to give them all up, and Suppose, *tho' not Granting*, that all which is suggested of them by the worst Temper, the most censorious Writer, the most scandalous Pamphlet or Lampoon should be true. (38)

He maintains his innocence, swearing that if the ministry were for the Pretender, he 'did not see it', or 'ever see Reason to believe it', and that certainly he 'never took one step in that kind of Service'. Defoe admits his self-interest: 'It may be Objected to me, That they might be in the Interest of the Pretender for all that: *It is true they might*; But that is nothing to me, I am not Vindicating their Conduct, but my own' (41). The bottom line, for the Defoe of the *Appeal*, probably represents his actual mindset during

---

[99] Furbank and Owens, *Political Biography*, p. 143.
[100] The *Appeal* is printed by Furbank and Owens in *Political Biography*; quotation at p. 209, and denial of having been in Harley's pay or having 'written [by] his Direction' is at p. 210.

1711–1714: enemies accused the ministry of being for the Pretender, and 'God forbid this should be true' (43).

One final piece of evidence is important in judging Defoe's attitude toward the Harley ministry – to wit, his role in the Whig journal *The Flying-Post and Medley*. The paper was launched on 27 July 1714 – the day of Harley's dismissal – and was 'the first outlet for Defoe's pen after the fall of the Tories'. Furbank and Owens describe it as 'a vigorous and trenchant Whiggish journal, highly censorious about the ousted ministry'. *The Flying-Post* went after Ormonde and commended Marlborough, and its verdict on Anne's last ministry is clear. What it does not do, however, is 'attack Lord Oxford personally'.[101] Whether that is owing to Defoe is impossible to guess, but his restraint is in keeping with his other pamphlets, where he contrasts Harley's moderation with noxious high Toryism.

There is no reason to believe that Defoe hero-worshipped Harley; we know from his panegyrics on William III what his idolatry sounds like, and at no point does Defoe acclaim him with similar passion. The two men were different in a number of respects, though Defoe does share something with the man who earned the epithet Robin the Trickster. Both were sneaky, secretive, and coy, prepared to manipulate others to achieve their ends. A distinct possibility is that Defoe imagined himself able to use his proximity to Harley to influence the ministry. *The Review* was sweeping in its coverage, both more multi-dimensional and more global than Swift's *Examiner*, which is by comparison narrow and single-minded. Defoe addresses all kinds of issues related to partisan politics, the war, European balance of power, the Union with Scotland, and religious controversy; he also deals with moral reform, Presbyterian baptism, African trade, the treatment of insolvents, and the lamentable shortage of engineers in England. To describe his paper as a ministerial organ devoted to upholding and promulgating Harley's policies is misleading. In the overwhelming expanse of Mr. Review's prose, whatever pro-government work is being done never looms large. Novak's conclusion is fair: 'Harley, Godolphin, and Sunderland allowed [Defoe] to say what he wanted on most issues, but now and then they wanted a particular viewpoint expressed'.[102]

Quite probably, Defoe was prepared to make concessions to the government's agenda, to support those positions he could support in order to keep

---

[101] Furbank and Owens, *Political Biography*, p. 138.
[102] Novak, *Daniel Defoe*, pp. 211–12.

the ministers' occasional payments coming in. Even more important than the subsidy, moreover, is the fact that *The Review* represented a powerful outlet for Defoe, a widely read paper in which he could argue his various causes and through which he might imaginably influence his respective employers and have an impact on policy. Whatever support he lends to the ministry's cause, Mr. Review always seems to have his own agenda – and there is more work to be done to explicate and contextualise his topical and ideological interventions in the high-stakes political controversies of the reign of Queen Anne.

Chapter 4
Swift, Oldisworth, and St. John: The High Toryism of *The Examiner*

Between 2 November 1710 and 14 June 1711, Jonathan Swift contributed thirty-three weekly issues of *The Examiner*,[1] a ministerial journal that most contemporaries understood 'to be writ by the Direction, and under the Eye of some Great Persons who sit at the helm of Affairs.'[2] Queen Anne had changed her ministry in August 1710, and one of *The Examiner*'s principal aims is to defend the new leaders (Robert Harley and Henry St. John) and lambaste the old (the Whig junto led by Sidney Godolphin and the Duke of Marlborough). That Swift was writing at the ministry's 'Direction' is undeniable, but the position of Mr. Examiner vis-à-vis the administration was not uncomplicated. Scholars have stressed the fundamental disagreements between Harley and St. John about what the government's objectives and policies should be. Harley called for moderation and was determined to achieve shared governance between Whigs and Tories; St. John pushed for more radically high-Tory measures and the exclusion of all Whigs. Mr. Examiner, critics have argued, had to be either Harley's or St. John's man. As W. A. Speck concludes, this conflict is what ultimately led to Swift's decision not to carry on in this capacity: '*The Examiner* began to justify St. John's proceedings more than Harley's until Swift came to realise that he was caught in the firing line between the rival ministers, and stopped contributing . . . when the end of the Parliamentary session gave him a convenient excuse.'[3] J. A. Downie has more explicitly attributed Swift's

---

[1] Swift wrote 32 issues solo, and co-authored another with Delarivier Manley.
[2] Gay, *The Present State of Wit* (London, 1711), p. 9.
[3] W. A. Speck, '*The Examiner* Re-Examined', in Downie and Thomas N. Corns (eds.), *Telling People What To Think: Early Eighteenth-Century Periodicals from* The Review *to* The Rambler (London, 1993), 34–43, p. 34.

abandonment of the examining role to Harley, who dismissed him when the paper became too much a vehicle for St. John's extremism.[4]

Is this a fair representation of what happened with Swift and *The Examiner*? In this chapter, I want to revisit the common story about Swift's instalment as Mr. Examiner and his stepping down from that role. The bulk of my discussion will be devoted to an analysis of *The Examiner* in its entirety – that is, the paper that existed before Swift took over and (with a brief lapse) ran for three years after he ceased being the sole author. Scholars have had singularly little to say about the pre- and post-Swift phases of the journal, despite the fact that Swift evidently continued to participate in – perhaps even direct – it between December 1711 and July 1714. Leo Damrosch's succinct dismissal reflects the general attitude: the paper was 'carried on for a while, not very well, by others'.[5] Part of my objective here is to re-read Swift's *Examiner* within the context of the paper as a whole, which turns out to be helpful in assessing the politics of Swift's contributions. Such a re-reading also raises questions about the nature of Harley's involvement in the management of *The Examiner*.

By way of conclusion, I shall also briefly consider the place of the *Examiner* within the culture of partisan journalism in the last years of Anne's reign. *The Examiner* was the object of especially fierce denigration from opposition writers; the frequency and bitterness of the complaints about it are exceptional. Though Swift's role in the paper has bestowed upon it a special importance among scholars, the distinctiveness of its contemporary reception has received little comment. Most broadly, I wish to make the case for engaging with the whole of the journal, and for appreciating Swift's collaboration with St. John on the paper that continued after he ceased to be sole author. What does Swift's evolving role in *The Examiner* tell us about both his and the paper's relationship to the Harley-St. John ministry?

'very great *Hands* have *Fingers* in it': the rise and fall of *The Examiner*

The Examiner commenced publication on 3 August 1710, five days before the Earl of Godolphin was dismissed from his post as Lord High Treasurer.[6]

---

[4] J. A. Downie, *Robert Harley and the Press: Propaganda and Public Opinion in the Age of Swift and Defoe* (Cambridge, 1979), pp. 135–37.
[5] Leo Damrosch, *Jonathan Swift: His Life and His World* (New Haven, 2013), p. 210.
[6] '[L]ike *The Tatler*, [*The Examiner*] was priced at a penny'; Ian Gadd, '"At four shillings per year, paying one quarter in hand": Reprinting Swift's *Examiner* in Dublin,

Godolphin's fellow Whig, the Earl of Sunderland, had been sacked in June, and though the Whig ministry's removal was not complete until September, by early August the Tory *Examiner* is already anticipating a major turnover. The inaugural issue addresses the Queen's right to select her ministers, and mocks the notion that the Whig Marlborough will refuse to serve as general upon such a change. Authorship of numbers one through 13 is difficult to establish with any precision, but Dr. William King, Francis Atterbury, Dr. John Freind, Matthew Prior, Delarivier Manley, and St. John himself were involved in the enterprise at the outset.

The Examiner was from the first a potent vehicle of Tory propaganda, as the Whig response makes clear. In John Oldmixon's telling, 'The old Ministry [Godolphin's] saw it was absolutely necessary to set up a Paper in Opposition to the *Examiner*, to dispel the Mists it cast before the Peoples Eyes'.[7] To that end, Arthur Mainwaring recruited Joseph Addison for *The Whig-Examiner*, which began on 14 September 1710 and ended a month later. Mainwaring then decided on 'a new Paper with a new Title, the sole Business of which should be to watch the Motions of the *Examiner*, and guard against the ill Effects of them', as he announced in the first issue of *The Medley* (5 October). In other words, the *Whig-Examiner* lived and died, and *The Medley* was well launched, before the Irish vicar took up his quill as Mr. Examiner. Frank Ellis's edition of *The Medley* and *The Examiner* opens with Swift's first issue, and then prints *The Medley*'s response, giving a somewhat misleading impression. Swift was enlisted to oppose Mainwaring, not the other way around.[8]

Was *The Examiner* Harley's or St. John's brainchild? Scholars disagree. Ellis, the editor of the modern standard edition of Swift's contributions, suggests that Harley 'recruited' King to undertake the venture but was dissatisfied by the ultra-Tory nature of the early contributions.[9] David Nokes attributes the project initially to St. John, while maintaining that 'Harley was anxious' for the paper to 'express his own, rather than his Secretary's views',[10] and he hoped to use Swift as his mouthpiece. On the last point,

---

1710–1711', in Kirsten Juhas, Hermann J. Real, and Sandra Simon (eds.), *Reading Swift: Papers from The Sixth Münster Symposium on Jonathan Swift* (München, 2013), 75–93, p. 79.

[7] John Oldmixon, *Memoirs of the Press* (London, 1742), 8. Subsequent quotation at p. 9.

[8] A good account of Mainwaring is to be had in Frank H. Ellis, 'Arthur Mainwaring as Reader of Swift's *Examiner*', *The Yearbook of English Studies* 11 (1981), pp. 49–66.

[9] Ellis, Introduction, *Examiner*, pp. xxiv–xxv.

[10] David Nokes, *Jonathan Swift, A Hypocrite Reversed: A Critical Biography* (1985; Rpt. Oxford, 1987), p. 122. Downie likewise suggests that St. John 'sponsored the

Nokes agrees with other Swiftians, who assume that by involving Swift Harley was looking to establish the paper as 'his'. The lord treasurer wished to use the paper to advance a more moderate platform, the story goes, and so he enlisted the Irish vicar, someone 'whose understanding of Harley's propaganda needs was almost clairvoyant'.[11] Downie goes further, hypothesising that 'the original authors, including St John, were not consulted' about Swift's appointment as Mr. Examiner.[12]

We have precious little contemporary comment about the establishment of the paper. The most extensive is Oldmixon's retrospective account, which suggests Swift's early involvement and describes St. John as one of 'the *Harleians*' who collectively launched *The Examiner*.[13] Swift and St. John evidently did not meet until 11 November, when the two of them dined with Harley, Erasmus Lewis, and Freind,[14] though this does not absolutely preclude the possibility that both Swift and St. John were already engaged with the paper. On 10 October, Swift had written to Archbishop King about Harley's warm reception of him, adding, 'He says, Mr. Secretary *St. John* desire[s] to be acquainted with me, and that he will bring us together'.[15] Exactly how and why Swift got involved in *The Examiner* we can only speculate. In the *Memoirs* written after Anne's death, Swift recounted Harley's telling him, in fall 1710, that 'the Queen was resolved to employ none but those who were friends to the constitution of church and state', and that the ministry's 'great difficulty lay in the want of some good pen, to keep up the spirit raised in the people, to assert the principles, and justify the proceedings of the new ministers'.[16] Here Swift identifies Harley as the man responsible for his recruitment – but throughout the *Memoirs* he takes pains to overemphasise his connection with Harley and de-emphasise St. John, and for good reason. By the time Swift was composing the *Memoirs*, the new king had arrived, and the Whigs were out for Tory blood; that Swift wanted to decouple himself from the more extreme St. John is eminently reasonable. In any case, that Harley enlisted him to moderate the tone of the paper is plausible, though what moderation Swift managed to achieve was always limited, and – as Speck has pointed out – he soon abandoned

---

launching of the ultra-tory *Examiner*, and he gave the paper a purpose in his *Letter to the Examiner*' (*Robert Harley*, p. 122).

[11] Ellis, Introduction, *Examiner*, p. xxxi.
[12] Downie, *Robert Harley*, p. 127.
[13] Oldmixon, *History of England*, p. 456.
[14] Abigail Williams (ed.), *Journal to Stella* (Cambridge, 2013), p. 64.
[15] David Woolley (ed.), *The Correspondence of Jonathan Swift, D. D.* (4 vols., Frankfurt am Main, 1999–2007), vol. 1, p. 302.
[16] *Memoirs, Relating to That Change . . . in the Year 1710*, (Swift, *PW*, vol. 8, p. 123).

it.¹⁷ Another explanation is that the *Examiner* continued to be St. John's enterprise despite the change of hands, and that Harley introduced Swift to St. John as 'their' new man, not his own. After all, as of November 1710, the split between the ministers had not happened; H. T. Dickinson places St. John's rejection of Harley's moderate policies in the early months of 1711.¹⁸

Swift apparently enjoyed his seven months as Mr. Examiner, and how willing he was to relinquish control is impossible to know. His last solo issue was 7 June 1711, where he not very compellingly waxes triumphal: 'And now I conceive the main Design I had in writing these Papers, is fully executed. A great Majority of the Nation is at length thorowly convinc'd, that the Qu[een] proceeded with the highest Wisdom, in changing Her Ministry and Parliament', and so on (470). Swift claims that his 'main Design' has been 'fully executed', but most Swiftians have presumed this to be insincere. They tend to explain his resignation as compulsory rather than voluntary: he fell more and more under the influence of the hot-headed St. John, increasingly using the paper as a vehicle for high Toryism; Harley was displeased, and took action.¹⁹ The essay that seems most likely to have upset Harley, however, appeared three months before Swift stepped aside. In *The Examiner* for 15 March, Swift recounted the stabbing of Harley by the French refugee the Marquis de Guiscard. Problematically, he reported that Guiscard had 'confessed in *Newgate*, that his chief Design was against Mr. *Secretary St. John*' – a lie, the source of which was almost certainly St. John himself, emerging as a rival to the lord treasurer and resentful of his celebrity in the wake of the stabbing.²⁰ Swift's naïve falsehood, critics plausibly suggest, must have frustrated Harley, who was none too eager to share the victim's spotlight with his ministerial adversary. Because of this particular occasion, and/or because of the generally increasing Toryism of *The Examiner*, Downie *et al.* conclude that Harley had had enough: 'Swift had been told that if he intended to write without consulting the general policies of the government, then his services were no longer required.'²¹

---

[17] W. A. Speck, '*The Examiner* Examined: Swift's Tory Pamphleteering', in C. J. Rawson (ed.), *Focus: Swift* (London, 1971), pp. 138–54; see also Speck's '*The Examiner* Re-Examined'.

[18] H. T. Dickinson, *Bolingbroke* (London, 1970), pp. 76–78.

[19] Downie, *Robert Harley*, p. 135.

[20] Swift's quotation is *Examiner*, p. 303. See Ellis's notes to ll. pp. 110 and 113–24 on St. John's fabrications about this episode. As Irvin Ehrenpreis observes, 'Harley was unlikely to feel consoled for his near-murder by an assurance that the intended victim was his hated rival'; *Swift: The Man, his Works, the Age* (3 vols., London, 1962–1983), vol. 2, p. 470.

[21] Downie, *Robert Harley*, p. 137.

Scholars assume that Swift was unhappy about giving up his role, and that may have been true. In the *Journal to Stella* for 7 June, he foretold the abrupt depreciation of the journal:

> As for the *Examiner*, I have heard a whisper, that after that of this day . . . you will hardly find them so good. I prophecy they will be trash for the future; and methinks in this day's *Examiner* the author talks doubtfully, as if he would write no more, so that if they go on, they may probably be by some other hand, which in my opinion is a thousand pities. . . . (225)

Reading tone is not necessarily easy here. Is Swift voicing serious alarm about the fate of the paper? Or is he being playfully self-aggrandising, disingenuously distancing himself from the venture? If he did feel pushed out, then the distinct lack of *ex post facto* complaint is decidedly uncharacteristic. Swift is rarely reticent about his life's disappointments, especially when he feels wounded by those in power.

The unfortunate reality is that we have no record of any conversation between Harley and Swift about *The Examiner*, and the question of subsidy remains cloudy as well. We do not know what if any role Harley played in Swift's relinquishment of the role. The most likely reason is the simplest one: he had other ministerial work to do. Harley and St. John both needed his pen, but for *Conduct of the Allies* rather than *The Examiner*. *Conduct* was a difficult, time-consumptive piece, and Swift no doubt enjoyed occupying a still-central role in the ministry's propaganda machine.

In any case, that Swift and Manley co-authored the 14 June issue, and then she carried the paper on for six weeks; it temporarily lapsed after issue no. 52, but was revived in December 1711 by William Oldisworth. The last issue appeared on 26 July 1714, which unfortunately deprives us of Mr. Examiner's commentary on both Harley's fall from power (he was officially removed on the 27th) and Anne's death on 1 August.[22] *The Examiner*, in other words, ends at more or less the same time that Swift too was going quiet, at least in the realm of public pronouncement.

---

[22] The paper was briefly revived at the beginning of George I's reign, but suppressed. As Brian Cowan explains, 'Warrants were issued for the arrest of the publishers and the author of the paper, and by May 1715 the crackdown had reached the coffeehouses who supplied the *Examiner* to their customers'; *The Social Life of Coffee: The Emergence of the British Coffeehouse* (New Haven, 2005), p. 219. I have seen only one issue, dated 14 September 1715.

What about the issue of subsidy? Who paid for *The Examiner*? That turns out to be a difficult question. Downie has contended that, 'Despite his close association with Swift, and with Roper and the *Post Boy*, Bolingbroke's role in relation to the press was a minor one. All financial backing for government propaganda came, officially, out of the prime minister's tiny intelligence fund. Oxford made up for this deficiency by digging deep into his own pocket'.[23] Downie cites Harley's payment of £100 to Swift in response to the prosecution of the printers of *The Publick Spirit of the Whigs* in 1714,[24] but this is for legal protection, not payment for propagandistic production. Downie reports that Manley 'also received remuneration for her services to the ministry', but from whom and how we do not know.

The more interesting fragment of evidence we have concerns an apparent payment to Oldisworth from Harley, or at least offered on Harley's behalf. Downie has published a 'manuscript of a bill sent by [John] Barber to Oxford when the former Lord Treasurer was being confined in the Tower' in 1715.[25] This bill itemises the purchases of 100 copies of *Examiner* nos. 5–50 (before Swift took over and shortly after his run 'ended'), as well as a payment to 'Mr O. for writing the Exam'. Downie explains the problem of determining the precise sum involved, but it appears to have been substantial. The invoice includes an appended passage, which strikes a sceptical note: 'The last Article [the payment to Oldisworth] is humbly submitted to y^r Lordship; but for the Truth of his Demand refers to the Dean of St Patricks'. In other words, in order to verify the legitimacy of the sum owed to Oldisworth, Swift will need to be consulted. The bill was not settled directly by Harley but instead by his former undersecretary, Erasmus Lewis, friend to both the ex-minister and Swift. Downie takes this as demonstrating Harley's close involvement in – and sponsorship of – *The Examiner* from soon after its commencement until well beyond Swift's tenure as its primary author. This may be correct, though there are some puzzles – even if we ignore the considerable one represented by the extremely high Tory politics of the paper. Why is Barber settling up on a debt from 1710–1711 (nos. 5–50) some five years later? And if Swift were removed from his post as Mr. Examiner, why did Harley need to rely upon him in order to settle his debt to Oldisworth?

---

[23] Downie, *Robert Harley*, pp. 181–82.
[24] See Harley to Swift, 3 March 1714: 'a friend of mine, an obscure person, but charitable, puts the enclosed Bill in yr hands to answer such exigencys as their case may immediate[e]ly require. and i find he wil[l] do more, this being only for the present' (*Correspondence*, vol. 1, p. 589). Swift's endorsement (589n) tells us the amount.
[25] J. A. Downie, 'Swift and the Oxford Ministry: New Evidence', *Swift Studies* 1 (1986), 2–8, p. 4.

A related episode is reported in the *Journal to Stella* for 12 March 1713: 't[h]e Chancell[r] of t[h]e Exchequ[r] sent the Auth[r] of th[e] Examiner 20 Guineas' (511). At this time, the Chancellor of the Exchequer was Robert Benson, made Lord Bingley in 1713; he was also Her Majesty's Spanish ambassador. The particulars of Bingley's relationship to Harley and St. John are uncertain; one source suggests, 'Although shortly after being raised to the peerage Bingley was reported to be discontented with Oxford, it seems that he remained loyal to his former leader'.[26] That Bingley is doing Harley's bidding in offering a (substantial) sum to Oldisworth is far from clear. The other problem is that, if Harley could 'dig . . . deep into his own pocket', no doubt St. John could as well, even if his 'private income was much smaller' than Harley's.[27] And we know that Arbuthnot 'sollicited both Ld Tr & ld Bolingbroke' for Parnell, presumably looking for patronage for his friend.[28]

Harley's settling of the debt to Barber could conceivably reflect nothing more than the fact that by 1715 he was concerned about his own neck. If he happily subsidised *The Examiner* during much of its run then the bottom line would seem to be that we have no reason to credit the usual tale of Swift's removal. Surely Harley would not fire Swift for his high Toryism and then bankroll the revived high Tory work of Swift's successor. What follows details both change and especially continuity across the life of *The Examiner*, but one conclusion must be offered here. If Harley was actively supporting *The Examiner* throughout its Swift and 'post'-Swift stages, we cannot assume that his politics were as moderate as some scholars have supposed. At the very least, we have to grant that he was willing to support the dissemination of high Tory propaganda while simultaneously advocating a broader bottomed government.

The political evolution of *The Examiner*

For our purposes, *The Examiner* can be divided into three phases: pre-Swift, Swift, and 'post'-Swift. The standard accounts of Swift's installment and then dismissal as Mr. Examiner presume some ideological and/or tonal shift between the first and second, and between the second and third, of those phases. In other words: something changed when Swift took over,

---

[26] See the online history of parliament site (http://www.historyofparliamentonline.org), under 'Benson, Robert'.
[27] Downie, *Robert Harley*, p. 182.
[28] Arbuthnot to Swift (*Correspondence*, vol. 1, p. 625); 26 June 1714.

and, by implication, something else happened when he quit. Virtually no ink has been spilled on the content of *The Examiner* before and after Swift, and the untested assumption has been that his contributions are distinct from those of his predecessors and successors, and not only in qualitative terms. Is this true?

Consistent themes and attitudes

Examiner no. 1 includes a prefatory announcement of the journal's principal aim: '*I meet with a great Variety of Papers, neither so Correct, so Moral, nor so Loyal as they ought to be*', and '*Some of these Papers I intend to* Examine'. This statement anticipates the antagonistic nature of the new weekly, which Addison sharply observed 'wou'd have been more properly entitled the *Executioner*',[29] but does little to signal the actual content of the subsequent issues. What themes were established in the early weeks of this venture?

Ideologically, the paper was aggressively high Tory. Oldmixon explains that the 'weekly Libel' was initiated principally 'in order to prepare the Way for this astonishing Change in the Ministry'.[30] Issue no. 3 anticipates a parliamentary and ministerial upheaval: the defence of the change is a defence of the prerogative, and Mr. Examiner reproaches those who, though asserting '*Friendship* and *Fidelity* to the *Chief Ministers*', forget their '*Duty to the Crown*'. In the upcoming election, landowners are encouraged to choose those 'Men that hold Her Majesty's Hereditary Right' over 'those who plainly deny it to Her' (no. 10). The writers call for obedience from subjects, caution against revolution, and affirm that '*Hereditary Right . . .* is *Fundamental* to our *Constitution*' (9). No. 13 rebukes those who have 'Condemn'd, Curs'd, Exploded and Ridicul'd' the doctrine of non-resistance, and passionately objects to the 'precarious Principle . . . *That the Good of the People is the ONLY End of Government*'. Authority comes from God, not from the people, and when 'Subjects [become] the Governours', government ceases to exist. The political philosophy of the paper as Swift inherited it is authoritarian, conservative, and nostalgic – adjectives all applicable to Swift's own contributions.

Much of the attitude established in the early issues turn out to be consistent across the life of *The Examiner*. The hostility toward the Dutch introduced in no. 4 persists throughout Swift's tenure and beyond. So do the intolerance of Protestant dissenters and the rejection of the association

---

[29] *The Whig-Examiner*, no. 1 (p. 6).
[30] Oldmixon, *History of England*, p. 456.

of 'high church' with 'popery' and the Pretender. From inception to termination, *The Examiner* defends the royal prerogative against encroachments from below, and characterises the Whigs as a routed party practiced in 'the Art of *Political Lying*'.³¹ A desire to unite the Tories and divide the Whigs is evident throughout the duration of the paper. There are some changes, to which we will return, but in general there is marked consistency of political outlook.

The Examiner is anti-populist and anti-resistance. In no. 13, the last before Swift took over, the author concludes, 'I suppose the Authority of Governors to be deriv'd only from *God*; which I am sensible will never be granted by those who place the Original of it in the *People*'. In no. 9, Mr. Examiner had asserted divine right, while cagily qualifying his claim: 'It is manifest that the Power and Authority of Governors is *from God.* . . . But *indefeisible* [sic] or *inalienable* Right is quite another Thing'. In his third contribution, Swift goes further than his predecessor:

> 'Tis as plain as the Words of an Act of Parliament can make it, That her present Majesty is Heir to the Survivor of the late King and Queen her Sister. Is not that an *Hereditary Right*? What need we explain it any further? . . . Suppose we go further, and examine the Word *Indefeasible*, with which some Writers of late have made themselves so merry: I confess it is hard to conceive, how any Law which the supream Power makes, may not by the same Power be repeal'd: So that I shall not determine, whether the Queen's Right be *indefeasible* or no. But this I will maintain, that whoever affirms it so, is not guilty of a Crime. For in that Settlement of the Crown after the Revolution, where Her present Majesty is named in Remainder, there are (as near as I can remember) these remarkable Words, *To which we bind our selves and our Posterity for ever.* Lawyers may explain this, or call them words of Form, as they please: And Reasoners may argue that such an Obligation is against the very Nature of Government; but a plain Reader, who takes the Words in their natural Meaning, may be excus'd, in thinking a Right so confirm'd, is *indefeasible.* (pp. 41–42)

Mr. Examiner seems certain that those who promulgate indefeasibility – i.e, the notion that the monarch's power can never be annulled – are

---

³¹ Swift uses this phrase in no. 15 (p. 20); Oldisworth uses it as well in *The Examiner* of 7 February 1712. All citations of Oldisworth's *Examiner* will be to the volume number and issue number; the 7 February issue is vol. 2, no. 10. The second volume begins when Oldisworth revives the paper (6 December 1711); the last issue is vol. 6, no. 19.

completely within their rights. He sanctions a political philosophy based on non-resistance. His attitude toward the 'Reasoners' who advocate a more contractual idea of power is not admiring. I must respectfully disagree with David Oakleaf, who concludes that Swift 'dismisses' the notion of passive obedience 'as pedantry'.[32] Defending those who presume indefeasibility is not the same thing as preaching passive obedience – but we are a long way, here, from reducing high Tory convictions to foolish dogma. Throughout his *Examiner*, Swift treats the prerogatives of the prince as sacred, and his attack on the Whigs has everything to do with their having 'no very great Veneration for *Crowned Heads*' (345).[33] He may moderate the high Tory tone of the early *Examiner*s, at least for a little while, but the fundamental outlook does not change.

The authoritarian tendencies of Swift's *Examiners* persist long after his official involvement with the paper has ended. Oldisworth is explicit in his rejection of Whig ideology: he takes for granted that 'the *Queen* is Supream over all Orders of the Realm', and upbraids the Whigs for 'mak[ing] *Obedience* the Duty of the Sovereign' (vol. 3, no. 16). Swift and Oldisworth likewise share the view that freedom is a perilous concept. Although it would become a buzzword for inalienable personal rights later in Swift's career, as of 1710–1714 'liberty' represents something menacing. In *Examiner* no. 37, he cautioned against the Whigs who operate according to 'false Notions about *Liberty*' (360), and in no. 32 he presented 'Liberty' as '*the Daughter of* Oppression', responsible not only for arts and learning but also for faction and unrest (285). In February 1712, Oldisworth would attest that the 'Word . . . has more Witchcraft in it . . . than it has real Charms'. Although 'Liberty is . . . an invaluable Blessing', the Whigs have perverted it, using the battle cry of freedom 'to introduce a Tyranny of the worst sort, and to share the Bulk of Power among themselves' (vol. 3, no. 27). Like Swift in his 1701 *Discourse*,[34] Oldisworth depicts Julius Caesar as the symbol of tyranny achieved 'by Popular Arts', tyranny arrived at when 'The Power of the People to dictate to the *Senate* [is] openly Asserted and Encouraged' (vol. 3, no. 47). He scorns the 'Mock Sovereignty' of the mob, disdaining

---

[32] David Oakleaf, *A Political Biography of Jonathan Swift* (London, 2008), p. 111.
[33] For this argument, see Ashley Marshall, *Swift and History: Politics and the English Past* (Cambridge, 2015), esp. pp. 181–91.
[34] In Frank H. Ellis (ed.), *A Discourse of the Contests and Dissentions Between the Nobles and the Commons in Athens and Rome* (Oxford, 1967), Swift writes of Caesar's (dangerous) 'Arts of pleasing the People', and of his 'publick and avowed Pretensions for beginning the Civil-War', which 'were to restore the Tribunes and the People opprest (as he pretended) by the *Nobles*'. The consequences of Caesar's rise included the 'entire Subversion of the *Roman* Liberty and Constitution' (pp. 109–10).

the Whig tendency 'to make *Noses* equivalent to a *Vote*, and *Numbers* to a *Freehold*' (vol. 3, no. 49).

Oldisworth is as staunchly conservative as Swift, perhaps more so. He brands the Whigs irreverent innovators rather than upholders of the sacred constitution. His history of '*Modern Whiggery*' (27 July 1713) is sneering: Whigs were once upon a time powerless Puritans, but the '*Jesuits*' 'took care to Infuse into [them] several pernicious Notions, relating to the Rights of Nature, the Subjection of Governors, and the Power of the Subject, on purpose to make this little One a Thorn in the Sides of the Nation'. The Whigs became politicised, working 'against the Power and Person of their Sovereign' in 'the Name of *Republican*[s]'. Only around the time of the Revolution do Whigs 'declar[e] for Monarchy, but such a Monarchy, so restrained and limited, as to make the Sovereign the Creature and Servant of the People'. This account is meant to demonstrate a singular lack of principle: the Whigs have 'Turn'd, and Tack'd, and Chang'd to fine Purpose', and 'can no more call themselves a *Party* . . . than a *Chaos* is a *World*, or a *heap of Ruins* a *compleat Piece of Architecture*'. But Oldisworth also associates them with a dangerous, destabilising form of government, precisely because they 'never could be reconcil'd to the *Regal Power*' (vol. 4, p. 21). In ideological terms, Swift's *Examiner* and Oldisworth's are of a piece – though the latter outdoes the former in the frequency and extensiveness of his arguments about power and authority. Oldisworth styled his contributions 'Essays on Government',[35] and indeed the last Mr. Examiner is committed to offering a political philosophy – yet another tendency that marks him as more St. John's man than Harley's.

One major component of the battle between *The Examiner* and the rival *Medley*, as Ellis has explained,[36] concerns interpretation of 1688, and Swift is not the only Mr. Examiner to voice ambivalence about that climactic event. In his first *Examiner*, Swift describes the 'Nobility and Gentry' who orchestrated the Revolution as 'true Lovers of their Country' who were compelled 'to yield to those Breaches in the Succession of the Crown . . . out of a regard to the Necessity of the Kingdom' (5). Swift's assessment of 1688 is, then, that it was perhaps necessary but still a 'Breach', one not to be lightly replicated. The first authors of *The Examiner* had reached a similar conclusion: 'About twenty Years since, we had a *Revolution* in *England*, which had some *very good Consequences*, and some *not so good*: Therefore we must *now* talk,

---

[35] *Examiner*, 9 February 1713 (vol. 3, no. 23).
[36] Ellis, Introduction to the *Examiner*, p. xxi.

write, and think of nothing else' (9).[37] Oldisworth likewise cites the events of 1688–1689 as introducing a lamentable new political reality: 'Since the *Revolution*, there seems to have been a studied Design carry'd on for many Years to deprive the Crown, not only of the Art, but even the Power of Preferring' (vol. 3, no. 15).

From Swift and Manley to Oldisworth, the position of *The Examiner* continues to be polarising, fiercely antagonistic to the Whigs and supportive of the High Church landed gentry. The elitist contempt is familiar to readers of Swift's journalism: 'I have often heard it made a wonder, how an obscure Sort of Men, dissenting from the Establishment both in Church and State, should ... become so Rich, so Numerous, yet so Obnoxious to the true Interest of their Country' (vol. 2, no. 1). Oldisworth scolds 'the *Mutinous* Party' of Whigs, 'with their limited Politicks, or very much extended Knavery' (vol. 2, no. 23). He also carries on the old attack on the Godolphin–Marlborough junto: any rational man knows that 'the Insolence of the late Men in Power to the Q[uee]n was such, as was never offered to any Crowned Head before', that 'a General for Life was intended', and that 'the Prerogative ... was openly struck at' (vol. 2, no. 44). As he observes in the next issue, 'EVERY time I reflect upon the Conduct of the late Ministry, still I discover more Abuses'. The ministerial change is by this point two years past, but the anti-Junto offensive continues strong. 'Father *Time*' is, we are told, obviously 'a most inveterate *Tory*; for he has detected more Iniquities of the People called *Whigs*, than all the honest Zeal of their Inspectors could ... pry into' (vol. 3, no. 17). Whigs are virtually sub-human, the 'Insects and Venomous Reptiles of the *Political World*' (vol. 4, no. 1).

Many of the fundamental convictions of Mr. Examiner, then, seem consistent, but some things change over the life of this paper. What is the nature of the relationship between Swift's contributions and the rest of *The Examiner*? What happens when he takes over, and what happens when he steps down? How does the paper's voice evolve, and how does that evolution correspond to alterations in political circumstances?

From St. John's Tories to Harley's Swift?

Swift assumes the role of Mr. Examiner in early November 1710, immediately after the Tory rout of the Whigs in the October General Election. The

---

[37] The language of this critique is echoed in Swift's 1721 epistolary *apologia*: 'the Prince of Orange's expedition' might have been justified by 'the publick good', but 'in the consequences it produced some very bad effects, which are likely to stick long enough by us' (*Correspondence*, vol. 2, p. 360).

election results were no surprise: by the spring, the majority of Anne's subjects were weary of the expensive, seemingly interminable war that Whig leadership was determined to continue. Oppressive taxes, the bloodbath of Malplaquet, and the bill for the naturalisation of foreign Protestants all intensified the anti-Whig sentiment. By the time Swift took up his pen, the Tories found themselves to be the people's choice. How does he respond to this new political climate, and what changes does his takeover produce?

The partisanship of Swift's contributions, as we have seen, corresponds fairly closely to that of the preceding numbers. According to the standard explanation, Swift was assigned to this position in order to restore some degree of moderation to the paper, to neutralise the High Church polemics of the preceding issues. In his inaugural number, Mr. Examiner does indeed signal a change: he apologises for having, 'for some Weeks past . . . been forc'd in my own Defence, to follow a Proceeding that I have so much condemn'd in others' (1). The audience is evidently to assume continuity of voice: the author of no. 14 does not introduce himself as new, merely as mildly repentant. His apology is for manner rather than content: he does not recant any of the previous positions. In any case, the following sentence highlights the grudging nature of this self-criticism: 'several of my Acquaintance among the declining Party, are grown so insufferably Peevish . . . and represent the State of Things in such formidable Idea's, that I find my self dispos'd to share in their Afflictions, though I know them to be groundless and Imaginary'. For his 'peevishness', then, the opposition has itself to blame. Significantly, Swift maintains the language of the early *Examiner*s, characterising the Whigs as 'the declining Party' (1), and insinuating that they are masters of the art of political lying. He complains unequivocally about 'the Malice of a ruin'd Party', meant 'to render the Queen and Her Administration odious, and to inflame the Nation' (3). That said, the tone of no. 14 is much calmer and more reasonable than the previous issues; Swift does not sustain the accusatory indignation with which the pre-Swift *Examiner* had closed.

The essays written by King, St. John, *et al.* are emotional, indignant, defensive; the attitude toward anyone who dares question the Queen's right to make a ministerial change is unapologetically judgmental. Swift is not without judgment, even from the beginning, and he does not tend toward contrition – but he is more conciliatory in his language. Initially, he gives the appearance of explaining Anne's decision in rational terms: 'it was the most prudent Course imaginable in the Queen, to lay hold of the Dispositions of the People for changing the Parliament and Ministry at this Juncture' (9). The non-defensive tone is effective. Throughout, Swift assures his readers that he is attempting to achieve a *via media*, that he wishes to avoid 'entring into the Violences of either Party'; he can go so far in that direction as to describe the 'two parties' as 'both pretend[ing] a mighty Zeal for our Religion and Government, only they disagree about the Means' (34).

Swift's moderation is mostly a matter of broadening his audience, from the rigidly high Tory to all Tories (and 'Old' Whigs, whom he treats as essentially Tories). He appeals broadly to the landed gentry, lamenting 'that *Power*, which according to the old Maxim, was us'd to follow *Land*, is now gone over to *Money*' (pp. 4–5). In no. 15, he reflects that, 'We have seen a great part of the Nation's Mony got into the Hands of those, who by their Birth, Education and Merit, could pretend no higher than to wear our Liveries' (25). On one occasion, he appears to challenge both the war-mongering, freethinking Whigs as well as the highest-flying Tories. In no. 16, he denounces the Whig *Review* and radical Whig *Observator*, and brands the Jacobite Charles Leslie's *Rehearsal* 'yet more pernicious' (35). Swift criticises the extreme Tory position here, but in fact he merely pays lip service to moderation. He has nothing of substance to say against Leslie, and his attitude toward the high-flyers is not disparaging. He maintains the legitimacy of the 'church in danger' cry so common among high Tories, and he depicts Sacheverell as 'a faithful Subject' whose loyalty has been branded disaffection (39).

At no point does Swift kowtow to the Whigs, and – *pace* Downie – neither does he peddle the same propaganda we find in Simon Clement's Harleyite *Faults on both Sides* (1710). That pamphlet argues 'that both parties were partly to blame for inciting conflict in the nation'.[38] The furthest Swift goes in this direction is in announcing a desire to 'converse in equal Freedom with the deserving Men of both Parties' – but within a handful of paragraphs he hails the change at court necessary to end the (Whig-favoured) war, complains about the 'Malice of a ruin'd Party', laments that the moneyed class has gained on the landed, voices ambivalence about 1688, and casts aspersions on Godolphin's fiscal practices.[39] Mr. Examiner does say once that his aim is 'to let the remote and uninstructed part of the Nation see, that they have been misled on both sides' (36) – but Swift's unsustained attempt at the rhetoric of moderation could not have fooled the Whigs, and did not. His first issue (no. 14) is provocative and polarising – in a skillfully non-inflammatory way, perhaps, but courting potential Whigs is not Swift's game. Neither is criticising the Tories. *Faults* describes 'the Generality of the *Tories*' as 'a looser and less thoughtful sort of People, who look no further than the Outside of things, and take up with Notions

---

[38] Downie, *Robert Harley*, p. 119.
[39] Swift, *Examiner*, pp. 1, 3, 5, 6.

they don't understand' (46). Swift would never adopt such a position. If Harley was afraid that the 'tory resurrection was in danger of becoming a rout', and wished to enlist some moderate Whigs in support of the new ministry, *The Examiner* was not the paper meant to help smooth the way.[40]

In his seminal work on *The Examiner*, Speck notes that Harley must have disliked the original *Examiner*'s treatment of the war and of England's allies: it ran the risk of 'alarm[ing] the allies against his ministry', expressing lack of support for continuing the war and frustration with the Dutch for providing less than England and standing to gain more.[41] Swift softens the tone, but in his first issue he reiterates much of the message: the allies are not 'upon the same Foot with us', and 'the greatest part of the Money circulates among' the continental powers, 'whereas ours crosses the Sea . . . and every Penny of it . . . is so much lost to the Nation for ever'. The bottom line, for the new Mr. Examiner, is clear: the Queen needed to 'extricate[e] . . . Her self, as soon as possible, out of the Pupilage of those who found their Accounts only in perpetuating the War' (8, 9).

Swift's position is, in fact, not so different from that of St. John in *A Letter to the Examiner* (1710), written to guide the authors of the early issues. St. John assumes the role of counsellor: 'these are the Things, Sir, that deserve to pass under your Pen' (16). In the *Letter*, St. John deals extensively with the mismanagement of the war and with the inordinate dependence of the allies upon English men and money: 'We engag'd as *Confederates*, but we have been made to proceed as *Principals*' (6). I would argue that his tone, coolly rational rather than severe, resembles that of issue no. 14 (Swift's) more than that of the preceding numbers: 'From hence it appears probable enough, that if the War continue much longer on the present Foot . . .' (9). He proceeds, like Swift, to praise the Queen and voice concern about the disloyal opposition who seek 'to *Limit* the *Allegiance* of the Subject' (14). St. John is not fiery hot; he is regretful, lamenting the state of affairs and hoping that the situation can be set right. Reading the *Letter* alongside Swift's early contributions to the *Examiner*, one finds continuity – and still more reason to suspect that Swift was not imposed upon St. John by Harley, or brought in to replace and silence the secretary.

Swift's adoption of a more conciliatory tone perhaps reflects, to some extent, an unusual political reality. When he takes over *The Examiner*, the Tories appear to be the stronger party, with good prospects under Anne and with considerable popular support. In February 1711, he gloated about 'a Flourishing Ministry, in full Credit with the Q[uee]n, and belov'd by

---

[40] The quotation is Downie, *Robert Harley*, p. 128.
[41] Speck, '*The Examiner* Examined', p. 145.

the People' (211), and throughout his *Examiner* he swore the Tories to be the choice of the majority.[42] The 'truest way of judging the Dispositions of the People', he contended, 'is by computing the County-Elections; and in these, 'tis manifest that five in six are entirely for the present Measures' (181). Hence the supreme self-confidence of Mr. Examiner, who often relies on declarative statements that leave readers little room to dissent. In no. 22, for example, he characteristically dictates the proper sentiments of his audience: 'Whoever is a true Lover of our Constitution, must needs be pleas'd to see what successful Endeavours are Daily made to restore it in every Branch to its ancient Form' (125). He coerces readers into accepting his interpretation of the present and the recent past. A couple of issues later, he announces, 'I Am satisfy'd, that no reasonable Man of either Party, can justly be offended', and so on (163). The 'I am ready to allow' formulation (166) signals his desired rhetorical relationship to his readers: what he asserts they may accept as true. Take his positive declaration, in no. 46, that 'the People may be convinced, that five parts in six of what the *Examiners* have charg'd on the late M[inist]ry and Faction is right' (482).

The shift we see from the pre-Swift phase of the *Examiner* to the Swift phase perhaps has something to do with the Tory leadership's desire to capitalise on this new popularity, to build the party's base. Swift's persona, unlike that of the earlier essays, is that of a fairly moderate Tory gentleman, one duly antagonistic toward the Whig faction but neither too little nor too much a conservative churchman. If this is the case, then we need not assume that Harley installed Swift as a block to St. John's high Tory initiatives. Uniting the Tories against the Whigs – as Swift does in his contributions – was more St. John's strategy than it was his rival's. By the spring of 1711, says Dickinson, St. John was almost monomaniacally driven by 'his concern for the welfare and the future prospects of the Tory party', impatient with Harley's leniency toward the Whigs, and 'frantic . . . to keep the Tories together and in power'.[43]

The crux here is that, though Speck *et al.* believe that Swift was increasingly doing St. John's bidding, there is some possibility that as Mr. Examiner he was *always* doing St. John's bidding.[44] Significantly, Dickinson locates St. John's rejection of Harleyite moderation not in the autumn of 1710 but in the early months of 1711 – meaning that the secretary's own trajectory, vis-à-vis moderation, roughly corresponds with that of Mr. Examiner's. 'The

---

[42] The author of *The Britain* mocks Mr. Examiner for this fiction in no. 24. In no. 22, he complains that *The Examiner* 'is so free with the Government, as to tell us the *State is Tory*.'
[43] Dickinson, *Bolingbroke*, p. 80.
[44] Speck, '*The Examiner* Examined', p. 152.

more [St. John] saw Harley's . . . moderation alienating the Tory rank and file, the more he was tempted' to join the rebellion.[45] Swift, to be sure, never actually rebels against Harley; the closest he comes is in his identification of St. John as Guiscard's intended victim. But he does ultimately use *The Examiner* on behalf of principles that are not Harley's, and not only at the end of his tenure as sole author. In any case, the paper continues to be aggressively Tory under Oldisworth – and arguably even more so.

Swift's 'constant Drudge': Oldisworth as Mr. Examiner

The premise has been that Swift was removed from his examining role because he was tending too far toward high Toryism. If that was the cause for Swift's dismissal, then we might reasonably expect the post-Swift *Examiner* once more to swing toward the political centre, or at least to shift meaningfully in either tone or content. Is this what happened?

Swift's immediate successor was not Oldisworth but Manley, who collaborated with him on the 14 June issue and then contributed five more issues; her last was 26 July 1711. Manley's essays are comparatively dull; they attack the Whigs and the late ministry, but without Swift's sharpness and sense of urgency. Manley's authorship does raise an interesting question. If Swift were removed because Harley was uncomfortable with the paper's increasing high Toryism, why would Harley then install Manley, who was probably involved in the early, ultra-Tory *Examiner*? Soliciting Manley's pen sounds more like the work of St. John and Swift than of the lord treasurer. In any case, the paper suspended publication in late July and lay dormant for three and a half months. Why was it revived, and what is the relationship between Oldisworth's *Examiner* and Swift's?

The first of the new *Examiner* papers appeared on 6 December 1711, and the timing is significant. As Oldisworth announces in a swaggering opening paragraph, he is recommencing the journal 'upon the Second Meeting of the present Parliament', and he invites his '*Old Adversaries*' to 'prepare their Pen and Ink' to contend with him. On 7 December, Parliament sat, and the Whigs scored a major victory against the ministry. Harley and St. John had secretly negotiated a peace treaty with France, ending England's involvement in the War of the Spanish Succession – but which made what the Whigs believed to be outrageous concessions to the French. The treaty did not require the Spanish throne to be entirely restored to the house of Austria, and the Whigs considered it a betrayal of England's allies. The Whig cry of 'no peace without Spain' represented an ultimatum, and on 7 December, the

---

[45] Dickinson, *Bolingbroke*, p. 78.

Earl of Nottingham carried a vote to that effect in the House of Lords. In the *Journal to Stella*, Swift wrote desperately of the 'melancholy' turn of events. He describes the 'no peace without Spain' vote as 'a mighty blow and loss of reputation to lord treasurer', portending that it 'may end in his ruin' (340). Swift remained on edge for the rest of the month; on 29 December, he writes giddily, 'we are all safe; the queen has made no less than twelve lords to have a majority' (356). Anne's constitutionally dubious manoeuvre saved the Tory peace – allowing the ministry to proceed with their treating, despite Spain – but only heightened the controversy surrounding the negotiations. For our purposes, the key is that Swift was apprehensive about the parliamentary session: the revival of the *Examiner* was manifestly about cultivating support for the outcomes that Swift and St. John favoured.

The major difference between Oldisworth's *Examiner* and Swift's is not fundamental political outlook but focus and subject matter. Swift had written almost exclusively of domestic circumstances, with occasional references to the war and its costs; for Oldisworth, the peace is the thing. He is relentless in his defence of the ministry's treaty, and in his criticism of the warmongering Whigs and of England's ungrateful allies. Throughout the winter, he laments that the English 'might have been a *Rich*, a *Peaceful*, and a *Happy* People, which glorious State they voluntarily exchanged for *Poverty*, *War*, and *Desolation*' (12). He blames the Whigs for their 'Warlike Spirit' (14), and reflects on the bittersweet nature of Marlborough's success: he 'hath ... been Victorious, but for whom? we are poorer at the end of a ten Years successful War, than we could have been by being only fairly Beaten' (9). Oldisworth highlights the human cost of war (lingering on images of 'Men with their Limbs shot off, lying upon the Field' [20]), but his particular gripe is with the fiscal irresponsibility of those who would have England keep fighting.

That Oldisworth advertises, cites, and concurs with Swift's *Conduct of the Allies* (published in November 1710) is not surprising. On 20 March 1712, he maintains flatly that, 'whatever hath been charged upon the Allies, by the Author of the *Examiner*, of *The Conduct*, &c. ... might be proved, beyond all Contradiction.' Echoing *Conduct*, Oldisworth voices outraged incredulity at the exorbitant share England has had to bear, attributing any 'Disunion of our Allies' to the negligence of the Dutch, by whose 'Behaviour they have forced our Nation to shew their Weakness and Inability to support any longer the Burden of the War' (vol. 2, no. 30). The arguments and conclusions correspond to those of Swift, and Mr. Examiner is capable of sounding a good deal like his distinguished predecessor: 'AMONG a thousand popular Expressions which have lately been very much used, and very little understood; that of a *Separate Peace* is none of the most Inconsiderable.... Are these Gentlemen ... really of the Opinion, that when we entered into the War, we obliged our selves never to make Peace, unless when the *Dutch* should be pleased to give us leave?' (42). By July 1712, in the wake of a French victory at Denain that effectively ended Dutch resistance to the Tory peace, the great majority of Anne's subjects were eagerly anticipating peace.

Oldisworth's papers reflect this change: talk of the treaty becomes much less prominent, and he carries out instead a broader indictment of the Whigs. A Tory in religion as well as politics, he targets the freethinkers in general and Anthony Collins in particular (vol. 3, no. 12), and curses the Whigs for 'their excessive want of Faith in matters of Religion' (13). He deems the Whigs to be vile in 'every Article of their Infidel No-Creed' (vol. 4, no. 22), recalling Swift's earlier description of that group as 'a very odd mixture of Mankind', having been 'forced to enlarge their Bottom by taking in every Heterodox Professor either in Religion or Government' (*Examiner*, 314). If we expect the post-Swift *Examiner* to shift toward a more moderate position, we must be disconcerted by Oldisworth's relentless polarisation: 'The only true material Distinction of Persons with regard to the Church, is that of its real *Friends*, and its real *Enemies*'. The former are '*for*', the latter '*against* their own Native Country' (vol. 2, no. 37). In 1712–1713, Oldisworth disparages Whig populism, Whig hypocrisy, Whig irreligion, Whig history as written by Bishop Burnet, and in general the absurd and pernicious nature of '*Whig-Logick*' (vol. 3, no. 30). By the spring of 1713, he is sparring with Richard Steele, whose *Englishman* (1713–1714) was principally devoted to challenging *The Examiner* and to neutralising High Church propaganda.

The point here is not to provide an exhaustive analysis of Oldisworth's *Examiner*, but to observe that it represents an effective complement to Swift's coterminous polemics. What Oldisworth's tenure as Mr. Examiner makes crystal clear is that Swift was not dismissed so that the paper would sound like someone other than Swift. That Harley removed him in order to re-establish a moderate Tory mouthpiece is highly implausible given the directions in which the paper went after Oldisworth took over – and given that Swift stayed intimately involved with it. As he suggests in the *Journal to Stella*, he and St. John were instrumental in the revival the Tory periodical: on 5 December 1711, he announced, 'I have got an under spur-leather [Oldisworth] to write an *Examiner* again, and the secretary and I will now and then send hints'. If Harley had ordered Swift to step down, why did Swift and St. John continue to dictate the contents of the paper? Other explanations for his abandonment of the role are more credible, including the one he himself proffers: he had become recognisable as Mr. Examiner,[46]

---

[46] In *The Present State of Wit*, Gay had named Swift as the author and listed Atterbury and Prior as his primary assistants (p. 10).

and ideally the new persona would be 'a little upon the Grubstreet, to be a match for [Whig] writers' (pp. 338–39). Conceivably, Swift simply wanted to turn to other kinds of work, to serve the ministry through his polemical poetry and pamphleteering. Another possibility is that he was unsettled by the growing rivalry between Harley and St. John – something to which we will return. There is some chance that the *Examiner* was suffering an identity crisis: its *raison d'être* had been to defend the ministerial change, and by summer 1711 that subject could have seemed thoroughly exhausted. Writing in the fall of 1714, Swift explained his decision in evasive and disingenuous terms: 'my stile being soon discovered, and having contracted a great number of enemies, I let [the paper] fall into other hands, who held it up in some manner till her Majesty's death'.[47]

Whatever made Swift step down, the notion of a 'post-Swift' *Examiner* is misleading. We have no reason to assume that his involvement in the paper ended, and the politics of the *Examiner* were sufficiently consistent from its Swift to its Oldisworth phase that contemporaries continued to connect it with him. Oldmixon would later suggest that Swift too was involved in 'the First *Examiner*',[48] suggesting either that the vicar was part of the project from its beginning or that Oldmixon made no distinction between the first and second phases of the paper. The latter seems more probable. Steele never ceased to associate the *Examiner* with Swift, and he made a game out of insinuating Swift's authorship.[49] The anonymous author of *The Publick Spirit of the Tories* (1714) described Swift as 'Supervisor to that Weekly Lampoon upon Honesty, the *Examiner*'. Oldisworth ('Timothy') is merely 'a constant Drudge', whose 'Master is labouring in the Vineyard, like an honest Parson, with two or three Friends, and only steps in to help when *Timothy* is at a Loss'.[50] In 1735, Oldmixon would record that, 'The common Drudge for [the paper] was one *Oldesworth*, an obscure Person; but Mess. *St. John*, *Swift*, and *Prior*, were Fellow-Labourers in supporting it.'[51]

Swift and Oldisworth were seen as allied Tory tools – usually as St. John's Tory tools – and though Swift might not have approved of all of his successor's efforts, the content of the paper continued to be what we can safely call 'Swiftian' in important respects. Oldisworth's *Examiner* represents not a break from but an extension of Swift's, albeit one written in

---

[47] *Memoirs*; *PW*, vol. 8, p. 124.
[48] Oldmixon, *History of England*, p. 456.
[49] Charles A. Knight discusses this at some length; *A Political Biography of Richard Steele* (London, 2009), pp. 117–19.
[50] *The Publick Spirit of the Tories* (London, 1714), pp. 6, 9.
[51] Oldmixon, *History of England*, p. 456.

evolving political circumstances and therefore with different emphases and concerns.

Swift, Oldisworth, and the Tories

An important context for Swift's and Oldisworth's *Examiner* is what is happening (1711–1714) within the ministry and within the Tory party more broadly. Both Swift and Oldisworth are keen to serve the Tory party, and to varying degrees they each reflect on the tensions within that party, tensions reflected in the rivalry between the moderate, Whig-courting, Old Whig Harley and the hot-headed High Church St. John. What is the attitude of Swift's *Examiner* toward the ministry? And how does Oldisworth respond as the fissures become more apparent between 1712 and 1714?

A theme of Swift's essays is that the 'Old Whigs' are more closely aligned with his Tories than with the new Whigs. One has to wonder whether he is – ineffectively – trying to build a bridge between Harley and St. John and their respective followers. On 22 March, he professes, 'I am not sensible of any material Difference there is between those who call themselves the *Old Whigs*, and a great majority of the present *Tories*' (314). Earlier he had made a similar point: if one examines not an extremist but 'a reasonable honest Man of either side, upon those Opinions in Religion and Government, which both Parties daily buffet each other about, he shall hardly find one material Point in difference between them' (37). The impression created by this middle-ground-finding passage is that the ideological differences between two parties – Tories and *proper* Whigs – are not profound. What does Mr. Examiner gain by establishing continuity between present-day Toryism and pre-1688 Whiggism? Perhaps he is trying to augment the legitimacy of the Tory party, or at least to make it more appealing to conservative Whigs who might wish to dissociate themselves from the modern fanatics who share their name. Oldisworth would make a similar argument in the later *Examiner*, inviting 'the *Old Whigs* [to] consider, how far these degenerate Wretches are gone off from the best Principles of their Forefathers' (vol. 3, no. 2). Later, he addresses the '*Remnant* among the *Whigs . . .* who profess to follow their Forefathers', urging them to acknowledge that the 'Men, call'd *Tories*' have 'answer'd all the great Ends, which even an *Old Whig* could propose for the Security and Repose of the State' (vol. 4, no. 23).

Swift, like Oldisworth, makes the case that the real successors to the Old Whigs are not the new Whigs but their Tory 'rivals'. He is waxing moderate, highlighting the reasonableness and widespread currency of a set of conservative, traditional, core ideals – while also trying to divide (and conquer) the Whigs. Mr. Examiner's nemesis took exception to this tendency and highlighted its malicious intent. In *Medley* no. 18, Mainwaring and Oldmixon complained that the Examiner 'will, like the rest of the Faction, confound *Whig* and *Tory*, by dividing the Whigs into *Old* and *Modern*; a wicked Distinction invented by their Enemies to ruin those by *Divisions*, they cou'd never have contended with without them' (205). Defoe had raised a similar objection in *The Review*: the Tories hope 'to make an irreconcilable Breach among the *Whigs*' by introducing 'foolish Distinctions of *Old* Whigs and *New* Whigs', and unfortunately 'these Distinctions have prevail'd so far, and that some are so warm upon the Division, that they cannot see the Hand that divides it' (vol. 6, pp. 504, 506).

Swift's objective is straightforward: split the Whigs, unite the Tories. On 1 March, he admits that the Tories are not all like-minded – '*some* are thought too warm and zealous; *others* too cool and remiss' – but grumbles that 'these Divisions are industriously fomented by the discarded Faction' (273). He implicitly warns the Tories to stand together: the 'Discontent' of those out of power is 'apt to breed Differences among those who are in Possession', and the Tories must resist squabbling and pulling apart (274). Over the course of Swift's tenure in the examining role, the divisions within the Tory party become increasingly apparent. The most important conflict was between St. John's October Club – High Church country Tories – and Harley, whom they considered too moderate, too willing to pay court to the Whigs. Harley was in turn suspicious of St. John's intensity and extremism. Swift was worrying about these tensions by early 1711. In the *Journal to Stella* for 18 February, he reports that, 'We are plagued here with an October Club', and stresses the divide between the ministry ('for gentler measures') and 'the other Tories', who want 'more violent' policies (145, 146). On 27 April, he expresses his apprehension that Harley and his allies 'take things ill of Mr. St. John, and by some hints given me from another hand that I deal with, I am afraid the secretary will not stand long'. He resolves to 'tell [St. John] my opinion, and beg him to set himself right, else the consequences may be very bad' (194). By the spring, Harley had regained some of his popularity, and St. John had failed to rally the Tory backbenchers against his rival. The rumors that he 'would be fortunate to survive as Secretary of State' had clearly reached Swift.[52]

By the end of his reign as Mr. Examiner, Swift was evidently seeking, however ineffectively, to unite the ministers and the Tories. In the 24 May issue, he appears to be trying to persuade the High Church interest that Harley is serving them as well: 'The Clergy, and whoever else have a true Concern for the Constitution of the Church, cannot but be highly pleas'd

---

[52] Dickinson, *Bolingbroke*, p. 83.

with one Prospect in this new Scene of Publick Affairs' (440). Two weeks later, he praises Harley for his effective debt control measures and for having 'obtain'd of Her Majesty a remission of the First Fruits and Tenths to the Clergy of *Ireland*'. That affirmation is clearly meant to endear Harley to men of the October variety; in this *Examiner*, Swift's last as sole author, he highlights 'my Lord High Treasurer's Concern for Religion' (468).

Oldisworth was every bit as alarmed as Swift about the state of the Tory party. His inaugural *Examiner* rebukes the Tories for being 'stupid Animals', who 'know not how to come up to . . . *Unanimity*'. In January 1714, he praises the 'Cause' of the Tories, but targets those among them who 'set up against their own Friends'. Any Tory who, 'at this time of Day especially, endeavours at any thing that may Divide his own Party, or create Misunderstandings between them, takes the shortest, the surest, and the only way to Ruin them' (vol. 5, no. 11). A few weeks later, he complains that '*Quarrels at Court*' are 'Judgments . . . upon the *Ministry*', and concludes that any '*Tory*, who wishes to Displace any one but a *Whig*, is really a *Whig* of the worst sort' (15). His sentiments are obviously a good deal closer to those of St. John than to those of Harley. On 14 May, Mr. Examiner takes the present ministry to task for 'a plain notorious Mistake in their Conduct' – to wit, that they 'have not yet alter'd their gentle Treatment of their Adversaries' (48). In his emphatic rejection of the Whigs, and in his desire to consolidate Tory power, Oldisworth is a fellow traveller of St. John's and Swift's. Elsewhere I have traced Swift's response to the collapse of the Tory party, *circa* 1712–1716, and cited his frustration with Tory passivity: 'I have been told, that for two Years past it hath been the Politicks of that Party to let every thing go as it would, without interposing'.[53]

Oldisworth, writing before the crisis of Anne's death, tries to cultivate a sense of Tory concord: 'I remember the Time, when the *Tories* at the Helm, were but a handful of Men, in comparison of the *Whigs*; and yet how Weighty was that *little Body*? What a glorious Stand did they make? . . . Such was the Power of Concord and Unanimity' (vol. 6, no. 2). Oldisworth was evidently willing to fight for the Tory cause in life as in letters. In 1715, Oldisworth joined the Scottish Jacobites. The author of *The Weekly Packet* falsely reported that the former Mr. Examiner met his end in the rebellion: 'Some People assure, that Mr. Oldsworth [*sic*], suppos'd to have writ or assisted in writing the last Examiner, was kill'd with his Sword in Hand in the late Engagement at Preston, in Company with several others who had the same Fate, having resolv'd not to survive the Loss of the Battle' (no.

---

[53] *Correspondence*, vol. 2, p. 285. See Ashley Marshall, '"*fuimus Torys*": Swift and Regime Change, 1714–1718', *Studies in Philology* 112 (2015), pp. 537–74.

183). In fact, Oldisworth died in 1734, in prison for bankruptcy – but he was clearly seen by contemporaries as a militant Jacobite.

That Oldisworth was St. John's man is difficult to deny. I have been arguing that Swift, at least as Mr. Examiner, was also St. John's man, and not just gradually or eventually. At the outset of his examining, he had no need to think of himself as either one politician's or another's, but when the choice needed to be made, he followed the secretary. Swift's personal dealings with, and his relationship to, his ministerial masters is important to our speculations about his decision to abandon the role of Mr. Examiner, and to that subject we need briefly turn.

Swift, St. John, and Harley

Our best insight into these connections is the *Journal to Stella*, always, of course, with the caveat that Swift is every bit as playful and elusive in these intimate letters as he is revealing. From December 1710 throughout the spring and early summer, Swift makes frequent reference to visiting with St. John, and the two seem to get along swimmingly. In his encounters with Harley, on the contrary, one senses some strain. On 12 December, he reports having been 'at the secretary's office' (85). Two days later: 'I went to-day to the court of requests . . . in hopes to dine with Mr. Harley', but was told that Harley 'did not dine at home', so 'met with Mr. secretary St. John, and went home and dined with him' (90). On 22 December, irked by Harley's constant unavailability, he announces, 'I am going now to Mr. Harley's Levee on purpose to vex him; I'll say I had no other way of seeing him, &c' (96). Four days later: 'I called at Mr. Harley's, who was not within' (101). On 29 December, he recounts an evening with Harley and St. John, explaining that after the lord treasurer left, the other two spent another hour together: 'I took the secretary aside, and complained to him of Mr. Harley, that he had got the queen to grant the First-Fruits, promised to bring me to her, and get her letter to the bishops in Ireland; but the last part he had not done in six weeks, and I was in danger to lose reputation, &c' (103). Though Swift would attribute the First Fruits success to Harley, here he seems to esteem St. John a more helpful ally, and two days later he comments that St. John 'has promised to [get results] in a very few days' (104). On 2 January, St. John tells Swift (he reports) 'that the warrant was now drawn, in order for a patent for the First-Fruits....he assures me 'tis granted and done, and past all dispute, and desires I will not be in any pain at all' (109).

Swift's proximity to St. John is clear. Downie has suggested that both ministers 'had a happy knack of avoiding the scrounging Doctor', [54] but in the *Journal* only Harley's evasiveness is on display. On 5 January, Swift reports, 'Mr. secretary St. John sent for me this morning so early that I was forced to go without shaving' (112), and two days later, something similar: 'Mr. secretary St. John sent for me this morning in all haste; but I would not lose my shaving' (115). The next day he announces that he 'promised to be with Mr. secretary St. John', but he decides not to oblige; he goes two days later instead (116). On the twelfth, Swift was again 'upon some business with Mr. secretary', who 'made me promise to dine with him, which otherwise I would have done with Mr. Harley, whom I have not been with these ten days' (118). Swift would be responsible for *The Examiner* for another five months, and yet he already seems distant from his ostensible master. On 25 January, he spends the morning with St. John upon 'some business' again (130), and yet once more a week later (131). On 4 February, Swift says St. John has promised to find a place for Swift's young friend, William Harrison (133). The following night he visited with Harley from six until eleven, and then vowed to Stella, 'henceforth I will chuse to visit him in the evenings, and dine with him no more if I can help it. It breaks all my measures, and hurts my health' (134). 'It breaks all my measures' might simply be a reflection of their late-night revelling, of a piece with 'hurts my health', though on 6 February Swift expresses deeper frustration with the lord treasurer. 'Mr. Harley desired I would dine with him', he writes, 'but I refused him, for I fell out with him yesterday, and will not see him again till he makes me amends' (pp. 134–35).

The falling out had to do with Harley's offering Swift a bank note for £50,[55] a sizeable sum that the vicar refused. Abigail Williams explains, 'Swift was outraged, and refused to visit Harley until ten days later',[56] but this is not wholly accurate. On 12 February (six days later), he reports sending 'Mr. Harley into the house to call the secretary, to let him know I would not dine with him if he dined late' (142). He ended up spending the evening with St. John, and perhaps his using Harley as a go-between was meant as a passive-aggressive rebuke – but he did see Harley. On the 15th, he again contemplated and half-attempted to connect with Harley: 'I went to the court of requests, thinking if Mr. Harley dined early, to go with him', but

---

[54] Downie, *Robert Harley*, p. 131.
[55] This is an enormous amount of money, amounting to more than the average household annual income at the time. Retail price index value would be *circa* £6700; 'labor value' something like £100,000; and income value roughly £130,000 in 2015 (measuringworth.com).
[56] *Journal to Stella*, p. 135n14.

others 'invited me to dine with them, and away we went' (143). The next day, he and Harley 'made up our quarrel'; the following night he dined with Harley and St. John together (144), but on the 18th and the 26th, and again on 4 March, he is with St. John, not Harley. There is a definite trend in his socialising, and, if the *Journal* is to be trusted, in his talking politics and doing 'business' with St. John. His growing distance from Harley seems difficult to deny, between the long gaps in contact and the miscellaneous tensions and reproaches. On 9 February – three days after the £50 incident – Swift tells Stella, with obvious disappointment, that:

> Mr. Harley of late has said nothing of presenting me to the queen: – I was overseen [mistaken] when I mentioned it to you. He has such a weight of affairs on him, that he cannot mind all; but he talk'd of it three or four times to me, long before I dropt it to you. (138)

One has to wonder whether the bank note represented an attempt to pull Swift back from St. John, a kind of unofficial patronage meant to cultivate loyalty.

Whatever Harley's motivations, the *Journal* makes clear that Swift remained more closely connected to St. John, at this point, and that he tended to view the secretary as a more reliable benefactor. His *Examiner* is more and more in line with St. John's politics; he spends more and more time in St. John's company; and he and St. John appear to have been involved in the continuation of the paper under Oldisworth. Wherein lies the evidence suggesting Harley's alleged responsibility for Swift's removal as Mr. Examiner?

Mr. Examiner among the journalists

The Examiner was a big deal in the last four years of Anne's reign, a paper that incited the creation of rival journals and fuelled considerable controversy. Addison's *Whig-Examiner* and *The Medley* (penned primarily by Mainwaring with assistance from Oldmixon and Steele) began in response to the pre-Swift *Examiner*. Steele's *Englishman* made Oldisworth's *Examiner* a major target, and much of Steele's late Stuart journalism is taking aim at that rival paper. Anonymous Whig pamphleteers and journalists heaped scorn upon what Mainwaring and Steele called an '*Orthodox* Libel' and a '*Protected* Paper'.[57] Opposition commentators voiced much exasperation with the paper, and Steele expressed a sense of piqued futility: 'THERE is no Possibility of applying any Remedy to the Evils which this Rascal commits twice a Week'.[58] Why the fuss over *The Examiner*, and what can we learn from its critics?

Modern scholars have stressed the Harleyite dimension of Swift's *Examiner*, at least in its beginnings, an emphasis helped by associating the paper with Defoe's Whiggish *Review*. Critics are fond of quoting the Whig historian Oldmixon, who in 1715 would reflect that '*Foe* and *Swift* [were] fellow Labourers, in the Service of the *White-Staff*'.[59] I challenged in this association in the previous chapter, and here wish merely to observe that Oldmixon's pairing is anomalous. Almost all writers instead couple Swift and Abel Roper, the editor of the thrice-weekly *Post Boy*. On 25 September 1712, Oldisworth points out that, 'It hath been a very frequent Topick of Wit, among my Brother-Authors of the *Whig* Party, to couple honest *Abel* my Fellow-Labourer and Me together'. Oldisworth's observation is accurate. The author of *High Church Aphorisms* (1711) targeted Mr. Examiner and his brother Abel as 'Two Political Lyars', twin '*UNDERTAKERS*' who bury 'People's *Reputations*' (1). The same language recurs. In *Bouchain: In a Dialogue Between the Late Medley and Examiner* (pub. September 1711, after Swift's tenure had ended), the author (Francis Hare?) has Mr. Examiner refer to 'my Fellow-Labourer *Abel*' (17). *The Flying Post* for 3 February 1713 – like Steele, continuing to associate the *Examiner* with Swift – berates '*Abel* and his Brother the *Examiner*'. The Whig paper mocks those Tories who 'want nothing but the Sanction of *Abel* and the *Examiner* to publish [anything] as *Gospel*'. The connection between the *Examiner* and the *Post Boy* is one Swift himself announces, proudly, in the *Journal to Stella*: 'Roper is my humble Slave' (412). He also contributed to *The Post Boy*.[60] The point here is that contemporaries spotlighted the high Tory nature of *The Examiner* by linking it with *The Post Boy*, a paper Henry L. Snyder has justly described as 'a tool of Bolingbroke, who wrote pieces to be inserted

---

[57] *The Medley*, pp. 281, 282 (no. 23, a collaborative effort); throughout, he denounces 'such Scriblers as *Abel* and his Brother' (349). These issues of *The Medley* appear in Frank H. Ellis (ed.), *Swift vs. Mainwaring: The Examiner and The Medley* (Oxford, 1985).

[58] Steele, *The Englishman*, p. 56.

[59] [John Oldmixon], *The Life and Posthumous Works of Arthur Maynwaring* (London, 1715), p. 276.

[60] See *Journal to Stella*: 'I have been drawi[n]g up a Paragraph for t[h]e Post boy, to be out to morrow, and as malicious as possible, and very proper for Abel Roper th[e] Printer of it' (p. 460).

in it and directed many others'.⁶¹ Perhaps Oldmixon was trying to damage Defoe by dubbing him a fellow traveller of Mr. Examiner's – but whatever his motives, taking his partisan swipe as representative of contemporary judgments is problematic.

What did the Whigs find so objectionable about *The Examiner*? Obviously they disliked its ideological commitments, taking exception to its high Toryism and its virulent and personal abuse of Whigs. Like Steele in *The Englishman*, *The Medley* disputes its rival's arguments about the basis of power, from the beginning attempting to devalue the core principles contemporaries associated with the *Examiner*. In *Medley* no. 3, Mainwaring alludes to 'a great deal of Bustle about the *Hereditary*, &c', deprecating the 'dangerous' doctrine promulgated by the Examiner and his 'Fellow-Labourers'.⁶² The cross examinations of *The Examiner* make plain that contemporaries *always* understood it to be a polarising, High Church paper alarmingly capable of disseminating ultra-conservative dogma. If they connected the 'weekly Libel' with Harleyite moderation, no trace of that association remains.⁶³

But objections to *The Examiner* were about more than ideology. As Heinz-Joachim Müllenbrock suggests, 'the Examiner's arrogant self-assurance was often denounced by his adversaries', and his paper 'became the leading opinion-journal, setting the pace for public debate and relegating the other papers in the Tory interest to a subsidiary role'.⁶⁴ *The Examiner* does seem to have been uniquely upsetting. Whig critics frequently use words like 'libelous', 'impudent', 'scurrilous', 'dull', and 'false'. Mr. Examiner's treatment of Marlborough was, for the Whigs, unconscionable;⁶⁵ his remarks on Godolphin, Wharton, and Somers represented the kind of personalised abuse that did not belong in print. The author of *High Church Aphorisms* includes an epitaph on the late Mr. Examiner, one which mimics the defamatory language associated with the paper:

---

⁶¹ Henry Snyder, 'The Circulation of Newspapers in the Reign of Queen Anne', *The Library* 5th series 23 (1968), 206–35, p. 211.

⁶² The last quotation is from the inaugural issue of *The Medley*.

⁶³ Those who connect Harley with the politics of the *Examiner* tend to be trying to brand him more of a high Tory than an Old Whig. This is certainly true for Steele, who generally expresses hostility to Oxford's treatment of Marlborough and who assumes that the *Examiner* is written 'under Oxford's direct control' (Knight, *Political Biography*, p. 141).

⁶⁴ Heinz-Joachim Müllenbrock, 'Swift as a Political Essayist: The Strained Medium', in Richard H. Rodino and Hermann J. Real (eds. with assistance from Helgard Stöver-Leidig), *Reading Swift: Papers from The Second Münster Symposium on Jonathan Swift* (München, 1993), 151–58, pp. 157–58.

⁶⁵ See for example Steele, *The Guardian*, no. 63 (p. 241).

> *Thus Insects, that from Dunghills rise, And are to flies prefer'd,*
> *Descend soon after their Demise, To their Original a Turd.*[66]

The same author looks back to the original *Examiner*, making no distinction between the pre-Swift and Swift phases of the journal: 'He was to maul the Whigs. . . . [K]nowing he had very little good to say of his Masters that employ'd him, he could do no less than promise to write a great deal of Ill of their Opponents' (3). He goes on to complain that *The Examiner* uses 'the only Language that they take pleasure in reading' (13), a language of insolence and contempt. In *Medley* no. 23, Mainwaring and Steele had similarly disparaged Swift for passing 'Ribaldry . . . for Wit', for being 'foul-mouth'd' and 'scurrilous in an extraordinary degree' (280). To be sure, Swift and the Tories in turn accuse the Whigs of similar impertinence, but the degree of disapprobation of Mr. Examiner's audacity is remarkable. Even the high-flying *Rehearsal* does not warrant such censure.

What especially infuriates Whig writers is the fact that this 'libel' is not only permitted but endorsed by the ministry. The author of *Essays Divine, Moral, and Political* (1714) disparages Mr. Examiner as '*a Creature of Power, a Spaniel that Fetches and Carries at the Command of his Master*' (v).[67] In *The Publick Spirit of the Tories*, the writer marvels at the fact that such a virulent paper 'should meet with a Toleration under so excellent a Government' (10) – and expresses the country's expectation 'that the *Examiner* . . . be silenced' (12). The pamphleteer behind *Two Letters Concerning the Author of the Examiner* (1713) indirectly counsels the ministry 'to bring that Wretch to open Shame and Punishment'. Their 'Forbearance' is what 'has given Occasion to some unthinking Persons to suspect them for the Encouragers, nay the Patrons of this Wretch' (21).

This is a constant theme of anti-*Examiner* polemic. In *The Englishman* for 7 November 1713, Steele grumbles that the 'unexampled License' of 'loose Papers' such as this one signifies a more general 'Corruption' at court. Mr. Examiner 'transgress[es] the Rules of Decency . . . with respect to Persons distinguished by high Stations' – and, what is worse, Steele supposes the paper to be 'supported by a Peer of the Realm' (pp. 62–63).[68] In January 1714, Steele includes a 'letter' addressed to the Englishman, urging him to 'attack' *The Examiner*: he should not be allowed to take such 'indecent Liberty . . .

---

[66] This quotation is at the end of the epitaph, on the last page of prefatory matter.
[67] The author of *Essays* is obviously targeting Swift throughout, clearly associating him with the *Examiner*, even though this volume appears three years after Swift ceased to be 'Mr. Examiner'.
[68] Gay makes this point as well, and goes further: the paper is 'look'd on as a sort of publick Notice which way [the ministers] are steering us' (*Present State of Wit*, p. 9).

with Great Men out of Power', and 'if he has any Encouragement from [the ministry] to demean himself as he does, 'tis illegal and criminal' (pp. 171–72). Oldmixon would later reflect similarly, though he specifically faults St. John for allowing *The Examiner* to be so egregious. Mainwaring, he recalls, 'had a very mean Opinion not only of Mr. *St. John*'s Honesty, but of his Capacity ... and, with very great Indignation, observ'd how he suffer'd the best Men in the Nation to be bely'd, and vilify'd in his *Libel*'. And, he continues, Mainwaring 'never doubted Mr. *St. John*'s being a main Promoter of that detestable Libel'.[69]

Whig writers also attested, unhappily, to the journal's potency. The *Examiner* was from its beginning viewed as toxic. In his *History of England*, Oldmixon describes a conversation with Mainwaring about this new paper: 'he began with Complaints of the Villainy and Insolence of the *Examiner*, saying, *It did a World of Mischief*.'[70] The Whig answerers, however, did nothing to diminish the journal's effectiveness, which remained considerable well after Swift ceased to be sole author. In *The Englishman* for 15 February 1714, Steele coldly pronounces *The Examiner* to be one of the 'Oracles of Policy' (233). The 1715 *Letter to the Examiner*, a Whig polemic, singles out Mr. Examiner as a crucial disseminator of Tory opinion: 'this is the Man on whom they lay so great a stress; this is him from whom they pick their Argument, whom they quote, whom they refer to: His Papers are sent into every Corner of the Kingdom, received as Oracles' (12). This author links the paper with Oldisworth (17), but also cites his 'Master, the *Irish* Dean' (20) – presumably hoping that both men will be in difficulties in the new reign, and keen to publicise their utility to the treasonous ministry of Harley and St. John.

The critical consensus has been that *The Examiner* was less interesting and less important after Swift 'left' the paper. Damrosch's casual dismissal, cited above – 'carried on for a while, not very well, by others' – is only the most explicit statement of a longstanding assumption. This notion, however, is flat wrong. Swift continues to pull the strings, to some degree and in some fashion, and contemporaries continue to connect him with the venture. *The Examiner* also remains a powerful Tory outlet, one with which the Whigs continue to do fierce battle and about which they sharply complain well after Anne's death.

◆

---

[69] Oldmixon, *History of England*, p. 456.
[70] Oldmixon, *History of England*, 456. Keith Feiling describes the paper as 'the life of Tory politics during the first half of 1711'. It 'was read aloud to village congregations by country clergy' (*History of the Tory Party*, p. 429).

The middle phase of *The Examiner*, from November 1710 to June 1711, is, as critics have suggested, different from what preceded and followed – though the differences have been overstated, and the presumption that Harley was responsible for removing Swift turns out to be implausible. This standard explanation also tends to ignore other changes in circumstances. When Swift took control of *The Examiner*, the Tories had just won a whopping majority in the general election; that he tries to be less polarising, and to cultivate the notion of a popular Tory party, is not astonishing, and it might or might not have had anything to do with Harley's preferences. Swift stepped down in the summer of 1711, but he was involved in its revival and three-year long continuation, and Oldisworth's *Examiner* looks enough like Swift's that contemporaries seemed unaware of any operational change. *The Examiner* of later 1711–1714, moreover, functions as a complement to Swift's polemical contributions to ministerial defence and Tory unity. The phases of the paper would seem to have as much to do with the changing needs of the Tory party than they do with Harley's attempt to wrest control from St. John. *The Examiner* never paid court to the Whigs, not for a day, and contemporaries never took it to be anything other than high Tory, a paper with a 'great ... Reputation among *Churchmen*'.[71] If Swift were assigned by Harley 'to take the wind out of tory sails',[72] then we can only conclude that he failed. And if Harley removed him because the paper had fallen under St. John's influence, then the installation of first Manley and then the Jacobite Oldisworth is utterly inexplicable. There is, in point of fact, very little solid evidence connecting Harley to the management of *The Examiner* – nothing like what we have to associate him with the inception of the *Review*. On the contrary, we have excellent reasons to see *The Examiner* as St. John's project – and thus to rethink Swift's complicated and frustratingly obscure relationship with the ministry during the fraught last years of Queen Anne's reign.

---

[71] *The Thoughts of a Tory Author, Concerning the Press* (London, 1712), p. 3.
[72] Downie, *Robert Harley*, p. 135.

Chapter 5
Steele's Party Journalism

Scholarship on Richard Steele continues to be dominated by his collaboration with Joseph Addison on *The Tatler* (1709–1711) and *The Spectator* (1711–1712; 1714). Surprisingly little has been said about his other journalistic enterprises, including *The Guardian* (1713), *The Englishman* (1713–1715), *The Theatre* (1720), and lesser-known but scarcely less ephemeral papers like *The Lover* and *The Reader* (both 1714). Steele's contributions (1707–1710) to *The London Gazette*, the official government newspaper, probably deserve the neglect they have had; no editorialising was tolerated in that paper, and Steele himself found the enterprise 'very innocent and very insipid'.[1] Though Charles Knight and Nicola Parsons have published good work on Steele's politics, in common critical imagination he remains a cultural ally of Addison, the producer of literary periodicals offering ethical instruction and promoting good sense and benevolence.

Some of the best recent discussions of Steele (and Addison) have been devoted to the role of *The Tatler* and *The Spectator* in either fostering or challenging the emergence of a Habermasian public sphere. Brian Cowan has contended Addison and Steele 'were not so enthusiastic about the potential for public politics', at least in 'the *Spectator* project',[2] and in general scholars have assumed that both men wished to distance themselves from their contemporary news-writers. The presence of news in *The Tatler* is often marginalised by modern commentators; most critics conclude that Addison and Steele rely primarily on indirection, implicitly advocating a Whig culture without engaging directly in specific civic controversy. When Steele appears in accounts of early eighteenth-century journalism, he is kept well distant from his more argumentative, deep-in-the-muck counterparts like Defoe and Swift. Scholars see him

---

[1] *Mr. Steele's Apology* (1714) (*Tracts and Pamphlets*, p. 339).
[2] Brian Cowan, 'Mr. Spectator and the Coffeehouse Public Sphere', *Eighteenth-Century Studies* 37 (2004), 345–66, p. 346.

more as a champion of Whig culture, in other words, than a participant in partisan Whig politics.

The questions addressed in this chapter are simple ones. What sort of political work does Steele do as a journalist, and what change if any do we find across his periodical *oeuvre*? What happens if we read him not only as Addison's ally but also as a party player crossing swords with the likes of Defoe and Swift? Knight's *Political Biography* is the only study produced in the last generation that pays significant attention to any Steele paper other than *The Tatler* and *The Spectator*. Developing the work done in Calhoun Winton's sound two-volume biography, Knight offers an account of the content of Steele's papers and characterises their degrees of politicality. What follows is indebted to both Winton and Knight, but my focus is specifically on Steele's evolving role as a party journalist.

My contention is that Steele's attitudes toward power and authority, and toward popular politics, have been oversimplified or misunderstood because too small a sample of his journalism gets consulted, and because what is studied is too often divorced from the context of early eighteenth-century partisan journalism. His more ephemeral papers have been irrelevant to modern (non-biographical) accounts of his journalism, but we should remember that his entire periodical canon consists of short-lived ventures. *The Tatler* ran for 21 months; his involvement in *The Spectator* lasted a year and a half. Granting the popularity and influence of those better-known papers, they occupied Steele only for a little while and they were succeeded by other relatively brief enterprises that also matter to how we understand his journalism and its fundamental objectives. Reading all of his periodicals highlights the pervasive partisanship of his concerns: the tendency to present Steele's journalism as the work of a cultural commentator rather than a party pen has led to considerable distortion. Without denying his role as critic and moraliser, we need also to appreciate that as a journalist he was doggedly committed to peddling Whig propaganda. Contemporaries were well aware of his partisanship: when the author of the assertively Whig *Patriot* (1714–1715) closes his journal, he insinuates that readers had wrongly – but understandably – attributed the work to Steele.

The bulk of this chapter is devoted to analysis of the aims and strategies of Steele's party periodicals, meant to demonstrate conceptual and formal shifts as well as fundamental continuity. He turns out to be a remarkably versatile journalist, one who adapts his strategies, content, and tone to respond to evolving political circumstances. His multiple successive papers each call into question some aspect of Tory policy or propaganda. After a consideration of Steele's shifting agendas in his various journals, I offer a brief comparative discussion of Steele and Defoe's Mr. Review. He and

Defoe share many values and agree on many issues, but Defoe represents an instructive contrast; reading them together highlights Steele's distinctive manner of engagement with his readers. The final section traces some of the consistencies and inconsistencies of Steele's journalism, arguing that whatever the variations in his approach he consistently fixated on the issue of authority – in politics and in the press. Steele was consistently politically engaged. My argument here is that his canon of Whig journalism represents a deliberate challenge to Tory journalism – a sustained and strategic assault on the credibility of Tory politicians and of their champions in the pulpit and the press.

The politics of *The Tatler*

Scholars have emphasised *The Tatler*'s miscellaneous nature, literary style, preachment of civility and decorum, and pervasive geniality,[3] concluding that that the partisan moments in *The Tatler* are anomalous, somehow at odds with 'the *Spectator* project'. As J. A. Downie has wryly observed, few scholars of periodical literature have wanted 'to taint' Addison and Steele's 'deathless prose . . . with the dirty world of the politics of Queen Anne's reign'.[4] Knight has convincingly described *The Spectator* as having 'replaced propaganda with ideology as a mode of political discourse', as carrying 'on a political discourse without appearing to do so'.[5] Among Cowan's many solid contributions to our understanding of Addison and Steele is his contention that they introduce 'a truly reformed coffeehouse . . . as a respectable alternative to the Sacheverellite Tory claim that only the Church of England can offer a solid foundation for the moral revitalization of society'.[6] That is, they deny the Church's exclusive claim on morality. Most scholars have suggested, rightly, that Addison and Steele 'demonstrate quietly that

---

[3] The subtitle of Richmond P. Bond's 1971 study of *The Tatler* is *The Making of a Literary Journal* (Cambridge, 1971), and most studies of early eighteenth-century journalism treat *The Tatler* and *The Spectator* primarily as the finest exemplars of the literary periodical.
[4] Downie, 'Periodicals and Politics in the Reign of Queen Anne', in Robin Myers and Michael Harris (eds.), *Serials and their Readers 1620–1914* (New Castle, 1993), 45–61, p. 51.
[5] Charles A. Knight, '*The Spectator*'s Generalizing Discourse', in Downie and Thomas N. Corns (eds.), *Telling People What To Think: Early Eighteenth-Century Periodicals from* The Review *to* The Rambler (London, 1993), 44–57, pp. 54–55, 44.
[6] Cowan, 'Mr. Spectator and the Coffeehouse Public Sphere', p. 349.

Whiggism was the natural consequence of the public values and attitudes that they articulated'.[7] Though critics acknowledge the presence of the news in *The Tatler*, they usually stress not its presence but its diminution, sometimes attributed to pressure from Addison. In general, *The Tatler* is seen not as apolitical but as oblique and generalised in its ideological message. If *The Tatler* had been followed by the more aggressive *Englishman* rather than by *The Spectator*, I suspect that critics would characterise it differently. *The Tatler*'s association with the less politically engaged *Spectator* has encouraged scholars to downplay its partisanship; had it been succeeded by *The Englishman*, they would probably instead treat those moments as presaging Steele's later and louder Whig propaganda.

Anyone familiar with the critical consensus on *The Tatler* must be somewhat surprised by the degree to which the early numbers are saturated by news reportage and explicit political commentary.[8] Robert Waller Achurch acknowledges Steele 'regarded the news department [of *The Tatler*] as quite an important component'[9]; at the outset the paper resembles *The Review* and other newspapers more than *The Spectator*. During the early months of *The Tatler*, Steele was also in charge of the official government paper, *The London Gazette*. The news printed in *The Tatler* to some extent reflects his access to dispatches in his capacity as the Gazetteer, as well as his reading of *The Daily Courant*.[10] Originally, then, *The Tatler* functioned essentially as a ministerial paper, and that Whig ministry comes in for quite a lot of praise from Isaac Bickerstaff. Like most contemporary Whig papers, *The Tatler* is obsessed with the progress of the war. Like Mr. Review, Steele defends the continued waging of that war, insisting that the Allies have France on the ropes, and that the battle must be fought until the French are weakened enough to agree to the most favourable possible terms. A theme of the early issues is that French agents have attempted 'to break the good Understanding of the Allies' – in vain (vol. 1, p. 28). Another is the heroism of Marlborough, the 'Illustrious Man, who . . . has pass'd through all the Gradations of Human Life, 'till he has ascended to the Character of a Prince' (vol. 1, p. 58). In no. 25, Bickerstaff asserts that 'all Things tend . . . to a vigorous and active

---

[7] Abigail Williams, *Poetry and the Creation of a Whig Literary Culture, 1681–1714* (Oxford, 2005), p. 160.

[8] Downie notes that 'the actual opening of the first number of *The Tatler* . . . is too easily forgotten. It is only after Steele has thus set out his stall in *political* terms that he mentions his other, more celebrated, resolution '*to have something which may be of Entertainment to the Fair Sex*''' ('Periodicals and Politics', p. 51).

[9] Robert Waller Achurch, 'Richard Steele, Gazetteer and Bickerstaff', in Richmond P. Bond (ed.), *Studies in the Early English Periodical* (Chapel Hill, 1957), 49–72, p. 54.

[10] Charles A. Knight, *A Political Biography of Richard Steele* (London, 2009), p. 46.

Campagne', a campaign he glorifies (vol. 1, p. 198). Andrew Lincoln has usefully reminded us of the paradox of *The Tatler*'s – and *The Spectator*'s – 'commitment to gentler civil manners on the one hand, and their support for military aggression on the other.'[11] Knight recognises that what news Steele includes in 1709 mostly has to do with the war,[12] but the key is the *pervasiveness* of the warmongering in these early issues. The early *Tatler* is a work of political propaganda.

The obliqueness of Steele's political commentary has been overstated. Knight suggests that, 'Political discourse in the *Tatler* operates almost entirely through indirection,'[13] but I suspect that contemporaries regarded Steele's partisanship as a good deal more explicit than modern scholars have. Steele devotes three issues to the battle of Malplaquet, a costly win for the Allies (31 August 1709); he describes the result as 'the intire [*sic*] Defeat of the Enemy' (vol. 1, p. 441). Desperate to prevent the Whigs from using the victory to prop up their pro-war arguments, Tories contended that it had been too little to justify the loss of life. Steele does not invoke the Tory position, but he pre-emptively counters it by highlighting 'the Greatness of the Action' (443). His conclusion is unequivocal: 'This wonderful Success, obtain'd under all the Difficulties that could be oppos'd in the Way of an Army, must be acknowledged as owing to the Genius, Courage and Conduct, of the Duke of *Marlborough*' (pp. 445–46). No less than Mr. Examiner and Mr. Review, he sets himself up as the spokesman of truth. In no. 65, Steele contemns the 'Battle-Critick', who feels that he must 'examine the Weight of an Advantage before [others] will allow it' (448). He introduces Sir George England to respond to this Battle-Critick (the latter clearly a Tory detractor of Marlborough): 'The Action you are in so great doubt to approve of, is greater than ever has been perform'd in any Age' (449).

This is not the forceful polemic of either Swift or Defoe, but neither is it amiable or particularly circumspect. How a journalist assessed Malplaquet revealed his or her partisan commitments. The following year, Steele again glorified a controversial battle, Stanhope's victory in Catalonia (27 July 1710), in *Tatler* no. 210. For his account, he was attacked in *The Examiner* no. 5. Knight's conclusion that Steele wished not 'to drive away Tory readers' does not reflect the contentious reality of 1709–1710. Knight reasons that though *The Tatler* 'celebrated behaviours, values and attitudes that it

---

[11] Lincoln, 'War and the Culture of Politeness: The Case of *The Tatler* and *The Spectator*', *Eighteenth-Century Life* 36 (2012), 60–79, p. 60. These periodicals, Lincoln continues, 'represented war as an activity that did not conflict with benevolent principles of polite society but rather promoted those principles' (p. 73).
[12] Knight, *Political Biography*, p. 47.
[13] Knight, *Political Biography*, p. 64.

associated with Whigs . . . it did so with a genial good nature that was attractive to all.'[14] Steele's Tory antagonists, however, were not likely to be keen to read Bickerstaff's (frequent) praise of Marlborough, or to suffer his resolute support of the war. In *The Importance of the Guardian Considered* (1713), Swift reflects that initially *The Tatler* was 'equally esteemed by both Parties, because it meddled with neither. But, sometime after *Sacheverell*'s Tryal, when Things began to change their Aspect; Mr. St[eele] . . . would needs corrupt his Paper with Politicks.'[15] Before Sacheverell's trial, of course, Swift was not yet involved in ministerial politics, and the second half of his quotation shows that the Tories came to find Steele's position anything but 'attractive'. Steele adopts the pose of impartiality, but as Ophelia Field has observed, he 'slipp[ed] in a good deal of Whig editorializing. He avoided the usual tone of the propagandist', but he did not avoid propaganda.[16]

In late 1709 and early 1710, Steele engages less directly with political controversy than he had previously, but that shifts during the controversial ministerial change of summer 1710. While the Whigs were in power, Steele wrote from a position of comfortable superiority, celebrating 'the *British Nation*' for being 'at a greater Height of Glory . . . than it ever was before' (vol. 2, p. 170). Steele basks in the glow of a nation well led by his idols: 'It is . . . a particular Happiness to a People, when the Men of Superior Genius and Character are so justly disposed in the high Places of Honour', and so on (vol. 2, p. 256). This was February 1710. By June, *The Tatler*'s outlook had darkened. In no. 183, Steele has Bickerstaff grumble about the 'universal Degeneracy from that publick Spirit, which ought to be the first and principal Motive' for human actions (vol. 2, p. 491). Up to this point, Bickerstaff has very occasionally protested moral laxity, but without a trace of political sourness. Throughout the rest of the life of *The Tatler*, he reflects on the failures of patriotism and implies distrust of the powers that be. That no. 183 finds Bickerstaff rereading Tacitus – cynical historian of Roman power politics – is not surprising.

The Tatler is inconsistent. It is always Whig in orientation, but as Whig fortunes change, naturally so does Steele's mood. As Knight and others have noted, Steele is conspicuously silent about the Sacheverell trial, but in the wake of that *cause célèbre* he does sharply observe that the world has turned upside down: 'the whole People are taken with a Vertigo, great and popular Actions are received with Coldness and Discontent, ill News hoped for with Impatience, Heroes . . . are treated with Calumny, while

---

[14] Knight, *Political Biography*, 51.
[15] Swift, *English Political Writings 1711–1714*, p. 221.
[16] Field, *Kit-Cat Club*, p. 196.

Criminals pass through . . . with Acclamations' (vol. 3, p. 16). This passage comes from a letter from 'Pasquin of Rome' to Bickerstaff,[17] in which Steele has Pasquin puzzle over 'the Words *Indefeazable* and *Revolution*', reflecting his manifest unhappiness about the renewed currency of high-Tory dogma (16). Pasquin goes on to allude to the story 'of *Hanno* the *Carthaginian*, and his irreconcilable Hatred to the glorious Commander *Hannibal*' (17). Hannibal clearly represents Marlborough, and the 'Faction at Home' that 'recal[ls] him from the midst of his Victories' stand in for the Tories.

Little has been said by critics about Steele's response to the ministerial change. At the time of this *Tatler*, the Whigs had not yet been entirely removed from office: Godolphin fell in August, the Whig dismissal was complete in September, and in October the Whigs were routed in the General Election. Writing in June, Steele shows his awareness of the way in which the political winds are blowing, likely hoping to revive and/or foster support for the Junto. Pasquin's letter concludes with an ominous warning to English readers: Hanno '*will Smile to have purchased the Ruin of* Hannibal, *tho' attended with the Fall of* Carthage' (18). *The Tatler* here functions as pro-Marlborough propaganda at a time when the general was increasingly vulnerable, as pro-Whig propaganda on the eve of the Whig fall from power. The Tory *Moderator* of 3 July targets Steele for this issue, and more generally for entering the political fray. *The Tatler* had previously 'diverted the Town', but now 'hath joined in the cry with' *The Observator* and *The Review*, 'in hopes . . . that by his additional strength they shall become such a formidable Triumvirate that all opposition must fall before them'. In no. 191, Steele offers a portrait of the 'Cunning' *Polypragmon* (vol. 3, p. 33), which might or might not have been meant to satirise Harley; no. 193 also includes oblique criticism of Harley's management. In July 1710 – still before Godolphin's removal – Steele includes a letter from 'Cato Junior', scolding him for 'turn[ing] Politician'. The letter-writer refuses to believe that Steele has been 'bribed by the Staggering Party', but cannot understand why he would so foolishly 'offend the very better Half of the Nation' (50). Steele's response is neither defensive nor apologetic: 'This Gentleman and I differ about the Words Staggering and Better Part' (51). The Tory ascendance was (we now know) imminent, but in a moment of crisis, Steele evidently sought to bolster support for the endangered Whig regime. This issue precedes the account of Stanhope's victory – a reminder that the Allied forces are helping the Whig administration fulfill its promise of a good peace.

Steele's Tory opponents were quick to savage him for his escalating partisanship. In his *Annotations on the Tatler* (2 parts; Aug–Sep 1710), William

---

[17] In *The Review*, Defoe also has the Scandal Club receive letters from Pasquin (no. 7).

Oldisworth – who took control of *The Examiner* in late 1711 – devotes himself to sensitising readers to the nature and extent of Steele's politicking. As I argue in the next chapter, Oldisworth not only highlights the presence of abuse in Steele's works, but he also implies the partisanship of Steele's moralising. Oldisworth seeks both to affirm (perhaps to exaggerate) *The Tatler*'s political objectives and to undermine the legitimacy of Bickerstaff's prognostications. His 'Politicks and Predictions... make an admirable Medley', since he is 'not too particular' about what he is prophesying. Bickerstaff can confidently declare '*There will be a Peace*' because he does not 'insist... on Chronological Niceties' (vol. 1, p. 73). When Oldisworth sneers at those '*Romantick* Writers' who 'make even Impossibilities *Credible* and *Real*' (vol. 2, p. 97) we know of whom he speaks. Bond dismisses Oldisworth's remarks as 'rather pointless',[18] but Oldisworth – not unlike his ally Swift – contests Whig political prophecy. He also alerts readers to the relationship between language and politics, to the ways in which words and phrases can suggest more 'Design' than we might imagine. What the *Annotations* make crystal clear, moreover, is that as of August 1710, Tories were no longer able to ignore the popular *Tatler*'s increasing partisanship.

A commonplace about Addison and Steele is that they mock newsmongers and a generally news-crazed populace, but Steele's disparagement becomes much more prominent in the second half of *The Tatler*. His critique of the 'Battle-Critick' concludes with a denigration of those 'Malecontents, in the only Nation that suffers profess'd Enemies to breath in open Air' (vol. 1, p. 450). This is one of a very few instances in which Steele voices scepticism about 'free' speech – but it specifically targets Tory decriers of Marlborough's victory. In October 1710, after the dismissal of the Whig ministry, Steele scorns the news-hungry Upholsterer, but that Upholsterer is devouring *Tory* papers, *The Moderator* and *The Post Boy* and the 'admirable' *Examiner* (vol. 3, p. 201). Steele disapprovingly wonders 'how it should be possible that this Turn to Politicks should so universally prevail, to the Exclusion of every other Subject out of Conversation' (202). Again, timing matters: the strength of popular Toryism on display in the wake of the Sacheverell trial must have alarmed Steele. Parsons's conclusion is spot on: 'While the *Tatler*'s bias against the public's use of news was evident from its very first number, it was reinvigorated by the trial, particularly by the role the press played in engaging the general reading public with the serious issues under debate.'[19] What this means is that we

---

[18] *Tatler*, vol. 1, p. xxiii.
[19] Nicola Parsons, *Reading Gossip in Early Eighteenth-Century England* (Basingstoke, 2009), p. 106.

should not assume that Steele's position on public politics in 1710 accurately reflects his settled opinion on the subject. To Steele's assessment of popular political engagement, we will return in the next section.

Steele's critique of satire likewise emerges relatively late in *The Tatler*. Because *The Spectator* is so outspoken in its rejection of Hobbesian laughter and mean-spirited satire, scholars have tended to overstate the presence of such censure in its predecessor. In fact, for a long while Bickerstaff has nothing bad to say about satire. In November 1709 (no. 92), Steele defends it by dissociating it from libel: 'the Satyrist and Libeller differ as much as the Magistrate and the Murderer', as the former 'never falls upon Persons who are not glaringly faulty', and the latter 'on none but who are conspicuously commendable' (vol. 2, p. 74). Only near the end of *The Tatler*'s life does Bickerstaff pronounce 'Good-Nature' to be 'an essential Quality in a Satyrist' (vol. 3, p. 241). Bickerstaff warns that satire only works when the satirist 'throws himself quite out of the Question' (244). Steele's advocacy of ego-less satire is related to his characteristic sponsorship of ego-less (public-minded) politics. His insistence upon benevolent satire comes only after he has begun to squabble with his Tory rivals, and after his complaint that Mr. Examiner's 'Method of Criticism' involves 'turn[ing] into Ridicule any Work that was ever written' (vol. 3, p. 229). Steele implicitly links Tory satire with the factious un-patriotism of Swift *et al.*, which anticipates his and Addison's strategy in *The Spectator*. In that periodical, as Ronald Paulson has shown, Addison and Steele denounce satire as a way of satirising the Tories. They define satire as Juvenalian, targeting Tory lampoonery and insinuating the superiority of their own Horatian *sermones*.[20] In *The Tatler*, though he does so only briefly, Steele is beginning to make a similar argument – and, crucially, only after the emergence of *The Examiner* onto the journalistic scene.[21]

After Bickerstaff: Steele's political aims as a journalist

How did Steele's journalistic role evolve after *The Tatler*? His first venture was the much more collaborative *Spectator*, an enterprise even less directly engaged with politics than its predecessor. Before turning to *The*

---

[20] Ronald Paulson, *The Fictions of Satire* (Baltimore, 1967), pp. 216, 218.
[21] See Ashley Marshall, 'Steele's Rhetorical Duel with the Authors of *The Examiner*', *Swift Studies* 34 (2019), pp. 67–89.

Guardian, The Englishman, and Steele's other later party journals, something needs to be said about the nature of political commentary in Steele's contributions to *The Spectator*.

Steele as 'very busy Spectator'[22]

The Tatler abruptly ended on 2 January 1711, and *The Spectator* commenced two months later (1 March). Addison and Steele were involved in the first series of *The Spectator* (nos. 1–555), helped by others; the second series was carried out by Addison and others but without Steele. Of the first 555 issues, Bond definitively attributed 251 contributions each to Addison and Steele, though he accentuated the inequity of their roles. 202 of Addison's numbers are independent essays; 162 of Steele's consist of letters, probably genuine submissions from other people.[23] The longer pieces tend to be by Addison. Perhaps Steele was less engaged with *The Spectator*, less committed to using it as a repository for his reflections. His reliance on outside letters also signals a different attitude toward the public sphere: whereas Addison tends to 'tell people what to think', Steele's polyphonic contributions model not only dialogue but also inquiry, encouraging commoners to ask questions in a public forum. Bond offered a tonal difference between Addison's and Steele's numbers, as well: the former is more various and comedic, the latter more serious (vol. 1, p. lx).

What is the politics of *The Spectator*? Unlike *The Tatler*, this new venture included no news reports. Most scholars have described it as indirectly ideological, representing Whig values positively. *The Spectator* project, in Cowan's telling, was a 'response to the crisis of Whig political fortunes in the later years of Queen Anne's reign', a reaction to Tory resurgence. Addison and Steele, he continues, deny the Church's exclusive ability to serve as a moral guide, offering the 'reformed coffeehouse' as an alternative foundation.[24] Downie has highlighted the politicisation of the early numbers of *The Spectator*s, which call attention to a potential credit crisis faced by Anne's new Tory ministry. Downie conjectures, plausibly, that the timing of the launch of *The Spectator* could signal Addison's intentions 'to perpetuate the period of political instability which the change of government had precipitated'.[25] Had *The Spectator* closed after a dozen issues, scholars would not be as inclined to de-politicise its initial aims.

---

[22] *Spectator*, vol. 1, p. 22.
[23] *Spectator*, vol. 1, pp. lviii–lix.
[24] Cowan, 'Mr. Spectator and the Coffeehouse Public Sphere', p. 349.
[25] Downie, 'Periodicals and Politics', p. 54.

My concern is with Steele's contributions. His position on public politics is not, in *The Spectator*, what it will become in later papers, but as usual he shows more approval of popular political education than Addison. Without appealing to the people to be outspoken, Steele does insinuate the failings of the regime in a way that fosters public scrutiny and judgment-rendering. In no. 103, he complains, 'The World is grown so full of Dissimulation and Compliment, that Mens Words are hardly any Signification of their Thoughts' (vol. 1, p. 430). He had earlier described a 'good Courtier's Habit and Behaviour' as 'hieroglyphical' (pp. 275–76), highlighting a disparity between appearance and reality and inviting readers to be sceptical and critical. I agree with Terence Bowers, who regards *The Spectator* 'as a fundamentally enfranchising political project', establishing 'the protocols of the public sphere', 'redefin[ing] citizenship, and show[ing] eighteenth-century readers the way to civic enfranchisement'.[26]

That Steele disapproved of the Tory regime is to be expected, but the sourness of *The Spectator* has not been sufficiently appreciated. As Bickerstaff, Steele had initially enjoyed writing from a position of comfortable Whig superiority; during the life of *The Tatler*, Anne changed her ministry and Bickerstaff grew discontented, defensive of the ousted Whig leaders and unable to resist sparring with the Tory *Examiner*. The first series of *The Spectator* was written during the period of Tory dominance, and Steele must have recognised the futility of challenging the popular new administration head-on. Instead, he is quietly subversive, portraying power as corrupt: 'The Ambition of Princes is many times as hurtful to themselves as their People' (vol. 2, p. 282). Steele again invokes Tacitus, who found the political world to be dominated by hypocrisy, self-interest, malice, and sycophancy.

Steele's disapprobation is mitigated by the genial banter and easy moralism of *The Spectator*, but there is no denying the essential darkness of his portrayal of the powers-that-be. In no. 294, he describes those 'drawn in Pomp and Equipage', who 'with an Air of Scorn and Triumph overlook... the Multitude that pass by them'. On the same street, he continues, one sees 'a Creature of the same Make crying out in the Name of all that is good and sacred to behold his Misery' (vol. 3, p. 47). Empathy permeates the whole of *The Tatler* and *The Spectator*, but Steele also highlights the fact that the well-to-do (including the powerful) are singularly unreceptive to the suffering commoners. That the miserable 'Creature' begs not only for food but to be seen ('behold') seems telling. Though this is not a partisan passage, Steele does appear to

---

[26] Terence Bowers, 'Universalizing Sociability: *The Spectator*, Civic Enfranchisement, and the Rule(s) of the Public Sphere', in Donald J. Newman (ed.), *The Spectator: Emerging Discourses* (Newark, DE, 2005), 150–74, pp. 152–53.

position himself as an outsider, as a spokesman for the marginalised. Bowers argues that 'Addison and Steele extended to plebeian depths the opportunity for individuals to participate in polite forms of association and become members of the public',[27] a compelling conclusion. Throughout Steele's political journalism, he takes pains to represent the meanest subjects, validating their own right to demand such representation.

Steele's hostility to flattery, another prevalent theme of his *Spectator* papers, is specifically political, if not obviously partisan. In language not unlike that of Trenchard's and Gordon's in *Cato's Letters* (1720–1721), he frequently glances at the sycophantic courtier, the excessively 'obsequious' men who fancy themselves significant but are in fact 'in the fifth or sixth Degree of Favour with a Minister' (vol. 2, p. 508). The bootlicker is contemptible, as is the man demanding that his boots be licked: 'AMONG all the Diseases of the Mind there is not one ... more pernicious than the Love of Flattery' (424). Elsewhere Steele offers the pointed reminder that 'the Character of the Person who commends you is to be considered, before you set a Value upon his Esteem' (238). That last line seems key, especially when read in the context of Steele's ongoing feud with Mr. Examiner, whom he continually reviles as a ministerial toady. Did he have his erstwhile friend Swift in mind? The upshot of Steele's reflections is straightforward: the world of power is corrupt, and the Great – who are not good – have to be propped up by fawning hangers-on. The sycophants include public propagandists such as Mr. Examiner, and their pronouncements are at best suspect.

At a time when direct partisan engagement must have seemed futile, Steele is mostly able to avoid direct confrontation. But I have no doubt that his systematic exposure of the debasement of the court and the perniciousness of self-interested and dissimulating sycophants was politically motivated. In the context of c. 1711, Steele evidently (probably wisely) reasoned that negative implication served as a more potent weapon than direct abuse. The bottom line: Steele's *Spectator* contributions were meant, among other things, to condition readers to distrust both those at the helm and also the zealous pens who defended them.

Moral politics: The Guardian

The Guardian (12 Mar–1 Oct 1713) appears in retrospect to have been a transitional enterprise – partly political, partly socio-moral – between *The Spectator* and the more forceful *Englishman*.[28] More than any of Steele's

---

[27] Bowers, 'Universalizing Sociability', p. 159.
[28] John Calhoun Stephens concludes that Steele was sole author of at least 57 of *The Guardian* numbers; my discussion here is based upon those contributions. Other

other Stuart journals, *The Guardian* focuses upon the ethical obligations of citizens and leaders; its politics have more to do with morality than political expediency.

The effect of *The Guardian* depends upon the persona of Nestor Ironside, who calls to mind Homer's wise King of Pylos (Nestor of Gerania) and who assures readers that he is without bias. In the inaugural issue, he promises, 'I shall be impartial, tho' I cannot be Neuter' (43). Steele's position in *The Guardian* connects, however indirectly, to his and especially Addison's critique of satire in *The Spectator* and *The Tatler*. Their criticism often highlights the problem of ego in public discourse: in *Spectator* no. 35, Addison looks down upon those whose 'Ridicule is always Personal' (vol. 1, p. 148). *The Tatler* no. 242 insists that effectual satire cannot be subjective: 'There is no Possibility of succeeding in a Satyrical Way of Writing or Speaking, except a Man throws himself quite out of the Question' (vol. 3, p. 244). Although *The Guardian* has little to say, directly, about ridicule, Steele does attempt to establish his authority – and to contest that of Mr. Examiner *et al.* – by presenting himself as selfless and impartial. The pose is affirmed in no. 76, when Ironside voices his desire 'to preserve Peace and Love', to be a 'Universal *Guardian*' who looks for common ground between 'the Landed and the Trading Interests' in an effort 'to make them both sensible that their mutual Happiness depends upon their being Friends' (280). No other Steele eidolon achieves the same kind of self-effacement as the anonymous Mr. Spectator, who seeks social invisibility, but the impulse is present in much of his journalism.

The context in which Steele's occasional partisan commentary appears is important. John Calhoun Stephens points out that only a dozen of the 175 *Guardian* issues explicitly 'deal with party matters'.[29] Given what Steele evidently wished to do in *The Guardian*, this is an effective strategy. The seemingly grudging nature of Ironside's foray into party politics lends moral authority to his judgments. He is a reluctant partisan, compelled by love of country to offer intermittent, necessary warnings and reflections on current affairs. This pose – recalling Juvenal's *difficile est saturam non scribere* – represents a powerful alternative to Mr. Examiner, whom Steele portrays as insolent, contentious, and unrelentingly antagonistic.

Appeals to public spirit and patriotism are more central to *The Guardian* than to *The Englishman* or Steele's contributions to *The Spectator*. The

---

contributors include Addison, Pope, Budgell, Gay, and Parnell; Stephens (ed.), *The Guardian* (Lexington, KY, 1982), p. 23. When Steele decided to run for Parliament, Addison essentially took control of *The Guardian*.

[29] *The Guardian*, p. 35.

title of this venture signals a crucial feature of Ironside's aspiration: his job is to protect the country and the reputations of good men savaged by the likes of Mr. Examiner. In no. 41, an anonymous letter-writer voices disapprobation of *The Examiner*'s insolent allusions to the Earl of Nottingham's daughter: 'If Life be (as it ought to be with People of their Character, whom the *Examiner* attacks) less valuable and dear than Honour and Reputation, in that proportion is the *Examiner* worse than an Assassin' (168). In no. 53, 'Steele' offers similar censure: in a letter to Ironside, waxing self-sacrificial, he warmly defends the venerable the Whigs, including Marlborough. Mr. Examiner:

> is welcome from henceforward to treat me as he pleases; but as you have began to oppose him, never let Innocence or Merit be traduced by him. In particular, I beg of you, never let the Glory of our Nation, who made *France* tremble . . . be calumniated in so impudent a manner. . . . Let not a Sett of Brave, Wise and Honest Men, who did all that has been done to place their Queen in so great a Figure . . . be treated by ungenerous Men as Traytors and Betrayers. To prevent such Evils is a Care worthy a Guardian. (210)

Steele's selflessness is part of the point: the true patriot will risk partisanship, and the inevitable abuse from his rivals, in order to defend the best men from defamation.

The apolitical numbers often concern sympathy and empathy, pity and conscience. These more philosophical, socio-moral reflections have the effect of lending the political commentary considerable moral weight. As scholars have argued in their discussions of *The Spectator* and *The Tatler*, Steele's dichotomy is clear: on the one side, aggressive polemic and ministerial flattery; on the other, patriotism and benevolence. If Steele's *Spectator* essays indirectly expose the unprincipled sycophancy of the ministerial hacks like Mr. Examiner, then *The Guardian* complements that critique by claiming the moral high ground over those ego-driven rivals. Mr. Examiner was, at this time, fixated on Steele and Ironside, which should caution us against underestimating the partisanship of *The Guardian*. The 22 May 1713 issue of *The Examiner* notes Oldisworth's and Steele's mutual obsession: 'I Begin to apprehend, that *The Guardian* and I shall do little Service to the Publick, if we go on in Skirmishes against each other' (vol. 4, p. 2). Oldisworth connects *The Guardian* to the perceived anti-Harley satire in *The Tatler*, recalling Steele's Polypragmon portrait in numbers otherwise devoted to animadversions on *The Guardian*. Throughout the fall and winter of 1713, he mocks Steele, who 'hath for some time labour'd to Quarter the *Guardian* upon the *Examiner*' (vol. 4, p. 35).

On power and public politics: The Englishman *(I)*
The Englishman (first series, 6 Oct 1713–15 Feb 1714) reflects Steele's increasing outspokenness about political power and his escalating commitment to politicising the public. Scholars have limited their discussions of Steele and the public sphere to analyses of *The Tatler* and especially *The Spectator*, usually concluding that neither Addison nor Steele were particularly comfortable with public politics. Cowan suggests that they sought 'to close off and restrain, rather than to open up, venues for public debate . . . on matters of political concern'.[30] Cowan acknowledges that differences between 'the *Spectator* project' and Steele's other writings, but little has been said about those works or Steele's evolving position on public politics.

In the spring of 1713, Steele's polemics somewhat abruptly begin to feature assertions about royal authority and its limits. In his *Letter to Sir M[iles] W[harton] Concerning Occasional Peers* (March), he reflects upon Anne's dubious manoeuvre of creating a dozen new peers in order to secure a vote in favour of the Tory ministry's peace treaty. Though 'Sovereigns upon Earth' are hailed as 'Fountains of Honour', they are 'alas! . . . themselves diminished in Proportion to what they grant out of themselves'. The arbitrary creation of peers 'is the greatest Wound that can be given to the Prerogative', and invites justified popular dissension.[31] *The Examiner* tends to collapse the distance between royal prerogative and popular will, portraying the interests of the people as naturally in line with those of the sovereign. Steele does the opposite. In *The Importance of Dunkirk* (1713), he complains that the 'word Prerogative' has come to be employed by Tories 'to frighten Men from speaking what they lawfully may upon publick Occurrences'.[32] Not only does he suggest conflict between the will of the Queen and that of her people, but he also advocates popular engagement with politics. Again and again, Steele asserts a populist position: 'the Executive Power is a Prerogative . . . vested in the Head of the Constitution, for the Good of the whole'. He goes so far as to remind readers that when he and Anne perish, 'the Remains of Her Sacred Person [will be] as common Dust as mine'.[33]

To find Steele espousing basic Whig ideology is not surprising, but the degree to which this political philosophising dominates his late Stuart journalism needs to be recognised. So does the radical nature of his pronouncements about popular politics. As a political journalist, Steele's role – at least

---

[30] Cowan, 'Mr. Spectator and the Coffeehouse Public Sphere', p. 346.
[31] Steele, *Tracts and Pamphlets*, pp. 74, 75.
[32] Steele, *Tracts and Pamphlets*, p. 113.
[33] Steele, *Tracts and Pamphlets*, pp. 115, 123.

in 1713–1714 – is to remind readers of their (ancient) constitutional rights and of their patriotic duty to be a check on governmental excesses. As the inaugural issue of *The Englishman* makes clear, Steele appreciated that the time of civic passivity had passed: 'It is not ... now a Time to improve the Taste of Men by Reflections and Railleries of Poets and Philosophers, but to awaken their Understanding' (5). No. 3 opens with a message for Anne's subjects: 'It is the Happiness of an *Englishman*, that his Property is fenced about with Laws and Privileges, into which no Power can make any Incursion, except it is encouraged by his own Stupidity or Cowardice' (14). Steele acts as legal counsellor. He also empowers the people he advises: his first issue concludes, with remarkable defiance, 'I am accountable to no Man, but the greatest Man in *England* is accountable to me' (10).

Later in *The Englishman*, he includes an unsigned letter from a concerned citizen insisting that though the prince may choose his ministers, 'it is the Privilege of the People by their Representatives, to judge of, and even to arraign the Conduct of [the] Ministers' (pp. 75–76). The subject can be penalised for overstepping, but so can authorities: all are 'equally punishable by Law' (76). This patriotic missive eloquently endorses the use of journalism to provoke the people toward righteous defence of their liberties: 'An *Englishman* may speak his Opinion *without Doors* as well as *within Doors*: He may, nay he ought to have a jealous Eye upon the Officers and Servants of his Prince: He may, and he ought to alarm his Fellow-Subjects'. The letter-writer urges Steele on: 'I conjure you ... to cry aloud and spare not whenever you shall see Occasion' (75). The Englishman's job is 'to inculcate' such 'Notions ... frequently to ... Readers'. By 'making them publick' in his journal, Steele can 'put every *Englishman* a little upon this Train of thinking, for the Security of his Religion and Property to himself and his Posterity' (76). Throughout *The Englishman*, Steele reminds readers that England is a limited monarchy, that the sovereign is easily tempted toward absolutism, and that in this '*Capital of Liberty* ... the Property of the meanest Subject is ... strongly guarded by our Laws' (115).[34] Later, in the four numbers of *The Plebeian* (1719), Steele obsesses again over balance of power issues, asserting the sanctity of the ancient constitution and the divisions of power it establishes.[35]

Obedience and disobedience figure prominently in *The Englishman*. No. 55 includes a letter from 'Constant Churchman', who chastises pulpit-politicians like Sacheverell for 'perverting ... the Notions of Right betwixt Kings and their Subjects'. Steele had glanced at this subject in *The Tatler*

---

[34] See also *The Englishman*, pp. 115–16, 128, 167–68, 184.
[35] See for instance *Tracts and Pamphlets*, pp. 474–76.

no. 44, where he comically likens those practicing passive obedience to the dolls controlled by a puppeteer named Martin Powell. Here, in *The Englishman*, Steele has the churchman express his own scepticism about the Tory belief in non-resistance. He complains about those 'foolish Strains of Obedience without Reserve', which prevent a country from 'defend[ing] it self against Tyranny and Oppression'. Significantly, he looks back to the ministerial change: 'the Change proceeded from Approbation of the passive side, and Dislike of that of Resistance', which meant that 'young Clergymen and Time-servers made their Court by throwing themselves into the Scale of unlimited Loyalty' (219). Steele defines the Tories as sycophants – an implicit theme of *The Spectator* – and gives moral primacy to patriotic resistance over passive obedience. 'Constant Churchman' reappears in the following issue, where he sternly observes, 'I Believe our Church never did either receive, determine, or teach Passive-Obedience dogmatically, as a positive Doctrine' (224). The churchman's missive expounds the reasons for rethinking the Tory commitment to such credenda. Steele's *Romish Ecclesiastical History of Late Years* (May 1714) targets high-flyers committed to divine hereditary right and non-resistance, but (recalling 'Constant Churchman') he dedicates the pamphlet to the son of Nottingham – a loyal churchman who was adamantly supportive of the Hanoverian succession.

The Englishman not only gainsays Steele's Tory opponents; it raises questions about the value and limits of obedience. Steele's strategy is twofold: undercut Tory notions of passive, unpatriotic, loyalism; and remind citizens of their obligation to defend their rights. In no. 8, Steele prints a letter from 'Anglo-Britannicus' urging him to continue in his galvanisation of the people: 'I hope, Sir, you will . . . let [your countrymen] know it is their Duty to study Politicks as well as Ethicks or Morals' (37). The best-known instance of Steele's presumptuousness, vis-à-vis authority, occurs in *The Guardian* no. 128: 'The *British* Nation expect the immediate Demolition' of Dunkirk (426). This passage is typical of his 1713–1714 attitude toward the relationship between the governors and the governed. In the same number, he maintains that, 'the very Common People know, that within three Months after the signing of the Peace, the Works towards the Sea were to be demolished' (426). Steele repeats this position – and this language – in *The Importance of Dunkirk Consider'd* (1713).[36] As in his role as 'Tatler' and 'Spectator', here he stresses surveillance, in this case civic surveillance, not only passing his own judgment but also doing two other, crucial things: taunting authorities with the knowledge of an aware and righteously disappointed public; and inviting that public to feel and express outrage. Swift

---

[36] *Tracts and Pamphlets*, p. 96.

took exception to Steele's politicisation of the people: in *The Importance of the Guardian Considered*, he complained of Steele's temerity in reflecting on the government, and of his insistence that 'it is every Man's Right to find fault with the Administration in Print, whenever they please' (230).

Steele's encouragement of popular politicisation is an effective complement to his distrust of blind obedience. In the second issue of *The Englishman*, he asserts, 'AMONG us it is so far lost, that it has been made a kind of political Faith to submit to the Infringement of Liberty' (12). That paper depicts lawful resistance as public spirit, clearly insinuating that the present regime's actions invite righteous opposition. In the preface to the second series of *The Englishman*, Steele would highlight this agenda: 'THE Former Volume ... was written with a direct Intention to destroy the Credit, and frustrate the Designs of Wicked Men, at that Time in Power' (252). Steele's use of journalism to undermine the ministry is perhaps more radical than it now seems. Read alongside *The Examiner* and other obedience-preaching journals, his insistence that the authorities are answerable to the people seems remarkably progressive. Swift and other Tory writers argued that subjects had no right to reflect upon governmental proceedings; Steele does not call for rebellion, but to contend that the people should be vigilant judges of ministerial actions represents an entirely different sense of journalistic mission.

Challenging the ministry and ministerial propaganda: The Lover and The Reader

In the first half of 1714, Steele launched two short-lived, overlapping periodicals, both of which challenge the Harley ministry and have been completely ignored by scholars. *The Lover* appeared on 25 February 1714, ten days after the conclusion of *The Englishman*'s first series; it ran to 40 tri-weekly numbers, concluding on 27 May. A month earlier, Steele had introduced *The Reader*, which lasted only a couple of weeks, terminating before *The Lover* ended. Neither of these ventures gets much attention; even in Winton's admirably thorough account of Steele they are barely alluded to even *en passant*.

The Lover – 'in imitation of the Tatler' and penned by Sir Marmaduke Myrtle – is almost exclusively devoted to manners and morals.[37] Almost exclusively, but not exclusively. Knight hypothesises that *The Lover* served as 'a relief from the intensive politicking and *Examiner* examining of the

---

[37] *The Lover* and *The Reader* were reprinted together in 1715 in a single collection.

Englishman',[38] though the fact that Steele started the pointedly political *Reader* during the course of *The Lover* suggests that he was not weary of partisan battle. As Steele was writing *The Lover*, Harley appeared to be losing his contest with St. John; his domestic alliances were broken or breaking (e.g., with Lady Masham); his position vis-à-vis the Queen was precarious. Steele's sudden turn back to *Tatler*-esque socio-moral reflections might reflect hopefulness about the fragility of the Tory ministry. The paper's most significant political agenda involves mockery of Harley, perhaps an attempt to capitalise on the lord treasurer's vulnerability. In no. 11, Steele depicts the Crabtree family as having been 'bred Presbyterians', though they are now disingenuously 'set up for High Church-men. They carry it admirably well, and the Partizans do not distinguish that there is a difference between those who are of neither side, from generous Principles, and those who are disinterested only from having no Principles at all' (42). Harley was at this point rapidly alienating High Church Tory followers of St. John, which means that Steele's ridicule of his religious hypocrisy has timely propagandistic value. No. 14 continues the attack on the Crabtrees, who are again linked with 'the Phanaticks' (51).

Sir Anthony, 'that merry cunning Fellow' (53), has a talent for 'making Fools of Mankind' (58). In this respect, he resembles the whole 'mischievous . . . Race of the *Crabtrees*', who use 'Arts and Stratagems . . . to impose upon many wise, brave and learned Gentlemen in this County' (58). Steele's charge anticipates that of the 1715 *Englishman*: Harley and his ilk have swindled the nation, misleading otherwise rational citizens into believing that they are protecting the interest of the people. An inept politician, Sir Anthony derives his policies from all the wrong sources: 'his Knighthood has conceived a mighty Opinion of *South* Sea Stock, not from the National and solid Security . . . but from [a] . . . memorable Passage in . . . a Book called *a Tale of a Tub*' (59). The allusion to *A Tale* might well have been meant to implicate Swift, with whom Steele continued to associate *The Examiner*. In no. 21, Steele exposes Sir Anthony as a false friend to the landed class, probably another attempt to appeal for Tory readers to acknowledge their prime minister's charades.

Why drop such particularised political satire into an otherwise non-partisan paper? At a guess, Steele envisioned *The Lover* as a true sequel to some of his earlier periodicals, including *The Tatler* and *The Guardian*. The moralistic aims can be sincere enough, but they also represent an important context for what political argument he wishes to make. The apolitical parts of *The Lover* establish Sir Marmaduke as a trustworthy, dispassionate

---

[38] Knight, *Political Biography*, p. 158.

ethical authority, a reliable arbiter of socio-moral situations. The effectiveness of the targeted criticism of Harley depends upon the establishment – at considerable length – of a disinterested, not-politically-motivated persona.

The Reader is thoroughly polemical and political. Winton describes this new venture as 'a dull paper, totally engaged in wrangling, issue by issue, with the two Tory opponents [*The Examiner* and *The Monitor*]; all the old subjects: the new converts, the succession, Dunkirk, are revived and thrashed once more.'[39] Steele's arguments are not new: he defends the naturalisation of foreign Protestants (144); objects to the creation of new peers (164); and continues his campaign for the demolition of Dunkirk. But his choice of title implies a different focus: he presents himself not as 'guardian' or 'Englishman' but as reader, and specifically as a consumer of daily papers. In the opening issue, his speaker offers this 'Account to the Publick . . . [of] why I appear':

> YOU must know I have a long Time frequented Coffee-houses and read Papers, and spent my Money upon Coffee for the Advantage of Reading the Papers; tho' the Coffee and the Papers also are meer Dryers, and do but hinder my natural Capacity by a forced Liveliness as to the Coffee, and a false Gravity as to the Papers; for as to the former, I have afterwards found my self dispirited thereby, as to the latter, misled rather than enlightened. (143)

Characteristically, Steele's speaker presumes to represent a populace: 'I humbly desire all who, like my self, have been patient or gentle Readers, to take in me, who set up in Behalf of all Persons who . . . have been imposed upon. . . . I step out to do all of those good People Justice' (143). What follows will expose some of the writings that 'have most offended that innocent part of the World' (144).

As elsewhere, Steele is establishing himself (through a persona) as an unbiased observer acting in the interests of all good and loyal citizens. *The Reader* continues his ongoing attack on *The Examiner*, whose author 'has no Conscience' (146), and who 'has a great while had nothing else to utter but meer Words of Passion' (147). The objection, then, is partly tonal: as Mr. Spectator indirectly denied the value of Tory satire, so Steele contests the credibility of 'passionate' journalism. In no. 2, he observes that, 'it has been the Trick . . . to let drop Hints in the *Examiner* . . . of what has been openly avowed afterwards: The Way to any unwelcome Circumstances has been

---

[39] Calhoun Winton, *Captain Steele: The Early Career of Richard Steele* (Baltimore, 1964), p. 208.

paved by some received political Writers' (149). Steele encourages readers to take seriously the troubling intimations of Tory propaganda, and to resist before they become policy. In any case, he seems keen to convince readers to attend to the import of what the ministry's pens are publishing. He goes on to print a particular passage, prefacing it thus: 'The Words which raise my Jealousy are these' (149). We need not get too deep into the particulars of his dispute with Oldisworth, but I do wish to highlight how close to the text he stays in *The Reader*. He is among other things offering a model of textual engagement, promoting and demonstrating a kind of deconstructive analysis. If Steele was, in *The Spectator*, wanting to tell readers what to think rather than pushing them to think for themselves, that is no longer his *modus operandi*. In no. 6 he asserts that 'A Reader that has any Understanding is naturally a Commentator' (164), calling not only for private critical consumption of partisan propaganda but also for public judgment-rendering on it. *The Reader* is Steele's most text-oriented work, engaging at a micro-level with *The Examiner* and its allies. Though his animadversions necessarily lead him to hold forth on the ministry's policies, his primary focus is on the props that support that regime.

These seemingly minor papers have never significantly figured in the modern critical sense of who Steele was a journalist, which is a problem. *The Lover* and *The Reader* help us appreciate the degree to which Steele relied upon a succession of short-lived periodicals: he changes course, adapts, and evolves. They help us recognise not only his persistence in the role of opposition journalist but also his pervasive interest in popular political education. Steele evidently wished these enterprises to be received as separate and distinct, not all the work of the same Whig pen. Significantly, some Tory contemporaries laboured to connect these ventures in the public mind. The author of *A Letter from Will. Honeycomb to the Examiner* (1714) reflects on the 'various Shapes' Steele has 'been dress'd in, to serve a ruin'd Party' (6). Mr. Spectator first gave way to the '*Guardian* of the Liberties of *Great-Britain*' (9), and then 'in an Instant . . . *presto pass*, by a kind of magical Stroke . . . from a Native of *Dublin* turn'd into a True-born *Englishman*' who 'writes and converses with himself' (10). But he 'does not stop here: *Englishman* he'll be no longer . . . and in his Melancholy and Dotage turns *Lover*' (12), before changing yet again into 'a *Reader*' (13).

What would have been the polemical value of connecting these papers? One conceivable explanation is that, like Oldisworth in *The Examiner*, this author sought to reduce what seemed like multiple Whig critics into a single, sad anti-ministerial voice. The author of *A Letter from Will. Honeycomb* also translates Steele's polite civilities into something darker: 'In this character of *Guardian* the Disorder rages violently' (9). His Steele is a bit mad, a Quixote tilting at non-existent Jacobite windmills: 'he ... now and then starts suddenly, and cries out *The Pretender! The Pretender!*' (10).

Popularising the Hanoverian regime: The Englishman *of 1715*

The second series of Steele's *Englishman* (11 Jul–21 Nov 1715) is more focused and polemical than his earlier journalistic ventures. The paper commenced five days before Harley's imprisonment in the Tower, preliminary to his impeachment proceedings; much of this new *Englishman* is devoted to aggressive denunciation of Harley, Anne's last ministry, and their pen-and-pulpit tools. Steele is firm in his own conviction: 'This is ... the State of the Case; and he that will not allow ... *That we and our Allies have been basely Betrayed*, must be in the Interests of the Pretender' (277). Despite that premise, however, *The Englishman* II was evidently meant not only to preach to a choir but to court moderates, to persuade potential defenders of the former ministry to share his judgment. Steele's tone is always sober, restrained, matter-of-fact: he writes, as he reminds readers on occasion, 'without Railing' (325). His earlier varyingly partisan papers had offered ideological conditioning or indirectly opposed the government via seemingly abstract political philosophising. *The Englishman* II announces its aim at the outset and names its targets.

The fact that Steele felt the need to expose the treachery of the previous ministry in July 1715 is important to understanding the impetus behind *The Englishman* II. Harley was in the Tower; St. John and Ormonde were soon to flee to France. By all appearances, the ministry was going to get the comeuppance that Steele thought they so richly deserved for their dealings with France. But as we saw in Chapter 2, the Tories remained the popular party upon George's accession. Steele's revived *Englishman* reflects, then, not vindictive triumphalism or gratuitous partisan abuse but an attempt to cultivate support for the government's proceedings against Anne's last ministers. In no. 1, Steele complains that Harley and his henchmen had 'blinded their Fellow-Subjects with specious Names and Pretences', and have unfortunately 'left ... an Unwillingness in the People to hear the Proofs of their Falshood' (253). The language of this *Englishman* tends to be emotional, and Steele seems eager to convince his not-yet-converted readers to feel hoodwinked: 'We know We have been Betrayed' (254). His choice of the first-person plural – rather than the more divisive second person – is effective here.

What follows is devoted to the recent past, to rehearsing particular problematic episodes (e.g., the Restraining Orders), reprinting and annotating controversial passages from the Tory treaty, and so on. From beginning to end, Steele seeks 'to Explain the false Arts which have been used against this injured Nation, and the false Men who used those Arts, by a plain State of Facts' (254). Variations on this promise – 'plain State of Facts' – recur, signaling Steele's desire to persuade readers of his objectivity and of the historical rather than polemical nature of his argument. The journalist operates as a courtroom lawyer, vowing to 'make good this Charge [of treason against the former ministers] to the Conviction of every Man living' (255). The first number of *The Englishman* II sets out the principal charges against the accused; the second offers as background a historical understanding of treason laws; in the rest, Steele slowly, strategically makes his case. Though neither St. John nor Ormonde are blameless, *The Englishman* attributes the greatest portion of villainy to Harley: 'there is no Crime in the whole Treaty . . . in which he does not appear to have had the principal Part' (271). After disparaging the former lord treasurer, Steele pauses to affirm the justice of his critique: 'This would be a railing Accusation, if it appeared . . . that the Errors of this Gentleman, and the rest employed by him, were the Mistakes of Men who intended honest things' (257). Steele's tonal control in *The Englishman* II is masterful: he manages to seem neither spiteful nor smug, to write more in sorrow than in anger, to depersonalise his condemnation of the former government.

Steele's antagonism toward Harley here continues a thread evident at the end of Anne's reign. *The Tatler* had, in the summer of 1710, offered what now appears to have been indirect criticism of the 'Cunning' politician. *The Englishman* no. 57 (first series) likewise glances obliquely at Harley, bringing his 'famed evasiveness and his allegedly equivocal attitude toward the Church together in an anecdote'.[40] In *The Lover*, in the spring of 1714, he portrayed Harley as Sir Anthony Crabtree and caricatured some of Harley's relatives, emphasising their religious hypocrisy and self-importance.[41] His October 1714 *apologia pro vita sua*, like the second *Englishman*, censures the now-fallen minister.[42] In June 1715, shortly before the commencement of *Englishman* II, Steele's *Political Writings* were published; that volume 'served as a reminder of the evils of the Oxford administration'.[43] In all of his writings upon Anne's ministry, Steele is conspicuously more hostile to Harley than he is to the high-Tory-turned-Jacobite St. John. As Winton has pointed out, he held Harley personally responsible for his own expulsion from the House of Commons in spring 1714, which contributed to his

---

[40] Calhoun Winton, 'Steele and the Fall of Harley in 1714', *Philological Quarterly* 37 (1958), 440–47, p. 443.
[41] Rae Blanchard discusses this in *Steele's Periodical Journalism*, p. 275.
[42] For example, see *Tracts and Pamphlets*, p. 281.
[43] Knight, *Political Biography*, p. 209.

animus. Winton also notes that Steele's frequent attacks on Harley's dubious religious conviction were meant 'to turn both Dissenting and High Church support away from the Tory Minister'.[44] That Steele hoped to contribute to Harley's fall seems clear, and that aspiration probably partly explains his relative reticence about St. John (Harley's rival, as of spring 1713). It might also account for his association of the libelous *Examiner* with the prime minister,[45] despite its closer alignment with St. John's politics.

The Englishman II contains Steele's most direct denunciation of Harley, though he targets not only the ministry but also the propagandists who propped it up. In no. 13, he reminds readers that, 'THE Treason practised against these Nations was carried on by Persons who had lost all Sense of Honour and Conscience, and their Tools, who never had any Notion of those Motives' (303). The following issue calls out those 'Incendiaries, superficial Wits, and the worst Kind of Men, Ministers of the Gospel', who 'tainted with Avarice and Ambition, were the Instruments made use of to divert the People from a Sense of their true Interest' (309). The reproach of the dissimulating ministerial partisans – the likes of Mr. Examiner as well as high-flying pulpit politicians such as Sacheverell – is not astonishing. It does, however, connect to another part of Steele's agenda, one relevant to our discussion of his attitude toward public politics.

As in his late Stuart papers, Steele encourages readers to read critically and carefully. The fundamental premise behind *The Englishman* II is that the ministers and their hacks have duped – one might fairly say brainwashed – English subjects, and Steele's job is to un-enchant them. In no. 17, he expresses his resentment for the government and its tools, who 'diverted Mankind from making Examinations which the Ministers knew their Actions could not bear'. The '*Populace*' has been misled, he continues, and then he defines his term: 'I mean by the *Populace*, all People who do not think for themselves' (318). Implied here is the demand that readers try to be less susceptible to such trickery, that true English citizens separate themselves from the gullible masses by exercising their critical thinking. In *The Englishman* II, Steele simply states overtly something that is a part of his agenda from *The Tatler* on. To wit, he is always concerned with cultivating better habits of reading, and that reading is rarely entirely apolitical. As in the first series of *The Englishman*, moreover, Steele here calls into question the value of obedience. While shrewdly maintaining that George

---

[44] Winton, 'Steele and the Fall of Harley', pp. 443, 444.
[45] Steele perceived *The Examiner* 'not only as a paper supporting Oxford and the Tory ministry, but as a paper that is, in effect, under Oxford's direct control, so that he is responsible for its scurrilous attacks [on] Marlborough, Wharton, and Steele himself' (Knight, *Political Biography*, p. 141).

has 'a better Title to the Throne ... than any Prince in any Country, in any Age' (339), he reiterates his warning against assuming 'that the Nature of Government requires an absolute Submission' (338). The revived *Englishman* is manifestly an attempt to lay bare the crimes and misdemeanours of the former regime, but his project is not merely backward-looking. Instead, Steele appears determined to expose some of the mechanisms by which a corrupt ministry had managed to convince English subjects of its patriotism. He is trying, in other words, to train better, warier citizens.

Let me briefly mention *Town-Talk* (17 Dec 1715–16 Mar 1716), which follows the second *Englishman* series and continues its attack on high Toryism. Though *Town-Talk* was written in part 'to promote interest in the stage',[46] Steele could not avoid partisan politics. The Pretender's doings in January 1716 provoked him to speak out against the Jacobite threat. He rebukes Anne's last ministry for their Jacobite aspirations: 'being resolved' to install James III, they 'became, instead of Guardians of the People, their Betrayers' (223). *Town-Talk* is for a while preoccupied by the rebellion, by the threat of the Pretender, and by legitimate and illegitimate notions of succession. Continuing the argument he had been making since at least the initial *Englishman*, Steele objects to Tory proponents of passive obedience and non-resistance. Their followers 'are made to believe' that such ideas 'have something of a venerable and religious Meaning in them', whereas in fact 'they only imply, that a King of *Great Britain* has a Right to be a Tyrant, and that his Subjects are obliged in Conscience to be Slaves' (234). After *Town-Talk*, Steele's next periodicals were *Chit-Chat* (3 numbers; March 1716) and *The Plebeian* (4 numbers; spring 1719). Shortly after George I's accession, he was also serving first as licencee and then as patentee of Drury Lane, and as the Governor of the Royal Company of Comedians.

Self-defensive journalism: The Theatre

On 2 January 1720, Steele launched what turned out to be his last periodical, *The Theatre*, which ran for three months. In its final number, its author reflected on his initial objective: 'THIS Paper was first undertaken, to avert a Clamour, at that time industriously rais'd against the Stage' (121). Steele's governorship of the Royal Company of Comedians, along with his knighthood, constituted his share of the spoils of the new Whig government. In 1720, the Duke of Newcastle suspended Steele from his governorship. *The Theatre* anticipates and objects to Newcastle's interference with him and with the stage more generally. (He was restored to the post by Walpole in

---

[46] Knight, *Political Biography*, p. 179.

1721.) *The Theatre* is a vehicle for self-defence, as well as – significantly – for what Winton calls his broader disapprobation of 'arbitrary authority and bullying'.[47] Its ostensible author is Sir John Edgar, the name of the character who would become Sir John Bevil in *The Conscious Lovers*.[48]

The conflict between Steele and Newcastle – who had become Lord Chamberlain in 1717 – had much to do with the question of the theatre's independence. As Lord Chamberlain, Newcastle was in charge of regulating the theatres, and the quarrel between him and Steele was primarily jurisdictional, 'turning on the ambiguous legal relationship between Lord Chamberlain and patentee'.[49] In 1715, Steele and his actor-manager colleagues – Colley Cibber, Robert Wilks, Barton Booth – had attempted to declare their independence from the (earlier) Lord Chamberlain. Among their acts of defiance was the decision not to submit their plays to the Master of the Revels, who worked for the Lord Chamberlain, for review and approval.[50] When Newcastle took over, he pressed Steele and the actor-managers to resign the royal patent that gave them more independence, in exchange for a theatrical licence ('a less authoritative and durable legal instrument' [xi]). The group naturally refused.

However unhappy Newcastle was with the perceived impingement upon his prerogative, he let the matter go until late 1719, when he and Steele found themselves on opposite sides of the debate over the Peerage Bill. The Bill sought to limit the king's power to create new peers; Steele opposed it, and Newcastle, like Steele's old friend Addison, supported it. While this controversy was playing out, Cibber published his tragedy *Ximena* along with a dedication to Steele, 'in which he combined praise of Steele's political independence with a charge that Steele had been ungenerously treated by the Whig ministry' (xiii). A month later Cibber added insult to insult, defying a directive from Newcastle about casting. In December 1719, Newcastle demanded that Steele, Wilks, and Booth sack Cibber; Steele

---

[47] Calhoun Winton, *Sir Richard Steele, M.P. The Later Career* (Baltimore, 1970), p. 176. Steele also offers devotes several issues to the South Sea Company's proposal to fund the national debt, and his own counter-proposal (see from no. 17 on).

[48] John Loftis discusses *The Theatre*, briefly, as 'in a measure (and much more in unrealised design), a companion piece to the play'; Loftis (ed.) *The Theatre* (Oxford, 1962), p. xxi. For example, 'The scheme for the board of theatrical auditors, described in . . . No. 3, is motivated by the concern with dramatic reform which provided the primary impulse for *The Conscious Lovers*' (p. xx).

[49] Loftis, Introduction to *The Theatre*, p. x. The background information here is a précis of what is offered by Loftis.

[50] The Master of the Revels protested their refusal to pay his fees; see Judith Milhous and Robert D. Hume, 'Charles Killigrew's Petition about the Master of the Revels' Power as Censor (1715)', *Theatre Notebook* 41 (1987), pp. 74–79.

responded with a letter of protest; Newcastle vowed imminent legal action against Steele's patent. As Loftis explains, Steele commenced *The Theatre* 'at this juncture – an order of silence threatened but not yet issued' (xiv).

At the same time, Steele wrote *The State of the Case Between the Lord-Chamberlain . . . and the Governor of the Royal Company of Comedians* (1720), where he accuses Newcastle of overstepping. The Duke had, he complained, 'contrary to Law and Justice, dispossessed me of my Freehold in a manner as injurious to the King his Master, as to me his Fellow-Subject.'[51] His pamphlet reprints the royal patent bestowed upon him and his colleagues, insisting that the patent 'no way opposes or impairs the Authority of a Chamberlain', and insinuating that Newcastle's actions are an attack on the royal prerogative (600). Steele refutes his opponent's right to meddle with his patent, as 'there is no Power which can make it void or ought to frustrate it, except the Patentee. . .'. (604). The indignation carries over from *The State of the Case* to *The Theatre*, despite the introduction in the latter of a persona meant to seem like someone other than Steele.

The Theatre is the work of Sir Richard the martyr, and the self-defence is scarcely made more palatable by the thin disguise of the fictional Sir John's authorship. Few if any of the paper's 28 issues eschew implicit or explicit praise of the patriotic, self-sacrificing Steele. In no. 4, Sir John describes the figure of the '*Whimsical*', someone 'who governs himself according to his own Understanding, in Disobedience to that of others, who are more in Fashion than himself'. The Whimsical 'is, at different times, call'd a Renegade, a Confessor, and a Martyr. . . . This happens from his sticking to Principles, and having no Respect to Persons' (15). Sir John insists that 'Reason . . . is on the side of the derided *Whimsical*', decrying (as Nestor Ironside had in *The Guardian*) those sycophants who offer 'general and slavish Adulation to those that are present' (16). That Steele is patting himself on the back seems obvious: 'Fortitude in a Man's Behaviour, without Distaste, Envy, Malice, or any other indirect Motive, will . . . be crown'd with its due Reward' (17). In the last installment of *The Theatre*, Steele abandons Sir John and writes in his own voice, explaining the rationale of his self-defence and highlighting his own honourable methods: 'I have [not] attempted to raise Indignation against those who have labour'd my Ruine', but have instead been 'contented to say no more than what was absolutely necessary for my Justification, without returning Rage for Rage' (121).

For most of *The Theatre*, Steele appears either (occasionally) as letter-writer or (more frequently) as an upstanding, hardly-done-by character. He is '*THE injur'd Knight*', who 'wants [Sir John's] Favour and Protection' (47).

---

[51] Steele, *Tracts and Pamphlets*, p. 595.

In no. 13, we are told that, '*THE injur'd Knight* has his greatest Complaint still to make, to wit, that he is represented as not having show'd Zeal to his Majesty's Service, in this his Government' (58). Later in *The Theatre*, '*THE injur'd Knight*' returns, a man wrongly 'dispossest of a large Estate, libelled, calumniated, and abused in Speech, Manuscript, and Print' (109). Sir John's incessant acclamation of the ousted-Governor-turned-martyr complements his juster-than-thou reflections about humanity: 'A Man would imagine, that nothing but the utmost Need and Necessity could possibly urge or prompt Man to do Injury to Man' (40).

Steele evidently wished *The Theatre* either to be or at least to seem motivated by something more important and more widely beneficial than self-defence or self-promotion. On several occasions he has Sir John invite readers to find broader meaning: 'my Business, as I take Care of the THEATRE, is to make a Survey of all Humane Nature' (20). Or, as he maintains elsewhere, 'the World and the Stage . . . have been ten thousand times observ'd to be the Pictures of one another' (28). Other than Steele's own plight, then, what is *The Theatre* 'about'? Two answers seem relevant here. One is his message about theatrical independence. Steele confronts, says Loftis, 'the problem of the nature and proper limit of the government's responsibility for the stage' (xvi), something we see particularly clearly in no. 7, where Steele insists that, 'The theater cannot be managed . . . either as an ordinary business is managed, or as a department of the state'.[52] He sets himself up as an 'Advocate' for the theatre (6), and his impulse is clearly to promote English liberty and to object to inappropriate interference.

Both Sir John and Steele also figure in *The Theatre* as spokesmen for the relatively powerless, for the marginalised. Sir John stresses the primacy of character over station: 'a rich Man is only a poor Man supply'd; and . . . all the Pomps and Vanities of haughty and superior Life are but thin Disguises . . . to hide the Weakness and Poverty of humane Life' (64). He underscores the 'difference between Title and Honour', between 'Heraldry and Morality', and between 'a Man's Person and his Cloaths' (71). *The Theatre* no. 25 prints a letter from a commoner to a peer of the realm, and the plebe schools his ostensible better in real nobility: 'Contempt of unjust Gain, which is naturally inherent to generous Minds, brings you at once to the Summet of humane Grandeur' (108).

In the final issue, Steele drops the mask, depicting himself as a representative of ordinary, ill-treated men:

---

[52] Winton, *Sir Richard Steele*, p. 173.

> I took for my Defence the only Method a friendless Man could, to wit, a Method of showing that my Case was that of every Subject in these Dominions. My powerful unprovok'd Adversaries wanted Wit enough, in their Anger, to reflect, that a generous People have always a Concern for the Oppress'd, and Detestation of Oppressors. (121)

The notion that Steele's antagonists – Newcastle foremost among them – were somehow chastened by his journal is a fanciful one, but they are perhaps not his primary concern here. Instead, he seems keen to buoy ordinary citizens, to establish himself as the browbeaten Everyman subjugated by the unjust Great. *The Theatre*, no less than some of Steele's late Stuart papers, is preoccupied with the misuse of power. This particular paper is more desperate than his others; not for nothing does Loftis describe it as 'journalistic shouting' (xv). Among the critics of this paper was the author of *The Commentator* (1720) – Defoe? – who counters Steele's critique of the South Sea Plan and his disaffection from the government more broadly.[53]

Eight numbers of *The Theatre* challenge the South Sea Company's proposal to fund the national debt. Steele addresses this issue in pamphlets, too: both *The Crisis of Property* and *A Nation a Family*, invoked in *The Theatre* no. 17, contest 'the morality of the proposal'. In *The Theatre*, he offers his own alternative plan, 'by which money to pay off the national debt would be raised by selling a large number of life annuities, these to be financed by the government in conjunction with the South Sea Company and to be administered according to a complicated actuarial system'.[54] In opposing the South Sea proposal, Steele is opposing the ministry; he was, however, on the side of Walpole, who would become First Lord of the Treasury and Chancellor of the Exchequer in spring 1721, promptly restoring Steele to his governorship at Drury Lane. Steele's rejection of the South Sea scheme is offered, characteristically, in the name of '*Publick Spirit*' (94). He highlights the hazards 'of putting the Funds for the discharge of the publick Debts, into the Care and Management of the Directors of the *South-Sea*', objecting to the fact that 'the Project undoes the greater [the majority] to inrich the smaller Number' (98). Steele criticises this 'applauded Project' (98), but the fact that it will hurt the many and benefit the few is at the heart of his criticism. His financial arguments, in other words, are inextricably connected to his broader complaint about 'THE Impudence and

---

[53] Daniel Defoe, *Religious and Didactic Writings of Daniel Defoe*, vol. 9: *The Commentator*, ed. P.N. Furbank (London, 2007), p. 10.
[54] Loftis, Introduction to *The Theatre*, pp. xxiii, xxiv.

Injustice with which the Money'd Part of the Mankind behave themselves towards the rest of the World' (101). In *The Theatre*, Steele writes as both patriotic martyr and defender of the common man against the avaricious power-holders. That Knight treats *The Theatre* in a section entitled 'Steele Agonistes' is fitting.

Steele, Mr. Review, and the reader

The differences between Steele and Defoe as journalists are many and important. *The Review* is vastly longer-lived than any of Steele's periodicals, and more comprehensive in its coverage. Defoe's treatment of trade (for him, a global issue) is extensive, and his polemical reports on the war and the peace are more direct and detailed than anything in Steele's oeuvre. Steele has more to say about literary and cultural affairs, and includes more in the way of instructive social tales and encounters. As John McVeagh also points out, 'alluding to Addison and Steele, Swift and Maynwaring . . . [Defoe] declines to dress up political discussion in allegorical Roman dress and opts instead for "a down-right Plainness" which speaks home "both in Fact and in Stile".'[55] Defoe's complicated, equivocal relationship to Harley is of course also categorically unlike Steele's increasing distrust and resentment. Indeed, in February 1714, Defoe complained to Harley about 'The New Champion of The Party', Steele, whose 'Virulent writeings' should be reckoned 'Seditious' and lead to his expulsion from Parliament.[56] The comparison between Steele and Defoe, however, remains a productive one, and Defoe's journalism arguably represents a more helpful context for Steele's late Stuart writing than Addison's.

When Steele launched *The Tatler* in spring 1709, *The Review* was no doubt an important model. Bond aptly describes Defoe's paper as 'the only essay journal to be predecessor, contemporary, and successor to the *Tatler*' and 'the first eminent essay periodical in England to treat political, economic, ecclesiastical, social, and ethical themes'.[57] Defoe had chosen to eschew the popular dialogue form, instead relying upon the essay, which

---

[55] *Review*, vol. 7, pp. xxv–xxvi.
[56] George Harris Healey (ed.), *The Letters of Daniel Defoe* (Oxford, 1955), p. 430 (19 February 1714). *Circa* 10 March 1714, Defoe writes another long missive to Harley, in which he details all the scandalous passages in Steele's *Englishman* and *The Crisis* (pp. 433–39).
[57] Bond, *The Tatler*, p. 128. Bond discusses some of the connections between *The Tatler* and *The Review* (p. 129).

could then integrate letters, lists, and other forms within it. Steele followed suit. McVeagh hypothesises mutual influence: 'Twelve days after Defoe closed his fifth volume ... Steele began the *Tatler*, which ... began defining a new era of polite literature in periodical essay form. Did Defoe sense the shift in the air and steer into new water as a result?'[58] McVeagh points out that 'Defoe acknowledged himself outdone in polite wit by Addison and Steele, saying on one occasion, '*I do not pretend to be famous for my Concern at pleasing you*' but adding that 'If I can serve you it will do every way as well.'[59]

Both *The Review* and *The Tatler* claim reformative purposes, seeking to enlighten and guide the public on a wide range of subjects. Following Dunton's early model, Defoe's Scandal Club allows for broader representation, printing as it does voices other than that of Mr. Review; Steele's public letters, in *The Tatler* and later, function similarly. As Walter Graham warned in 1934, however, we need to be careful in what we assume about influence: dozens upon dozens of periodicals appeared in London at the time of *The Tatler*'s conception, many of them using questions and answers, offering advice, highlighting a reformative agenda, remarking upon a wide range of cultural and political issues, and so on.[60] Without overstating two-way influence, we can probably safely assume that Steele and Defoe were reading each other in 1709–1710. For the purposes of orientation: Defoe's *Review* ended in June 1713; Steele was at that time publishing *The Guardian*, and in October he commenced *The Englishman*.

That Steele and Defoe share similar values is well known, though scholars almost never connect them as similar kinds of writers. Both are prolific pamphleteer-journalists and committed Whigs dedicated to the defence of parliamentary sovereignty, Revolution principles, and Protestantism. *The Review* creates a kind of Protestant public sphere, and at least by 1713 Steele seems actively concerned to do the same. In *The Guardian* no. 90, he has an anonymous letter writer voice outrage that the Francophiliac *Examiner* can publish freely when a loyal Protestant is held in check: 'Is it then become a Crime for a Protestant to speak or write in Defence of his Religion? Shall a Papist have leave to Print and Publish in *England* what he pleases in Defence of his own Opinion, with the *Examiner*'s Approbation; and shall not a Protestant be permitted to write an Answer to it?' (323).

Steele would no doubt sympathise with Mr. Review, who felt the need for a robust and vocal Protestant public sphere to combat high Tory

---

[58] *Review*, vol. 5, p. xxvi.
[59] *Review*, vol. 6, p. x; the Defoe quotation is in *The Review* for 13 October 1709 (vol. 6, p. 409; McVeagh adds emphasis).
[60] Walter Graham, 'Defoe's *Review* and Steele's *Tatler* – The Question of Influence', *The Journal of English and Germanic Philology* 33 (1934), 250–54, p. 250.

propaganda. In *The Englishman*, Steele's narrator defines himself as a champion of the religion of freedom: 'It is essential to my Character, as an ENGLISHMAN, to have a particular Regard to the Protestant Interest in the World' (209). Both polarise the populace on one point: *'there were no other Distinction among us, but of those who are hearty and zealous for the Protestant Religion and present Establishment in Church and State, and those who are Popery and a French Government'* (*Englishman*, 62). Or as Mr. Review suggests, on one side are 'the *Papists*, the *Atheists*, the *Drunken, Swearing*, and most *Vicious* of the people', on the other the solid citizens and good Protestants (vol. 2, p. 191). Like Defoe, Steele advocates the naturalisation of foreign Protestants.[61] He celebrates 'that glorious Instrument of . . . Providence the great and memorable King WILLIAM', in Defovian manner lamenting the fact that England as 'not only . . . forgotten the Deliverer, but even the Deliverance it self'.[62] In his dogged defence of the Hanoverian succession, in 1713–1714, Steele also seems an ally of the equally outspoken Defoe. By comparison Addison is conspicuously reticent on the subject.

Both Steele and Defoe, despite the intensity of their partisan commitments, use the rhetoric of party neutrality and call for peace at home. The inaugural issue of *The Guardian* notes that 'The Parties among us are too violent to make it possible to pass them by without Observation' (43), a point Defoe routinely makes as well: 'The *Pulpit*, the *Press*, the *Exchange*, the *Market*, all were Debauch'd with the Contagion of Parties'.[63] Both accuse party zealots of having 'debauch'd' the 'Minds of the People',[64] Steele and Defoe are loud defenders of Marlborough, promoting his glories in battle and endorsing him against the false charges of the Tories. *The Review* and *The Tatler* both comment, to different degrees, on the abrupt, inauspicious ministerial change of 1710.

In many respects, the early *Tatler* connects with *The Review* of that time.[65] By the time Steele begins *The Tatler*, Defoe has been arguing for while in favour of a continuation of war rather than for an unsatisfying or unsafe peace (e.g., vol. 5, p. 687). Bickerstaff adds his voice to Mr. Review's in no. 1: 'The late Offers concerning Peace, were made in the Style of Persons who think themselves upon equal Terms: But the Allies have so just

---

[61] *The Reader; Steele's Periodical Journalism*, p. 144.
[62] *The Crisis; Tracts and Pamphlets*, p. 138.
[63] *Review*, vol. 3, p. 237.
[64] *The Crisis; Tracts and Pamphlets*, p. 173.
[65] Louis T. Milic has compared *The Tatler*'s style to that of *The Review* and *The Examiner*; 'Tone in Steele's "Tatler"', in Donovan H. Bond and W. Reynolds McLeod (eds.), *Newsletters to Newspapers: Eighteenth-Century Journalism* (Morgantown, WV, 1977), 33–45, pp. 35–40.

a Sense of their present Advantages, that they will not admit of a Treaty, except *France* offers what is more suitable to her present Condition' (21). Steele lingers on the subject of French suffering, like Mr. Review hoping to rouse the English public's support of carrying on the war. We could draw a similar conclusion about the late *Review* and *The Englishman*: Defoe is, in summer 1713, deeply concerned with the Pretender and with loyalty oaths. Steele's *Englishman* is, among other things, preoccupied by questions about allegiance and obedience.

Despite shared values, however, Mr. Review serves as an instructive contrast to Steele. One significant disparity has to do with Steele's eidolons, especially the developed, dynamic, sophisticated Isaac Bickerstaff and Nestor Ironside. The trouble Steele took to create personae signals their importance to his objectives and to his attempt to establish for himself a different kind of journalistic authority. In each of his periodicals, Steele supplies his readers with a guide, usually though someone other than himself – clearly an attempt, among other things, to remove some of the ego from journalism, or rather to seem to do so. Steele's handling of journalistic narration, in other words, functions similarly to his and Addison's critique of satire. By distancing himself, he implicitly challenges the ego-driven polemical journalism practiced by the likes of Mr. Examiner. The guide's rapport with readers is not entirely consistent: in *The Reader*, for example, the persona addresses his audience more frequently than Bickerstaff or Ironside had, and he seems particularly determined to keep that audience very conscious of itself. In a paper fostering critical consumption of Tory propaganda, this constant reminder to the audience of their own agency seems strategic.

Steele's relationship to his readers also diverges significantly from that of Defoe. Steele's eidolons are affable: 'I am call'd forth by the immense Love I bear to my Fellow Creatures, and the warm Inclination I feel within me, to stem, as far as I can, the prevailing Torrent of Vice and Ignorance' (*Tatler*, vol. 1, p. 278). He connects with his readers as equals, especially after *The Tatler* and *The Spectator*. Erin Skye Mackie suggests that in his earliest collaborative ventures, Steele wishes 'not to engage with [readers] in a debate among equals, but to prescribe his thoughts and opinions to them'.[66] This seems half right. He does not debate with his readers, and when he prints letters that do not fully agree with his own position, he does not rebut them. Relations between Steele and his audience rarely seem strained. I agree with Stuart Sherman, who concludes that '"Tattling" . . . necessitates

---

[66] Erin Skye Mackie, 'Being Too Positive About The Public Sphere', in Donald J. Newman (ed.), *The Spectator: Emerging Discourses* (Newark, DE, 2005), 81–104, p. 91.

community; it requires both listeners and speakers, often in alternating roles. Steele's title implies that the paper's "Action and Discourse" will be addressed *to* its readers, and more important, undertaken *with* them'.[67] My sense is that Steele encourages patriotic, lawful dissent, but he does so while also demonstrating polite discourse. This, too, cultivates trust: a rabble-rouser like Mr. Examiner will always be rabble-rousing, but when a tolerant, gracious, learned, non-divisive spokesman suggests the need for critical inquiry, his scepticism carries weight.[68]

The contrast between this rhetorical relationship and that we find in *The Examiner*, *The Rehearsal*, and other Tory papers is to be expected: Swift, Leslie *et al.* tend to be a good deal preachier. They eschew the 'we' that the Whig writers more commonly use. But Steele's voice must also be distinguished from that of Mr. Review, who on multiple occasions shows his exasperation – whether genuine or performative – toward his audience. He might preach moderation, but he is not well described as calm or controlled himself. Defoe at times seems uncertain about his readers' reason, and he manages both to interest and to vex his audience; especially in the latter half of *The Review*, his addresses to the 'ENGLISH FOOLS!' become prevalent (vol. 7, p. 265). Steele almost always writes as though he trusts his readers to follow him to the right conclusion. This is true even where he seems to be appealing to moderate Tories, as in *The Englishman* II. One of the reasons that Steele's opposition to Mr. Examiner's aggression is so effective is that he himself manages to adopt and comfortably sustain the Horatian voice. When he and Addison ostensibly reject satire, they are passing judgment on the Tory rhetoric of exclusion. As Addison observes in *The Freeholder* no. 19, 'The *Examiner* would not allow such as were of a contrary Opinion to him, to be either Christians or Fellow Subjects' (121).[69] Steele's journalistic practice seems informed by a desire to do the opposite, an impulse toward inclusivity and tolerance. We would never find Steele

---

[67] Stuart Sherman, *Telling Time: Clocks, Diaries, and English Diurnal Form, 1660–1785* (Chicago, 1996), p. 127.

[68] Mark Knights reminds us that politeness – like reason – 'could be a political tool, a way of denying legitimacy to a rival point of view'; *Representation and Misrepresentation in Later Stuart Britain: Partisanship and Political Culture* (Oxford, 2005), p. 57.

[69] Michael G. Ketcham discusses this passage as well, rightly concluding that, 'Mr. Spectator does not heighten the antagonism between himself and his adversaries but, through a rhetorical sleight of hand, assimilates them into his own 'Community' and 'make[s] them happy in the same Government with [himself]. The aim . . . is to draw men together into a cohesive community'; *Transparent Designs: Reading, Performance, and Form in the* Spectator *Papers* (Athens, GA, 1985), p. 161.

echoing the polarising Mr. Review: 'The Designs of the *Episcopal* and *Jacobite* Party, *for they are but one Party and one People*'.[70]

Ideologically, Steele is an ally of Defoe's, then, but they envision their roles in very different ways. *The Moderator*'s complaint that Steele had 'joined in the cry' with Mr. Review and Mr. Observator is deserved; that Tory author worried that Steele wanted to help form a stronger opposition to the Church party.[71] Rhetorically and tonally, Steele and Defoe diverge. Defoe cannot quite manage to avoid the idiom and manner of Mr. Examiner and other partisan controversialists; his métier is provocation and preachment. Steele is consistently labouring to oppose and subvert his Tory rivals, but he does so in a series of papers that (mostly indirectly) contest foundational values rather than battling over (many) particular issues. Most partisan journalists are fighting over the interpretation of the ministerial change, over trade, over war and peace, over toleration. Steele does not ignore these controversies, but he seems always preoccupied with the broader question of Tory authority – in social, ethical, cultural, religious, and political realms.

The authority of political journalism

Steele was among the most versatile Whig journalists of the early eighteenth century, arguably more active and adaptable in that role than any of his contemporaries. He was unusual in producing multiple papers, contesting his rivals' from a variety of angles and through different personae. Whereas Defoe devoted years to *The Review* and Tutchin and Ridpath to *The Observator*, Steele offered a succession of relatively short-lived enterprises. His reliance on a series of back-to-back periodicals has probably contributed to the relative critical neglect of his journalism – but it likely reflects a deliberate strategic choice. He introduces the public not to one Whig critic of Toryism, but to multiple Whig critics, each with a somewhat different perspective and with his own axe to grind. Whatever Steele's intentions, the cumulative effect is to suggest a broader culture of polite journalistic Whiggism. In any case, he clearly preferred to change his tack, and taken together his periodicals suggest a multi-pronged attack: claiming moral authority for the Whigs, denying the morality of Tory politics, undermining Tory definitions of obedience and loyalty, caricaturing the

---

[70] *Review*, vol. 8, p. 679.
[71] Quoted by Bond (*Tatler*, vol. 3, p. 16n10).

'Cunning' Harley, and inviting readers to dissect and refute the propaganda on which the Harley's ministry depended. Even after George's accession, Steele continues to do battle with Tory ideology and with Anne's last ministry, not pointlessly tub-thumping but instead labouring to popularise and bolster Whig ideals at a time of great political uncertainty.

By way of conclusion, I want briefly to note some of the inconsistencies and continuities in Steele's political periodical writing, hoping ultimately to demonstrate that one of the fundamental constants is a commitment to defining both journalistic and political authority. Steele is skilled at moving back and forth between the seemingly (sometimes actually) apolitical and the overtly political, and the former tends to lend credibility to the latter. He is always interested in the practice of reading, and increasingly concerned to train his readers to be careful consumers of (Tory) texts. To say that for the entire life of *The Examiner* Steele always had that paper in view would not be an exaggeration. The degree of his fixation on *The Examiner* has not, I think, been sufficiently appreciated. Sometimes his challenge is direct quotation and animadversion; elsewhere it comes in the form of a critique of unprincipled fawners seeking the favour of the great. Contemporaries highlight the battle between Steele and Mr. Examiner, and justly so.[72] The author of *The Character of Richard S[tee]le* (1713) opens his sketch with a waggish mock-apology to his fellow Tory: 'It will be no Injury . . . to the *Examiner* to borrow [Steele] a little while, upon Promise of returning him Safe, as Children do their Play Things, when their Mirth is over' (2).

Partisans on both sides clearly recognised – in a way modern scholars have not – the centrality of Mr. Examiner to Steele and vice versa. In *The Examiner* for 12 March 1714, Oldisworth again targets Steele, and his characterisation is astute: 'this Writer has all along been a gentle and courteous Enemy to the *Examiner*: He would never yet enter into the Merits of the Dispute between us, or weigh any of those Articles, that are Controverted by the *New Ministry* and the *Government* on one side, and the *Faction* and *Old Ministry* on the other. He durst not offer to lay hold, or gripe me any where; but bark'd and snarl'd at a distance'. Oldisworth recognises Steele's partisanship, in other words, as well as the artifice of Steele's pretence of politeness. He mocks and reinterprets Steele's civility (his 'distance' from the fray) as either a false pose or timidity.

The formal variations among Steele's periodicals are subtle but noteworthy. The most obvious distinction is in degree of epistolarity: his

---

[72] *The Case of Richard Steele* (London, 1714), pp. 12–13; *A Letter to Mr. Steele, Concerning the Removal of the Pretender from Lorrain* (London, 1714), pp. 7–8; and *A Letter to Mr. Steele, Concerning His Crisis* (London, 1714), p. 12.

Spectator contributions, for example, like *The Guardian* and the first *Englishman*, rely heavily upon letters from others, whether authentic or fabricated by Steele himself.[73] The epistolary format allows Steele to model a certain kind of public inquiry; the printing of letters from 'Ralph English' and other commoners validates those ordinary citizens who wish to engage in public political debate. In *The Englishman* II, on the contrary, he writes almost entirely in his own voice, which highlights the polemical nature of that paper. *The Tatler*, *The Spectator*, and *The Guardian* all use personae who seem convincingly distinct from the author; though there is much less distance in *The Englishman* I and *The Theatre*, Steele almost always takes care to signal that the narrative voice is not 'Steele'. As Italia observes, he 'rarely allows his dramatis personae to voice his political views', instead tending to print letters from 'Steele' within papers ostensibly authored by someone else. 'This allows Steele to maintain a fiction of editorial political impartiality', Italia concludes, 'while including political commentary within the papers'.[74] But Sir John Edgar, tireless (and tiresome) advocate of Steele, does not provide the same cover that Nestor Ironside does, and the final issue of *The Theatre* abandons the fiction completely. For the most part, the putative authors of Steele's Hanoverian journalism are less distinct from the actual author than was the case in Anne's reign.

Steele's journalistic modes vary as well. The familiar essays of *The Tatler*, *The Spectator*, and *The Guardian* represent a meditative, non-argumentative approach. In *The Guardian* and *The Englishman* I, though, he anticipates some of his later journalistic aggression by shifting, occasionally, into a more interrogative mode. In *Englishman* no. 46, for example, 'Steele' accuses Mr. Examiner *et al.* of Jacobite intentions, nobly professing to 'publish the Rules by which I govern my Judgment of Men and Things in the present Conjuncture'. Those rules consist of questions, each of which gets at a similar point: 'Does this Position open a way to the Pretender? Or does it further secure the Protestant Succession?' These questions, Steele maintains, 'I make the Test of Men and Opinions' (187). *The Guardian* no. 90 similarly relies upon queries, a device Steele uses more prominently in these 1713–1714 papers than he had previously, and one which seems to encourage readers' engagement. In any case, Steele's journalistic registers are meditative or interrogative or declarative; they

---

[73] For a good discussion of the public letter in *The Spectator*, see Greg Polly, 'A Leviathan of Letters', in Donald J. Newman (ed.), *The Spectator: Emerging Discourses* (Newark, DE, 2005), pp. 105–28.

[74] Iona Italia, *The Rise of Literary Journalism in the Eighteenth Century: Anxious Employment* (New York, 2005), p. 69.

vary from the not-wholly-innocent mode of subtle ideological conditioning to the outright polemical.

Steele's canon of political journalism, whatever its inconsistencies, reflects an unwavering commitment to Whig values and an abiding concern for the abuse of authority. Steele is always an advocate for popular and parliamentary sovereignty, for the sanctity of Revolution principles and the Protestant succession. He writes often on the appropriate limits of royal and ministerial power and on the liberty of English subjects, who are free assert their civic rights. The subject of familial and political authority is central to his journalistic oeuvre. He stresses the responsibility of those in power – those who represent official authority – to model moral practices and to punish those who behave dishonorably. He often complains that the ministry allows Mr. Examiner to abuse his betters with impunity.[75] His frustration with Mr. Examiner, in fact, has much to do with authority: not only does the Tory propagandist 'transgress the Rules of Decency', but he also does so in a paper that pretends to be and evidently is 'supported by a Peer of the Realm'.[76] In *The Medley*, Steele and Mainwaring refer to contemptuously to *The Examiner* as a '*Protected* Paper' (282).

Steele's discussions of political power, and his exasperation with Mr. Examiner's claim to represent authority and thus to serve as an authority, complement his reflections on his own right to speak out. He comments regularly on the justice of public pronouncements, whether his own or those of his readers. As Knight notes, 'The problem of defining royal prerogative quickly shades into the broader question of who is authorised to discuss matters of state and what the grounds for such authority are'.[77] In Steele's hybrid papers – where political reflections are diluted by sociomoral ruminations offered by an upstanding narrator – he seems eager to establish himself as a moral authority. This is not only a way of lending credibility to his political commentary, but it certainly has that effect. In the opening of the first *Englishman*, his unnamed editor refers back to *The Guardian*: 'Though I cannot pretend to come up to the Authority which that venerable Gentleman has so deservedly enjoyed, I hope I shall not appear his unworthy Disciple' (6). His affirmation of Ironside's clout is pointed.

Steele as a political journalist seems always conscious of the fact that the partisan battle is primarily about authority. While editing the *Gazette*, he wrote in a letter (perhaps to Lord Sunderland) that his objective was largely 'to raise the Value of the paper written by Authority, and Lessen the

---

[75] See for example *Englishman*, pp. 171–72.
[76] *Englishman*, pp. 62–63.
[77] Knight, *Political Biography*, p. 129.

esteem of the rest among the Generality of the People'.[78] Steele labours to establish the integrity of his own narrators and editors, and to undermine that of his rivals. This is not unique to him, but no other contemporary – not Mr. Review or Mr. Examiner, not Leslie or Tutchin or Ridpath – seems so thoroughly preoccupied with this issue. Steele often privileges the questions about authority over issue-based argumentation. Especially in his late Stuart journalism, we find him attacking Tory authority from different perspectives and through disparate strategies. In *The Tatler* and *The Spectator*, as Cowan has shown us, he offered the well-regulated, polite coffeehouse scene as a counter to the Church's notion that only it could provide 'a solid foundation for the moral revitalization of society'.[79] In *The Guardian*, he (again indirectly) questions the morality of the political game being played by Mr. Examiner and his fellow travelers. In *The Englishman* I, Steele disputes Tory dogma, and in particular voices scepticism about the value and appropriateness of passive obedience. He takes the Tories to task on particular issues, and systematically queries the methods and motives and veracity of their propagandists. But from paper to paper he also raises broader questions about the rationality, morality, civility, and sociability of the Tories – and thus about that party's authority to represent and lead a nation.

Steele was a major player in late Stuart and early Hanoverian partisan controversy, though this part of his career has been almost entirely eclipsed by the modern scholarly tendency to see him as urbane, Addisonian cultural critic. The political import of his journalistic canon has never been sufficiently appreciated, despite the fact that his contemporaries clearly worried about his periodical presence and felt compelled to do battle with him in the press. That he has been mostly divorced from the early eighteenth-century culture of partisan journalism is unfortunate – not least because he was as aware as anyone of the relationship between power and the press, of the role of journalism and journalistic personae in cultivating or challenging political authority.

---

[78] Rae Blanchard (ed.), *The Correspondence of Richard Steele* (Oxford, 1941), p. 23.
[79] Cowan, 'Mr. Spectator and the Coffeehouse Public Sphere', p. 349.

PART III

Envisioning and Engaging Readers

Chapter 6
The Journalists on Popular Politics and Public Engagement

'This was the *Dawn* of *Politicks* among the Common People....'[1]

A study of political journalism should explore how journalists appeal to and imagine the 'public', what they say about and how they attempt to encourage or limit political engagement.[2] How do the authors and editors of newspapers and periodicals imagine their roles vis-à-vis the populace? What are their attitudes toward a public sphere that encourages participation, questioning, and judgment-rendering from subjects? Scholars have highlighted the widespread anxiety about popular political education, citing writers who feared the destabilising polarisation created by a more extensive news network. In *The Review*, Defoe routinely complains about 'that Universal Pen and Ink Strife': 'Never was Nation in the World, so intollerably worried from the *Press*' (vol. 2, p. 711). Most discussions of the press and the Habermasian public sphere in this period have focused predominantly on Addison and Steele, specifically on *The Tatler* and *The Spectator*, reading those journals as revealing their authors' desire to limit rather than enhance popular involvement. As Brian Cowan notes, Addison and Steele 'were not so enthusiastic about the potential for public politics'.[3] Cowan offers a broader conclusion: 'All parties, both Whig and Tory, shared an aversion to widening popular participation in the political public sphere', and 'the politicization of the public sphere remained a

---

[1] Daniel Defoe, *Religious and Didactic Writings of Daniel Defoe*, vol. 9: *The Commentator*, ed. P.N. Furbank (London, 2007), p. 24 (4 Jan 1720).
[2] Throughout, when I speak of 'the people' or 'the populace', I mean primarily the electorate. Very few writers, even among the Whigs, appealed to the masses – though some authors do at least rhetorically include the most common of commoners in their writing.
[3] Brian Cowan, 'Mr. Spectator and the Coffeehouse Public Sphere', *Eighteenth-Century Studies* 37 (2004), 345–66, p. 346.

move that was only made *in extremis*.'⁴ One object of this chapter is to test that supposition, and to restore to the discussion those newsmen who provoked and taught readers to play the role of active, attentive, inquisitive citizens.

Scholars have emphasised negative attributes of the relationship between the press and the public. Not only were contemporaries uneasy about politics 'out of doors', but they also worried that the press functioned to manipulate and mislead rather than to clarify. Mark Knights's excellent *Representation and Misrepresentation in Later Stuart Britain* (2005) studies the ways in which 'the involvement of the public . . . raised questions about the capacity of the people to make informed, rational, political judgements', as well as about writers' partisan misrepresentations and deceptions (3). The proliferation of text, like the increase in coffee-house discourse, alarmed contemporaries, since the 'emphasis on free speech was feared to be the first step on the road to free thought': to extend the list of topics warranting critical scrutiny and uninhibited dialogue was ultimately to risk the spread of atheism.⁵ A flourishing periodical culture introduced many problems, hence the widespread 'critique of the . . . emergence of an avid, news-craving, politically engaged sector of the newspaper consumer market'.⁶ Addison and Steele delight in mocking *Quidnuncs* ('what news?') and the burgeoning tribe of state-pedants too 'wrapt up in News' to attend to their own lives and businesses.⁷ The crux is that, on the strength of these contemporary tendencies, scholars often depict the press's relationship to the public sphere as a paradoxically adversarial one: journalists discourage popular engagement even as they by their very existence foster it.

My contention in this chapter is that such characterisations do not do justice to the range of rhetorical relationships between journalists and their readers. This is partly because so few exemplars tend to be represented; Swift and Defoe are scarcely mentioned, Charles Leslie and Arthur Mainwaring virtually never, and Addison and Steele only for their most celebrated productions. What follows is an attempt at a fuller, more nuanced account of the ways in which partisan newswriters and essayists

---

4   Cowan, 'Mr. Spectator and the Coffeehouse Public Sphere', p. 351.
5   Cowan, 'What was Masculine about the Public Sphere? Gender and the Coffeehouse Milieu in Post-Restoration England', *History Workshop Journal* 51 (2001), 127–57, p. 140.
6   Uriel Heyd, 'News Craze: Public Sphere and the Eighteenth-Century Theatrical Depiction of Newspaper Culture', *The Eighteenth Century: Theory and Interpretation* 56 (2015), 59–84, p. 60.
7   *Spectator*, vol. 1, p. 438.

constructed a 'public'. Such treatment requires some confrontation with the 'public sphere' that Jürgen Habermas identifies as emerging around the turn of the eighteenth century, and that is where the chapter begins. But Habermas's concern, like that of many of his sharpest critics, is with the political-historical reality, with the actual measure of inclusivity of coffeehouse culture, with how participatory this new public really was. My concern is more rhetorical, one that reflects a truth most scholars now agree upon: 'A public appears, with a shape and a will, via the various claims made to represent it'.[8] How did journalists represent and dictate to the public, and how did they invite and train readers to behave? I treat Addison and Steele alongside Swift, Leslie, Tutchin, Defoe and others, distinguishing among the attitudes toward popular politics exhibited or implied in their respective papers. I then consider, briefly, the dramatic reversal in the relationship between Whig and Tory journalists and their readers in early Hanoverian England, before moving on to the ways in which periodical writers attempt, rhetorically, both to establish their own authority and to undermine that of their rivals.

Throughout, I attempt to read the ideological implications of rhetorical and formal choices, and to consider how those choices reflect writers' attitudes toward public politics. Few of the newspapers and periodicals covered in this book have been read closely (or at all), and the rhetoric of early English journalism continues to be a surprisingly understudied subject. The major exceptions are *The Tatler* and *The Spectator*. *The Review* and *The Examiner* have been mined for content by students of Defoe and Swift, but have enjoyed surprisingly little literary-critical analysis. But not all political journals engage with readers in the same way, and distinctions need to be made. One object of this chapter is to highlight some of those distinctions.

Habermas and the press

Habermas's *Structural Transformation of the Public Sphere* (pub. 1962) was the first extensive account of the evolution of a virtual public community that was *in theory* both all-inclusive and rational. As Habermas tells the story, around the turn of the eighteenth century, as a result of the conflict between absolute states and an emerging bourgeoisie, a new

---

[8] Thomas F. Crow, *Painters and Public Life in Eighteenth-Century Paris* (New Haven, 1985), p. 5.

public sphere developed. This reasoning public's authority and influence gradually expanded, allowing public opinion to function politically as a check on institutional power. In previous societies, 'the ruler's power was merely represented *before* the people'; this is a world in which the French king can confidently pronounce *l'etat c'est moi*. That political model was replaced, *circa* 1700, by one in which 'state authority was publicly monitored through informed and critical discourse *by* the people'.[9] The bourgeois public sphere is a collective, imaginary space, but is also 'situated in concrete social spaces, in debate in coffee houses and salons, in newspapers and periodicals, and there 'public opinion' is formed'.[10] Though not denying that previous societies had some element of representative publicness, Habermas concludes that only around 1700 did subjects imagine 'a forum in which the private people . . . readied themselves to compel public authority to legitimate itself before public opinion' (2526). Part of the change was the lapsing of the Licensing Act in 1695,[11] which ended pre-publication censorship – though the fear (and reality) of post-publication punishment remained strong throughout our period.

Most scholars of late Stuart Britain have adopted some version of Habermas's account as 'convenient shorthand for an apparent broadening of political participation',[12] though he has had no shortage of critics. Karin Bowie argues that our conclusions about the public sphere need to derive from more than coffeehouses and newspapers; they need also to reflect pamphlets, meetings, sermons, and letters, as well as petitions and riots and other forms of political expression.[13] J. A. Downie has been the most persistent and sceptical: 'it would not be putting the matter too strongly to say that one can quibble about the accuracy of almost every sentence

---

[9] Thomas McCarthy, Introduction to Jürgen Habermas, *The Structural Transformation of the Public Sphere: An Inquiry into a Category of Bourgeois Society* (1962), trans. Thomas Burger with assistance from Frederick Lawrence (Cambridge, MA, 1995), p. xi.

[10] Ian Atherton, 'The Press and Popular Political Opinion', in Barry Coward (ed.), *A Companion to Stuart Britain* (Malden, MA, 2003), 88–110, p. 95.

[11] Other changes include the increase in critical discussion of culture, the emergence of a concept of 'economy' beyond the private, and the evolution of a kind of sociability that encourages discussion and debate; Michael Warner, *Publics and Counterpublics* (New York, 2010), p. 47.

[12] Tony Claydon, 'The sermon, the 'public sphere' and the political culture of late seventeenth-century England', in Lori Anne Ferrell and Peter McCullough (eds.), *The English Sermon Revised* (Manchester, 2000), 208–34, p. 209.

[13] Karin Bowie, *Scottish Public Opinion and the Anglo-Scottish Union, 1699–1707* (Woodbridge, 2007), p. 6.

[Habermas] writes about seventeenth- and eighteenth-century "Britain".[14] Downie and others object to Habermas's presumption of inclusivity, rightly noting that not only were women and the lower ranks of society excluded from meaningful political participation, but so were Roman Catholics and many dissenters. England and Wales were home to some 5.5 million inhabitants in 1701, out of which roughly 200,000 formed the electorate.[15] Cowan has shown that, though women were allowed to and did frequent certain coffeehouses, those spaces were widely regarded as masculine.[16] Historians have also objected to Habermas's dating of the starting point for this new kind of society. Downie contends that the appeal to public opinion 'had already been made earlier in the [seventeenth] century, both during the civil wars, then in 1659 and 1660 . . . then again during the Exclusion Crisis . . . and once more in 1688–1689'.[17] Peter Lake and Steven Pincus trace the development of a 'post-Reformation public sphere', though they highlight a major difference between post-Reformation and post-Glorious Revolution publicness. The former 'began as occasional and opportunistic openings and shuttings-down of debate on a limited set of issues', but in the 1640s and 1650s, more regular appeals to the public crucially transformed 'the occasional into the normal', creating 'political actors with an increasingly self-conscious and sophisticated sense of the way to play politics in this new public arena'.[18] This conclusion is affirmed by Jason Peacey's excellent study of *Print and Public Politics in the English Revolution*. Peacey focuses on the role of pamphlets and newspapers in promoting engagement with national affairs and in fostering an 'enhanced participatory culture' in the 1640s (399). His book demonstrates that 'by virtue of becoming engaged with parliament and educated about its processes, proceedings and personalities, contemporaries from all walks of life developed the tools and skills with which to participate' (402). I share Peacey's concern with the 'interactive nature' of certain kinds of periodical writing (261),[19] and more

---

[14] J.A. Downie, 'How useful to eighteenth-century English studies is the paradigm of the "bourgeois public sphere"?' *Literature Compass* 1 (2003), 1–19, p. 2. See also his 'The Myth of the Bourgeois Public Sphere', in Cynthia Wall (ed.), *A Concise Companion to the Restoration and Eighteenth Century* (Blackwell, 2005), pp. 58–79.

[15] Downie, 'How useful', p. 3.

[16] Brian Cowan, 'What's Masculine about the Public Sphere?', Gender and the Coffeehouse Milieu in Post-Restoration England'. *History Workshop Journal* 51 (2001), pp. 127–57.

[17] Downie, 'How useful', p. 15.

[18] Peter Lake and Steve Pincus, 'Rethinking the Public Sphere in Early Modern England', *Journal of British Studies* 45 (2006), 270–92, pp. 289–90.

[19] Jason Peacey rightly emphasises the way in which 'Civil War newspapers offered ordinary citizens the perfect vehicle for making themselves heard'; *Print and Public*

broadly with the relationship between print culture and subjects' self-perception as engaged citizens – as well as print's role in helping subjects cultivate the capacity for such engagement. In the period upon which my own study is focused, the news culture has become much more extensive and formalised, with more interchange among rival journalists implicitly or explicitly about what politicising role the press should (or should not) have.

Habermas and those responding to his work tend to be concerned with the realities of public participation. They also focus more on the coffee-house dimension of this public sphere than on the role played by particular periodicals, with the exception, again, of Addison, Steele, and a few of their imitators and critics. Habermas *et al.* treat 'newspapers' as a collective force, one great tool by which political information is disseminated; the periodicals represent, *en masse*, an agent of popular politicisation. Habermas's overview of the English press begins with an acknowledgement that, despite governmental and popular unease about too much freedom of speech, it 'enjoyed unique liberties' compared to its European counterparts. He then summarises Harley's use of hired pens to advance ministerial ends, making 'party spirit' a 'public spirit'. Habermas briefly cites *The Review*, *The Observator*, and *The Examiner*, all of which were 'discussed in clubs and coffee houses, at home and in the streets' (59). Problematically, he assumes that those and other journals functioned similarly vis-à-vis the public. To date, analyses of the press and those of the public sphere fail to offer a sufficiently nuanced account of the relationship between the press and street politics. Habermas and his critics are admittedly dealing with the actual effect of journalism and coffeehouse discourse, with the responses of subjects and with their levels of potential engagement. But beyond issuing generic denunciations of the pernicious freedom of the press, how do journalists position themselves in this new kind of politicised society?

The Tatler, The Spectator, and The Englishman: *degrees of vigilance*
Addison's and Steele's two most celebrated ventures have served as a touchstone for measuring both journalistic production in the early eighteenth century and the promotion of public politics. As Cowan notes, 'One of the main sources for Habermas's concept of the public sphere was the ideal image of the coffeehouse society presented in' *The Tatler* (1709–1711) and

---

Politics in the English Revolution (Cambridge, 2013), p. 264.

The Spectator (1711–1712, 1714).[20] Cowan's discussion of what he terms the '*Spectator* project' and its commitment to non-participatory publicness is sound, and I agree with most of his conclusions. This collaborative scheme, reflected in *The Tatler* and *The Spectator*, and to some extent Steele's *Guardian* (1713), 'put the reform and the discipline of public sociability at the heart of its agenda'. It 'did not encourage or even condone Habermas's "political public-ness" (*politische Öffentlichkeit*)', instead seeking 'to tame it and make it anodyne'. Most students of late Stuart journalism make little distinction between *The Tatler* and *The Spectator*. How similar are their philosophies about Habermas's *politische Öffentlichkeit*, and how well does Steele's later Stuart periodical ventures correspond to them?

Steele was a more aggressive polemicist than his milder-mannered friend and collaborator. His corpus of partisan journalism is more extensive than Addison's and, on several occasions, he got himself into trouble for his virulence. Steele spilled a lot of ink in his battle with Mr. Examiner; he was a ministerial gadfly in the reign of Anne and carried on his fight against the Harley government well into George's reign. *The Tatler*, though, is no *Englishman*. Its ethos is one of tolerance and restraint. In no. 6, Steele encourages his audience not to be too caught up in current events: 'While other Parts of the Town are amus'd with the present Actions, we generally spend the Evening at this Table in Inquiries of Antiquity, and think any thing News which gives us new Knowledge' (56). Isaac Bickerstaff's authorial persona is civic-minded without exception, motivated by 'the immense Love I bear to my Fellow Creatures' (278). His goal is 'the Benefit and Instruction, as well as the Diversion', of his audience (271). Like Addison, he wonders 'how it should be possible that this Turn to Politicks should so universally prevail, to the Exclusion of every other Subject out of Conversation' (vol. 3, p. 202). Steele mocks the newsmonger, the Upholsterer, though he does so in partisan terms: that figure is a follower of the leading Tory papers, *The Examiner*, *The Moderator*, and *The Post Boy* (201). He likewise expresses his disapproval of 'Coffee-house Orators' (350) and for 'Volunteers in Politicks': 'Our Streets swarm with Politicians, and there is scarce a Shop which is not held by a Statesman' (vol. 2, p. 394). His most caustic comments on this subject, however, date from the period during which the Whig junto he admired was under attack. That he scorned sceptical public politics in the spring of 1710, with the Godolphin ministry under pressure during and after the Sacheverell trial, is not astonishing.

---

[20] Cowan, 'Mr. Spectator and the Coffeehouse Public Sphere', p. 345. Subsequent quotation at p. 346.

Mr. Spectator is if anything more an advocate of polite distance from the political fray. As Anthony Pollock observes, he 'repeatedly removes himself from urban scenes that threaten to overwhelm him'. The 'spectators' we find in Addison and Steele, Pollock continues, 'will do the seeing for you – leave the seeing to us, they say. Bickerstaff and Mr. Spectator often insist that ordinary citizens are easily led astray when left to their own aesthetic faculties'. Like Mr. Review, Addison and Steele exhibit frustration with the deluders, partisan promulgators of untruth who dupe a credulous readership. In Pollock's telling, 'Addison and Steele send readers home from coffeehouses and public assemblies to consume their periodicals' in private spaces.[21] We might consider, though, whether this is merely an acknowledgement of a (temporary) political reality, a recognition that in a time of Tory dominance, the social spaces are as corrupt as the court. Ronald Paulson's take on the 'polite' journalism of Addison and Steele likewise seems significant here: Addison in particular contests the legitimacy and civility of satire, but his criticisms in fact serve as satire on the Tories. In challenging Tory polemical satire, he insinuates his own – Whig – superiority, and the pre-eminence of Horatian *sermones* to Juvenalian diatribe.[22] We can reasonably extend this to the realm of popular politics. *The Spectator*'s projection of a sociable, clubbable, non-contentious ideal of publicness represents indirect critique of prominent Tory notions (as in *The Examiner*) of vitriolic public discourse – especially one that privileges institutions over the community of citizens.

Both Addison and Steele overtly censure certain kinds of public involvement, depicting the sites of political discussion as fraught and uncivil. That said, *The Tatler* in particular cannot be described as reluctant to offer a political education. Steele freely alludes to public events; his attempt to offer national and international news sets him apart from Addison. For the most part, Bickerstaff addresses himself less to 'subjects' than to readers, often (evidently) in an effort to make those readers more sceptical consumers of text, not passive recipients of partisan propaganda but active analysts.[23] In no. 18 (by Addison and Steele), Bickerstaff expresses mock sympathy for the 'Fraternity' of newsmen:

---

[21] Anthony Pollock, 'Neutering Addison and Steele: Aesthetic Failure and the Spectatorial Public Sphere', *ELH* 74 (2007), 707–34, pp. 707, 713, 727.

[22] See Ronald Paulson, *The Fictions of Satire* (Baltimore, 1967), pp. 216–18. See Ashley Marshall, 'Thinking about Satire', in Paddy Bullard (ed.), *A Handbook of Eighteenth-Century Satire* (Oxford: Oxford University Press, 2019), pp. 475–91.

[23] For another instance of inviting readers toward critical interpretation, see *Tatler* no. 212 (vol. 3, pp. 119–20).

> The Case of these Gentlemen is, I think, more hard than that of the Soldiers, considering that they have taken more Towns, and fought more Battles. They have been upon Parties and Skirmishes, when our Armies have lain still; and given the General Assault to many a Place, when the Besiegers were quiet in their Trenches. They have made us Masters of several strong Towns many Weeks before our Generals could do it; and compleated Victories, when our greatest Captains have been glad to come off with a drawn Battle. Where Prince *Eugene* has slain his Thousands, *Boyer* has slain his Ten Thousands. (vol. 1, pp. 148–49)

The point here is not only the ironic disparagement of journalists who fabricate, falsify, and overdramatise, but also the implications for readers of their works. Bickerstaff implicitly promotes questioning, doubting, disbelieving. This is the opposite of abjuring the role of engaged public citizen; on the contrary, it promotes scrutiny both of the peddlers of lies and of the authorities who employ them.

The roles of 'Tatler' and 'Spectator' (like that of 'Censor', as Bickerstaff fancies himself[24]) are, after all, hardly non-judgmental. All suggest an element of surveillance. The official job of the state Censor was to carry out the census, though of course the term also recalled classical magistrates charged with overseeing public morals; Cato the Elder was known as Cato the Wise and Cato the Censor, no doubt an attractive precursor for Steele. In no. 144, Steele explains that as Censor he 'observe[s] upon Things which do not fall within the Cognizance of real Authority' (vol. 2, p. 319); he sets himself up as an alternative to the (Tory) authorities. As observer and judge, his role connects well to that of spectator and tatler, though 'censor' also has a textual dimension; he functions as an arbiter of cultural production. Generally speaking, the eidolons of *The Spectator* and *The Tatler* are associated with active inspection. In no. 4, Mr. Spectator brags about having 'a more than ordinary Penetration in Seeing', and 'flatter[s]' himself that he has 'looked into the Highest and Lowest of Mankind', assessing their actions and motives (vol. 1, p. 20).[25] But (*pace* Pollock) neither Addison nor Steele suggests that they alone have such capacities for perception: 'so many Men', Steele concludes, 'so many *Spectators*' (vol. 4, p. 52). The Lockean epistemology informing *The Spectator* privileges

---

[24] *Tatler*, vol. 2, p. 318.
[25] Michael G. Ketcham discusses the ways in which Addison and Steele promote 'forms of penetration by which the observer or reader reads through outward manners to penetrate to the actors' secret selves'; *Transparent Designs: Reading, Performance, and Form in the* Spectator *Papers* (Athens, GA, 1985), p. 13.

individual perception[26]; in the political climate of late Stuart Britain even that is a political commitment. Erin Mackie concludes that, in *The Tatler*, Steele attempts 'not to engage with [his readers] in a debate among equals, but to prescribe his thoughts and opinions to them.'[27] I disagree. Like any partisan journalist, Steele seeks to persuade and to guide, but reading him alongside the truly submission-preaching papers of Swift and Leslie, one appreciates how much he encourages rational and independent thought. He and Addison both create a public of readers, who can apply their skills – for observation and interpretation – to texts and to the events and issues such texts are meant to 'explain'.

Pollock describes Mr. Spectator as teaching 'not an ethics of dialogue ... but an ethics of visibility'.[28] The point, though, seems less about his own visibility than about the visibility of a polite Whig citizenry, and the 'spectator' role implies, to my mind, not inaction but deferred action – subjects watching, thinking more than discursive decorum (and political reality) allows them to say, and awaiting their turn. Bickerstaff's namesake, after all, was a prophet, a fortune-teller contesting his target's partisan predictions and envisioning an alternative future. Steele's use of Swift's soothsayer suggests partisan astrology: reading and interpreting and predicting political (as well as celestial) phenomena. Steele would later be more direct in his endorsement of a critical public.

The first series of Steele's *Englishman* (1713–1714) represents a strikingly different enterprise than what we find in the 'Spectator project', one that calls into question Steele's promotion of non-participation. *The Englishman* includes many letters ostensibly written to the editor by concerned citizens (including 'Richard Steele' himself), encouraging their spokesman to address what he has not yet addressed, to object to happenings and attitudes to which he might not otherwise object. Far more than either *The Tatler* or *The Spectator*, this venture appears to be a 'paper for the people'. Among the letter-writers are commoners as well as MPs, including Ralph English and the corn-cutter John Smith. Another loyal citizen, one Theophilus Deacon, implores Steele to remember that he speaks for a significant part of the populace: 'when you set up for ENGLISHMAN in the aggregate Sense of the Word, you take us with you' (30). And Steele does write as a representative, one determined that his countrymen should be mindful of their rights and brave enough to defend them. The next issue

---

[26] Ketcham, *Transparent Designs*, p. 23.
[27] Erin Skye Mackie, 'Being Too Positive About the Public Sphere', in Donald J. Newman (ed.), *The Spectator: Emerging Discourses* (Newark, DE, 2005), 81–104, p., 91.
[28] Pollock, 'Neutering Addison and Steele', p. 713.

opens with Juvenalian judgment: 'THE many and great Evils into which this Nation is involved...' (18). The inflammatory rhetoric is a long way from *The Tatler*'s equanimity, and it invites a much different kind of response from its contemporary audience.

Throughout *The Englishman*, Steele underscores the need for a politicised citizenship. Instead of appealing to polite readers and sceptical interpreters of news, he writes to 'civil and political' beings. Every Englishman must 'stand by the free Constitution of his Country with his Discourse, with his Pen, and with his Sword' (75). Steele collapses any boundary between private and public protest, appealing to his audience to imagine themselves as part of a public community of free civil discourse. He represents England as on the eve of crisis; 'it behoves every Man who loves his Country, himself, his Family, or his Fortune, to be very vigilant' (25). Neutrality is unacceptable: 'IT is the most abject Meanness to be cold or indifferent upon this Occasion' (26). No. 8 includes non-specific election advice, and combines the language of civic responsibility with an epithet less commonly used than one might expect by Queen Anne's journalists: 'Fellow-Subjects' (37).

One of Steele's allies is the author of *The Patriot* (1714–1715), a paper worth mentioning here. In the final months of Anne's reign, the author – like Steele – appeals to his 'Fellow Subjects' (no. 1), urging them to 'employ both their Tongues and their Pens in opposing . . . oppressive Schemes' (7). True citizens will 'exert [themselves] to the uttermost. . . . It is the Business of every one, from the highest to the lowest, to stand up. . . .' (8). Throughout the author argues explicitly that engagement and righteous opposition are vital civic duties: 'Nothing has contributed more . . . to the imminent Danger both of our Religion and Liberty, than a Slavish Resignation of the Mind to the Opinion of others' (43). He expresses surprise that his fellow citizens:

> act as if they believ'd the Search after Truth was confined to such and such a particular Cloth and Quality, as if a Reasonable Soul was not breath'd into all the Sons and Daughters of *Adam*, but only into Half a Dozen Prime Ministers and Two or Three State Divines.

The author voices frustration with those who at times of national crisis assume 'that there are Wiser Heads at Work than ours'. His arguments are not identical to Steele's, but both writers are use their journalism as a vehicle for politicising English subjects.

An anonymous letter-writer exhorts the author of *The Englishman* to 'inculcate' Whiggish notions about the sacred rights of the people 'to your Readers . . . by making them publick in your Paper' (76). This phrase seems significant, an acknowledgement of the role of the journal in publicising ideology that fosters an engaged citizenship. *The Englishman* is empowering, insisting among other things that England is 'the *Capital of Liberty*, where the Property of the meanest Subject is ... strongly guarded' (115). Again and again, Steele prints letters purportedly from real citizens articulating their expectations that their fellow subjects prove ready to act: 'it is high Time for every *Englishman* to exert himself', one demands, before defending those 'who were most shamefully condemned without being heard ... and barbarously treated' for supporting the country (171). The subtleties of the Spectator project, like its apparent unease about too politicised a public, are not only irrelevant but even counter to the objectives of *The Englishman*. Steele goes out of his way to politicise the people, to persuade readers of the wisdom 'of *Governing All by All*' (113). Most Whig journals object to the dogma of non-resistance, but *The Englishman* of 1713–1714, unlike *The Medley* and some others, actively argues for a populist basis of power.

Steele's epistolary form in *The Englishman* connects with this message. Among the major journalists in this period, he relies the most upon 'outside' letters, whether authentic or not. Even in *The Spectator*, his preference for the epistolary form distinguishes his contributions from Addison's. The first series consisted of 555 issues, and Richmond Bond definitively attributes 251 essays each to Addison and Steele – but 162 of Steele's contributions feature letters from outsiders (apparently mostly genuine).[29] In *The Englishman*, Steele distances his editors from the most polemical parts of his message: instead of delivering controversial judgments themselves, they receive and publish the opinions of their readers. One anonymous letter-writer emphasises that the monarch is not above the law (76), offering an eloquent defence of the citizen's role as a check on governing institutions: 'An *Englishman* may speak his Opinion *without Doors* as well as *within Doors*: He may, nay he ought to have a jealous Eye upon the Officers and Servants of his Prince: He may, and he ought to alarm his Fellow-Subjects'. The correspondent also encourages the editor of *The Englishman* 'to cry aloud and spare not', using his paper to help maintain a watchful populace (75). Steele has shifted here from an authorial model of journalism to an editorial one, which implies broad popular support for the editor. It gives the impression of a whole community of government critics – not one disaffected writer operating alone.

Steele's epistolary journalism has another important effect: to model public political behaviour for his audience. His outside contributors are also his readers, and who have been invited to weigh in, to voice strong

---

[29] *Spectator*, vol. 1, pp. lviii–lix.

opinions, to think critically about state matters. As much as any of his contemporaries, Steele creates in his journalism a sense of shared public discourse, where 'Steele' (a frequent letter-writer) participates alongside the editor and other commentators of all stripes. His contributors – again, whether real or fictional – represent a wide-demographic. 'Constant Churchman' (*Englishman* no. 55) denounces high-flyers like Sacheverell, and 'Ralph English' (no. 42) likewise challenges high Tory dogma; MPs write to Steele's editors, but so do commoners like 'John Smith, Corn-Cutter'. The levelling effect is crucial: all citizens have a right, indeed a duty, to be active participants in a textual public sphere. Epistolary journalism serves as an effective vehicle for late Stuart Whig populism.

Steele's party periodicals are emphatically oriented toward readers and texts. His epistolary journalism makes a space for readers to participate directly, and more generally he acknowledges that the public sphere is a textual one. Nowhere is this more apparent than in *The Reader* (spring 1714), whose title signals a distinctly Whiggish commitment. In *The Reader*, he reiterates themes that run throughout his late Stuart journalism: Dunkirk, the naturalisation of foreign Protestants, the problem of monarchical overreaching, and so on. His guide, however, is not a 'guardian' or a censor or a patriotic 'Englishman' but, specifically, a consumer of texts – and of daily papers in particular. In the inaugural issue (22 April), his speaker announces that he has for 'a long Time frequented Coffee-houses and read Papers', but has found himself 'mis-led rather than enlightened' by the press. The persona speaks not only for himself but for all English subjects: 'I humbly . . . desire all who, like my self, have been patient or gentle Readers, to take in me, who set up in Behalf of all Persons who . . . have been imposed upon. . . . I step out to do all of those good People Justice' (143). His aim, then, is exposure – and he sets his sights on *The Examiner* and other Tory outlets. Steele has his narrator address the audience more frequently than either Bickerstaff or Ironside had, reflecting his desire to remind his audience of their agency and their ability to consume Tory propaganda critically. *The Reader* reveals Steele's awareness of the relationship between texts and policy: 'I, who have been a careful Reader, have observed that it has been the Trick, for some Time past, to let drop Hints in the *Examiner* . . . of what has been openly avowed afterwards: The Way to any unwelcome Circumstances has been paved by some received Writers' (149).

Steele conditions readers to pay attention to the import of what the ministry's pens are publishing, and he stays close to the texts he is critiquing – principally Oldisworth's *Examiner*. He quotes passages and explains the rationale behind his disapproval, encouraging what we would now call deconstructive reading. In no. 6, Steele's narrator insists that, 'A Reader that has any Understanding is naturally a Commentator' (164) – a premise key to the nature of his enterprise. Crucially, he moves from private consumption of partisan propaganda to public criticism: the civically responsible way to read is *publicly*. Wise readers should be commentators, and commentators have audiences. Steele and other late Stuart Whigs recognised that the establishment of a vigilant, constitution-defending populace depended to some extent upon encouraging subjects to be discerning consumers and critics of the propaganda on which corrupt ministries depend. Journalists who speak directly to readers are often those who also show awareness of – and create – a textual public sphere. In *The Patriot*, for example, the Whig narrator announces his aim of 'tak[ing] notice of every thing I hear, see or read', and he freely 'recommend[s]' texts 'to the Perusal of [his] Readers' (20). Addison and Mainwaring's *Whig-Examiner* (1710) devotes its five numbers to analysis and interpretation of *The Examiner*; the authors remind readers that 'impudent Assertions must pass for Arguments' (1), training them to be discerning in their interactions with texts. Almost everything *The Whig-Examiner* includes is offered so 'That the Reader may see. . . .'. (2). Contemporaries conceived of the textual and political public spheres as intimately connected: critical thinkers make engaged citizens. Kate Loveman has suggested – in response to Barbara Benedict's association of scepticism and transgression – that 'supporters of the government and the established Church were prepared to encourage a wary, questioning attitude in the reading public'.[30] This may be true in pamphlet and sermon literature, but within the canon of periodicals conservative writers almost never speak to readers in a way that promotes sceptical curiosity.

What can we conclude about how *The Spectator* and *The Tatler* functioned in terms of the creation of a Habermasian public sphere? First, the degree to which they promote non-participation has been overstated; they invite a kind of surveillance that leads naturally to the active vigilance later demanded in *The Englishman*. Second, Addison and Steele's most famous papers have represented the major test case for Habermas's paradigm of a new model of publicness, which is a problem: they epitomise neither Steele's later Stuart periodical writings nor contemporaneous papers by others. Third, *The Tatler* and *The Spectator* have recently been reinterpreted

---

[30] Kate Loveman, *Reading Fictions, 1660–1740: Deception in English Literary and Political Culture* (Aldershot, 2008), p. 34.

as seeking to limit rather than foster public politics, but if we place them alongside the Tory journalism of Swift and Leslie, they no longer seem restrictive. Addison and Steele do not challenge those promoting rowdy street politics; they instead offer alternatives to those like Swift who call for submission and dutiful non-reflection. *The Examiner* and other high Tory outlets taught readers that even to 'reflect' upon the government represents a violation of civic duty. In *The Importance of the Guardian Considered* (1713), Swift takes Steele to task for irreverently supposing 'it is every Man's Right to find fault with the Administration in Print, whenever they please' (230). In a world where critical rumination is an act of disloyalty, Addison's and Steele's promotion of public spectatorship is more partisan than it may appear to modern scholars.

Mr. Examiner and the rhetoric of assent

Though Swift would in the 1720s and 1730s find himself playing the role of patriotic champion of liberties, his attitude toward 'the people' was never positive. As many of his students have observed, he was temperamentally authoritarian, and while working for Queen Anne's last ministry he defended the prerogative of the monarch and the government against populist demands and inquiries. Those who wrote for *The Examiner* before he took over – including Dr. William King, Francis Atterbury, Matthew Prior, and Henry St. John – shared his prejudices about what we now call 'the fourth estate', as did his principal successor as Mr. Examiner, William Oldisworth. Not surprisingly, what we find in *The Examiner* is essentially the opposite of what we find in Steele's *Englishman*: pressure to behave, obey, acquiesce. Swift never directly tells his readers to be passive subjects, but his rhetorical choices throughout establish the values of reticence and compliance.

Swift's formal and tonal choices are significant. In *A Tale of a Tub* and *An Argument against Abolishing Christianity*, he deliberately misleads and disorients, forcing readers to be constantly on guard, sceptical about the veracity of texts and authors. In journalism, that vexing manner would be out of place and self-defeating. *The Examiner* is meant to seem authoritative, to discourage certain kinds of incredulity. This could be why Swift eschews extensive quarrelling with his party rivals. Steele, Defoe, and others do battle, in their papers, with other journals – not only responding critically but also offering readers examples of how to do so. Swift, as we shall see, largely avoids animadversion, partly because (unlike Steele) he does not want his audience to see themselves as engaged and critical readers; in fact he mentions 'the Reader' only once (p. 185), whereas the language of reading is prevalent in the Whig journals of Steele, Defoe, *et al.*

In *The Examiner*'s inaugural issue, probably pre-dating Swift's involvement, the author announces his aim: to 'Examine, *and set People right in their Opinions: My chief Business will be to instruct my Country-men*'. The point is not to awaken or engage, but to tell English subjects what to think. Swift's contributions reflect the same objective. One repeatedly finds in his essays an invitation for readers *not* to be critical inquirers but to trust him for the truth: 'the People may be convinced, that five parts in six of what the *Examiners* have charg'd on the late M[inist]ry and Faction is right' (482). Swift's successor, Oldisworth, carries on the language of passive reception. In election season, Oldisworth – contra Steele, Tutchin, and other Whigs – promotes an acquiescent populace: 'If the Generality of our People, whose Station is fix'd in middle Life, and who are by Nature Plain, Honest, and Well-meaning', do not feel capable of judging, 'I know not where they can apply themselves better, or with a fairer Prospect of being set right in their Measures . . . than by consulting the Clergy of the *Church of England*' (vol. 4, no. 26). In December 1713, Oldisworth characterises Whig writing as a series of threats, utterly predictable and groundless: 'An Author's usual *Exordium, is the Danger of his Country. A State* must be *in Danger* every Time these *People of Importance* write'. Whig writers wish to make English readers and subjects into '*tame negligent Creatures*, whom they are sent to *Warn* and *Admonish*' (vol. 5, no. 3). The implication is that English subjects do not need to be roused; if Whigs wish to incite the people to action, Mr. Examiner seeks to anesthetise.

Throughout his *Examiner*, Swift naturalises assent and radicalises innovation. That will not come as news to Swiftians, but the way he manages to communicate this attitude toward the fourth estate deserves attention. In no. 25, Mr. Examiner explains, 'It is *Machiavel's* Observation, that the People when left to their own Judgment, do seldom mistake their true Interests; and indeed they naturally love the Constitution they are born under, never desiring to change but under great Oppressions' (180). The subtext: our natural, inborn inclination is to resist change and follow our leaders. Any alternative tendency is therefore unnatural, the product of manipulation and delusion. As Swift frames his argument here, to think Whiggishly is to be under an outside influence, 'under great Oppressions'. To submit is, paradoxically, to act according to one's 'own Judgment'. Independence, then, looks like compliance, and vice versa. Swift consistently pathologises popular political action, treating it as a sign only of lunacy: 'the Madness of the People hath [in the past] risen to such a height as to break in pieces the whole Frame of the best instituted Governments' (180).

The Tory sympathies on display of late represent not 'a new Madness' but a 'Recovery from an old One' (181). Obedience signals recuperation from a collective Whig malady; commitment to conservative ideology is a sign of mental health.

Swift has much to say about the proper behaviour of the people: they are either true subjects or part of a mob. In no. 17, he calls for 'entire *Submission and Respect*, to Her Sacred Person and Commands', anticipating 'universal Hatred' toward those who would usurp power from the queen (51). The presumption is that English subjects will turn against the disaffected, aligning their interest with that of state and monarch. Swift is fond of describing the Queen and Ministry as 'belov'd by the People' (211), of affirming that 'those who are now at the Helm, are entirely in the true Interest of the Prince and People' (432).[31] In no. 22, he maintains that the Queen's decision to change her ministry was 'suitable to her own Wisdom, and the Wishes of her Subjects' (132). He insinuates that the moment those 'People' are anything other than contently respectful, they become an unruly and/or deluded mob. In no. 30, as elsewhere, Swift elides the distance between 'the Prince and People', treating that relationship as mutually beneficial and natural (259). In theory, a bad king can overstep, but for Swift the more immediate danger is in the other direction, when the people separate themselves from their monarch. The faction, those who unnaturally challenge 'the old Establishment', tend to 'strengthen' themselves by enlisting 'the lowest of the People' (286).

One of Swift's rhetorical manoeuvres involves describing loyalty as essentially passive. Active verbs are bad, as far as the people are concerned, in the world of Mr. Examiner. In no. 38, he suggests that support for Anne and her decisions has been made 'plain . . . by the visible Disposition of the People', but the 'visible Disposition', for Swift, manifests itself invisibly. True subjects show their allegiance through acceptance. He describes 'a wise and good Prince, at the Head of an able Ministry, and of a Senate freely chosen; all united to pursue the true Interest of their Country'. The '*Vox Populi*', he continues, is 'indisputably declarative on the same Side' (464). Once again, 'declarative' suggests vocal backing, something active and engaged. But read in the context of the whole *Examiner*, 'declarative' sponsorship seems suspiciously like silent assent – the withholding of judgment and the cooperation in Swift's erasure of any distance between genuine subjects and Her Majesty. Even to 'reflect upon the Q[ueen] and the Ministry' is treachery (165).

---

[31] Or, as Oldisworth concludes, 'the Prerogative of the Prince and Liberties of the People [have been] brought to an exact Consistency' (*Examiner*, vol. 4, no. 50).

Mr. Examiner is explicit about the fact that citizens do not need to know all that happens at the state level: 'it is certain, that a wise and good Prince will not change his Ministers without very important Reasons; and a good Subject ought to suppose, that in such a Case there are such good Reasons, tho' he be not appris'd of them' (pp. 83–84). Elsewhere, he takes exception to his rival Abel Boyer's peddling the parliamentary news in the *Political State of Great Britain*: because Boyer has 'more *Whig*-Customers than *Tories*', he has insolently 'take[n] it into his Head to write Politick Tracts of our Affairs' (433). The fault lies with the Whig consumers as much as Boyer; all are committed to the unnatural principle that state policy should be subject to public consideration and coffeehouse chat. This is consonant with Swift's comments elsewhere about 'those absurd notions of civil power', and about the problem of public opinion: 'this Way of every Subject interposing their Sentiments upon the Management of foreign Negotiations, is a very new Thing among us, and the Suffering it, has been thought in the Opinion of wise Men, too great a Strain upon the Prerogative'.[32]

Mr. Examiner's disapproval of a Habermasian public sphere sounds a bit like that critics find in Mr. Spectator and Bickerstaff. Reading them alongside one another, however, brings some key disparities into specific relief. *The Tatler* and *The Spectator* both endorse a kind of citizen perception. They do not deny the right of subjects to follow politics, and Steele can rarely resist offering 'news', even as he and Addison acknowledge that the political climate of 1710–1714 will not reward the civic engagement of honest Whigs. If we want to talk about a partisan journalist truly committed to popular civic non-participation, then we should look to Swift, not to Addison and certainly not to Steele. When in *The Englishman* Steele addresses his 'Fellow-Subjects', he is integrating readers into a shared community, the same virtual public sphere in which he is operating himself. He invites readers to identify his public commentary as a model. He and Addison do not go so far in *The Tatler* and *The Spectator*, but the difference seems a matter of degree.

Neither Addison nor Steele would ever accept Mr. Examiner's definition of 'subject'. For Swift, at least in 1710–1714, a subject is subordinate, not only to the government but also to its spokesman, Mr. Examiner. Thinking himself an insider and the ministry's man, he does not imagine a public sphere in which he participates on a level with his readers. *The Englishman* represents a particularly potent contrast. Steele's periodical takes to the virtual

---

[32] *A Sermon upon the Martyrdom of K. Charles I* (1726; *PW*, vol. 9, p. 223); David Woolley (ed.), *The Correspondence of Jonathan Swift, D. D.* (4 vols., Frankfurt am Main, 1999–2007), vol. 1, p. 472.

streets; Mr. Examiner is, on the contrary, a pulpit journalist conditioning his flock to receive in silence. But Swift turns out to be adept at using rhetoric to neutralise his ideas, at communicating high Tory values in a style and manner that seems more moderate – and more participatory – than it is. *The Examiner* is in this way opposite of the '*Spectator* project', which appears to be more discouraging of public politics than Addison and Steele really were. Irvin Ehrenpreis describes Mr. Examiner's 'constant positive theme' as 'the will of the people',[33] a surprising summation considering the manifest authoritarian, anti-populist tendencies of the paper. Ehrenpreis, however, is not entirely wrong. What Swift does so masterfully is to create the fiction of speaking *for* the people while in fact speaking *to* them.

A comparison with Charles Leslie's high Tory *Rehearsal* will illustrate my point. Leslie and Swift are broadly sympathetic with one another, both intolerant of dissent and fully committed to a deeply conservative politics, but *The Rehearsal* represents a useful contrast to *The Examiner*. The distinction has less to do with ideology than with approach. Leslie preaches to the choir, and his message is unequivocal: no circumstances ever justify resistance to church and state. One either gives oneself wholly to monarchical and episcopal authority – in complete obedience – or one dangerously separates oneself and endangers one's mortal soul. In November 1707, as elsewhere, Leslie asserts, 'There is no *Rebellion* but for *Power*. Other things, as *Religion, Liberty,* &c. are made the *Pretence*, to stir up the *People*' (vol. 2, no. 13). Legitimate popular protest is an oxymoron; civic rights represent a perilous Whig fancy. *The Rehearsal* reads like a handbook on how to breed and maintain submission.

Leslie has nothing but contempt for Whig writers who 'infect' (vol. 3, no. 19) or 'Gull' (vol. 4, no. 7) the people. Any appeal to or engagement with the populace is tantamount to rebellion, and when he speaks of them, he does so in the third person. Rather than warning them or appealing to them to behave – as Swift often seems to do – Leslie merely fulminates for the benefit of like-minded readers. For Leslie, subjects are largely irrelevant to the workings of government; he shows little patience for voting or for parliamentary representation. He is inflexible on the point: 'The *People* cannot *Derive* their *Authority*. They ever were, and must be in *Subjection*' (vol. 3, no. 28). Leslie's periodical represents a deliberate counter to the Whig papers, whose popularity among the plebeians he laments:

---

[33] Irvin Ehrenpreis, *Swift: The Man, his Works, the Age* (3 vols., London, 1962–1983), vol. 2, p. 411.

> Their *Books* and *Pamphlets* have been solidly and seriously Answer'd. But their *Papers* have been neglected, that is their *weekly penny Papers*, which go through the Nation like *News-papers*. And have done more *Mischief* than the others ... the greatest Part of the *People* do not Read *Books*, Most of them cannot *Read* at all. But they will Gather together about one that can *Read*, and Listen to an *Observator* or *Review* (as I have seen them in the Streets) where all the *Principles* of *Rebellion* are Instill'd into them.[34]

The crux here is Leslie's patent antagonism toward public politics, toward the whole notion of (reading) politics out of doors.

Mr. Examiner would agree with most of what Leslie concludes, but the two adopt significantly different rhetorical stances. Rather than indiscriminately scorning 'the people', Swift offers two models: the respectable, principled subjects who live in obedience, and the rabble. Leslie makes no such distinction: when he invokes 'the people', he almost always does so as rebels or would-be rebels, active or potential rabblers of church and state. He shows his disdain for readers' capacity for reason or discernment. Mr. Rehearsal's conversation partner, Countryman, functions as a kind of stand-in for the common reader, and Leslie makes clear Countryman's exemplary docility. Countryman's short speech in the 3 April 1708 issue offers considerable insight into Leslie's attitude toward his rhetorical relationship with his readers:

> Now, *Master*, you have sometimes a Short way to Determin a Point, and give one a Clear thought of a thing, such as one may fit Common Capacities like mine, and make it Easy to us, without sending us to Learned Books, and things we do not Understand. I wish you may be so Happy in this, and not to carry me out of my Depth for an Answer, for that will but Perplex the Cause the more.... (vol. 3, no. 1)

Countryman serves as deferential student and sycophant, utterly dependent upon his '*Master*' for instruction and moral clarity. As this passage suggests, Leslie invites the reader to identify with Countryman – that is, to be submissive and to heed (and remember) the lessons of his sage counsellor. One notices a pattern in Countryman's self-effacing comments: 'I Shall not forget a good while, *Master*, that *Rule* you gave me in

---

[34] Leslie, *The Rehearsal*, preface to vol. 1; quoted in Downie, 'Stating Facts Right About Defoe's *Review*', p. 17.

your Last....'. (vol. 2, no. 3); 'What you said last time, *Master*, has made a Great *Impression* upon me' (vol. 2, no. 7); 'But yet, *Master*, I wou'd know a little, if you please to tell me....'. (vol. 2, no. 16); 'you have Instructed me better', and so on (2:30). Countryman is a model of intellectual submission. Countryman is tiresomely diffident, even needy, as the preface to the final volume highlights: '*Must I part with my Dear* Master *– When shall I get such another?*' The dialogue functions catechistically; readers are encouraged to respond as though to a preacher before them in a pulpit. Leslie's quasi-Catholic tendencies are on display here, and aesthetics again complement and parallel ideology: the journalist serves as mediator between the sacred institutions and the uncomprehending people, who should be denied direct access to the mysteries of state. Whether or not Leslie sought to demoralise his readers, his paper has that effect. He repeatedly insists that too much complexity, or too many words, might 'Confound ... the Reader' (vol. 2, no. 3). Leslie's critics bristled at this treatment. In 1707, one author complained that Countryman was made to 'ask *silly Questions*, and you [Mr. Rehearsal] answer them *wisely*, if you can; but not to dispute things above a Clownish Understanding'.[35] The Whig *Observator*, on the contrary, dwells upon the Countryman's reading: he routinely brings pamphlets along to discuss with Mr. Observator, and he comes having already read and reached a verdict on those texts.[36]

Leslie's heavy-handed preachment is tonally and rhetorically distinct from his ally's. *The Examiner* is not exactly lenient or forbearing, but Swift operates as much by way of conditioning as of straight denunciation. Both Swift and Leslie want obedience and loyalty from the public, but Leslie denies, wholesale, any legitimate public voice. His authority derives not from reason or popular affirmation but from the righteousness of the Christian code; he is an imposing figure, not a likeable one. In the wake of a Tory landslide in the fall 1710 election, Swift can afford to write as though he personally were backed by the powers-that-be and by the people, and he assumes rather than argues for the authority of his positions. His *Examiner*, despite being thoroughly anti-populist, sometimes *appears* to represent the people. Swift gives the impression of empowering a subgroup of subjects, while in reality encouraging them only to submit.

[35] Lloyd, *Muzzle for a Mad Dog*, 6. Leslie's journalism was not as frequently targeted as *The Examiner*, presumably because the latter claimed to be 'official' in a way that Leslie did not.
[36] See for example nos. 52 and 56.

The Medley and *The Observator*: Whig politicisation of the people

The public sphere as envisioned in *The Medley* and especially in the more radical *Observator* is fundamentally unlike that hopefully projected by Mr. Examiner and Leslie. Not surprisingly, Mainwaring, Oldmixon, Tutchin, and Ridpath (the major contributors to these two papers) share many of Steele's values.

The Medley (1710–1712) was the principal rival to the Tory *Examiner*, and Mainwaring and Oldmixon contest Swift *et al.* on virtually every point, including their notions of public politics. They see the journalist's job as raising consciousness among the people. For his 'Itch of meddling with matters', Mainwaring is unapologetic (no. 2), and throughout he invites readers to ask questions of the government and the writers who defend it. Its inaugural issue responds to Defoe's *Essay upon Publick Credit* (1710), complaining that the author had chosen not to '*examine what politick Reasons induc'd her M[ajesty] to change*' her ministry: 'this I am sure you will regret as I do, because it is the thing in the World which I verily believe he could have given most Light into'. The 'you' here is specifically the *Whig-Examiner*, but the pronoun has broader resonance. Whig writers like Mainwaring and Steele rely on the second person in a way Leslie and Swift do not, directly engaging their audience and rhetorically constructing a community of debate that includes themselves and their readers on a level with each other.

Unlike Swift, Mainwaring and Oldmixon create rather than collapse distance between prince and people. In *Medley* no. 13, Mainwaring challenges Mr. Examiner's affirmation that '*the People join'd as one Man to wish the Ministry chang'd*', maintaining on the contrary that 'every Man of Business or Intelligence in *Great Britain* was alarm'd at the late Changes' (119). The tidy equation of the royal prerogative and subjects' liberties so prominent in Swift is absent from *The Medley*, where readers are instead reminded of their connection to parliamentary representatives (e.g., p. 91). In no. 30, Mainwaring and Oldmixon cite 'the *Elections* . . . and . . . the late Choice of an Alderman in one of the City-Wards, which had been long in Tory Hands' as clear evidence that the Whig ministry was 'not *hated by the People*' (384). They challenge Swift's assertion of Tory popularity, and their index of popular support is also distinct from his. Like Steele in *The Englishman*, Mainwaring speaks of his 'Fellow-Subjects', writing as one enlisted not just to protect their interests (which Swift would say of Mr. Examiner, too) but also to teach them to guard those interests themselves. Swift's and Leslie's journalistic personae are figures of authority, standing in for and answerable to church and state; Mainwaring and Oldmixon position themselves as monitors of the government, answerable to the subjects living under it.

The Observator is in every respect a more radical Whig journal. Its endorsement of a participatory public is manifest from beginning to end. Scholars have emphasised the 'shared ... aversion to widening popular participation in the political public sphere',[37] and a related anxiety about the free press – but Tutchin is an exception. Though 'the Press needs ... Regulation', he concludes, it needs 'but so little, that we need not trouble our Heads about it' (vol. 4, no. 73). If modern critics are looking for their liberal counterpart in the early eighteenth century, Tutchin and his fellow *Observator* authors seem most closely to foreshadow modern liberal thought. Tutchin's use of the dialogue form itself opens up the possibility for deliberation and inquiry. The rhetorical situation is not one authority telling readers, authoritatively, what to think, but modelling the mutual – and mutually self-respecting – engagement of author and readers. Tutchin's Observator and his Countryman enjoy a relatively smooth rapport, and while the latter's role is subordinate, his conversation partner treats him with affection: 'thou art Honest *Roger*, my Country Friend' (vol. 3, no. 42). Countryman at times shows his innocence: 'Pray, Sir, what is a *High-Churchman*?' (vol. 1, no. 25). But he also reads, listens, and forms opinions: 'I vow, Mr. *Observator*, I don't like these *High Churchmen*, as they call themselves; they Rail at the *Moderate Churchmen*, which I esteem the only true Members of the Church of *England*' (35). When he passes judgment on the high-flyers, he seems all the more credible because he did not begin as a rabidly partisan figure; Tutchin presents him as an unindoctrinated, well-meaning chap who arrives at the truth through rational dialogue. Countryman feels entitled to his own opinions, and – significantly – nothing in his relationship to Mr. Observator undermines that conviction. When Leslie launches *The Rehearsal* in response to *The Observator*, he drastically revises this dynamic. Both Tutchin and Leslie seem to use the Countryman figure to represent a good subject; unlike Bayes, dramatised as Marvell's opponent in *The Rehearsal Transpros'd* (whose title Leslie invokes), Countryman stands in for the reader. Leslie models proper submission, Tutchin rational political conversation among equals.

Neither Tutchin (who operated the journal until his death in 1707) nor Ridpath (who took over at some point in 1710) – nor anyone involved in the interim – has much to say about monarchs or about subjects' obedience to traditional authorities. The emphasis is on parliaments, though Tutchin grants more popular than parliamentary sovereignty: 'We do trust our Representatives' to guard our liberties, he argues, but if they fail to do so to our satisfaction, '*They have Betray'd their Trust*' (vol. 4, no. 5). His position on

---

[37] Cowan, 'Mr. Spectator and the Coffeehouse Public Sphere', p. 351.

popular authority is more extreme than that of moderate Whig contemporaries: 'the People have a Natural Power Inherent in them to chuse their own Governours, and to settle 'em in Succession, Reversion, Election, or other wise'.[38] Tutchin endorses the more traditional Whig philosophy that 'The Affections of the People are the best Security to the *Crown*', and that the 'Title' alone 'cannot Support it self' (vol. 5, no. 22). The royal prerogative and the people's liberties should be bound together, as Swift also argued, but for Tutchin the burden is upon the monarch to ensure the allegiance of her subjects.[39]

Both Tutchin and Ridpath work to create an informed electorate ready to act collectively for its own good, whether peaceably or no. On 4 November 1704, Tutchin proclaims to 'have as good a Right to use my Pen' in the fight for English liberties as any one has to write against them. 'I have better hopes of the Citizens of *London*', he continues, than to suppose that they will live under oppression: 'they have seen the ill Effects of Party-Prosecutions in former times, and I believe are better inform'd than to tear off a Member from their Body out of a Humour of pleasing a Party' (vol. 3, no. 66). His right to speak is matched by the right of Whig subjects to stand up to their high-flying enemies; he both acknowledges their voice and invites them to use it. Earlier, he had reflected on historical episodes of tyranny and persecution, observing that the '*Folly*' of the victims was 'not *Defending* their *Rights*' (vol. 1, no. 12). The moral, for present-day readers, is clear. Our assumptions about late Stuart writers' widespread discomfort with public politics – about the apprehensions even among those journalists who were fostering public debate – do not much help with *The Observator*.

Mr. Review's Protestant spectacles

Defoe perhaps does more than any other contemporary journalist to appeal to and create 'public opinion', though his attitude toward his readers and their capacity for rational political participation is complicated. The opening sentence of his long-running *Review* clarifies part of his relationship to his audience: '*When Authors present their Works to the World, like a Thief*

---

[38] 'Vindication', p. 2.
[39] Carnell has observed that Defoe does something similar in *Robinson Crusoe*: 'When the voice of "the people" is literally one and the same as the voice of the sovereign, social-contract theory achieves its ideal representation. Robinson Crusoe, both subject and king, embodies not just a parallel between household and state, but an exact identity between the two realms' (*Partisan Politics*, p. 86).

at the Gallows; they make a Speech to the People. The Author indeed has something like this to say too, Good People all take Warning by me' (vol. 1, p. 1). Throughout, Mr. Review fashions himself a friend to the people; he writes as guide, informer, and enlightener, though in the later years of the paper he seems increasingly uncertain about the reasoning faculties of his 'poor blinded' fellow subjects (vol. 7, p. 56). If his attitude toward 'the people' shifts, what stays consistent is his determination to depict high-flyers as separate from 'the nation', to construct, rally, and unify a Protestant public sphere threatened by immoderate Tories.

At different times in *The Review*, Defoe addresses both his allies and his enemies, but he consistently asserts a distinction between the interests of high Tories and those of the nation. In election season, he appeals 'to all the People of *England,* that if they will secure the Church and Government, there is no better Rule for Poor Men to guide their Votes by, than not to Vote as the *Papists* and *Non-jurors* do' (vol. 2, p. 215). When he maintains, 'we are Brethren', the plural pronoun encompasses all true Protestants and only true Protestants (216). His mission, as declared in 1705, is to cultivate 'the Publick Peace of *Protestants*' (245). Lecturing the high-flyers, Mr. Review insists that 'the Queen, the House of Lords, the Bishops, the Moderate Clergy, and all the Gentlemen of *England,* that are troubled with the Faculty of Thinking, are so Engag'd against your Design', and so on (163), clearly defining rational English citizens as part of a united public to which high Tories do not belong. Later he contends that 'the Gentlemen of the High-Church' can expect 'the Nations Resentment' (482).

Throughout, Mr. Review disputes Leslie's understanding of who does and who does not represent 'the nation', who are the patriots and who the rebels.[40] Though 'A *Whig may be false* to the Nation', under enough pressure, 'a *High Flyer* must do it, he destroys his own Principle else' (vol. 4, p. 129). Defoe's ideal public is an electorate of Protestant voters who value Protestant unity, fear Catholicism and Jacobitism, and resist the rabbling violence of the Tory mobs. His most violent language is directed at the Sacheverellite horde, 'The vilest of the People, the Scum of the Earth, the Drunken, Swearing, Damning, and most Hellishly Debauched' (vol. 7, p. 99). Like Mr. Examiner, Defoe divides the populace into true citizens and disruptive rebels, though they disagree about which group is of which party.

Defoe is of course contemptuous of his high-flying contemporaries, but what of his attitude toward 'the people' more broadly conceived, that Protestant citizenship to which he appears to be appealing? In the early volumes, Defoe is (like Steele) ever conscious of his readers and of their

---

[40] For example, *Review*, vol. 3, p. 411.

habits of reading. No. 5 opens with a 'DIGRESSION to the READER', something one would never find in the Tory journals of Anne's reign (vol. 1, p. 36). The Scandal Club of 1704–1705, a subsection of *The Review*, begins as a vehicle with which Defoe can critique his brethren of the quill. Initially, the mission of the Scandal Club was to 'the Correction of News-papers', a 'Burthen' that proved so 'constant and intolerable' that Mr. Review laid it aside for a while. But, he explains, 'the Importunity of such Gentlemen as are daily offended with the Blunders and Errors of these Sons of the Incorrigible, calls [the Society] back again to this Work' (vol. 1, p. 160).[41] Defoe is taking on his journalistic adversaries, as well as fostering a world of readers exasperated by the 'Blunders and Errors' in the press.

Mr. Review repeatedly reminds his readers that they are readers. When he disputes *The Post Man* and *The Rehearsal*, he sets up a culture of debate, and he assures his readers that the right to question is universal: 'We now live under a Government that will hear Truth, and the freedom of the Press intimates any Man may write it' (vol. 1, p. 606). Defoe writes in an accessible, reader-friendly way: he makes cases rather than delivering judgments, offers lists and step-by-step reasoning. His form corresponds with his rhetoric: he seems to want his readers to be persuaded, to follow his logic rather than merely accepting his conclusions. He may not be democratic in the modern sense of the term, but he both demonstrates 'demotic vigor'[42] and eschews elitism: 'It is easie to tell you the Consequences of Popular Confusions, Private Quarrels, and Party Feuds, without Reading *Virgil*, *Horace*, or *Homer*' (vol. 2, p. 227).[43]

Although Defoe relies upon biblical authority, the ethos of his speaker derives largely from his (seemingly) transparent reasoning, his use of historical sources, and his political 'logic'. Few papers are more historically-minded, in Anne's reign, than the Whig *Review* and *Observator*; they relentlessly appeal to history and use past-based polemic. Defoe's apparent lack of artifice is an effective strategy, a powerful complement to his commitment to colloquialism. He makes a point of reminding readers that he is speaking plainly: '*Let not those Gentlemen who are Criticks in Stile, in Method or Manner, be angry that I have never pull'd off my Cap to them in humble Excuse for my loose way of treating the World as to Language, Expression, and Politeness of Phrase*' (preface, vol. 1). Defoe is not, of course, as frank as he seems, but the persona he projects in *The Review*

---

[41] In the 22 March 1705 issue, Defoe prints a letter from a concerned citizen encouraging the Scandal Club, '*Pray Revive your Endeavours of Reforming our* News-Writers; *let Publick Faults receive as Publick Censures*' (vol. 2, p. 51).

[42] Richetti, *Life of Daniel Defoe*, p. 99.

[43] Cowan makes this point ('Daniel Defoe's *Review*', p. 98).

depends upon that pose. The appearance of forthrightness is given credibility by Defoe's decision – like Tutchin in *The Observator* but unlike Swift, Leslie, Steele, *inter alia* – to speak as himself in *The Review*. He renounces anonymity, collapsing the distance between author and persona. Having no mask, he implies, means having no fiction. As much as any other journalist of his time (perhaps excepting Steele) he is ever conscious of the reader, and explicit in his intention to be accessible.

By 1707–1708, Mr. Review has begun to stress not the rational powers of 'the people', but instead their dangerous credulity. On 29 November 1707, he describes man as 'a short-sighted Creature, and weak in his politick Opticks' (vol. 4, p. 650), insinuating that his role is to lead rather than to enable self-leadership. The 18 December issue continues this theme, focusing on the manipulation, in the pulpit and the press, of a gullible populace: 'I confess, we are a Nation willing to be deluded, willing to be imposed upon, and nothing is so absurd, but we are pleased with it, rather than not have some News' (696). Mr. Review complains about the Tory 'Forgeries' and 'scandalous News', reflecting dolefully on the reception such misinformation receives:

> really the Infirmity of our People is remarkable; in that they seem pleased with melancholly Reports, and willing to have things made worse to them than they are, that they appear gratify'd with the Phlegmatick Part, and love to be poring upon their Misfortunes, with the magnifying Glass of their own Hypocondriack Vapours; of these People I shall speak by themselves hereafter, but at present my Observations are not so much upon the Deluded, as upon the Deluders. (694)

Between 1707 and the end of *The Review*, Defoe routinely bestows the epithet 'poor' upon the 'people'.[44]

The blindness of the people is a major theme of *The Review*, along with the systematic high-flying attempt to maintain popular ignorance. From the beginning, Mr. Review vows 'to Enlighten the Stupid Understandings of the Meaner and more Thoughtless of the Freeholders and Electors', to put 'this Age in Mind of the Injury they do themselves, by their constant misrepresenting Things to themselves' (vol. 2, p. 205, vol. 5, p. 284). But he becomes more adamant in later issues, as well as more explicit in blaming the high-flyers for hoodwinking good citizens. In the summer of 1710, he insists, 'That . . . this Nation be [not] overwhelmed by these rising Mists

---

[44] See for example *Review*, vol. 7, p. 56.

to the Ruine of her politick Senses, and particularly her *Eye sight*, is the
... single Design of Writing this Paper' (vol. 7, p. 188). Though he has earlier
seemed to despair of his chances to awaken an unthinking populace, here
he expresses his conviction that, 'their Eyes WILL be open'd, and ... all the
Peoples Eyes *do already begin* to be open'd' (244). A buzzword of 1708–1711
is '*Spectacles*', without which 'we must ... be quite Blind'; Defoe is concerned
that true patriots 'supply ... the poor People with them *Gratis*' (245). In July
1710, in the middle of the ministerial change that would reinstall the Tories,
Defoe describes the '*Party-Mists* and *State-Vapours*' that keep people in the
dark. Because 'BLINDNESS happens to be our Predominate, there cannot
be a greater piece of Service done to our Nation, than to assist them with
SPECTACLES ... which may clear up their *National* Eye-sight, and assist
them to convey right Notions to their Understandings' (260).

Defoe's apparently adversarial role – his angry addresses to the 'ENG-
LISH FOOLS!' (vol. 7, p. 265) – should not be read as scepticism about
the importance of popular politics. Instead, he seems determined to rouse
readers into exercising their own reason, maintaining his conviction that
'our People want nothing *but to see what they are doing*' (401). That last
comes from the 10 October 1710 number, where he objects again to the
'Senseless Contention' at home and the newswriters who confuse 'the
Country Freeholders and Electors':

> The Method they take to make the Poor People Understand, is by Rob-
> bing them of their Understanding. They appeal to the People; and that
> they may be good Judges, they Debauch their Judgments, blind their
> Eyes, that they may see; make them Drunk, that they may come to a
> sober Enquiry into the Thing, and doze their Heads, that they may be
> steady in Discerning. All the Arts and Engines imaginable are made
> use of, to bring the People to a wilful giving up themselves to Names
> and Parties, without Examining into Things, and into the Substance or
> Merits of the Debate. (399)

Defoe's hostility is primarily directed at the 'Deluders', who create such
chaos of misrepresentation and partisan distortion that subjects are hope-
less to distinguish fact from fiction. Significantly, this passage comes in the
wake of the controversial ministerial change. A few months earlier, Defoe
complained that no reasons for the removal of the Whig Sunderland had
been 'made Publick': 'I do not say the Queen had no Reason, or can give no
Reason ... But we find no Reproach cast, no Reflection made, no Reason
given in Justification of the Conduct' (vol. 7, p. 181). Mr. Examiner devotes
himself to persuading the people that they have no business inquiring into

the rationale for the ministerial change; Mr. Review's message is exactly the opposite.

Defoe obsesses over the problem of high Tory deceptiveness, and increasingly he uses the 'wolf in sheep's clothing' metaphor for his enemies. His object is to raise alarm among his fellow low-church Protestants, and to persuade readers of dangerous high-flying 'Subtilty'.[45] In May 1708, he complains, 'O the constant, steady Hypocrisie of *Jacobitism* and *High-Flying!* And O the Stupidity, Blindness and Madness of those who believe what they say!' (vol. 5, p. 101). Two weeks later, he again reflects on a 'Blind and stupid Generation!': 'Do you want Demonstrations of this [ill design]? Is this a thing that wants to be made out? Has not the whole Series of their Actions demonstrated that this is their Meaning?' (139) As elsewhere in his polemical writings, Defoe describes his moment as 'an Age of Plot and Deceit, of Contradiction and Paradox', a time in which 'the Nation can hardly know her Friends from her Enemies' (vol. 6, p. 656) – a reminder of the urgent need for discernment. Scholars like to quote Defoe's warnings about a free press, but we should not underestimate the partisanship of his admonitions: when he bemoans the 'horrid Cheats put upon us every Day in our publick Prints', he has his Tory rivals in mind (vol. 5, p. 284). Mr. Review's apprehensions about the deceptive rhetoric of his high Tory enemies compel him to establish himself as the true guardian of the people. His job is to translate Tory language – à la *The Shortest-Way with the Dissenters* – so that the people can know the designs of the high-flyers. That his allusions to that piece multiply in the middle years of *The Review* is not surprising.[46]

Mr. Review becomes increasingly aggressive toward his readers, less confident that merely affirming their right to participate will work. He tends instead to browbeat them, to din into them the tremendous difficulties of distinguishing between their allies and their adversaries. Some of this may reflect Defoe's defensiveness about the reception of *The Review*. By 1707, he reminds us that readers are finding him *'dull'*, that he has been 'bullied and bantered for . . . not conforming [his] Judgement to the hasty People of this Time' (vol. 4, pp. 1, 461). More broadly, Mr. Review seems alarmed by the credible untruths and pernicious 'Subtilty' of the high-flyers. If readers cannot distinguish between his facts and the enemies' fictions, then all he can do is badger them into accepting that they have no reliable judgment left. The upshot of his protest seems to be that the people must abandon their

---

[45] Defoe links 'Subtilty' with diabolical cunning in several texts, including *Memoirs of Count Tariff* (p. 17) and *The Political History of the Devil* (pp. 93, 103).

[46] For example, *Review*, vol. 5, p. 98, vol. 6, p. 710.

illusions about being able to navigate on their own and instead rely upon him their guide. 'In this wild Field', he concludes, 'leaving your *Examiners, Tattlers, Observators,* and a MEDLY of Moderns to toss the State in a Blanket among them; I shall for a while, talk to you. . . .' (vol. 7, p. 632). Defoe disparages both Whig and Tory papers, all of them contributors to the partisan cacophony, and stands alone, the sole source of impartial elucidation. Mr. Examiner and Mr. Review have this, at least, in common: they both excel at a kind of homiletic journalism, in which the people are schooled in the art of following their one true guide's leadership.

The crux, however, is not that Mr. Review doubts the legitimacy of popular politics. On the contrary, his anxiety about misrepresentation reflects his conviction that subjects need to be informed and engaged. In July 1710, he stresses the need for the Queen to attend to *'the Sense of the Nation'*, since in doing so one 'tacitely [sic] recognise[s] the Peoples concern in the Government'. Defoe deprecates those champions of non-resistance for whom 'it is Nonsense to trouble the Queen with what is the Sense of Her People; for her Majesty has nothing to do but to Command' (vol. 7, p. 222). On 29 November 1707, he imagines his readers asking him what can be done for the good of the country, and his response is a call to action: 'Indeed, Gentlemen, I never was of their Opinion, whose Faith in Omnipotent Power led them to put all the Work upon GOD, and make themselves only Spectators' (vol. 4, p. 650). Mr. Review challenges the assumptions made by Leslie and other Tories that subjects are meant to obey, lamenting the 'Simplicity' of those 'Poor misguided People [who] follow the Clergy' (vol. 2, p. 206). Defoe's self-proclaimed mission is to ensure that all true Protestants, all Englishmen or Britons worthy of the name, have the tools that allow them to see and judge fairly. His public sphere depends upon the provision not only of spectacles but of specifically 'Protestant SPECTACLES' (vol. 7, p. 260), the lens through which Jacobite treachery can be identified and thus defeated.

The press and the people, 1714–1720

As we saw in Chapter 2, Whig and Tory writers' attitudes toward the proper behaviour of subjects undergo something of a reversal in the immediate wake of the Hanoverian succession. George was not a king beloved by commoners, and popular Toryism was strong in the early years of his reign despite Whig success at the polls. Street politics were violent, and the response of the new regime was brutal; mobs protested in support of

Anne's last ministers, and anti-government disturbances were prominent.[47] The replacement of the triennial elections with septennial, the suspension of habeas corpus, the authorised culture of vigilantism, and the redefinition of protest as treason did not silence rebellion as much as it hardened hearts against the government. The authorities rewrote the law to mean that the injury or even murder of rioters would no longer be a punishable offence. Many moderates embraced Jacobitism as an attractive alternative to a ruthless Whig oligarchy. Jacobite papers encourage the people toward rebellion and present James III as a would-be deliverer from Hanoverian tyranny. The Whigs hardly enjoyed a comfortable ascendancy, and were instead anxious about the force of popular demonstrations. In other words, the Tories who preached obedience and submission under Anne now defend subjects' right to critique and act against the government under George I. The Whigs who advocated asking questions and holding the government accountable in the previous reign now call for loyalty.

A couple of examples should suffice. Addison's *Freeholder* (1715–1716) represents a telling contrast from *The Spectator*, particularly in terms of its direct political engagement. Addison's principal objective is to encourage allegiance to the new regime, and – à la Mr. Examiner – to discourage subjects from asking questions about what does not concern them:

> . . . my Readers as they are *Englishmen*, and as by that Means they enjoy a purer Religion, and a more excellent Form of Government, than any Nation under Heaven. . . . I shall only desire the honest, well-meaning Reader, when he turns his Thoughts towards the Publick, rather to consider what Opportunities he has of doing Good to his Native Country, than to throw away his Time in deciding the Rights of Princes, or the like Speculations, which are so far beyond his Reach. (59)

The rhetorical similarity to *The Examiner* is striking: subjects are to obey, not to exercise their critical capacities in terms of state affairs. In no. 55, Addison maintains without qualification that 'it [is] the Duty of every *Briton* to contribute his utmost Assistance to the Government' (271). Earlier he had complained of the 'late constant Application of the Press to the publishing of State-Matters', which has spread 'this Political Humour . . . among the People of *Great Britain*' (264). As in *The Spectator* and *The Tatler*, here subjects are warned against being too interested in the news: 'the making of the Politician is the breaking of the Tradesmen' (265).

---

[47] Rogers, 'Popular Protest in Early Hanoverian London'.

The disapproval of news-mongering quidnuncs is familiar from Addison's Queen Anne periodicals, but in most respects *The Freeholder* represents a very different enterprise. In *The Spectator*, Addison had to some extent attempted 'to close off and restrain, rather than to open up, venues for public debate . . . and especially . . . on matters of political concern'.[48] In *The Freeholder*, however, he mandates popular engagement with politics – as long as that engagement is loyalist.[49] In no. 13, we find the most forceful characterisation of his position: 'an avow'd Indifference is Treachery to our Fellow-Subjects; and a Luke-warm Allegiance may prove as pernicious in its Consequences as Treason' (98). Loyalty, he concludes, 'is of an active Nature' (65). What this means is that one cannot be a mere spectator; true citizens must not only support the government but also be prepared to battle its enemies. Kathleen Wilson describes Addison's paper as offering as:

> a cogent articulation of the principles that animated Whig street theater and rhetoric in the post-succession years and that would be elaborated by Court Whig apologists in ensuing decades, closing down the range of acceptable political positions that truly patriotic subjects could take. Loyal, manly citizens could only be Whig, whereas the rebellious, the effeminate, the unruly were by definition Tory, which here became identical with Jacobite and the 'rabble'.[50]

Addison not only requires patriotic behaviour but patriotic thought: 'the secret Promoter, or well-wisher of [the rebels'] Cause' is guilty 'before the Tribunal of Conscience' (66).

Throughout *The Freeholder*, Addison reminds readers of the King's 'undoubted Title', and he upholds the Whigs' constitutionally dubious and unpopular policies. His bottom line is simple: 'if every *Briton* . . . would sincerely desire to make his Country happy', George would have no disaffected subjects (60). The anti-Hanoverian street politics and rebellions are the product of faction, not a legitimate response to political circumstances. Addison is, crucially, offering rhetorical affirmation of what is implied by George's Riot Acts: there is no meaningful, rational basis for popular protest. What is '*natural*' and '*reasonable*' is 'Love of our Country' (56), and what that love looks like is public peace. *The Freeholder* is coterminous

---

[48] Cowan, 'Mr. Spectator and the Coffeehouse Public Sphere', p. 346.
[49] For an interesting discussion of the complex relationship between 'loyalty' and 'obedience' in late Stuart and early Hanoverian England, see Bowers, *Force or Fraud*, p. 153.
[50] Wilson, *Sense of the People*, pp. 94–95.

with violent Whig retribution against the Tories, and it reflects Whig loyalism to the new regime – but Addison is throughout calm, measured, and if not unemotional certainly not melodramatic. He cannily rejects the rhetoric of urgency and hyper-emotionality that such a crisis might inspire. His writing is artful and florid, verbose, carefully crafted, the opposite of an angry or defensive outburst. That he imagined his paper as a pacifying counterbalance to the government's brutal policies seems likely. *The Freeholder*'s actual conservatism is tempered – perhaps even cloaked – by its Whig rhetoric, and the crisis that inspired it is to some degree neutralised by Addison's composure.

Addison's vision of appropriate behaviour is startlingly narrow. His job, as he understands it, is 'to free the People's Minds from those Prejudices conveyed into them by the Enemies to the present Establishment' (273), 'to reconcile Men to their own Happiness' (107). Such a desire to help subjects understand that the present reality is the best of all possible political worlds seems surprisingly reminiscent of Mr. Examiner's conservative mission. The irony is that by 1716 Swift had, like many other Tories, found himself awkwardly defending political dissidence. In his marginalia on *The Freeholder*, he reviles Addison's position on public protest. Addison had complained about the methods used 'to infuse . . . groundless Discontents into the Minds of the Common People', to which Swift objects: 'Hath experience shown those Discontents groundless?'[51]

Steele's revived *Englishman* (1715) presents a useful contrast to Addison's loyalist enterprise. Steele is no less committed to the Hanoverian regime, and he underlines the legitimacy of the new king's title, obviously exasperated by Jacobite dissidents maintaining their allegiance to hereditary succession. But even as he encourages fidelity to the new regime, he never – like Addison – assumes that such fidelity should be automatic or boundless. Steele's primary aim is to justify the impeachment proceedings against Harley, St. John, and Ormonde, which requires convincing Englishmen that 'We have been Betrayed' (254). The proceedings against the Tory peace-makers of Anne's reign were not popular: mobs rallied behind those ministers, defying the government to punish them. Steele does not judge (or indeed even mention) the protestors. He does not accuse them of disloyalty. Instead he builds a case against the Tory leaders. In the preface, he explains that he will 'lay . . . together Facts which must convince all the World of the Methods [the ministry] had taken to accomplish' their traitorous ends (252). The key is 'convince': Steele recognises that defenders

---

[51] *PW*, vol. 5, p. 254; Addison's quotation is *Freeholder*, 173 (no. 31). Swift also remarks sardonically on the king's 'Prodigious clemency'.

of Anne's last ministry need to be converted, not coerced or bullied into obedience-based patriotism. He resolves to 'make good this Charge [his accusation against the Tories] to the Conviction of every Man living', but also to 'leave it to them to call the Guilty in this Case what they please' (255).

Though Steele does not in 1715 agitate for popular involvement the way he had in the earlier *Englishman*, the effect of his arguments is to promote civic engagement. In the inaugural number, he explains that he intends 'to Explain the false Arts which have been used against this injured Nation . . . by a plain State of Facts, in these little Half-Sheets, at a Time, when it is possible there may be found Readers who will be attentive, and give the Cause of their Country a Quarter of an Hour twice a Week' (254). This is not the position of *The Freeholder*. Steele wants his audience to be invested enough to track what is happening, to be involved in the political life of the nation. He stresses the pernicious deceptions of the previous ministry, who 'diverted Mankind from making Examinations which the Ministers knew their Actions could not bear'. Harley and his cohort 'had the *Populace*, (I mean by the *Populace*, all People who do not think for themselves) prejudiced in their Favour', which they accomplished by somehow persuading 'the Crowd' to think 'themselves insecure, except under the late Ministers' (318). Like Addison, Steele wishes to convince present readers that this illusion of security under the previous regime was false, and that their true happiness is possible only under a Protestant, Whig government. But while Steele does not energetically promote civic activism in 1715–1716, neither does he abandon the populist foundation of his politics. Some Whigs reversed their position on popular politics in the troubled early years of Hanoverian rule; Steele does not.

On the high Tory side, George Flint's *Robin's Last Shift* and its sequels serve to politicise the people, often in radical ways. On 3 March 1716, Flint wrote ominously that 'Blood will have Blood; Mischief will have Mischief; and the Barbarous and Cruel sooner or later perish'. A week later, reporting on Polish affairs, he celebrates those Poles who will 'reap the just Reward of their couragious [sic] Vindication of their Liberties. It has cost the Life of many a brave Polander before it came to this; but they were well bestow'd; *Dulce & Decorum est pro Patria mori*'. The application to English Jacobites is obvious. Throughout *Robin's Last Shift*, Flint contends that the actions of the Whig government have 'render[ed] his Majesty and his Family odious to his People', and that if the king wishes to prevent a coup, he must labour 'to retrieve the Affections of his People' (31 Mar). Not only does Flint insinuate the need for popular revolt, he also – in the inaugural issue of *The Shift Shifted* – implies that once such an overthrow has occurred the Jacks should have no mercy on their former oppressors: 'As no Ear was given to the Cries of the Poles when oppressed, I am humbly of Opinion, that now they are uppermost they will yield as little Attention to whatever Proposals are made them'. Flint presents himself as writing on behalf of the people, and his use of the vernacular – an idiom prominent in the Whig journalism of the previous reign – corresponds with that popular role (e.g., 'they had more need be willing to kiss their Backsides, were it possible thereby to appease them' [no. 10]). In the 31 March issue of *Robin's Last Shift*, Flint pointedly adopts as his models the Whigs Steele and Addison: reading their works leave one, he insists, 'fir'd with the Love of Liberty, and . . . ready to draw his Sword against Arbitrary Power'.

What we find, then, is a predictable shift in Whig and Tory positions on popular politics. The attitude put forward in Addison's *Freeholder* overlaps disconcertingly with the position of Mr. Examiner. Obviously there remain vast ideological discrepancies, and tonal ones as well, between Swift's Tory outlet and Addison's. But the promotion of assent, and the encouragement of loyalists to act only to suppress rebellion, is familiar from the conservative journals of Anne's reign. Jacobite Tories like Flint, too, start to employ the idiom of the Whigs ('*Dulce & Decorum est*'): that Flint cites (Stuart) Addison and Steele as the sources for his liberty-defending spirit should come as no surprise.

Journalists reading journals: the nature of the interaction

Journalists engage the reading public, and they are empowered to the degree that their readership finds them compelling. In *The Commentator*, Defoe (?) underlines the importance of knowing one's readership: 'every Body tells his News differently, with different Circumstances, and different Facts; and yet every Body's News is true. Methinks such a Disagreement among these *Retailers of History*, should alarm their Readers more . . . . But it is certainly otherwise; every Body writes to a particular Set of Men; and there are a proportionable Number of different *Believers* to every different *Writer*' (20). One concern of this chapter has been with how journalists attempt to win over – and teach, entertain, persuade – their respective sets of '*Believers*'. The urgent need to claim unassailable journalistic authority for themselves was apparent to Swift, Steele, Defoe, *et al.*, and to their readers. The effectiveness of their interpretations of events depended largely upon ethos. A feature of late Stuart periodical culture is frequent complaint about the proliferation of new papers and competing voices, about what Mr. Review called 'that Universal Pen and Ink Strife' (vol. 2, p. 711). Not only did they need to appear credible; they also needed – *plus ça change* – to undermine their adversaries' credibility. Journalists read each other privately, familiarising themselves with the arguments of their rivals; they also read each other publicly, construing such arguments in partisan fashion for the benefit of a reading public. As Knights points out, 'print was a dialogic medium: published claim provoked printed counter-claim, vindication, denial, or agreement'. Writers challenge the content of their antagonists' works, but also form and language: 'Political censure . . . often involved a process of extensive literary criticism, in which style and language were carefully scrutinized'.[52] Knights is no doubt right in his assessment. My argument is that, however widespread this tendency, not all writers practiced literary-critical analysis in the same way, and that some journalists – including Steele – suffered more of this kind of treatment than others. A comparison of the interactions among Mr. Examiner and his critics, and Steele and his, should illustrate some significant differences in the ways journalists respond to one another. Before turning to them, a brief précis of the near-universal battle over language is in order.

The language of politics

Knights's *Representation and Misrepresentation* is exemplary; no one has more carefully or systematically traced the anxieties surrounding 'slogans, words, and phrases' that were 'being given different meanings by each interest-group' (6). One of the aims of Knights's study is to show 'how public discourse operated to legitimize or undermine authority and allegiance' (8). His arguments and conclusions need not be rehearsed here, but some reminder of the nature of the problem is necessary, given the relationship between language and journalists' attempt to challenge the credibility of rivals.

One might fairly describe *The Examiner* as obsessed with language. In no. 8 – pre-dating Swift's involvement – the author reflects at length on 'how People have of late been amus'd and banter'd out of *Common Sense*, by the Sound of a few Words and Expressions, without any distinct Signification'. He proposes a new dictionary to expose 'the *fallacy* and *emptiness* of *popular Phrases*', one which will clarify language 'us'd in a *very loose* Signification, or in no Signification *at all*' – or 'in a Signification perfectly *New*', that last adjective a signal of 'new Whig' culpability. In no. 16, Swift would point to specific buzzwords employed strategically and speciously: 'the Word *Pretender* is a Term of Art in *their* Possession: A Secretary of State

---

[52] Knights, *Representation and Misrepresentation*, pp. 235, 356.

cannot *desire leave to resign*, but the *Pretender* is at bottom' (40), and 'the Word *Indefeasible*, with which some Writers of late have made themselves so merry' (41). The theme continues under Oldisworth, who describes 'The War at home' as:

> a mere *Logomachy*, a Battle of *Names* and *Phrases*. We have . . . *breath'd* nothing but Contention; have made our *Vocabularies* the Seat of War . . . *Words* of a very bad Meaning, or of no Meaning at all, have more effectually split . . . us, than the broadest Sword or most pondrous Battle Ax. (vol. 4, no. 19)

Oldisworth resents the fact 'that *New Meanings* for *Old Words* should obtain and come in vogue, and such as . . . perfectly contradict and overthrow an *Establish'd Signification*' (vol. 6, no. 10). For both Swift and Oldisworth, the war over definition belongs to the broader contest between tradition and modernity, between conservatism and dangerous innovation.

Whig writers often focus on the language of Tory dogma, targeting terms such as 'passive obedience' and 'hereditary' right. In *The Review*, Defoe labours to show that 'Entail' is only 'an inconsistent Jargon, empty in its Signification' (vol. 3, p. 463). The radical Whig *Observator* likewise takes issue with such language, challenging Mr. Examiner, whose 'Head is . . . so muddled . . . that he jumbles Indefeasible Hereditary Right and Passive Obedience together' (vol. 10, p. 24). The fifth and final number of *The Whig-Examiner* highlights the problem of connotation:

> *Passive-Obedience* and *Non-Resistance* are of a mild, gentle, and meek-spirited Sound: They have respect but to one Side of the Relation between the Sovereign and the Subject, and are apt to fill the Mind with no other Ideas but those of Peace, Tranquility, and Resignation. To shew this Doctrine in those black and odious Colours that are natural to it. . . . (5)

Addison and Mainwaring voice anxiety about the danger of such 'smooth ensnaring Terms', sweet-sounding but pernicious. They seek to expose the persuasive – or anesthetising – power of euphemism, a polemical goal akin to Defoe's attack on High Church 'Subtilty'.

Mr. Examiner and other Tories attempt to convince their readers of the trustworthiness of traditional notions of language and power; Whig rivals stress the sedating effect of Tory terminology and Tory attitudes. Political argument happens at the sentence-level. The Tories brand the Whigs dangerous innovators, using new language to create new – anti-traditional, anarchy-yielding – power structures. The Whigs charge the Tories with relying upon or reviving stale, archaic phrases to impose the old, exploded dogmas of passive obedience and non-resistance. The combatants' linguistic accusations mirror their more obviously issue-based allegations: one side is depicted as hypnotically lulling citizens into inattention, the other as needlessly alarming subjects and destabilising the state. For partisans on both sides, the battle over language is a battle over power: the fierce sparring over language vividly conveys fundamental disagreements about the extent of monarchical power, the rights of Parliament, and whatever limits might be appropriate concerning the involvement of the public press in debates about governance. The lexical controversies also anticipate the role of literary criticism in partisan paper wars – but not all writers were equally vulnerable to this kind of scrutiny. Neither do all journalists respond publicly to their adversaries in the same way.

The un-Examining Examiner

Swift's *Examiner* is unusual in resolving 'to take very little notice of other Papers'. He swears that he will 'by no means engage in so unequal a Combat' with *The Observator*, and he laments that subjects' 'Duty shou'd be convey'd to them thro' such *Vehicles* as those' (35). But otherwise he mostly ignores other journals, eschewing commentary on contemporary pamphlets just as he ignores 'the Reader' who consumes them. *The Examiner*'s most consistent critic is *The Medley*, written by Mainwaring with some assistance from Oldmixon and Steele; that paper devotes itself to animadverting on the ministerial *Examiner*. But the relationship is for the most part not a mutual one: during his tenure as Mr. Examiner, Swift has nothing to say about Mainwaring's enterprise and almost nothing about any other venture.[53] The strategic silence about other papers, however, characterises only Swift's contributions: his predecessors and successors in the role have more to say about competing texts. Swift's first successor, Delarivier Manley, routinely invokes 'my Friend the *Medley*' (no. 47).

Oldisworth's *Examiner* engages more frequently with other texts. His allusions to *The Daily Courant* (vol. 2, nos. 8, 22) and other newspapers represents a marked change from Swift's tendencies, and Oldisworth continues Manley's acknowledgement of 'the Medley and other scandalous Papers' (vol. 2, no. 33). He operates at a micro-level which Swift

---

[53] Swift's allusions are infrequent and dismissive; e.g.: 'I remember some time ago in one of the *Tatlers* to have read a Letter. . . .' (p. 95). His characterisations of other journalists are almost always generalised (e.g., p. 96).

scrupulously avoids: 'One *fiery* Paragraph of this Adversary I cannot but call to mind', and so on (vol. 2, no. 5). Later, he animadverts on Anthony Collins (vol. 3, no. 12) and on *The Observator* (vol. 3, no. 37). The issue for 11 December 1712 opens with a promise 'to *Examine* . . . a Book which is so far a Rarity in its Kind', and delivers (vol. 3, no. 7). Elsewhere Oldisworth reflects on Addison's *Cato* (vol. 3, no. 46) and still later on the *Memoirs of Count Tariff* (vol. 4, no. 32). On 24 April 1712, he comments at length on the state of the journalistic field, listing Whig and Tory papers in order to demonstrate that the Whig outlets outnumber their rivals.

Especially under Swift, Mr. Examiner has no interest in inciting readers to engage actively with texts. Like most Tory outlets, *The Examiner* mostly avoids printing letters from contemporaries, and Swift's contributions have only the slightest epistolary component.[54] In no. 48, Manley reflects retrospectively on Mr. Examiner's (Swift's) earlier decision not to solicit outside contributions:

> I Suppose some Wit, and much Leisure, have made it a Fashion among ingenious Persons, to send Letters, by way of assistance, to us Weekly Writers: 'Tis easy to imagine, that I have had my share of such Contributions, for which, tho' I am very thankful, yet I must confess, with some Vanity, That my Mind is rather burthened than relieved by those Intelligences.

The next number includes letters, which suggests that this passage is not a defence of Mr. Examiner's present *modus operandi* but of his past policy. Oldisworth includes letters to *The Examiner*, including 'A Letter from the Examiner to the Examiner' (vol. 5, no. 17) – almost certainly a parody of Steele's letters from 'Steele' to (for example) Ironside. No Mr. Examiner is enthusiastic about outside missives; Swift's reluctance clearly reflects his discomfort with encouraging a certain kind of popular engagement, or (more positively) his preference to play the preacher.

Swift pays no heed to his opponents, but they have plenty to say about him. *The Examiner* had as many critics as any late Stuart party paper, none of which was shy about explicitly contesting Mr. Examiner's claims. One potent rival was *The Medley*, whose response to Swift's *Examiner* seems primarily meant to puncture the supreme self-importance of the ministerial spokesman. In no. 13, Mainwaring mocks 'This Great Man, who seems to be Master of Press', and explains his approach: 'I am not for arguing with

---

[54] There is one exception: no. 29 includes two letters 'To the EXAMINER', one from a Whig and one from a Tory (pp. 243–46).

the *Examiner*, tho I endeavour to make my Readers merry with him' (120). His aim, then, is to render the ultra-pompous Mr. Examiner a comic figure, 'a Hero ... in a Farce of his own making' (472). The strategy is well-chosen.

Swift's Mr. Examiner presents himself as an authority because he is a spokesman for 'a Flourishing Ministry, in full Credit with the Q[uee]n, and belov'd by the People' (211). His repeated dismissal of the 'ruin'd' Whigs is part and parcel with his signature triumphalism. He does not doubt his superiority: 'it is highly requisite . . . that the People throughout the Kingdom, shou'd . . . be set right in their Opinions by some impartial Hand, which has never been yet attempted: Those who have hitherto undertaken it, being upon every Account the least qualify'd of all Human-kind for such a Work' (34).

Mr. Examiner is a compelling figure not least because he is non-defensive: eager to demonstrate that he speaks for the authorities and for the English majority, he shrewdly strikes a pose as one untroubled, unthreatened, secure in his convictions and in the reception they will receive. Had Swift indulged in the *saeva indignatio* for which he is celebrated, he would have undermined his own propagandistic aims: he who truly speaks for the nation need not bluster.

His critics dispute his complacency, and his assumption that the Whigs were defeated, never to rise again. As Mainwaring dryly observes, 'a Twelve-month hence will be a better time to make a Judgment of these matters' (120). Steele takes Mr. Examiner to task for his abusiveness and scurrility, but also for relying upon emotional bluster and vanity instead of logic and persuasion. He targets him, in other words, for failing to acknowledge those of another mind: *The Examiner* is 'full of that . . . usual kind of Argumentation which fills the Mouths of those who are for you, with more Words to vent their Passions and Prejudices, but affords no Reason to convince those who are against you.'[55]

Undermining Mr. Examiner's authority for the most part required puncturing that self-satisfaction, and Mainwaring rightly judged that bantering would be more effective than sober counter-argument. In no. 13, he makes this choice explicit: 'The *Examiner* seems to have a mind that somebody wou'd gravely dispute with him', but 'Who wou'd argue with a Man gravely, who says a great many Things in every Paper that he does not believe himself?' (118) Instead, *The Medley* makes use of ironic commendation, pretending to take Swift seriously but doing so in a way that is transparently disingenuous. 'I am aw'd, and kept at a distance by the importance of his Person', Mainwaring concludes, the importance of which Mr. Examiner

---

[55] In *Tracts and Pamphlets*, p. 271.

himself assures us (43). *The Medley* mocks Swift's 'modesty' and 'bashfulness', as well as his characteristic grasping familiarity with great men: 'his *John*, his *Oldfox*, his *Will*, his *Charles*, and his *Harry*' (105). Mr. Examiner 'has appear'd all along to be a person of profound Judgment' (73), Mainwaring ironically informs his readers, insinuating the opposite. Mainwaring as a public reader of Swift is taunting, brilliantly highlighting the hollowness of Mr. Examiner's extreme self-assurance. He also inspires all consumers of Swift's journalism to respond in kind, seeking to change the reception on which Mr. Examiner's power depends. Knights is correct in observing that 'the *Examiner* and ... the *Medley* ... were involved in an increasingly vituperative attempt to neutralize the poison of each other's words' – but the two responded to each other in significantly different ways.[56] *The Examiner* ignores his chief adversary, relegating him to irrelevancy; *The Medley* invites readers to laugh at a journalist whose arguments depend upon his gravitas (not so much the other way around).

The response of Swift's critics tends to be quite different from the response of Steele's, and the distinction is illustrative and important. The Whigs perceived Mr. Examiner's authority to derive from the confidence with which he wrote, the pretence of speaking for a ministry whose widespread popularity could be simply taken for granted. To debunk that triumphalist position is to undermine *The Examiner* and to raise doubts about the popularity of the government it supported. At least in *The Tatler*, *The Spectator*, and *The Guardian*, Steele's authority came on the contrary from his use of the language of politeness and the cultivation of upstanding, trustworthy personae. That his adversaries subjected him to more relentless 'literary' criticism is therefore not surprising.

Steele and his critics
In *The Tatler*, *The Spectator*, and *The Guardian*, Steele rarely alludes directly to other papers, though as we have seen, his arguments tend to insinuate criticism of the propagandistic props of the Harley ministry. In *The Guardian* no. 41, Steele offers his first direct opposition to *The Examiner*, voiced by an anonymous letter-writer who takes angry exception to Mr. Examiner's rough handling of the Earl of Nottingham's daughter. In no. 53, 'Steele' writes a stern missive to Ironside, in high-minded fashion denouncing Mr. Examiner's unjust treatment of 'a Sett of Brave, Wise and Honest Men'. Such patriots should not allowed to be treated like traitors, he continues, counselling Ironside on his journalistic duty: 'To prevent such Evils is a

---

[56] Knights, *Representation and Misrepresentation*, p. 279.

Care worthy a Guardian' (210). The point is that Steele's disapprobation of *The Examiner* and other rival papers is conveyed by someone other than the putative editor, either by common citizens or by 'Steele' himself. He clearly wished to create distance between his respectable eidolons and such animadversion or critique, to create a pretence that his personae were not casual participants in a grub-street paper war.

Steele receives more stylistic criticism than most of his contemporaries, and a theme among his rivals is the gap between what Steele says (or how he says it) and the true nature of his partisanship. Steele's journalism's trustworthiness comes from its *apparent* disavowal of polemic – and his critics sought to expose the personal animus behind his seemingly 'polite' discourse. As one contemporary protests, '*Publick Spirit, Charity, Benevolence to Mankind*, and *Disinterest*, are Virtues known to our *Mushroom Patriot* by Name only, and it raises the Contempt and Indignation of every honest Man, to hear a Person of the vilest Principles, and the most mercenary Hireling, who ever prostituted his Pen in the Defence of any Faction, giving himself such an Air of Sanctity and Virtue.' The same author explains that his focus has been upon the problematic nature of 'Mr. St[ee]le's Character, because it seems to be the main Argument at present'.[57] Such a formulation is distinct from what we find among Swift's critics; it signals the Tories' awareness of the importance of distinguishing between Steele's 'Character' and the characters of his righteous personae.

Among Steele's most unremitting critics is Oldisworth, who mocks him in the *Annotations on the Tatler* (2 parts; Aug–Sept 1710), and whose *Examiner* essays fixate on his Whig opponent. His attempt to appropriate Steele's language of politeness for the Tories seems significant, as does the more *Tatler*-esque scope of his contributions. He is first and foremost a political journalist in *The Examiner*, but he is noticeably more inclined toward cultural criticism than Swift had been. Throughout the fall of 1713, and the winter of 1713–1714, Oldisworth does battle – explicitly – with Steele's *Guardian* and *Englishman*. He prints advertisements for Swift works written against Steele, including *The First Ode of the Second Book of Horace Paraphras'd* and *The Publick Spirit of the Whigs* (both 1714).

Oldisworth's most focused engagement with Steele is in the *Annotations*, where he attempts to reveal the political designs behind Steele's seemingly innocuous comments, and indeed behind Steele's entire manner of presentation. One of Oldisworth's primary aims, evidently, is to encourage readers not to be bamboozled by Steele's '*Grammatical Popery*' (vol. 1, p. 37). That phrase is suggestive: Steele's propaganda reads

---

[57] *Character of Richard S[tee]le*, pp. 16, 17.

like polite, disinterested cultural criticism, but that smooth-tasting wine is still really only partisan water. Oldisworth seeks to expose the incongruity of Steele's high-minded pose and his rough-and-tumble partisan message. He warns readers that 'there is not one of [Steele's] Papers without a Design in it' (vol. 2, p. 21). In the dedication to Part I, Oldisworth coolly observes, 'A Sett of Rural Esquires did indeed misapply *Monsieur Bickerstaff*, by taking him Literally' – inviting readers to perform more deconstruction. Oldisworth alerts readers to the relationship between language and politics, to the ways in which words and phrases can suggest more 'Design' than we might imagine. Though Steele relies upon stylistic grandeur – 'Noble Exclamations', etc. – this is merely a strategy by which to make 'Others Little when Contending with' him (dedication). His pose is righteous; his language seems pretty; but Oldisworth will perform the still more honorable work of 'Unmask[ing] . . . Artifice and Hypocrisy' (dedication). His discussion of Bickerstaff alongside Grub Street newsmen like Abel Boyer (vol. 1, pp. 64–65) is meant to reduce the distance between them, to reveal the falsity of Steele's pretence that he is above the partisan fray.

Oldisworth puts Steele's prose under a microscope, dissecting it sentence-by-sentence, phrase-by-phrase. Under that microscope, even the 'Exalted Rhetorick' (Dedication) of *The Tatler* can read like nonsense; part of Oldisworth's point is that Steele uses language to disguise his partisan meaning or even his non-meaning. Swift would do something similar to Steele's *Crisis* in *The Publick Spirit of the Whigs* (1714), where he accuses Steele of 'Rancor and Falsehood, intermixed with plausible Nonsense', mocking 'the Flatness of his Style, and the Barrenness of his Invention' (248, 249). Part I of Oldisworth's *Annotations* comprises 100 pages' worth of catalogued infelicities. From *Tatler* no. 6, Oldisworth plucks the following passage: 'Standing, Sitting, Lying down, Fighting, Eating, Drinking, or any other Circumstance, however foreign or repugnant to Speed and Activity'. Our annotator need not work hard to show the unloveliness of this fragment, but he does comment upon one unfortunate implication of its content. 'The Placing the Business of *Fighting* among those Circumstances, that are foreign and repugnant to *Speed* and *Activity*, is an Admiral Reflection on those Heroes of the Moderns', etc. (24). Later, he quotes a snippet from *Tatler* no. 17, reducing it to so much claptrap: 'Not to know a Man, and yet to know of no Body more Deserving than he, is an Obligation of the highest Nature imaginable' (50). The effect here is to diminish Steele's authority as a cultural critic, and thus to undermine his status as a socio-moral and political authority. Steele's journalism depends heavily upon ethos, and that ethos Oldisworth targets, one syntactical blunder at a time.

Steele certainly felt that he had suffered from micro-level misappropriations of his writings. After his expulsion from the House of Commons in 1714 for his libels, he complained thus: 'It would be very unfair to separate my Words, and to pronounce a Meaning in them, which I have not expressed, when that I have expressed is a positive Denial of having entertained any such Meaning.... By this way of arguing, it is not in the Power of Words to be free from unwarrantable Hints and Innuendos'.[58] However accurate (or not) his self-defence, Steele was right to feel uniquely harassed in this respect. The contest over language was a feature of partisan controversy in this period, and accusations of wilful misuse of terminology were common on both sides of the divide – but Steele's prose is subjected to an exceptional degree of aggressively sceptical reading. He preached politeness and proper language, which left him open to charges that his civility was 'by Name only'.

Steele apparently wanted his multiple, short-lived late Stuart journals to be seen as separate ventures, not the work of one disaffected Whig writer. Though he did call *The Englishman* a 'sequel of the GUARDIAN', he also underscores the fact that the author is merely an admirer of Ironside and not a friend or collaborator.[59] His rivals worked to thwart Steele's desire, making a point of connecting these enterprises in the public mind. As one 1714 commentator pointed out, Steele had 'dress'd' himself in 'various Shapes... to serve a ruin'd Party'. Mr. Spectator had transformed into the '*Guardian* of the Liberties of *Great-Britain*', and then '*presto pass*, by a kind of magical Stroke... from a Native of *Dublin* turn'd into a True-born *Englishman*' who 'writes and converses with himself'. That last observation is a joke on Steele's tendency to submit letters 'from Steele' to the editor that he creates and controls – from himself, that is, to himself. Oldisworth parodies this manoeuvre in *The Examiner* of 25 January 1714. After playing the role of schizophrenic Englishman, Steele 'in his Melancholy and Dotage turns Lover', before shifting yet again into 'a *Reader*'.[60] Whatever the rationale

---

[58] *Apology*, in *Tracts and Pamphlets*, 307, 317. Steele's objection echoes that made by Sacheverell during his trial: the preacher grumbled that his original words had been distorted by '*Unnecessary Implications*, and *Strain'd Constructions*'; his enemies 'Piec[ed together] Broken Sentences ... Conjoyning Distant and Independent Passages, in order to make Me Speak what I never Thought of'; *The Speech of Henry Sacheverell, D.D. Upon His Impeachment* (1710), 2. Steele cites Sacheverell along these lines in his *Apology* (pp. 335–36).

[59] See *The Englishman* no. 1 (p. 5).

[60] *A Letter from Will. Honeycomb to the Examiner* (1714) pp. 6, 9, 10, 12, 13.

behind Steele's decision to rely upon a succession of comparatively ephemeral papers instead of one long-running Whig outlet, the effect is to suggest a variety of slightly differently motivated Whig critics of late Stuart political culture. His critics sought to reduce those several Whig voices into Steele's alone. This not only diminishes the sense of Whig opposition, but it also exposes the fictionality of Steele's approach. If he is deceiving readers on the subject of his relationship to his speakers, why should his arguments be considered credible?

Steele's pose of righteous, polite, ego-less civic-mindedness also inspired his rivals to highlight the actual measure of anger informing his journalism. The author of *A Letter from Will. Honeycomb* contends that Steele's polite civilities cloak something darker: 'In this character of *Guardian* the Disorder rages violently' (9). His Steele is a quasi-delusional figure, a sweet-talking Quixote nevertheless tilting at phantom Jacobite windmills (10), but the key is unbalance: contemporaries might find Steele's various personae to be persuasively high-minded, when in fact they all emanate from the same personally-motivated, spiteful, incensed, even obsessive mind.

Conclusion: the value of popular political education

What we find, in the early eighteenth century, is a wide range of competing notions about popular politics. *The Spectator* and *The Tatler* do not represent a sufficient index to what was actually happening in the public sphere or even to contemporary attitudes toward such changes. I will end with a broader conclusion about competing views on popular political education and participation that we find reflected in journalism. But first I wish to return to *The Tatler* and *The Spectator*, and to consider the 'public' envisioned in those papers alongside that projected by Mr. Examiner.

Addison and Steele have lately been treated as sceptics of the politicisation of their fellow subjects, but this scepticism has been overstated. Ketcham is right to highlight the 'rhetoric of assimilation' in *The Spectator*, and to contrast that with 'the rhetoric of exclusion' we find among Tory polemicists.[61] Addison's and Steele's rhetorical strategy is usually 'to draw men together into a cohesive community', to stress tolerance and empathy and to use the language of sociability and community-mindedness. Ketcham characterises the language and style of *The Spectator*, highlighting its tendency (among other things) toward 'structural redundancy', which enables

---

[61] Ketcham, *Transparent Designs*, p. 161.

a reader to 'readily pick up on the pattern of the sentence and anticipate its line of thought'.[62] This is a decidedly sociable syntactical choice, one that gives readers the sense of participating in the logic of the arguments being made. Swift and Leslie, along with many other Tory journalists in Anne's reign, are keener to marginalise; Swift relentlessly factionalises the opposition, treating it as a tattered group of malicious traitors who will forever be on the wrong side of history.

Both Addison and Steele criticise Swift for these exclusionary tendencies. In his 1714 *Apology*, Steele complains about Mr. Examiner's wrong notions of the political community and for his rhetorical mishandling of English subjects: 'This Man has represented half of Her Majesty's Subjects as a Different People who have forfeited the common Protection allowed them by the Constitution'.[63] Addison issues a similar reproach in *The Freeholder*:

> The *Examiner* would not allow such as were of a contrary Opinion to him, to be either Christians or Fellow Subjects. With him they are all Atheists, Deists, or Apostates, and a separate Common-Wealth among themselves, that ought either to be extirpated, or, when he was in a better Humour, only to be banished out of their Native Country. (121)

Addison and Steele challenge quite a lot about Tory rhetoric. They replace the mode of Juvenalian diatribe and personal abuse with that of politeness and Horatian decorum. They also implicitly discredit the idea that the (Tory) Church should or must dictate behaviour, replacing that model with one of self-restraint and (Whiggish) good manners. Finally, and crucially, they exchange the ethos of submission and assent (see Mr. Examiner), offering as an alternative a model of active scrutiny and self-governance. Addison and Steele hope to persuade, but they also promote a kind of independence of thought that runs directly counter to the ideology found in *The Examiner*. Scott Black describes the periodical essays of Addison and Steele as 'enabl[ing] a public space distinct from both church and state', and as helping 'a mundane public ... see itself in extra-legal and extra-theological terms'.[64] For many Tories, the public space was not distinct from but subservient to church and state; they promulgated a definition of citizenship that required loyalty to the authorities, aligning the interest of subjects

---

[62] Ketcham, *Transparent Designs*, p. 144.
[63] *Apology*, in *Tracts and Pamphlets*, p. 300.
[64] Black, *Of Essays and Reading*, pp. 86, 92.

and the interest of the state. Addison and Steele advocate a different kind of engagement.

They also stress the importance of clubbabilty and sociability. As Bowers concludes, 'Mr. Spectator's discourses on benevolence . . . and good-naturedness . . . seek to make people not only morally better but also civically functional by instilling within them the proper temperament of *fellowship* needed for participation in the processes of collective reasoning and mutual refinement.'[65] Such fellowship is not just among the audience, but between the authors and their readers. *The Tatler* and *The Spectator* dictate politeness and also practice it. That politeness is a *social* mode, in sharp contrast to the anti-social homiletics of Swift and Leslie. The same can be said of other Whig papers like *The Patriot*, whose author maintains that 'MAN is a sociable Creature' and defines a truly cooperative and happy society as one that operates according to Whig notions of power (no. 10).

Addison and especially Steele create warmer, more benevolent, more inclusive authorial personae. This represents a fundamentally different approach from Swift's and Leslie's distancing, their authoritarian chilliness. Addison and Steele not only reject the notion of the pulpit as moral arbiter; they also reject the pulpit oratory that reduces citizens to subjects. To challenge such rhetorical relationships is to challenge the ideas about power that inform those relationships. Swift conditions readers to be passive, not to inquire into the mysteries of state; Addison and Steele, however indirectly, school their readers to take some responsibility for their own behaviour, to be to some extent self-governing. Insofar as there are 'rules' to insure fellowship, those rules come from their fellow citizens, not from above.

Most of the debates about the value of the press had to do with whether or not partisan outlets were providing a useful political education – helping citizens make better decisions and/or cultivating loyalty to the right institutions – or misleading an easily misled populace into confusion and disaffection. Journalists and pamphleteers raise questions, too, about whether subjects could be counted on to read well enough, to cultivate sufficient perspicacity to recognise the misrepresentation of skillful liars. We might usefully distinguish between periodical essayists who highlight and strive to improve subjects' ability to read and see well, and those who privilege subjects' ability to listen. Mr. Review imagines himself as 'a mighty

---

[65] Bowers, 'Universalizing Sociability', p. 156.

Observer of Days and Hours' (vol. 3, p. 421), and observation is a key part of his mission.[66] His desperate plea for improved 'politick Opticks' or 'Protestant SPECTACLES'[67] is categorically different from (say) those who remind readers that 'it requires ... many years experience in Politicks ... to project or to penetrate into any of the sacred Mysteries of the State'.[68] Even some of our major journalists, moreover, alter their positions on public politics as historical circumstances and their own political fates change.

What we find reflected in early eighteenth-century journalism is a fundamental transition, and the tensions involved in the evolution of an intensely and consistently politicised public. Even the language used for subjects is contested. The choice of second- or third-person pronouns often reveals whether journalists imagine themselves addressing their 'fellow citizens' or subjects who should not presume to reason independently of their teachers and leaders (however defined). The range of rhetorical treatments of 'the public' signals an uncertain state of affairs. To call for docility and subjection is no longer entirely acceptable – but speaking of subjects' rights to monitor, reflect on, and challenge the state has hardly yet become the norm. Some of the dynamism of partisan journalism in these years comes from the fact that such rhetorical relationships are disputed. Propagandists on either side are arguing not only about policy or ideology, but also about the job of journalism and the ways in which it should be consumed. Should those who produce newspapers and periodicals be speaking to or for the people? Should they be representing the state to the subjects, as appropriate for the model replaced, in Habermas's telling, by the emergence of the bourgeois public sphere? Or should they be actively politicising the people, insofar as possible speaking truth to power? Should they, in other words, be popularising a paradigm of state accountability? The problems with Habermas's narrative have been effectively and justly detailed by his critics, but there is no doubt about the substantial expansion and redefinition of public politics.

The journalism of these years illustrates the conflict introduced by the continued entrenchment of a public sphere. The advent of a daily press helped create a politicised public, but it also served as one the major sites for the debates about the value or destructive potential for such politicisation. Those debates are often explicit, but they are also carried out at a

---

[66] *The Protestant Post-Boy*'s emphasis is similar. No. 74 (21 February 1712) opens thus: 'Heavens preserve every honest *Briton*'s Eye-sight; guard his Senses; and protect the Remains of his Understanding, that he may be able to unravel this present *Mistery* [sic] of *French Iniquity*'.
[67] *Review*, vol. 4, p. 650, vol. 7, p. 260.
[68] *Arguments Relating to a Restraint upon the Press*, p. 30.

rhetorical and stylistic level, which means that we have – as Swift and others certainly realised – to attend not only to what combatants were saying, but to the language in which they said it. The rhetorical battles are inseparable from the ideological battles, and journalists clearly wanted to defend not only their partisan positions but also their way of addressing the public. That public had not yet been clearly defined; its role was far from settled. Journalists were not only conveying partisan information and ideology to their readers; they were also labouring to create, promote, and establish expectations for a particular manner of public engagement. One could without much exaggeration argue that these writers played a significant role in how English citizens conceived of politics – and how they imagined or even realised their ever-evolving role in the political drama of the age.

Conclusion
Journalism and Authority

The culture of politics undergoes a radical change in the late seventeenth and early eighteenth centuries. The civil wars of the 1640s had challenged the centuries-old tradition that while a monarch's power might in theory have its limits, that power was widely accepted. One legacy of the wars was the notion of divided sovereignty between king and parliament, the idea that a parliament could act independently of the royal sovereign. What happened in 1688 represented, of course, another enormous transformation in English attitudes toward power. Evolving understandings of monarchical authority and its limits generated some anticipation of and demand for popular representation. The emergence of a clear-cut two-party system, with a governing party and an opposition, contributed to a new political landscape, as did the shift from septennial to triennial elections and the more constant culture of partisan debate that such a development fostered. The advent of a daily newspaper press combined with these and other changes to create an entirely different set of expectations about and parameters for public politics.

The daily press that started to come into existence in 1702 meant a huge expansion of what 'the people' knew. As late as 1690, readers could only assemble the news for themselves from distinctly limited resources: *The London Gazette* and *Votes of the House of Commons*, along with pamphlets, newsletters, and the foreign broadsheets found in coffeehouses and taverns. After 1702, a vastly larger percentage of the population had relatively affordable access to debate about the course of national and 'global' events. The weekly and daily news gave citizens more immediate insight into current affairs; it gave them not only a political education but an unprecedented presumption of a right to participate. Even those who could not read the papers could still engage. As the arch-conservative Charles Leslie complained, the Whig '*weekly penny Papers* . . . have done more *Mischief* than the others', and the sub-literate 'will Gather together about one that can *Read*, and Listen to an *Observator* or *Review* (as I have seen them in the

Streets) where all the *Principles* of *Rebellion* are Instill'd into them'.[1] Access to information changes the political dynamic between the people, parliament, and the monarch, and newspapers and periodicals provided not only reports but also interpretation of events. Journalists helped create a 'right to know' culture, and late Stuart Whig writers in particular also championed a right to monitor, question, and comment. Political journals become a more prominent part of the daily lives of English subjects – and they do so at more or less the time in which a fundamental critical debate was going on over the extent and limits of monarchical versus parliamentary (representative) power.

That early eighteenth-century newspapers and periodicals were invested in and contributed to debates about power and authority is a claim that few would question. Most accounts of journalism in this period, however, have either focused exclusively on a relatively small number of famous papers or have highlighted the presence of foreign news in English papers and downplayed the prominence of ideological debate. One object of this book has been simply to map some of the partisan positions of a wide range of both long-lived and ephemeral newspapers and periodicals, including the still under-studied contributions of Defoe, Swift, and Steele. Another has been to suggest that much of the dynamism of the early eighteenth-century periodical press comes from the evolving and contested status of that press: what was its authority to intervene in public discussion? did the daily politicisation of the people lead to socio-political justice, or did it endanger society and the state? what should the relationship be between the state and the people, and how could journalists responsibly define and cultivate such a relationship?

We need to appreciate the prominence of ideological debate in these newspapers and periodicals. That Mr. Examiner and Mr. Review contentiously reflect upon the nature and basis of power is perhaps well known, but the degree to which the daily press is obsessed with fundamental ideological issues – while also weighing in on topical events – has not been sufficiently recognised. Early eighteenth-century news and periodical writers live in and help create a culture of Whig versus Tory, establishment versus opposition. *The Flying Post* routinely appeals to 'our Origine and Constitution', maintaining that the English Crown is 'Elective and not Hereditary' (no. 1587). Like most Whigs, Ridpath takes to task those 'Monarchy-Men' who defend the prerogative above all things (3654). *The Observator* crucially defines the 'Constitution' as 'the *Power* of *Parliaments*', denouncing those '*High-Flyers*

---

[1] Leslie, *The Rehearsal*, preface to vol. 1; quoted in J. A. Downie, 'Stating Facts Right About Defoe's *Review*', in Downie and Thomas N. Corns (eds.), *Telling People What To Think: Early Eighteenth-Century Periodicals from* The Review *to* The Rambler (London, 1993), 8–22, p. 17.

in Government [who] ... teach Princes that they must make no Concessions to their People'.[2] *The Patriot* of 1714–1715 devotes considerable space to monarchical power and its limits, and – like his ally Steele – he accuses those who 'persuade ... Monarchs ... that they may do what they please' of the 'basest Flattery' (10). On the other side, Mr. Examiner and Leslie advocate obedience and criminalise dissent. Leslie's quarrel with Mr. Review *et al.* is never merely topical: with Defoe, Mr. Rehearsal complains, 'all *Rebellion* is the *Inspiration* of *God*' (vol. 3, no. 18), and 'The *Observator* Asserts a *Coercive* Power in the *Parliament* over the *Crown*' (36). The 'news' writers are as engaged in this battle as their essay-producing counterparts. *The Post Boy* routinely objects to those who 'revive the Doctrines of *Resisting* and *Deposing*' (no. 2368), preaching loyalty, obedience, and the sanctity of the prerogative.

The journalists fixate on authority – on that of the state, the church, and the press. Trenchard and Gordon's *Independent Whig* (1720) warns against the enchanting power of the term 'Authority'. It is, he concludes, 'a Word pregnant with Danger and Nonsense. It is a false misleading Light, or rather none at all; for those who follow it, do only grope in the Dark: When we blindly trust to another, our own Eyes grow useless, or may give offence' (212). Their critique is specifically directed at corrupted ecclesiology, not religion but the 'disfigured' dogma propounded by High Churchmen so that they can 'set themselves above the People' (302). Trenchard's criticism is directed at those like Leslie who presume the unassailable authority of the church and scripture (as interpreted by that church). Most journalists implicitly or explicitly establish their notions of authority, and many use their papers to caution against upsetting proper balances. *The Entertainer*'s admonition is typical: 'When Authority is brought into Subjection ... it portends the Consumption of the State' (no. 5). One function of the periodical press – evidently one appreciated by periodical writers – was to disseminate ideas about power. The author of *The Hermit* suggests his frustration with this endless debate: 'In Politicks every Man ... will go by his own Schemes; The World must be govern'd, but not Two out of Ten can agree in the Method' (no. 23). These journalists understood the ways in which 'public discourse operated to legitimize or undermine authority and allegiance'.[3]

The conflict between Whigs and Tories, government and opposition writers, is not only about their attitudes toward institutional authority but also about their attempts to claim journalistic authority. The conflict

---

[2] 'Vindication' prefaced to vol. 1 of the collected *Observator*s; vol. 3, no. 78.
[3] Mark Knights, *Representation and Misrepresentation in Later Stuart Britain: Partisanship and Political Culture* (Oxford, 2005), p. 8.

between Steele and Mr. Examiner is illustrative on this issue. Steele frequently balks at his main rival's claim to represent the government, a grievance repeated in *The Medley*: 'Another Reason against Disputing with him, is, the Excess of his Power, if you will take his own word for it. He plainly represents himself, as the sole Person into whose hands the Care of the Present M[inistr]y is committed: And his Libels came out with such an Air, that one wou'd think they were publish'd by Authority' (120). This argument is connected to the dispute about who genuinely speaks for the people. Whig critics of *The Examiner* contest his specious premise that 'the *State is Tory*'.[4] Mr. Examiner's pretence of Tory popularity is a significant part of his claim to journalistic authority: he represents traditional institutional authorities, and those presently in power enjoy the consent of the majority. He is credible because he promulgates ideals that are shared by the many. Partisans squabble over whose party is actually flourishing. In 1710, Swift dubs the Whigs the 'ruin'd Party' (p. 3),[5] an 'Impropriety of Speech' to which *The Medley* takes exception (207). *The Post Boy* mocks the Whigs' 'stinking Cause' (no. 2441). In *The Tatler* no. 195, Steele disagrees with an opponent about which party is 'Staggering' and which represents the 'better Half of the Nation' (vol. 3, pp. 50–51). The language of partisanship is in this case really 'about' who actually speaks for the majority of English subjects.

Attitudes toward the establishment and the opposition are not entirely stable either before or after Anne's death in 1714, but as we saw in Chapter 2 the parties do undergo a major reversal in the early months of Hanoverian rule. In *The Flying Post* for 1 November 1715, Ridpath took the Tories to task for their defiance of George I: 'Is it not the indisputable Prerogative of the Crown, to chuse its own Servants, or is that which was *Gospel* 4 Years ago, *Apocrypha* now?' Ridpath's query underscores the transformation: the Tories who had preached passive obedience under Anne found themselves, under her successor, adopting Whig language of critique and even resistance. Whigs like Addison, whose foundational principles included a commitment to limits on a monarch's power, became the spokespeople for loyalty and obedience. This represents a disconcerting turnaround, one that has not been sufficiently acknowledged by literary scholars.

A theme of establishment journalism after 1714 is that neutrality is no longer acceptable. If Anne's reign is dominated by (varying disingenuous, self-serving, or hypocritical) calls for moderation and party peace, in the half dozen years after her death one motif is that the people must

---

[4] *The Britain*, no. 22.
[5] In no. 24, Swift characteristically maintains that the Whigs 'have lost all Power and Love of the People' (p. 164).

be engaged. *The Freeholder* demands active participation, though with the important caveat that such participation be loyalist: 'an avow'd Indifference is Treachery to our Fellow-Subjects; and a Luke-warm Allegiance may prove as pernicious in its Consequences as Treason' (98). In *The Commentator*, Defoe (?) would distinguish:

> between *Impartiality* and *Neutrality*. It is far from being a commendable Part in any one who calls himself a *British* Subject, to be an idle Spectator at this Time of Day. Every Man has Opportunities enough, according to his Station and Abilities, to exert his Zeal; and so long as a just Government has unjust Enemies, there can be no such Thing as standing Neuter: It is in the mildest Construction, an unwarrantable Indolence; or, to term it more properly . . . a *Passive Rebellion* (18).

Those who do not defend a good administration against unfair criticism are merely '*Half subjects*' (18). In *The Censor* for 26 February 1717, the author describes 'INDIFFERENCE' at a time of 'Danger to our *Country*' as 'the most stupid and not-to-be-forgiven Crime'. By mere party quibbles a patriot may reasonably remain unmoved, 'But when the Difference lyes between the Faithful Subject and the Actual REBEL, the firm *Patriot* and the profes'd *Foe* to his Country; in short, between a *Popish* and a *Protestant* Line, then to be Indifferent is to be justly suspected to be *Guilty*'.

The press worried about political power, and about its own power, but how much power it had has proven a difficult question to answer. Jeremy Black rightly notes that the precise relationship between the press and politics needs more attention, but he has little answer to offer for the pre-1720 period.[6] J. A. Downie's *Robert Harley and the Press* is devoted to political literature more broadly, not only to periodicals, but he does as much as any scholar to demonstrate the government's desire to control a propaganda machine – their sensitivity, in other words, to the political uses to which such a machine could be put. He reflects with surprise on the administration's failure 'to sponsor the production and distribution of propaganda to ensure an electoral victory' in the 1708 general election. One 'illustration of the importance of extra-parliamentary opinion to the opposition propaganda campaign', for example, 'was supplied by the debates on the question of the invasion of Scotland in March 1708'.[7] In the periodical press, writers fought to control public opinion about specific bits of policy (e.g., the

---

[6] Jeremy Black, *English Press in the Eighteenth Century* (Philadelphia, 1987), p. 113.
[7] J. A. Downie, *Robert Harley and the Press: Propaganda and Public Opinion in the Age of Swift and Defoe* (Cambridge, 1979), pp. 104, 113.

naturalisation of foreign Protestants) and other events and issues, including the Sacheverell trial, the execution of the War of the Spanish Succession, and the merits or failings of the Harley ministry's peace treaty.[8] That journalists felt the need for claims and counterclaims is abundantly clear from the enormity of the journalistic canon and the nature of what it includes.

Contemporaries agreed about the power of the press to galvanise public opinion, which is no doubt why so many of them were compelled to comment on the problems or benefits of liberty of the press. Measuring the impact of newspapers and periodicals on particular issues is difficult to do with any precision, but the cumulative cultural change fostered by the rise of a daily press is undeniable. The author of *Reasons against Restraining the Press* (Matthew Tindal?) credited not only journalism but all published commentary – in very modern terms – for representing a check on political abuses. The press acts as 'a faithful Centinel', offering 'timely warning of any approaching Danger' (14). In May 1712, *The Observer* commented on the vulnerability of the Tories, who 'stand as much in need of a Cessation of Pens, as the *French* do a Cessation of Arms' (vol. 11, no. 42). Hannah Barker's conclusion seems useful: 'newspapers . . . did not dictate to individual politicians or governments as a rule, nor could they effect policy changes on a day-to-day basis', but 'as the political elite became increasingly sensitive to the tenor of extra-parliamentary politics, on certain occasions, and particularly during periods of political crisis, the press played a decisive role in altering or promoting existing governmental policy.'[9] Given writers' awareness of the power of the press, one of their positive agendas is also essentially negative: to undermine the authority of their rivals.

In *The Commentator* no. 5, Defoe (?) signals his sensitivity to the harm that even well-meaning public writers can do to the people's perception of the government: 'All who do not write directly against the Government call themselves Friends to it', and friends who are '*Enthusiasts* in the *State*' unintentionally do damage. They 'magnify and anticipate every Act of the Government, and promise more for it, than it is able to make good' (33). The 'Commentator' meditates on the different ways in which people interact (through the press) with government. The paper calls attention to the complicated interplay between discourse and the polity, to the increasingly sophisticated way of thinking about that interplay, and to seeming instability of the government's standing vis-à-vis the populace. The daily-ness

---

[8] For an example of such influence, see Mary Ransome, 'The Press in the General Election of 1710', *The Cambridge Historical Journal* 6 (1939), pp. 209–21.

[9] Hannah Barker, *Newspapers, Politics, and English Society 1695–1855* (2000; Rpt. London and New York, 2014), p. 5.

of the press created a perception of fluidity – and perhaps fostered that reality – which must necessarily have meant that citizens appreciated their own collective power to enact change. Their twenty-first century successors use Twitter polls and town halls to make their voices heard, issue-by-issue; the origins of such daily accountability, and daily awareness of the power of public opinion, are in the early eighteenth century.

The study of early eighteenth-century journalism makes clear that news- and periodical writers were arguing not only about policy, ideology, and control of public opinion. Whigs and Tories, establishment and opposition writers, Anglicans and dissenters, had very different notions about the proper form and degree of public engagement. They were battling with each other over representational authority: who speaks for the people? But they were also offering competing ideas and models for how best to mediate between the state and the people. Defoe, Steele, Swift and their contemporaries were directly and indirectly working out their ideas about the role of journalism should be, and attempting – often on the basis of their status as an either an establishment or opposition writer – either to limit or to foster an unprecedented degree of popular political participation and enfranchisement.

The study of early eighteenth-century political journalism resonates poignantly in our own moment. We understand the value of *argumentum ad verecundiam* – the argument from authority. In a world of social media profiling, hackers, botnets, and mercenary trolls pumping out target misinformation, citizens have to be scrupulously careful as readers. And journalists have to find ways to counter alternate (specious) political realities – and to help readers distinguish between fact and perhaps plausible but entirely unsubstantiated falsehood.

Early eighteenth-century periodical journalists could not have anticipated such advanced technology of misinformation, but the problem of competing narratives and reader credulity was a reality for them. One can imagine a version of Defoe's (?) 4 January 1720 lamentation as a perfectly timely tweet: 'I Believe I may venture to affirm, that the main Foundation and Support of most of the Evils we complain of, is *False News*: So that some attempt must be made to remove the Loads of Forgery, Infamy and Absurdity which pass daily under the Name of *News*'.[10] One particularly unsettling fact is that the daily news exists only for about a minute before the cries

---

[10] *The Commentator*, no. 2 (p. 21).

of distortion begin. We might feel that our own moment is a dark one for media integrity and trustworthy reportage, but the culture of daily information has always been a culture of misinformation. Representation and misrepresentation, as Knights's study richly demonstrates, have been twinned from the get-go. The charge of prevarication and fabrication is, of course, all about challenging credibility – challenging authority. That contemporaries relied upon metaphors of fakery and even witchery is not surprising: they wished to convey not only the guilt of partisan charlatans but also the victimisation of a gullible populace.

Arguably the greatest challenge facing twenty-first-century inhabitants of the western world is that posed by misinformation. The chicanery of trolls, the mass-produced 'alternative truth' stories disseminated by way of bots and endorsed by some of history's most unscrupulous 'democratic' leaders – this has created a crisis. The problem is discernment: readers believe what print culture tells them to be true, provided it syncs with their own biases, without fact-checking or testing conclusions against other more reputable sources. Early eighteenth-century writers as different as Swift, Defoe, Leslie, and Steele would have concurred in being horrified by the news culture to which their own moment has, eventually, led. They could not have visualised the twenty-first-century reality – but they knew enough to be alarmed. They saw the relationship between news and trickery, between informing and manipulating. They understood the vital role that daily and weekly periodicals played in telling people what to think and how to act, and they understood that such power could and would be abused. They recognised that they were living in a time of paradigmatic change, when the daily press could mobilise a populace, for better or worse, and could not only dictate the opinions of readers but could also make those readers see themselves as relevant participants in the political world around them. Early eighteenth-century periodical writers worried profoundly about how to gain authority for themselves – and how to discredit the narratives and interpretations and counsel of their rivals – precisely because they grasped, with savvy immediacy, the crucial relationship between journalism and power. They perceived in the present and prognosticated for the future the tremendous importance of daily news – in determining policy, driving election results, informing and engaging citizens, and, ultimately, shaping the course of local and global history.

Appendix
London Political Newspapers and Periodicals, 1695–1720: A Tabular Representation

This table includes the titles of London political papers circulating between 1695 and 1720 that I have been able to find. I have not listed all of the exclusively literary or diverting papers, of which there are many. I have included significant provincial papers in the list, *sans* characterisations, just to give some indication of that activity, though my primary concern here is with the London periodicals. The provincial press is the subject of G. A. Cranfield's *The Development of the Provincial Newspaper* (Oxford University Press, 1962) and C. Y. Ferdinand's *Benjamin Collins and the Provincial Newspaper Trade in the Eighteenth Century* (Clarendon Press, 1997). Irish and Scottish titles are not listed here.

For several of these titles, either few or no extant issues are to be found, in which case there is obviously very little information to be provided. Even if no issues survive, however, we do need to be aware that such journals existed. Column 1 lists electronic sources where available; the key is given below. Papers available from *Eighteenth-Century Collections Online* tend to be reprinted collected volumes. The number of issues available at that location are given in parentheses only where the number is less than 50. In some cases, of course, there are copies in multiple research archives; the location information given here is not exhaustive. I have included only the most significant instances of title changes. Columns 3 and 4 give commencement and termination dates where known. Where price is given (column 5), that information comes from issues of the paper in question unless otherwise stated. Column 6 gives frequency of publication: annual, monthly, weekly (1x), biweekly (2x), triweekly (3x), or daily (6x). Where two frequencies are given (e.g., 2x/3x), that indicates that a paper's publication schedule shifted at some point during its run. Contributors are named where known (column 7), sometimes tentatively (?), as in the case of some of the Defoe attributions. Column 8 provides printers, publishers, and/or booksellers where known; 'various' indicates that these figures changed several times across the life of the paper. The final column offers a very brief characterisation of content and ideology, based on the runs I have been able to survey.

In addition to relying upon the papers themselves, and upon the notes and introductions provided by modern editors, I have drawn from the headnotes available in the Digital Burney collection – though the reader should be wary of some of the authorial attributions supplied there. Other sources include the following, whose full publication information is given in the book's bibliography:

A Graphical Directory of English Newspapers and Periodicals, 1702–1714, ed. W. R. and V. B. McLeod, which includes a 'Chronological Index of Extant Newspapers and Periodicals.'

Census of British Newspapers and Periodicals, 1620–1800, compiled by R. S. Crane, F. B. Kaye, and M. E. Prior, which gives information about archival locations of copies of newspapers.

William Bragg Ewald, *The Newsmen of Queen*, which includes a non-exhaustive 'Descriptive List of Periodicals' (Appendix).

James Sutherland, *The Restoration Newspaper*, which ends with a list of 'The more important London newspapers' (1660–1720).

British Newspapers and Periodicals 1632–1800 ('A Descriptive Catalogue of a Collection at The University of Texas'), compiled by Powell Stewart.

NCBEL: New Cambridge Bibliography of English Literature, Vol. 2: *1660–1800*, ed. George Watson, which in most cases supplies all continuation titles.

Katherine Kirtley Weed and Richmond Pugh Bond's 'Studies of British Newspapers and Periodicals from their Beginning to 1800', a special book-length issue of *Studies in Philology*, which offers a bibliography of studies of newspapers through 1946.

Some titles derive from John Griffith Ames, *The English Literary Periodical of Morals and Manners*. Where Ames is the only source of title, no other information is available and no copies have been found.

Key

B = Digital Burney database (a Gale-Cengage database)
ECCO = Eighteenth-Century Collections Online (a Gale-Cengage database)
ECJ = Eighteenth-Century Journals online (an Adam Matthew collection)
NA = Newspaper Archive, available with a subscription at: https://newspaperarchive.com/uk/
1x = appearing weekly
2x = appearing biweekly
3x = appearing triweekly
6x = appearing daily

Appendix 260

Online Sources	Title	Start	End	Price	Frequency	Contributors/ Editors	Printers/ Publishers	Characterisation
ECCO (5)	The Annals of King George	1716	1721		annual		A. Bell; W. Taylor; J. Baker; et al.	Whig; vs. Tories, vs. Anne's last ministry; government line on topical events
ECJ (14 of 15)	The Anti-Theatre[1]	15 Feb 1720	4 Apr 1720		2x	'John Falstaffe'	W. Boreham	vs. Steele's The Theatre (Steele mocks it, p. 65)
B (27)	Athenian News: or Dunton's Oracle	7 Mar 1710	16 Sept 1710		2x	John Dunton	T. Darrack; sold by J. Morphew	in the tradition of The Athenian Mercury
B (10)	The Athenian Mercury[2]	17 Mar 1691	14 June 1697		2x	John Dunton		Q&A format; 1st periodical to claim that a club of editors was behind it; wide-ranging, but primarily socio-cultural
	Bristol Post-Boy[3]	1702?	1712?		1x	Wm. Bonny		[no copies consulted]
B (35)	The Britain	6 Jan 1713	≥13 May 1713	3 half-pence	2x		J. Pemberton; sold by A. Baldwin, J. Baker	moderate Whig; vs. the Examiner; popularising Harley's plan for Anglo-Dutch alliance[4]

[1] After the 4 April 1720 issue, this paper 'continued for eleven numbers under the title which Steele himself had used, *The Theatre* (reprinted in photographic facsimile by the Augustan Reprint Society [Los Angeles, 1948], with an introduction by John Loftis)' (Steele, *The Theatre*, p. 134).
[2] This paper began as *The Athenian Gazette or Casuistical Mercury*, but after protest from *The London Gazette* it changed its title (as of no. 2) to *The Athenian Mercury* (Burney).
[3] Succeeded by *Sam Farley's Bristol Post-Man* in 1713.
[4] David Harrison Stevens, *Party Politics and English Journalism 1702–1742* (1916; Rpt. New York, 1967), p. 71.

	Title	Start	End	Frequency	Price	Author	Publisher	Notes
	Britain's Genius: or the weekly correspondent	5 Feb 1719	9 Apr 1719	1x				[no copies consulted]
B (387)	The British Apollo	13 Feb 1708	11 May 1711	2x/3x		Marshall Smith; A. Hill; Garth? Arbuthnot? Gay?	J. Mayo	Whiggish; not topical; foreign news and a mix of other non-political stuff; in tradition of The Athenian Mercury
	The British Merchant	7 Aug 1713	30 July 1714	2x	3 halfpence	Henry Martin	A. Baldwin	Whig; designed to combat Defoe's Mercator
B (414)	The British Mercury by Jan 1715: British Weekly Mercury	27 Mar 1710	≥ May 1716	3x/1x		Aaron Hill; Stephen Whatley; et al.	H. Meere	miscellany; published by London insurance company; does little to signal partisan or ideological commitments
ECCO (2)	Cassandra (But I hope not)	1704		2 nos.		Charles Leslie	Booksellers of London	Tory; High Church; on power and authority; preaches non-resistance
B (1); ECCO	The Censor[1]	1 Jan 1717	≥ June 1717	3x	2d.	L. Theobald?	James Roberts	Addisonian moralising; Whiggish; occasionally explicitly politicised; defends Hanover and the Protestant interest

---

[1] On 11 April 1715, Lewis Theobald began writing a series of short essays ('The Censor') for *Mist's* weekly paper, done 'on the model of the *Spectator*'; these essays ran three times a week until June 1715. They were resumed on 1 January 1717 'as an independent publication running on to ninety-six numbers. When they were discontinued later in the same year, they were collected and published in three duodecimo volumes' (*Dictionary of National Biography*, vol. 56).

Appendix

Online Source	Title	Start	End	Price	Frequency	Contributors/ Editors	Printers/ Publishers	Characterisation
ECCO (1)	*Censura Temporum. The Good or Ill Tendencies of Books. . . . &c.*	Jan 1708	Mar 1710		monthly	Samuel Parker	H. Clements	Tory; renders judgments on books and other publications, evaluating their commitment to Anglican values
B	*The Charitable Mercury and Female Intelligence*	7 Apr 1716	7 Apr 1716	3 half-pence	1 no.	Eliz. Powell	Powell	vs. repressive Whig regime; Jacobite; see notes to *Orphan* and *Orphan Reviv'd*
	Chit-Chat[1]	10 Mar 1716	16 Mar 1716	3d.	1x	Steele	R. Burleigh	predominantly devoted to self-defense; chatty, gossipy [no copies consulted]
	The Church-man	29 Oct 1718	?					
B (3)	*The Church-Man's Last Shift, or, Loyalist's Weekly Journal*[2]	early June 1720?	≥ Nov 1720		1x		T. Bickerton	has a narrative component (entertainment); reports on politics (e.g., on schism and occasional conformity

---

[1] In *Steele's Periodical Journalism*.
[2] Became *The Church-Man or Loyalist's Weekly Journal* at some point; the only extant issue is dated 5 November 1720.

	Title	Start date	End date	Price	Frequency	Author	Publisher	Description
	The Commentator[1]	1 Jan 1720	16 Sept 1720		2x	Defoe?[2]	J. Roberts	Whig; defends administration and South Sea Company against Steele (Theatre) and others; complains about press; vs. Jacobitism; on trade, debtors' prison, stockjobbing
B (14) ECJ (2)	*The Controller, Being a sequel to the Examiner*	8 Oct 1714	>14 Jan 1715	2d.	1x		J. Morphew	anti-Whig; encourages defeated Tories to rally
ECCO	*The Court-Spy (in Christian's Gazette)*	spring 1713	spring 1713?		every 3 months	John Dunton	J. Baker	anti-Jacobite and anti-High Church; serves as warning to Protestants
ECCO	*The Criticks: Being Papers upon the Times*	6 Jan 1718	2 June 1718		1x	Thomas Brereton (ECCO)	W. Chetwood	Whig; pro-George I; engages with religious controversy, including the Bangorian controversy; pro-public politics
ECJ (23)	*The Daily Benefactor (becomes The Benefactor)*	2 May 1715	9 June 1715	3 halfpence	6x/3x		W. Wilkins; sold by J. Roberts	Whig; vs. divine right and Tory dogma; ideologically partisan; not a news outlet
B	*The Daily Courant*	11 Mar 1702	28 June 1735		6x	Samuel Buckley[3]	Buckley	first daily paper; Whig, increasingly so after 1714

---

1. Ed. P.N. Furbank, as volume 9 of *Religious and Didactic Writings of Daniel Defoe* (London, 2007).
2. In *A Critical Bibliography of Daniel Defoe* (London, 1998), P. N. Furbank and W. R. Owens consider this a probable attribution (though they also include it in their edition of the *Religious and Didactic Writings of Daniel Defoe*).
3. Before Buckley, the paper was very briefly edited by Elizabeth Mallet.

Appendix 264

Online Source	Title	Start	End	Price	Frequency	Contributors/Editors	Printers/Publishers	Characterisation
	The Daily Oracle [became *The Oracle*]	1 Aug 1715	Aug 1715					[no copies consulted]
B	*The Daily Post*	3 Oct 1719	14 Feb 1746		6x		H. Meere; sold by W. Boreham	Whig; Protestant; news and extensive book ads; becomes anti-govt. in the mid-1720s (B)
B (8)	*Dawks's Newsletter* [B: Dawk's]	23 June 1696[1]	22 Dec 1716	10s./ qtr;[2] 30s./yr.	3x	Ichabod Dawks	Dawks	printed to look like handwritten newsletter; 1st evening publication; reprints news from other papers in conversational style; Whig; Protestant; anti-French
	Dunton's Ghost	4 Mar 1714	Mar 1714?			Dunton		Whig; 'being the Hanoverian courant or merry observator' (NCBEL)
	Dyer's News-Letter[3]	1690?	Sept 1713		3x	John Dyer	Dyer	Tory; High Church; in 1710, follows Sacheverell's triumphal progress; covers domestic and foreign events; prints parliamentary news[4]
B (1)	*The English Courant*	25 May 1695	?		2x			[no copies consulted]

[1] *Dawks's* had existed as a scribal newsletter, but shifted to print – with its distinctive font and paper – in 1696.

[2] The quarterly price is listed on Burney, derived from no. 320; the yearly price is in a headnote printed on several but not all issues.

[3] See Henry Snyder, 'Newsletters in England, 1689–1715 With Special Reference to John Dyer – A Byway in the History of England'; in Bond and McLeod (eds.), *Newsletters to Newspapers*, pp. 3–19. Snyder focuses primarily on Dyer, 'the best-known and most influential newswriter in England during the quarter-century between the Revolution and the Hanoverian Succession' (p. 4).

[4] As Snyder points out, Dyer's parliamentary news was as full as that of any writer of the time. He reported briefly but accurately on events in both houses in each letter; often offering more information than could be had in the *Votes of the House of Commons* ('Newsletters in England', p. 12).

B (7)	*The English Examiner*	17 Feb 1715	≥ Mar 1715	2*d.*	2x		J. Roberts	pro-Holland, vs. France; vs. Harley ministry; insinuates un-patriotism of the *Examiner*
B	*The Englishman* (1st series)[1]	6 Oct 1713	15 Feb 1714[2]	2*d.*	3x	Steele	Sam. Buckley; sold by F. Burleigh	aggressively Whig; responds to the *Examiner*; opposition journal
B	*The Englishman* (2nd series)	11 July 1715	21 Nov 1715	3 half-pence	2x	Steele	R. Burleigh	establishment journal; anti-Jacobite; vs. Anne's last ministry, especially Harley and his propagandists, including Mr. Examiner
B; NA	*The English Post, giving an authentick account…*[3]	14 Oct 1700	≥ Oct 1709		3x	Nathaniel Crouch	R. Janeway; S. Bridge (?)	argues for Protestant unity; pro-dissenters; more anti-Catholic after 1702; insists on need to defeat French enemies
B (1)	*The English Spy; or the weekly Observator*	18 Aug 1699?	?		1x		Alan Banks?	1 no. consulted: anti-French; anti-Catholic; boasts of English military victories
B (1); ECJ (38)	*The Entertainer*	6 Nov 1717	27 Aug 1718	2*d.*	1x		N. Mist; T. Warner; A. Dodd; W. Heathcote	Tory; defends Church; pro-obedience, but (like most post-1714 Tories) insists on king's need to earn affections of his people

[1] Both series are collected in *The Englishman*.
[2] The lengthy final number was also issued as a pamphlet.
[3] *… with News Foreign and Domestick* (December 1700).

Appendix

Online Source	Title	Start	End	Price	Frequency	Contributors/Editors	Printers/Publishers	Characterisation
B (1)	The Evening Courant	July 1711	?				J. Baker	1 no. consulted: offers continental news; pro-Protestant succession and Hanover
B	The Evening Post	6 Sept 1709	5 Feb 1732[1]		3x	E. Berington, B. Berington	E. Berington, sold by J. Morphew	first paper to be called 'evening'; Whig; focuses on war and the French; insists on England's demands to the Allies
B (2)	The Evening Post, With the Historical Account[2]	Aug 1706	?				J. Morphew	
	The Evening Weekly Packet[3]	early 1716?	10 Mar 1716		1x		J. Roberts	[no copies consulted]
B (265); NA[4]	The Examiner	3 Aug 1710	23 July 1714[5]		1x	Prior, King, Atterbury, St. John, *et al.*; Swift; Manley; Oldisworth	J. Roberts, J. Morphew	vehemently high Tory; defends ministerial change of 1710; pro-peace, anti-Dutch, anti-Whig ideology; authoritarian

1. From 1732 to 1740, the paper ran under the title *Berington's Evening Post*.
2. Only two issues survive in Burney, nos. 3 (29 August 1706) and 5 (3 September). This paper may be an earlier version of the 1709 *English Post*, and both were printed by John Morphew. But as the Burney headnote explains, there is no evidence definitively to connect the two titles.
3. What information is given here about *The Evening Weekly Packet* derives from Paul Baines and Pat Rogers, *Edmund Curll, Bookseller* (Oxford, 2007), p. 338n42.
4. Frank Ellis's edition, *Swift vs. Mainwaring: The Examiner and The Medley* (Oxford, 1985), includes only Swift's contributions (2 Nov 1710–14 June 1711). Other issues, before and after Swift's editorship, are available on Burney.
5. The paper lapsed for roughly four months, late summer and fall of 1711; it was revived by Oldisworth on 6 December.

	Title	Start	End	Price	Freq.	Editor/Author	Printer/Publisher	Notes
	The Examiner	3 Nov 1714	11 Dec 1714	3*d.*	2x	Joseph Browne		short-lived attempt to revive old *Examiner*; savages the Whigs; defends High-Church; appeals to George to favour loyal Tories
B (4)	*The Exeter Mercury or, Weekly Intelligence*	1714	≥ 1722				Philip Bishop	derivative of London newspapers
B (1)	*Exeter Post-Boy* [*Jos. Bliss's*]	1709	?					[no copies consulted]
ECJ (111) NA	*The Female Tatler*[1]	8 July 1709	31 Mar 1710?		3x	Manley? Th. Baker?	B. Bragge	Tory; scandal-based
B (1)	*The Flying-Post and Medley*	27 July 1714	Sept 1714			Wm. Hurt; Defoe contributed	Wm. Hurt; sold by F. Burleigh	launched by Ridpath's printer after a quarrel; Defoe contributed; trenchantly Whig, against Anne's last ministry
B; NA	*The Flying Post: or, The Post-Master*	7 May 1695	25 Dec 1733	3 half-pence	3x	George Ridpath; Stephen Whatley	Ann Snowden; William Hurt; *et al.*	offers foreign news; Protestant propaganda; vs. the *Examiner*; depicts Tories as rabble-rousers; 'flagship of Whig propaganda'[2]
	The Foreign Post[3]	17 May 1697	≥31 Jan 1698?		3x			[no copies consulted]

---

1 *The Female Tatler*, ed. Fidelis Morgan (London, 1992).

2 P. B. J. Hyland, 'Liberty and Libel: Government and the Press during the Succession Crisis in Britain, 1712–1716', *The English Historical Review*, 101 (1986), 863–88, p. 868.

3 Continued as *Foreign Post: or, Historical Narrative* in October 1697.

Appendix

Online Source	Title	Start	End	Price	Frequency	Contributors/Editors	Printers/Publishers	Characterisation
	The Freeholder[1]	23 Dec 1715	29 June 1716		2x	Addison	S. Gray	calls for loyalty to Hanover; discourages popular protest; supports Septennial bill
B (1)	*The Freeholder Extraordinary*[2]	early 1717?	?	2*d.*		James Bettenham?	J. Morphew	responds to Addison's *Freeholder*?; 1 no.: revises *Freeholder* on Marcus Aurelius Antonius
	The Freeholder Extraordinary	early 1718?	?					Tory; quasi-Jacobite[3]
B (2)	*The Free-Thinker*	17 Nov 1711	≥3 Dec 1711				J. Baker	2 nos. consulted: apolitical; comprises philosophical essays
B (6); ECJ (55)	*The Free-Thinker*	24 Mar 1718	28 July 1721	2*d.*	2x	Ambrose Philips *et al.*[4]	W. Wilkins, T. Griffiths, J. Roberts (*et al.*)	Whig; religio-political; offers 'active support of the government'[5]; Lockean and Cartesian philosophy
	The Friendly Couriere	1711	?					invokes the *Tatler* throughout; lightweight; socio-moral with some news

---

1. *The Freeholder*, ed. James Leheny (Oxford, 1979).
2. The connection between this paper and the other *Freeholder Extraordinary*, if any, is not clear.
3. J. A. W. Gunn, *Beyond Liberty and Property: The Process of Self-Recognition in Eighteenth-Century Political Thought* (Kingston and Montreal, 1983), p. 143.
4. Other writers include (Bishop) Gilbert Burnet, Hugh Boulter (later Archbishop of Armagh), James Heywood, Zachary Pearce (later Bishop of Rochester), Leonard Welsted, Henry Stephens, and Richard West (later Lord Chancellor of Ireland); Nicholas Joost, 'The Authorship of the *Free-Thinker*', in Bond (ed.), *Studies in the Early English Periodical*, pp. 105–34, p. 106
5. Joost, 'The Authorship of the *Free-Thinker*', p. 106.

	The Gazette a-la-mode; or Tom Brown's Ghost	spring 1709			[no copies consulted]
ECCO (2)	*The General History of Trade*	Aug 1713	Sept 1713	monthly	6d.	Defoe involved?	J. Baker	gave way to Defoe's *Mercator*; defends Treaty of Commerce
B (2)	*The General Post; Apr 1716: Evening General Post*	July 1711	≥ 6 Dec 1716	3x			S. Popping	2 nos. consulted: claims non-partisanship and apoliticality; includes continental news and bland domestic reportage
B (33)	*The General Remark on Trade*	fall 1705?	≥Dec 1708	3x		Charles Povey	Matthew Jenour	offers trade, commerce, and shipping news; 'Perhaps the most famous of the early-eighteenth-century business advertisers'[1]
	The Generous Advertiser	early 1707?	≥ Apr 1707	2x				4K copies 'given away free "each day"'[2]
	Great Britain's Weekly Pacquet	23 June 1716	≥fall 1716	1x				[no copies consulted]

---

[1] James Raven, *Publishing Business in Eighteenth-Century England* (Woodbridge, 2014), p. 120.

[2] William Bragg Ewald, Jr, *The Newsmen of Queen Anne* (Oxford, 1956), p. 226.

Appendix 270

Online Source	Title	Start	End	Price	Frequency	Contributors/ Editors	Printers/ Publishers	Characterisation
	The Grouler; or, Diogenes Robb'd of his Tub	27 Jan 1711	≥15 Feb 1711		3x		S. Popping	whimsical; too small a sample to determine whether it has any ideological thrust
B (2)	*The Grumbler*	<28 Feb 1715	July 1715	3d.	2x	Th. Burnet[1]	W. Wilkins; R. Burleigh; J. Graves (*et al.*)	2 nos. consulted: pro-government; Whig; vs. the Harley ministry; prints abstract of 'Committee of Secrecy' report against Harley *et al.*
B	*The Guardian*[2]	12 Mar 1713	1 Oct 1713		6x	Steele and Addison	J. Tonson for A. Baldwin	Whig; only partly political; vs. the *Examiner*; discusses ethics of leadership, patriotism, public spirit
ECCO (3)	*A Help to History; or, A Short memorial...*	Sept 1709	1714	2d.	every 3 months		J. Morphew; T. Osborne; S. Butler; W. Lewis	moderate; catalogues events 'Which may be useful either in Conversation . . . or History' (TP)
	Heraclitus Ridens	1703	1704		2x	Wm. Pittis[3]		Tory [no copies consulted]

[1] David Nichol Smith (ed.), *The Letters of Thomas Burnet to George Duckett, 1712–1722* (Oxford, 1914), p. 92.
[2] *The Guardian*, ed. John Calhoun Stephens (Lexington, KY,1982).
[3] See Theodore F. M. Newton, 'William Pittis and Queen Anne Journalism (II)', *Modern Philology*, 33 (1936), 279–302, p. 279. Gunn suggests that Leslie contributed as well (*Beyond Liberty and Property*, 143).

	Title	Date	Date	Price	Freq.	Publisher	Description
	Heraclitus Ridens	13 Mar 1717				W. Boreham	absolutist, authoritarian, Jacobite[1]
B (30); NA	*The Hermit. Or, A View of the World, by a Person retir'd from it*	4 Aug 1711	23 Feb 1712		1x	J. Morphew	Tory preachment; pro-obedience; vs. Whigs; covers 'religious and ethical topics' (B)
ECCO (1714–15)	*The High-German Doctor*	30 Apr 1714	1717[2]	2*d.*	2x	Philip Horneck	Whig; criticizes Harley, St. John, Swift and others of Anne's last ministry
	The Historian	1712					[no copies consulted]
B (12)	*The Historical Account of the Publick Transactions in Christendom*[3]	11 Aug 1694	≥ Sept 1694		1x/2x	Richard Baldwin	bland; criticizes France and other safe targets; reports on military campaigns in Europe
	The Historical Journal	3 Feb 1697	?				[no copies consulted]

---

[1] See Gunn, *Beyond Liberty and Property*, p. 143.

[2] See Stevens on authorship and on the fact that Horneck likely carried the paper into 1717 (*Party Politics and English Journalism*, p. 112). As Stevens points out, this paper won Horneck 'a five hundred pound place in government service'; it was opposed by the Tory *Entertainer*.

[3] Initially appeared as *An Account of the Publick Transactions in Christendom*; it was incorporated with *The Post Boy* in spring 1695; James Sutherland, *The Restoration Newspaper and its Development* (Cambridge, 1986), p. 252.

Appendix 272

Online Source	Title	Start	End	Price	Frequency	Contributors/Editors	Printers/Publishers	Characterisation
ECCO	The Historical Register, Containing an Impartial Relation of all Transactions…	1717	1738	4s./5s.	annual		H. Meere, C. Meere; et al.	'Publish'd at the Expense of the Sun Fire-Office'
B (1); ECJ (23)	The Honest Gentleman	5 Nov 1718	22 Apr 1719	2d.	1x		J. Peele; sold by J. Roberts	Whig; loyal to George I; urges Protestant unity; dull, but perhaps attempting to diminish tension among Whigs
	The Idler	23 June 1714	28 July 1714?[1]			Th. O'Brien		[no copies consulted]
B (53); ECCO	The Independent Whig	20 Jan 1720	≥ 4 Jan 1721	2d.	1x	John Trenchard; Th. Gordon	J. Roberts; J. Peele	Whig; fiercely anticlerical; dissenting Protestant perspective; concerned about Church authority; supports Hoadly in Bangorian Controversy; defends primitive Christianity
B (13)	Intelligence Domestick and Foreign[2]	14 May 1695			2x	Benjamin Harris	Harris	Protestant; joins the battle between 'laws and liberties' and popery; supports William
B (8)	The Jesuite, with Political Reflections….	8 Aug 1719	≥ Oct 1719	3 half-pence	1x		T. Bickerton	moderate Tory; includes news about Great Northern War; criticizes George I

[1] J. A. Downie points out that only three issues are extant, numbered 1, 4, and 5; 'Periodicals and Politics in the Reign of Queen Anne', in Robin Myers and Michael Harris (eds.), *Serials and their Readers 1620–1914* (New Castle, 1993), 45–61, p. 46.

[2] With no. 8, Harris added 'with the Flying Post-Boy from the Camp in Flanders' to the title.

	Jones's Evening News Letter	29 Oct 1716	Nov 1716?	3x			[no copies consulted]
	The Kentish Post	1717	?				[no copies consulted]
ECJ (40)	The Lay Monk[1]	16 Nov 1713	15 Feb 1714		Richard Blackmore and John Hughes[2]	A. Baldwin	joins the *Spectator* tradition
	Leeds Mercury	1718	?				[no copies consulted]
B (1)	Lloyd's News	1 Sept 1696?	23 Feb 1697[3]	3x	Edward Lloyd	Lloyd	prints commercial, financial, shipping news and stock prices; papers like this 'probably started in Italy in manuscript form during the fifteenth century' (B)
B	The London Gazette	7 Nov 1665[4]	still running	2x/3x	Charles Delafaye; Steele; Wm. King; Charles Ford[5]	Tonson, Tooke, Buckley (*et al.*)	1st English newspaper; 'official' paper; mildly pro-government but not very political

---

1. These papers were reprinted in a volume entitled *The Lay Monastery*.
2. At Blackmore's suggestion, Hughes invited Addison to participate in this venture, but Addison declined; George A. Aitken, *The Life of Richard Steele* (2 vols., 1889; Rpt. New York, 1968), 1:406.
3. In 1726, the paper became *Lloyd's Lists*, a shipping paper well-known among contemporaries.
4. At its inception, entitled *The Oxford Gazette*.
5. Steele edited the *Gazette* between May 1707 and 1710; King edited it in 1711–1712, and he was succeeded by Ford (1712–1714). The editor of *The Daily Courant*, Buckley, became Gazetteer in September 1714, after the accession of George I (Ewald, *Newsmen*, p. 224).

Appendix 274

Online Source	Title	Start	End	Price	Frequency	Contributors/Editors	Printers/Publishers	Characterisation
ECJ	*The London Journal*[1]	6 Aug 1719	17 Mar 1744	3 half-pence	1x	John Trenchard, Th. Gordon, *et al.*; late 1720s: James Pitt	J. Roberts, J. Peele (*et al.*)	anti-ministerial until Walpole had the government buy the paper in 1722[2]; prints Cato's letters (1720–1723)
	The London Mercury	30 Dec 1695	21 June 1697					claims to be 'published for the promoting of trade'
B (23); NA	*The London News-Letter with Foreign and Domestick Occurrences*	29 Apr 1696	≥ 22 June 1696		3x		Francis Leach	
B (175)	[Parker's] *London-News, or the Impartial Intelligencer*[3]	1719	1725			George Parker	Parker	Whiggish; prints brief reports from various European countries; includes domestic executions (and behaviour of the criminals in question)
B (2)	*The London-Post*	1715?	≥ Jan 1716		1x		S. Keimer	2 nos. consulted: includes continental news; challenges the Pretender

[1] *The London Journal* succeeded *Thursday's Journal* (nos. 1–21), and quickly became *The London Journal or the Thursday's Journal* (as of 14 May 1720).

[2] Stevens, *Party Politics and English Journalism*, pp. 113–14.

[3] Became *Parker's London News* in spring 1719. In April 1725, the paper became *Parker's Penny Post*, under which title it ran until at least August 1733 (NC-BEL).

B; NA	The London Post, With Intelligence Foreign and Domestick¹	6 June 1699	8 June 1705?		3x/1x	Benjamin Harris	Harris	initially non-partisan; by 1704–1705, challenges the High Church an supports dissenters
B (2)	The London Post; or, the Tradesman's Intelligence	31 Mar 1717	≥ 12 June 1723		3x		W. Heathcote	2 nos. consulted: prints continental news and bland domestic reportage
B	The Lover²	25 Feb 1714	27 May 1714	2$d.$³	3x	Steele	F. Burleigh	only occasionally politicised; includes critical allusions to Harley; 'in imitation of the Tatler'
	The Loyal Post; with Foreign and Inland Intelligence	23 Nov 1705	?					[no copies consulted]
	The Loyal Weekly Journal, the phoenix or Sir Roger reviv'd	5 Jan 1717?	≥26 Jan 1717	3 half pence	1x			[no copies consulted]
B (11)	The Ludlow Post-Man. Or the Weekly Journal	9 Oct 1719	≥ Mar 1720		1x		W. Park(e)s	

---

1. No. 1 is entitled *The London Slip of News*.
2. In *Steele's Periodical Journalism*.
3. See *Steele's Periodical Journalism*, p. 318.

Appendix 276

Online Source	Title	Start	End	Price	Frequency	Contributors/Editors	Printers/Publishers	Characterisation
	The Manufacturer	30 Oct 1719	9 Mar 1721		2x/1x	Defoe		discusses London weavers and trade; commissioned by the London Company of Weavers
	The Master Mercury[1]	8 Aug 1704	25 Sept 1704		approx... 2x	Defoe		overlaps briefly with the *Review*; attacks Sir George Rooke, Admiral of the Grand Fleet
B (86)	*The Medley*[2]	5 Oct 1710	summer 1712		2x/1x	Mainwaring, Oldmixon, Steele[3]	A. Baldwin; J. Baker	Whig; anti-*Examiner*; somewhat miscellaneous in focus; challenges the ministerial change (1710); challenges the High Church and Tory ideology
ECJ (2)	*The Medley*	summer 1715	≥ fall 1715		2x		R. Burleigh; B. Mills	2 nos. consulted: vs. the Pretender; challenges the Church for pulpit promotion of rebellion
	The Medley: or, Daily Tatler	21 Apr 1715	≥ 7 May 1715[4]	3 half-pence	6x	'Jeremy Quick'; ed. Oldmixon?	R. Burleigh; B. Mills	toothless and miscellaneous; includes intrigue tales, gossip, poems
B (179)	*Mercator: or, Commerce Retrieved*	26 May 1713	20 July 1714	3 half-pence	3x	Defoe	Benj. Tooke, John Barber	Tory; defends Treaty of Commerce; challenged by *British Merchant*

1 A facsimile of nine issues of *The Master Mercury* (of the original 15) was published in the Augustan Reprint Society, with an Introduction by Frank H. Ellis and Henry L. Snyder (Los Angeles, 1977).
2 Ellis's edition, *Swift vs. Mainwaring*, includes only those issues that are coterminous with Swift's editorship of *The Examiner*, so those from no. 6 (6 November 1710) to no. 38 (18 June 1711). Others are available on Burney.
3 *The Medley* of the spring and summer of 1712 was probably the work of Oldmixon alone (Ellis, Introduction, *Swift vs. Mainwaring*, p. liv, n2).
4 The 7 May 1715 issue explains that subsequently the paper will appear three times a week instead of daily; I have not found any additional issues.

Source	Title	Start	End	Price	Freq.	Author	Publisher	Notes
ECCO	*Mercurius Oxoniensis; or, the Oxford Intelligencer*	1707	1707?	6d.	annual	M.G.	Egbert Sanger	Oxford intelligencer; prints with term dates, election days, preaching schedules; almanac-style news and charts
B (50)	*Mercurius Politicus; or, an Antidote to Popular Mis-representations*	12 June 1705	≥ 4 Dec 1705		2x	James Drake; Wm. Pittis?	Tho. Hodgson; James Orme; Samuel Briscoe	Tory; vs. toleration; proclaims/defends the authority of the Church; similar to *Rehearsal*
B (1); ECCO (1); ECJ (8)	*Mercurius Politicus; being Monthly Observations On the Affairs of Great Britain*	May 1716	Dec 1720	1s.	monthly	Defoe?[1]	J. Morphew; T. Bickerton; J. Moore	rivals Boyer's *Political State of Great Britain*; anti-Hanoverian government until 1718, when the paper becomes more Whiggish
	The Moderator	16 May 1705	≥ Dec 1705?		2x		S. Malthus; B. Bragg	1 no. consulted: 'For promoting of Peace; for reconciling Differences between Parties'; challenges party papers (*Review, Rehearsal, Observator*)
	The Moderator	22 May 1710	10 Nov 1710[2]		2x		J. Morphew	moderate to high Tory; advocates passive obedience and non-resistance; vs. the *Review* and *Observator*

---

[1] See Furbank and Owens, *Critical Bibliography*, pp. xxii–xxiii.

[2] *The Moderator* terminates shortly after the launching of *The Examiner*; the author opens his final issue (no. 50) with praise of *The Examiner* for doing some of the important work that he had considered necessary.

Appendix 278

Online Source	Title	Start	End	Price	Frequency	Contributors/ Editors	Printers/ Publishers	Characterisation
B (1)	The Moderator[1]	spring 1719	spring 1719	6d.	irregular	'By a Member of Parliament'	J. Roberts	seemingly neutral on the Peerage Bill but challenges it
B (3); ECJ (4)	The Monitor	22 Apr 1714	7 Aug 1714	3 half-pence	3x	Defoe?[2]	J. Morphew	does not advance Tory ideology but challenges freedom of speech as exercised by Steele, The Flying Post, and other government critics
	A Monthly Account of the Present State of Affairs	early 1700?	?		monthly			[no copies examined]
ECCO	The Monthly Journal of the Affairs of Europe	July 1704	?	6d.	monthly		George Sawbridge; sold by John Nutt	reflects on western European, Russian, Turkish governments and courts; prints English news, but none from Scotland or Ireland
	The Monthly Register; or Memoirs of the Affairs of Europe	1703	c. 1707		monthly		Sam. Buckley	[no copies examined]

[1] This paper is different from The Moderator of 1721 (no. 16 is dated 26 May), a triweekly printed by J. Peele.
[2] Furbank and Owens regard this as a probable attribution (Critical Bibliography, no. 253).

	The Muscovite	5 May 1714	2 June 1714	2*d.*	1x	Sam. Buckley	5 nos.: Whig; vs. 'Papal Usurpation and Civil Tyranny'; defends rights of private men to reflect on church and state (no. 4)
	The Newcastle Courant	1711	1884?		3x	J. White	
	The Newcastle Gazette	1710	1712?				
	The New Observator	Jan 1701	?			Anne Baldwin	anti-French; encourages English involvement in War of Spanish Succession
B (9)	*The News Letter*	7 Jan 1716	≤ 3 Mar 1716	3 half-pence	1x	Robert Mawson	headnote signed by the Jacobite Robert Mawson; openly Jacobite; succeeds Mawson's *Weekly Journal* after its suppression; suppressed[1]
B (66)	*The New State of Europe*[2]	23 May 1701	≥ Jan 1702		3x	J. Matthews; Eliz. Mallet	Whig; includes continental news and light editorialising; Protestant; anti-France
B (1)	*The Night Post*[3]	1711	≥ Nov 1713	3 half-pence	3x	John Nutt	1 no. consulted: offers news w/o pronounced bias

---

[1] Hyland, 'Liberty and Libel', p. 876.

[2] The subtitle shifts: the 23 May 1701 issue subtitle is 'Both as to publick Transactions and Learning'; and the 20 September one is 'Or a True Account of Publick Transactions and Learning.' Both of these issues are labelled 'no. 1.'

[3] What little we know about this is listed in Snyder, 'The Circulation of Newspapers', p. 212.

Appendix 280

Online Source	Title	Start	End	Price	Frequency	Contributors/Editors	Printers/Publishers	Characterisation
B (2)	The Norwich Gazette or Loyal Packet; 1722: Norwich Gazette	c. 1706?	1749		mostly 1x			'one of the greatest of all provincial papers'[1]
	The Norwich Mercury [The Weekly Mercury]	1714	?					
	The Norwich Post	Sept 1701?	1712?			Francis Burgis		1st known provincial paper[2]
B	The Observator	1 Apr 1702	30 July 1712		1x/2x	Tutchin, Ridpath, et al.	J. How; S. Popping; Wm. Hurt	radically Whig; challenged by the Rehearsal; dialogue form; argues the (parliamentary) basis of political power; extremely pro-resistance; after 1710, challenges the Examiner and the Harley ministry
B (2)	The Observator. Being a Sequel to the Englishman	25 Feb 1715	≥4 Mar 1715		2x		J. Roberts	3 nos.: challenges Tory ideology; criticises Swift; vs. Harley ministry

---

[1] G. A. Cranfield, The Development of the Provincial Newspaper 1700–1760 (Oxford, 1962), p. 19.
[2] Cranfield, The Development of the Provincial Newspaper, p. 13.

B (5)	*The Observator* [1718]	10 Feb 1718	≥ 17 Mar 1718	2x	3 half-pence	'Humph. Medlicot'	W. Boreham	Whig; attacks disaffected Tory party; raises spectre of Jacobitism; dialogue form
	The Observator Reformed	20 Sept 1704	11 Jan 1705	1x			Booksellers of Westminster and London	dialogue between 'the *Observator* and *Heraclitus Ridens*, With a *Moderator* between them'
B (1)	*The Observator Reviv'd*	fall 1707	≥ Dec 1707					1 copy consulted: ideologically indeterminate; dialogue form
	The Occasional Paper[1]	1716	1718	monthly; 36 issues	3*d.*	multiple[2]	R. Burleigh; J. Harrison; A. Dodd; *et al.*	defends dissenters and the Low Church; advocates Protestant unity; raises suspicions about the Catholic tendencies of the High Church
B (11)	*The Old Post-Master*	23 June 1696					George Larkin	includes continental news and some trading information; no editorialising
B	*The Old Whig*	19 Mar 1719	2 Apr 1719	[2 nos.]	6*d.*	Addison	J. Roberts, A. Dodd	responds to Steele's *Plebeian*; defends the Peerage Bill

---

[1] For a discussion of this paper and the later *Old Whig*, see Andrew C. Thompson, 'Popery, Politics, and Private Judgement in Early Hanoverian Britain,' *The Historical Journal*, 45 (2002), pp. 333–56.

[2] Thompson lists Benjamin Avery, Simon Browne, Jabez Earle, John Evans, Benjamin Grosvenor, Nathaniel Lardner, Moses Lowman, and Samuel Wright ('Popery, Politics, and Private Judgement', p. 336).

Appendix 282

Online Source	Title	Start	End	Price	Frequency	Contributors/Editors	Printers/Publishers	Characterisation
B (93)	(Applebee's) Original Weekly Journal[1]	9 Oct 1714	24 Dec 1737	3 half-pence	1x	John Applebee	Applebee	rivals Mist's and Read's weeklies; includes *Tatler*-esque essays, moralising columns, criminal biographies; Tory, but more moderate and cautious than Mist's
	The Orphan	21 Mar 1716	21 Mar 1716		1 no.	Eliz. Powell[2]	Powell	anti-government; Jacobite; suppressed after 1 no.
B (20)	The Orphan Reviv'd: or, Powell's Weekly Journal	winter 1719	≥ spring 1720	3 half-pence	1x	Eliz. Powell	Powell	'less openly antagonistic' than *Orphan*; but calls for clemency toward printer accused of treason[3]
	The Paris Gazette English'd	Feb 1704?	1704–05?					[no copies consulted]
B (4); ECCO (2)	The Patrician	21 Mar 1719	11 Apr 1719	3d.	1x		J. Roberts, A. Dodd	challenges Steele's *Plebeian* on the Peerage Bill

---

[1] The paper became *Applebee's Original Weekly Journal* in July 1720.

[2] Powell was the widow of the Jacobite Edmund Powell, who died in October 1716 while in hiding after being charged with treason. As Paula McDowell explains, 'While her husband was in exile,' Elizabeth Powell launched *The Orphan*, sufficiently offensive as to get her arrested after only one issue; *The Women of Grub Street: Press, Politics, and Gender in the London Literary Marketplace 1678–1730* (Oxford, 1998), p. 75.

[3] McDowell, *The Women of Grub Street*, p. 77. As McDowell explains, Powell voiced her support for the printer John Matthews, accused of treason and executed on 6 November 1719. *The Orphan Reviv'd* 'joined in the underground popular protest already under way, which eventually made young John Matthews a favourite in-house martyr of the eighteenth-century London press. But it was not, in fact, Elizabeth Powell's Jacobite and High Church sympathies that provoked this apparent concern for John Matthews. It was her fear that she might share his fate.'

B (124)	*The Patriot*	22 Mar 1714	22 Jan 1715	2*d.*	2x/3x	John Harris	J. Roberts	Whig; vs. Tory ideology; vs. the *Examiner* and especially the *Monitor*; supports Whigs as patriots, defenders of liberty
B (38)	*Pegasus: Being an History of The most Remarkable Events*	15 June 1696	1696 (40 nos.)		3x	John Dunton	Dunton	virulently anti-Jacobite; includes news and 'Observations'; more partisan than most Williamite papers
	The Penny-Post	19 July 1715	?					[no copies consulted]
B (17)	*The Plain Dealer*	12 Apr 1712	≥2 Aug 1712	1*d.*/2*d.*	1x	'Wm Wagstaffe'	J. Morphew	Tory; solely about war, peace, and allies; says nothing about the Church or Tory ideology
B (1)	*The Plebeian*[1]	14 Mar 1719	6 Apr 1719	3*d.*/6*d.*	1x	Steele	S. Popping	written against the Peerage Bill; defends royal prerogative but esp. rights of the Commons
B (20)	*The Plymouth Weekly-Journal: or, General-Post*	early 1718?	c. 1725	3 half-pence	1x		W. Kent; Eliz. Kent	
	The Political Courier	25 Apr 1716	?					[no copies consulted]
ECCO (8)	*The Political State of Great Britain*	Jan 1711	1729	1*s.*/1*s.*6*d*	monthly	Abel Boyer	J. Baker	publishes proceedings of Parliament and reports on debates; includes abstracts of publications and trade news

---

[1] In *Tracts and Pamphlets*.

Appendix 284

Online Source	Title	Start	End	Price	Frequency	Contributors/Editors	Printers/Publishers	Characterisation
	The Political Tatler	1716	1716?			'Joshua Standfast'		[no copies consulted]
B (4)	*The Politick Spy: or the Weekly Reflections on the... Present Dangers of Christendom*	30 July 1701	Aug 1701		1x	Anne Baldwin	A. Baldwin	4 nos. consulted: Protestant Whig; reflects on the war against France
B; NA	*The Post Boy*[1]	14 May 1695	30 Sept 1728	1718: 3 half-pence	3x	Roper, Boyer, et al.	B. Beardwell; L. Beardwell	leading Tory paper; rivals the Whig *Flying Post*; tool of St. John; includes foreign news and partisan advocacy
	The Post-Boy Junior[2]				3x			[no copies consulted]
B; NA	*The Post Man: And the Historical Account*[3]	24 Oct 1695	21 Feb 1730		3x	J. De Fonvive	Richard Baldwin; Fr. Leach; Dryden Leach	Whig; praised by Dunton and Defoe for its style, concision, quality; offers very detailed war coverage; anti-Catholic, anti-French; pro-war

[1] This paper began as *The Post-Boy Foreign and Domestick* and went through various subtitles before becoming simply *The Post Boy* in late September 1695. Between 19 Jan 1708 and at least 30 July 1712, George James edited *The Supplement* that appeared on the three days when *The Post Boy* was not published (Sutherland, *Restoration Newspaper*, p. 252). Some numbers are titled *Pax, Pax, Pax: or a Pacifick Post Boy*.

[2] Stanley Morison lists this paper as a triweekly; *The English Newspaper: Some Account of the Physical Development of Journals Printed in London between 1622 and the Present Day* (Cambridge, 1932), p. 84.

[3] *The Post Man*, a venture of Richard Baldwin's, which began in 1694 as *An Account of the Publick Transactions in Christendom*, was incorporated with the *Post-Boy* for about six months in 1695, and finally appeared as the *Post Man* on 24 October 1695; written by De Fonvive (Sutherland, *Restoration Newspaper*, p. 26). Continued as *Oedipus: or the post-man remounted* (February 1730).

	The Post-Master [Exeter]	1717	?		Andrew Brice	Brice	[no copies consulted]
B (24)	*The Post-master: or the loyal mercury* [Exeter]	summer 1720	≥ Apr 1725	1x	Andrew Brice	Brice	
ECJ (36)	*The Present State of Europe: or, The Historical and Political Monthly Mercury*	1686	1777	monthly		Henry Rhodes, John Harris, Eliz. Harris	licensed by the government
	The Protestant Medley, or Weekly Courant	17 Aug 1717	1720?				[no copies consulted]
B (3)	*The Protestant Mercury. Occurrences, Foreign and Domestick*	9 Mar 1696	Dec 1700?	3x	Ichabod Dawks	I. Dawks	3 nos. consulted: anti-Jacobite, anti-Catholic
	The Protestant Packet	21 Jan 1716	≥11 Feb 1716		Oldmixon?	J. Roberts, A. Dodd	4 extant nos.; anti-Jacobite, anti-Catholic[1]

---

[1] What information I have about this paper comes from Baines and Rogers, *Edmund Curll*. They suggest that 'Steele may have had a hand in' this short-lived periodical (p. 338n42).

Appendix 286

Online Source	Title	Start	End	Price	Frequency	Contributors/ Editors	Printers/ Publishers	Characterisation
B (41)	*The Protestant Post-Boy*	4 Sept 1711	≥ 12 July 1712		3x	Boyer[1]	S. Popping, Benj. Harris	Whig; vs. Tory ideology, anti-France, anti-Pretender; attacks Roper and Swift
	The Rambler	1712?	?					[no copies consulted]
	The Reader[2]	22 Apr 1714	10 May 1714		3x	Steele	Sam. Buckley	Whig; vs. the *Examiner* and other Tory writers; criticizes Tory propaganda and implies Jacobitism of ministerial supporters
B (17)	*The Reconciler*	30 Apr 1713	> 22 June 1713	1*d*./ 2*d*./3 half pence	3x (after 6 nos.)		Jonas Browne; sold by John Morphew	Whiggist; muddled; reflects on duty and rights of subjects
ECCO;[3] B (9); NA	*The Rehearsal*	5 Aug 1704	Mar 1709		1x/2x	Charles Leslie	Booksellers of London	High Church Tory; responds to the *Observator*; defends authority of Church (and monarchy); vs. populism, vs. right to resist; heavy-handed
	The Rehearsal Rehears'd, In a Dialogue between Bayes and Johnson	27 Sept 1706	≥ Nov 1706		1x		B. Bragge	features dialogue between Bayes (Tory) and Johnson (Whig) about the basis and nature of political power

[1] The most extensive discussion of this paper is Henry Snyde:, 'The Contributions of Abel Boyer as Whig Journalist and Writer of the *Protestant Post-Boy*, 1711–1712', in Robert B. White, Jr. (ed.), *The Dress of Words: Essays on Restoration and Eighteenth Century Literature in Honor of Richmond P. Bond* (Lawrence: University of Kansas Libraries, 1978), pp. 139–49.

[2] In Steele's *Periodical Journalism*.

[3] ECCO has volume 1, collected under the title *A View of the Times, their Principles and Practices: in the First Volume of the Rehearsals*.

	The Rehearsal Revived	22 Sep 1709	11 Nov 1709			E. Stacey [NCBEL]		[no copies consulted]
	The Re-Tatler	1709	1709?					[no copies consulted]
B	The Review[1]	19 Feb 1704	11 June 1713		1x/3x/2x	Defoe	initially, John Matthews	predominantly Whig; challenges the High Church and the French; supports war, dissent, and trade; miscellaneous in coverage
B (1)	The Rhapsody	1712?	1712?		2x			[no copies consulted]
B (5)	Robin's Last Shift: or, Weekly Remarks and Political Reflections	18 Feb 1716	spring 1716	3 half-pence	1x	George Flint	Isaac Dalton	Tory/Jacobite; challenges the Hanoverian government; pro-re-sistance against Whig tyranny; suppressed and followed by Shift Shifted and Shift's Last Shift
	Sam. Farley's Bristol Post-Man	1715?	1725?		1x			[no copies consulted]
	Sam. Farley's Exeter Post-Man	1704?	Sept 1715?		1x?			[no copies consulted]
B (1)	The Saturday's Post	29 Sept 1716	≤ Nov 1717	3 half-pence	1x		W. Charlton	1 no. consulted: includes conti-nental news and neutral domestic reportage

[1] A Review of the Affairs of France (1704–1713), ed. John McVeagh. 9 vols. in 18 books (London: Pickering & Chatto, 2003–2011). The original title was A Weekly Review of the Affairs of France: Purg'd from the Errors and Partiality of News-Writers and Petty Statesmen, of all Sides; after 7 nos., Defoe dropped 'Weekly'. In February 1705, the name changed to a Review of the Affairs of France, with Observations upon Transactions at Home; in 1707, the title became A Review of the State of the British Nation.

Appendix 288

Online Source	Title	Start	End	Price	Frequency	Contributors/ Editors	Printers/ Publishers	Characterisation
B (44)	*The Scourge*	4 Feb 1717	25 Nov 1717	2*d*.	1x	Rev. Thomas Lewis[1]	J. Morphew	high Tory; anti-dissent; defends Church of England
B (15)	*Shift Shifted*	5 May 1716	29 Sept 1716	3 half-pence	1x	George Flint	Isaac Dalton	Tory/Jacobite; anti-Hanoverian government; defends English Catholics; suppressed
B (1)	*Shift's Last Shift*	16 Feb 1717	spring? 1717		1x	George Flint		Tory/Jacobite sequel to *Robin's Last Shift* and *The Shift Shifted*; suppressed
B; NA	*The Spectator*[2]	1 Mar 1711	20 Dec 1714	1*d*./ 2*d*.	6x	Addison and Steele *et al.*	S. Buckley; sold by A. Baldwin	moralises; advocates Whig culture and Whig ideology
B (54)	*The Spectator* [1715]	3 Jan 1715	3 Aug 1715		2x	Wm. Bond		'a spurious continuation' (B)
B (1)	*The Spectator* [1716]	13 June 1716	8 Aug 1716					joins the *Spectator* tradition [no copies consulted]
ECCO (pt. 1)	*A Spy upon the Spectator*	1711	1711?				J. Morphew	Tory; criticizes the *Spectator*[3]
B	*The Stamford Mercury*	1713	1732[4]	3 half-pence	1x			
	The Stamford Post	1710	?					[no copies consulted]

1. Stevens, *Party Politics and English Journalism*, p. 112.
2. Joseph Addison and Richard Steele, *et al.*, *The Spectator*, ed. Donald F. Bond (5 vols., Oxford, 1965).
3. Charles A. Knight mentions this paper briefly in *A Political Biography of Richard Steele* (London, 2009), p. 101.
4. Succeeded (or rather put out of business by) *Howgrave's Stamford Mercury* (which ran until 1784).

	Title	Start	End	Price	Freq	Author	Publisher	Description
B (29)	*The St. James's Post*	21 Jan 1715	≥ 30 July 1722	3 half-pence	3x	Boyer?	J. Baker; S. Baker; T. Warner	1715–1716 copies consulted: Whig; vs. Tory disaffection; prints letters disapproving of Tory mob
	The St. James's Weekly Journal	7 Sept 1717	≥ 30 Nov 1717					[no copies consulted]
	The St. James's Weekly Journal: or Hanover Postman	31 Oct 1719	1720?					ministerial paper; claims to be impartial; includes news and opinion; founded during war with Spain
B; NA	*The Tatler*[1]	12 Apr 1709	2 Jan 1711		3x	Addison and Steele et al.	John Morphew	varyingly political; some news; promotes Whig culture and Whig ideology
	Tell-Tale	1710?	1710?					[no copies consulted]
B	*The Theatre*[2]	2 Jan 1720	5 April 1720	2*d.*	2x	Steele	W. Chetwood, J. Roberts, Charles Lillie	self-defense; vs. South Sea scheme; defends common man against powers-that-be; defends the theatre's independence from govt. control
	Titt for Tatt	early 1710	1710				B. Bragg	*Tatler* imitation [no copies consulted]
ECJ (16)	*The Tory Tatler*	27 Nov 1710	3 Jan 1711		3x		John Baker	Tory; socio-cultural, but mocks Whig fears about the royal prerogative

---

[1] Joseph Addison and Richard Steele, *et al.*, *The Tatler*, ed. Donald F. Bond (3 vols., Oxford: Clarendon Press, 1987).

[2] Richard Steele, *The Theatre* (1720), ed. John Loftis (Oxford, 1962).

Appendix 290

Online-Source	Title	Start	End	Price	Frequency	Contributors/Editors	Printers/Publishers	Characterisation
	Town-Talk[1]	17 Dec 1715	13 Feb 1716	3d./6d.	1x	Steele	R. Burleigh; J. Roberts, J. Graves, A. Dodd	gossipy; but vs. Pretender and the Jacobite threat; on the succession; challenges high Tory dogma
B (3)	The Useful Intelligencer. For promoting of Trade and Commerce	1711	≥ Jan 1712	free[2]	2x	John Houghton	E. Everingham. Samuel Jackson	includes commerce and shipping news; advertising sheet
B (3 for this period)	Votes of the House of Commons	30 Oct 1680[3]	present	2d. (1711)	6x[4]		Samuel Keble; Henry Clements (1711)	'a small halfsheet containing the status of bills, the king's speeches, and the kind of orders and resolutions that went into the House of Commons' journal'[5]
	The Weekly General Post	31 Mar 1716	≥2 Mar 1717					[no copies consulted]
B (166)	(Mist's) Weekly Journal, or, Saturday's Post[6]	15 Dec 1716	1728; as Fog's: 1737	3 half-pence	1x	Nathaniel Mist; Defoe (P); Charles Molloy	Mist	high-flying, tending Jacobite; popular opposition journal

[1] In Steele's Periodical Journalism.
[2] See Raven, Publishing Business, p. 120. Ewald reports that 4,000 copies were given away every day (Newsmen of Queen Anne, p. 226).
[3] 'The Votes were first published in 1680 as propaganda for the house of commons in its conflict with Charles II. They were again published in 1681.... Publication was ordered to be resumed on 23 October 1689' (Walker, 'The English Newspapers', p. 120n9)....
[4] Published daily during parliamentary sessions.
[5] C. John Sommerville, The News Revolution in England: Cultural Dynamics of Daily Information (Oxford, 1996), p. 93.
[6] The title became Mist's Weekly Journal in spring 1725; after Mist was forced to flee to France, Charles Molloy succeeded him, running the paper under the title Fog's Weekly Journal in 1728 (the latter operated by Charles Molloy).

	Title	Start date	End date	Price	Freq.	Publisher/printer	Notes
B	(Read's) Weekly Journal, or, British Gazetteer[1]	5 Feb 1715	1761	1d. / 3 half-pence	1x	James Read	Read	Whig; preaches Hanoverian loyalism; associates Toryism with Jacobitism
B (45)	[Mawson's] Weekly Journal; with Fresh Advices...[2]	Jan 1714	late Dec 1715	3 half-pence	1x	Robert Mawson	Mawson	Jacobite; vs. Hanoverian government; suppressed (followed by News Letter)
B (323)	The Weekly Packet	12 July 1712	≥ 29 July 1721		1x		H. Moore; sold by J. Graves	prints general news; arts and sciences, trade and shipping news; 1714–1715: loyalist
	The Weekly Post; or, A just account of all the principal news	1 Dec 1711			1x			[no copies consulted]
B (9); ECJ (12)	The Weekly Remarks and Political Reflections	3 Dec 1715	≥ Apr 1716	3 half-pence	1x		W. Heathcote	Tory; anti-Whig; vs. the Flying-Post; anti-dissent; prints continental news with commentary
	The Weekly Review: or the Wednesday's Post	14 Aug 1717	?		1x			[no copies consulted]

---

[1] The paper became known as *Read's Weekly Journal* in August 1730.
[2] See Sutherland, *Restoration Newspaper*, pp. 34–35.

Appendix 292

Online Source	Title	Start	End	Price	Frequency	Contributors/Editors	Printers/Publishers	Characterisation
ECCO	The Whig-Examiner[1]	14 Sept 1710	12 Oct 1710		1x	Addison and Mainwaring		Whig; vs. the *Examiner*; defends writers attacked by the *Examiner*; succeeded/replaced by *Medley*
B (1)	The Whipping-Post, At a New Session of Dyer and Terminer, For the Scriblers	summer 1705	≥ Oct 1705		1x	Wm. Pittis[2]	B. Bragg	vs. Whig papers; mistakenly attrib. to Dunton by contemporaries; 'Written in support of William Bromley's election as Speaker of the House of Commons; intemperate in tone' (B)
	The Whitehall Courant	2 May 1716	≥ 30 July 1716		3x			[no copies consulted]
B (73)	The White-hall Evening-Post	18 Sept 1718	1801		3x	Defoe contributed?	W. Boreham, B. Lintot, *et al.*	1718–1720: Hanoverian; expresses loyalty to the Whig leaders
	The York Mercury	1719						

---

[1] In *The Medleys for the Year 1711. To which are prefix'd, The Five Whig-Examiners* (London, 1712).

[2] See Newton, 'William Pittis and Queen Anne Journalism (II)', p. 279.

Bibliography

The bibliography does not list all of the newspapers and periodicals cited in this book. For a full list of titles, and information about dates and authorship (where known), see the Appendix. The only periodicals listed here are those available in a modern standard edition. In the case of Daniel Defoe, works that have been probably but not definitively attributed to him appear under his name with a 'P' beside the title.

Primary

Anon., *Arguments Relating to a Restraint upon the Press, Fully and Fairly handled in a Letter to a Bencher, from a Young Gentleman of the Temple* (London, 1712).

Anon., *An Attempt towards a Coalition of English Protestants . . . To which is added, Reasons for Restraining the Licentiousness of the Pulpit and Press* (London, 1715).

Anon., *Bouchain: in a Dialogue Between the Late Medley and the Examiner* (London, 1711). [By Francis Hare?]

Anon., *The Case of Richard Steele, Esq; being an Impartial Account of the Proceedings Against Him* (London, 1714).

Anon., *The Character of Richard St[ee]le, Esq; With some Remarks By Toby, Abel's Kinsman* (London, 1713).

Anon., *A Dialogue Between A Member of Parliament, a Divine, a Lawyer, a Freeholder, a Shopkeeper, and a Country Farmer; or, Remarks . . . upon the Liberty of the Press* (London, 1703).

Anon., *The Enigmatical Court: or, a Key to the High-German Doctor*, Part I (London, 1714).

Anon., *Essays Divine, Moral, and Political* (London, 1714).

Anon., *Hannibal not at our Gates: or, An Enquiry into the Grounds of our present Fears of Popery and the Pre[ten]der* (London, 1714).

Anon., *High-Church Aphorisms, Written by those Twin-Brothers in Scandal, the Author of the Examiner and Modest Abel* (London, 1711).

Anon., *The History and Defence of the Last Parliament* (London, 1713).

Anon., *A Letter from Will. Honeycomb to the Examiner, Occasion'd by the Revival of The Spectator* (London, 1714).

Anon., *A Letter to the Examiner, Suggesting Proper Heads For Vindicating his Masters* (London, 1714).

Anon., *A Letter to the Examiner; To which is Prefix'd, Preliminary Discourse and Preface* (London, 1715).

Anon., *A Letter to Mr. Steele, Concerning His Crisis* (Edinburgh, 1714).

Anon., *A Letter to Mr. Steele, Concerning the Removal of the Pretender from Lorrain, Occasion'd by the Crisis* (London, 1714).

Anon., *The Press Restrain'd: A Poem* (London, 1712).

Anon., *The Publick Spirit of the Tories, Manifested in the Case of the Irish Dean, and his Man Timothy* (London, 1714).

Anon., *Pulpit-Tyranny: or, Observations upon four High-Church Sermons* (London, 1710).

Anon., *Reasons against Restraining the Press* (London, 1704). [By Matthew Tindal?]

Anon., *Reasons for Laying some Restraint on the Licentiousness of the Pulpit. With A Few short Reflections on the present State of Affairs* (London, 1715).

Anon., *Reflections upon the Examiner's Scandalous Peace* (London, 1711).

Anon., *The Thoughts of a Tory Author, Concerning the Press* (London, 1712).

Anon., *Torism and Trade Can never Agree. To which is added, An Account and Character of the Mercator and his Writings* (London, 1713). [By John Oldmixon?]

Anon., *Two Letters Concerning the Author of the Examiner* (London, 1713).

Anon., *A Word to the Wise: or, Some Seasonable Cautions about Regulating the Press* (London, 1712).

Addison, Joseph, *The Freeholder*, ed. James Leheny (Oxford: Clarendon Press, 1979).

Addison, Joseph, and Richard Steele, *et al.*, *The Spectator*, ed. Donald F. Bond (5 vols., Oxford: Clarendon Press, 1965).

———. *The Tatler*, ed. Donald F. Bond (3 vols., Oxford: Clarendon Press, 1987).

Defoe, Daniel, *An Appeal to Honour and Justice* (London, 1715).

———. *A Collection of the Writings Of the Author of the True-Born English-Man* (London, 1703).

———. '*The Commentator*' (1720), in *Religious and Didactic Writings of Daniel Defoe*, vol. 9, ed. P. N. Furbank (London: Pickering & Chatto, 2007). (P)

———. *An Essay At a Plain Exposition of that Difficult Phrase A Good Peace* (London, 1711).

———. *An Essay on the Regulation of the Press* (London, 1704). (P)

———. *The Letters of Daniel Defoe*, ed. George Harris Healey (Oxford: Clarendon Press, 1955).

———. *The Master Mercury* (1704), facsimile with Introduction by Frank H. Ellis and Henry L. Snyder (Los Angeles: William Andrews Clark Memorial Library, 1977).

———. *Reasons why this Nation Ought to put a Speedy End to this Expensive War*, 2nd edn. (London, 1711). (P)

———. *A Review of the Affairs of France* (1704–1713), ed. John McVeagh. 9 vols. in 18 books (London: Pickering & Chatto, 2003–2011).

———. *The Secret History of the October Club* (London, 1711). (P)

———. *The Secret History of the White-Staff, Being An Account of Affairs under the Conduct of some late Ministers* (London, 1714).

The Diary of Dudley Ryder, 1715–1716, ed. William Matthews (London: Methuen, 1939).

Dryden, John, *Discourse Concerning the Original and Progress of Satire*, prefixed to *The Satires of Decimus Junius Juvenalis*, in *The Works of John Dryden*, ed. H. T. Swedenberg *et al.* (20 vols., Berkeley: University of California Press, 1956–2000), vol. 4.

Dunton, John, *The Life and Errors of John Dunton* (2 vols., London: J. Nichols and Son, and Bentley, 1818).

The Female Tatler, ed. Fidelis Morgan (London: J.M. Dent & Sons Ltd, 1992).

Gay, John, *The Present State of Wit, in a Letter to a Friend in the Country* (London, 1711).

Hill, Aaron, *The Plain Dealer: Being Select Essays on Several Curious Subjects* (2 vols., London, 1730).

Kennett, White, *The Wisdom of Looking Backward, To judge the Better of One Side and T'Other By the Speeches, Writings, Actions, And Matters of Fact on Both Sides* (London, 1715).

The Letters of Thomas Burnet to George Duckett, 1712–1722, ed. David Nichol Smith (Oxford: Oxford University Press, 1914).

Lloyd, Evan, *A Muzzle for a Mad Dog: or, Animadversions On some late Scandalous Papers call'd Rehearsers* (London, 1707).

Macpherson, James, *Original Papers; Containing the Secret History of Great Britain, from the Restoration to the Accession of the House of Hannover* (2 vols., London, 1775).

Mainwaring, Arthur, and John Oldmixon, *et al.*, *The Medley* (1710–1712), in *Swift vs. Mainwaring: The Examiner and The Medley*, ed. Frank H. Ellis (Oxford: Clarendon Press, 1985).

Oldisworth, William, *Annotations on the Tatler* (2 parts, London, 1710).

Oldmixon, John, *The History of England, During the Reigns of King William and Queen Mary, Queen Anne, King George I* (London, 1735).

———. *The Life and Posthumous Works of Arthur Maynwaring, Esq.* (London, 1715).

———. *Memoirs of the Press, Historical and Political, For Thirty Years past, From 1710 to 1740* (London, 1742).

Sacheverell, Henry, *The Speech of Henry Sacheverell, D.D. Upon His Impeachment at the Bar of the House of Lords in Westminster-Hall, March 7 1709/10* (London, 1710).

Steele, Richard, *An Account of the State of the Roman-Catholick Religion Throughout the World* (1715), in *Tracts and Pamphlets*.

———. *Chit-Chat* (March 1716), in *Steele's Periodical Journalism*.

———. *The Correspondence of Richard Steele*, ed. Rae Blanchard (Oxford: Clarendon Press, 1941).

———. *The Crisis: Or a Discourse Representing from the Most Authentick Records the Just Causes of the Late Happy Revolution . . . With some Seasonable Remarks on the Danger of a Popish Successor* (1714), in *Tracts and Pamphlets*.

———. *The Englishman: A Political Journal*, ed. Rae Blanchard (Oxford: Clarendon Press, 1955).

———. *The Guardian*, ed. John Calhoun Stephens (Lexington: University Press of Kentucky, 1982).

———. *The Importance of Dunkirk Consider'd* (1713), in *Tracts and Pamphlets*.

———. *Letter to Sir M[iles] W[arton] Concerning Occasional Peers* (1713), in *Tracts and Pamphlets*.

———. *The Lover* (Feb–May 1714), in *Steele's Periodical Journalism*.

———. *Mr. Steele's Apology for Himself and His Writings; Occasioned by his Expulsion from the House of Commons* (1714), in *Tracts and Pamphlets*.

———. *The Plebeian* (Mar–Apr 1719), in *Tracts and Pamphlets*.

———. *The Reader* (Apr–May 1714), in *Steele's Periodical Journalism*.

———. *Steele's Periodical Journalism, 1714–1716*, ed. Rae Blanchard (Oxford: Clarendon Press, 1959).

———. *The Theatre* (1720), ed. John Loftis (Oxford: Clarendon Press, 1962).

———. *Town-Talk* (Dec 1715–Feb 1716), in *Steele's Periodical Journalism*.

———. *Tracts and Pamphlets by Richard Steele*, ed. Rae Blanchard (1944; Rpt. New York: Octagon Books, 1967).

St John, Henry, viscount Bolingbroke, *A Letter to the Examiner* (London, 1710).

———. *Letter to Sir William Windham* (wr. 1717), in *Works*, vol. 1.

———. *The Works of Lord Bolingbroke* (4 vols., 1844; Rpt. London: Frank Cass and Company, 1967).

Swift, Jonathan, *The Conduct of the Allies, and of the Late Ministry, in Beginning and Carrying on the Present War* (1711), in *English Political Writings*, ed. Goldgar and Gadd.

———. *The Correspondence of Jonathan Swift, D. D.*, ed. David Woolley (4 vols., Frankfurt am Main: Peter Lang, 1999–2007).
———. *A Discourse of the Contests and Dissentions Between the Nobles and the Commons in Athens and Rome*, ed. Frank H. Ellis (Oxford: Clarendon Press, 1967).
———. *English Political Writings 1711–1714: The Conduct of the Allies and Other Works*, ed. Bertrand A. Goldgar and Ian Gadd (Cambridge: Cambridge University Press, 2008).
———. *The Examiner* (wr. by Swift, 1710–1711), in *Swift vs. Mainwaring: The Examiner and The Medley*, ed. Frank H. Ellis (Oxford: Clarendon Press, 1985).
———. *The History of the Four Last Years of the Queen* (wr. 1712–1713; pub. 1758), in *PW*, vol. 7.
———. *The Importance of the Guardian Considered* (1713), in *English Political Writings*, ed. Goldgar and Gadd.
———. *Journal to Stella*, ed. Abigail Williams (Cambridge: Cambridge University Press, 2013).
———. *A Letter to a Young Gentleman, Latley enter'd into Holy Orders* (1721), in *PW*, vol. 9.
———. *Memoirs, Relating to That Change which happened . . . in the Year 1710* (wr. 1714), in *PW*, vol. 8.
———. *Ode to the Athenian Society* (1692). In *The Poems of Jonathan Swift*, ed. Harold Williams, vol. 1 (3 vols., 1937; 2nd edn., Oxford: Clarendon Press, 1958).
———. *The Prose Works of Jonathan Swift*, ed. Herbert Davis *et al.* (16 vols., Oxford: Basil Blackwell, 1939–1974; various reimpressions, sometimes corrected). [*PW*]
———. *A Sermon upon the Martyrdom of K. Charles I* (1726), in *PW*, vol. 9.
———. *A Tale of a Tub* (1704), in *A Tale of a Tub and Other Works*, ed. Marcus Walsh (Cambridge: Cambridge University Press, 2010).
Toland, John, *The Second Part of the State Anatomy, &c.* (London, 1717).

Secondary

Achurch, Robert Waller, 'Richard Steele, Gazetteer and Bickerstaff', in Bond (ed.), *Studies in the Early English Periodical*, pp. 49–72.
Adburgham, Alison, *Women in Print: Writing Women and Women's Magazines from the Restoration to the Accession of Victoria* (London: Allen & Unwin, 1972).

Aitken, George A., *The Life of Richard Steele* (2 vols., 1889; Rpt. New York: Haskell House Publishers, 1968).
Ames, John Griffith, *The English Literary Periodical of Morals and Manners* (Mt. Vernon, OH, 1904).
Atherton, Ian, 'The Press and Popular Political Opinion', in Barry Coward (ed.), *A Companion to Stuart Britain* (Malden, MA: Blackwell, 2003), pp. 88–110.
Baines, Paul, and Pat Rogers, *Edmund Curll, Bookseller* (Oxford: Clarendon, 2007).
Barker, Hannah, *Newspapers, Politics, and English Society 1695–1855* (2000; Rpt. London and New York: Routledge, 2014).
Berry, Helen, *Gender, Society and Print Culture in Late-Stuart England: The Cultural World of the Athenian Mercury* (Burlington, VT: Ashgate, 2003).
Black, Jeremy, 'The British Press and Europe in the Early Eighteenth Century', in Harris and Lee (eds.), *The Press in English Society from the Seventeenth to Nineteenth Centuries*, pp. 64–79.
———. *The English Press in the Eighteenth Century* (Philadelphia: University of Pennsylvania Press, 1987).
Black, Scott, *Of Essays and Reading in Early Modern Britain* (Houndmills: Palgrave Macmillan, 2006).
Bloom, Edward A. and Lillian D. Bloom, *Joseph Addison's Sociable Animal: In the Market Place, on the Hustings, in the Pulpit* (Providence: Brown University Press, 1971).
Bond, Donovan H., and W. Reynolds McLeod, *Newsletters to Newspapers: Eighteenth-Century Journalism* (Morgantown: West Virginia School of Journalism, 1977).
Bond, Richmond P., ed., *Studies in the Early English Periodical* (Chapel Hill: University of North Carolina Press, 1957).
———. *The Tatler: The Making of a Literary Journal* (Cambridge, MA: Harvard University Press, 1971).
Bowers, Terence, 'Universalizing Sociability: *The Spectator*, Civic Enfranchisement, and the Rule(s) of the Public Sphere', in Newman (ed.), *The Spectator: Emerging Discourses*, pp. 150–74.
Bowers, Toni, *Force or Fraud: British Seduction Stories and the Problem of Resistance, 1660–1770* (Oxford: Oxford University Press, 2011).
Bowie, Karin, *Scottish Public Opinion and the Anglo-Scottish Union, 1699–1707* (Woodbridge: The Boydell Press, 2007).
Brewer, John, *The Sinews of Power: War, Money and the English State, 1688–1783* (New York: Alfred A. Knopf, 1988).
Bucknell, Clare, 'The Roman Adversarial Dialogue in Eighteenth-Century Political Satire', *Translation and Literature*, 24 (2015), pp. 291–318.

Bullard, Rebecca, and Rachel Carnell, eds., *The Secret History in Literature, 1660–1820* (Cambridge: Cambridge University Press, 2017).

Carnell, Rachel, *Partisan Politics, Narrative Realism, and the Rise of the British Novel* (New York: Palgrave Macmillan, 2006).

Caudle, James. 'Preaching in Parliament: Patronage, Publicity and Politics in Britain, 1701–1760', in Ferrell and McCullough (eds.), *The English Sermon Revised*, pp. 235–63.

Champion, Justin, 'Some Forms of Religious Liberty: Ecclesiology and Religious Freedom in Early Modern England', in Eliane Glaser (ed.), *Religious Tolerance in the Atlantic World: Early Modern and Contemporary Perspectives* (London: Palgrave Macmillan, 2014), pp. 41–72.

———. '"To govern is to make subjects believe": Anticlericalism, Politics and Power, c. 1680–1717', in Nigel Aston and Matthew Cragoe (eds.), *Anticlericalism in Britain, c. 1500–1914* (Stroud, Gloucestershire: Sutton Publishing, 2000), pp. 42–66.

Claydon, Tony, 'The sermon, the "public sphere" and the political culture of late seventeenth-century England', in Ferrell and McCullough (eds.), *The English Sermon Revised*, pp. 208–34.

Colley, Linda, *In Defiance of Oligarchy: The Tory Party 1714–1760* (Cambridge: Cambridge University Press, 1982).

Cowan, Brian, 'Daniel Defoe's *Review* and the Transformations of the English Periodical', *Huntington Library Quarterly*, 77 (2014), pp. 79–110.

———. 'Mr. Spectator and the Coffeehouse Public Sphere', *Eighteenth-Century Studies*, 37 (2004), pp. 345–66.

———. *The Social Life of Coffee: The Emergence of the British Coffeehouse* (New Haven, CT: Yale University Press, 2005).

———. 'What was Masculine about the Public Sphere? Gender and the Coffeehouse Milieu in Post-Restoration England', *History Workshop Journal*, 51 (2001), pp. 127–57.

Crane, R. S., F. B. Kaye, and M. E. Prior (compilers), *A Census of British Newspapers and Periodicals, 1620–1800* (Chapel Hill: University of North Carolina Press, 1927).

Cranfield, G. A., *The Development of the Provincial Newspaper 1700–1760* (Oxford: Clarendon Press, 1962).

Crow, Thomas F., *Painters and Public Life in Eighteenth-Century Paris* (New Haven, CT: Yale University Press, 1985).

Damrosch, Leo, *Jonathan Swift: His Life and His World* (New Haven, CT: Yale University Press, 2013).

De Beer, E. S., 'The English Newspapers from 1695 to 1702', in Ragnhild Hatton and J. S. Bromley (eds.), *William III and Louis XIV: Essays 1680–1720* (University of Toronto Press, 1968), pp. 117–29.

De Krey, Gary Stuart, *A Fractured Society: The Politics of London in the First Age of Party 1688–1715* (Oxford: Clarendon Press, 1985).

Dickinson, H. T, *Bolingbroke* (London: Constable and Co., Ltd., 1970).

——. *The Politics of the People in Eighteenth-Century Britain* (London: Macmillan, 1995).

Downie, J. A., 'Daniel Defoe's *Review* and Other Political Writings in the Reign of Queen Anne' (MLitt thesis, University of Newcastle upon Tyne, 1973).

——. 'The Development of the Political Press', in Clyve Jones (ed.), *Britain in the First Age of Party 1680–1750: Essays Presented to Geoffrey Holmes* (London: The Hambledon Press, 1987), pp. 111–27.

——. 'The Growth of Government Tolerance of the Press to 1790', in Robin Myers and Michael Harris (eds.), *The Development of the English Book Trade, 1700–1899* (Oxford: Oxford Polytechnic Press, 1981).

——. 'How Useful to Eighteenth-Century English Studies is the Paradigm of the "Bourgeois Public Sphere"?', *Literature Compass*, 1 (2003), pp. 1–19.

——. 'Periodicals and Politics in the Reign of Queen Anne', in Robin Myers and Michael Harris (eds.), *Serials and their Readers 1620–1914* (New Castle: Oak Knoll Press, 1993), pp. 45–61.

——. *Robert Harley and the Press: Propaganda and Public Opinion in the Age of Swift and Defoe.* (Cambridge: Cambridge University Press, 1979).

——. 'Secret Service Payments to Daniel Defoe, 1710–1714', *The Review of English Studies*, n.s. 30 (1979), pp. 437–41.

——. 'Stating Facts Right About Defoe's *Review*', in Downie and Corns (eds.), *Telling People What To Think*, pp. 8–22.

——. 'Swift and the Oxford Ministry: New Evidence', *Swift Studies*, 1 (1986), pp. 2–8.

——. 'Swift's Politics', in Hermann J. Real and Heinz J. Vienken (eds.), *Proceedings of The First Münster Symposium on Jonathan Swift* (München: Wilhelm Fink, 1985), pp. 47–58.

——. 'The Myth of the Bourgeois Public Sphere', in Cynthia Wall (ed.), *A Concise Companion to the Restoration and Eighteenth Century* (Oxford: Blackwell, 2005), pp. 58–79.

Downie, J. A. and Thomas N. Corns, eds., *Telling People What To Think: Early Eighteenth-Century Periodicals from* The Review *to* The Rambler (London: Frank Cass, 1993).

Ehrenpreis, Irvin, *Swift: The Man, His Works, the Age* (3 vols., London: Methuen, 1962–1983).

Ellis, Frank H, 'Arthur Mainwaring as Reader of Swift's *Examiner*', *The Yearbook of English Studies*, 11 (1981), pp. 49–66.

Emden, Cecil S., *The People and the Constitution: Being a History of the Development of the People's Influence in British Government* (1933; 2nd edn. Oxford: Clarendon Press, 1956).

Ewald, William Bragg, Jr., *The Newsmen of Queen Anne* (Oxford: Basil Blackwell, 1956).

Farooq, Jennifer, *Preaching in Eighteenth-Century London* (Woodbridge: The Boydell Press, 2013).

Feather, John, 'The English Book Trade and the Law 1695–1799', *Publishing History*, 12 (1982), pp. 51–75.

Feiling, Keith, *A History of the Tory Party 1640–1714* (1924; Rpt. Oxford: Clarendon Press, 1970).

Ferdinand, C. Y., *Benjamin Collins and the Provincial Newspaper Trade in the Eighteenth Century* (Oxford: Clarendon Press, 1997).

Ferrell, Lori Anne, and Peter McCullough, eds., *The English Sermon Revised: Religion, Literature and History 1600–1750* (Manchester: Manchester University Press, 2000).

Field, Ophelia, *The Kit-Cat Club* (London and New York: Harper Perennial, 2009).

Fraser, Peter, *The Intelligence of the Secretaries of State & Their Monopoly of Licensed News 1660–1688.* (Cambridge: Cambridge University Press, 1956).

Fritz, Paul S., *The English Ministers and Jacobitism between the Rebellions of 1715 and 1745* (University of Toronto Press, 1975).

Furbank, P. N., and W. R. Owens, *A Critical Bibliography of Daniel Defoe* (London: Pickering & Chatto, 1998).

——. 'Defoe and the Sham *Flying-Post*', *Publishing History*, 43 (1998), pp. 5–15.

——. 'The Myth of Defoe as "Applebee's Man"', *The Review of English Studies*, n.s. 48 (1997), pp. 198–204.

——. *A Political Biography of Daniel Defoe* (London: Pickering & Chatto, 2006).

Gadd, Ian,'"At four shillings per year, paying one quarter in hand": Reprinting Swift's *Examiner* in Dublin, 1710–1711', in Kirsten Juhas, Hermann J. Real, and Sandra Simon, eds., *Reading Swift: Papers from The Sixth Münster Symposium on Jonathan Swift* (München: Wilhelm Fink, 2013), pp. 75–93.

Gauci, Perry, *The Politics of Trade: The Overseas Merchant in State and Society, 1660–1720* (Oxford University Press, 2001).

Gerrard, Christine, *Aaron Hill: The Muses' Projector, 1685–1750* (Oxford: Oxford University Press, 2003).

Goldie, Mark, 'Civil Religion and the English Enlightenment', in Gordon Schochet, ed., *Politics, Politeness, and Patriotism*, vol. 5 of The Folger Institute Center for the History of British Political Thought Proceedings

(Washington, D.C.: The Folger Institute, The Folger Shakespeare Library, 1993), pp. 31–46.

Graham, Walter, 'Defoe's *Review* and Steele's *Tatler* – The Question of Influence', *The Journal of English and Germanic Philology*, 33 (1934), pp. 250–54.

Gregg, Edward, *Queen Anne* (1980; 2nd edn. New Haven, CT: Yale University Press, 2001).

Gunn, J. A. W., *Beyond Liberty and Property: The Process of Self-Recognition in Eighteenth-Century Political Thought* (Kingston and Montreal: McGill-Queen's University Press, 1983).

Habermas, Jürgen, *The Structural Transformation of the Public Sphere: An Inquiry into a Category of Bourgeois Society* (1962), trans. Thomas Burger with assistance from Frederick Lawrence (Cambridge, MA: MIT Press, 1995).

Handover, P. M., *A History of the London Gazette, 1665–1965* (London: H.M.S.O., 1965).

Hanson, Laurence, *Government and the Press 1695–1763* (1936; Rpt. Oxford: Clarendon Press, 1967).

Harris, Michael, *London Newspapers in the Age of Walpole: A Study of the Origins of the Modern English Press* (Rutherford, NJ: Fairleigh Dickinson University Press, 1987).

Harris, Michael, and Alan Lee (eds.), *The Press in English Society from the Seventeenth to Nineteenth Centuries* (Rutherford, NJ: Fairleigh Dickinson University Press, 1986).

Harris, Tim, 'Understanding popular politics in Restoration Britain', in Alan Houston and Steve Pincus (eds.), *A Nation Transformed: England after the Restoration* (Cambridge: Cambridge University Press, 2001), pp. 125–53.

Heyd, Uriel, 'News Craze: Public Sphere and the Eighteenth-Century Theatrical Depiction of Newspaper Culture', *The Eighteenth Century: Theory and Interpretation*, 56 (2015), pp. 59–84.

Higgins, Ian, 'Jonathan Swift and Charles Leslie', in Paul Monod, Murray Pittock, and Daniel Szechi, eds., *Loyalty and Identity: Jacobites at Home and Abroad* (Houndmills: Palgrave Macmillan, 2010), pp. 149–66.

———. *Swift's Politics: A Study in Disaffection* (Cambridge: Cambridge University Press, 1994).

Hill, Brian W., *Robert Harley: Speaker, Secretary of State and Premier Minister* (New Haven, CT: Yale University Press, 1988).

Holmes, Geoffrey, *British Politics in the Age of Anne* (1967; Rev. edn., London: The Hambledon Press, 1987).

———. *Politics, Religion and Society in England, 1679–1742* (London: The Hambledon Press, 1986).

Hone, Joseph, *Literature and Party Politics at the Accession of Queen Anne* (Oxford: Oxford University Press, 2017).

Horsley, Lee, '*Vox Populi* in the Political Literature of 1710', *Huntington Library Quarterly*, 38 (1975), pp. 335–53.

Hyland, P. B. J., 'Liberty and Libel: Government and the Press during the Succession Crisis in Britain, 1712–1716', *The English Historical Review*, 101 (1986), pp. 863–88.

Ingrao, Charles W., *In Quest and Crisis: Emperor Joseph I and the Habsburg Monarchy* (West Lafayette, IN: Purdue University Press, 1979).

Italia, Iona, *The Rise of Literary Journalism in the Eighteenth Century: Anxious Employment* (New York: Routledge, 2005).

Joost, Nicholas, 'The Authorship of the *Free-Thinker*', in Bond (ed.), *Studies in the Early English Periodical*, pp. 105–34.

Ketcham, Michael G., *Transparent Designs: Reading, Performance, and Form in the* Spectator *Papers* (Athens: University of Georgia Press, 1985).

King, Rachael Scarborough, 'The Manuscript Newsletter and the Rise of the Newspaper, 1665–1715', *Huntington Library Quarterly*, 79 (2016), pp. 411–37.

Kishlansky, Mark, *A Monarchy Transformed: Britain 1603–1714* (London and New York: Penguin, 1996).

Klein, Lawrence E., 'Joseph Addison's Whiggism', in David Womersley (ed., with assistance from Paddy Bullard and Abigail Williams),*'Cultures of Whiggism': New Essays on English Literature and Culture in the Long Eighteenth Century* (Newark: University of Delaware Press, 2005), pp. 108–26.

Knight, Charles A., *A Political Biography of Richard Steele* (London: Pickering & Chatto, 2009).

———. '*The Spectator*'s Generalizing Discourse', in Downie and Corns (eds.), *Telling People What To Think*, pp. 44–57.

Knights, Mark, 'History and Literature in the Age of Defoe and Swift', *History Compass*, 3 (2005), pp. 1–20.

———. *Representation and Misrepresentation in Later Stuart Britain: Partisanship and Political Culture* (Oxford: Oxford University Press, 2005).

Lake, Peter, and Steve Pincus, 'Rethinking the Public Sphere in Early Modern England', *Journal of British Studies*, 45 (2006), pp. 270–92.

Lincoln, Andrew, 'War and the Culture of Politeness: The Case of *The Tatler* and *The Spectator*', *Eighteenth-Century Life*, 36 (2012), pp. 60–79.

Loveman, Kate, *Reading Fictions, 1660–1740: Deception in English Literary and Political Culture* (Aldershot: Ashgate, 2008).

Mackie, Erin Skye, 'Being Too Positive About the Public Sphere', in Newman (ed.), *The Spectator: Emerging Discourses*, pp. 81–104.

Marshall, Ashley, 'Beyond Furbank and Owens: A New Consideration of the Evidence for the "Defoe" Canon', *Studies in Bibliography*, 59 (2015), pp. 131–90.

———. '"*fuimus Torys*": Swift and Regime Change, 1714–1718', *Studies in Philology*, 112 (2015), pp. 537–74.

———. 'Steele's Rhetorical Duel with the Authors of *The Examiner*', *Swift Studies*, 34 (2019), pp. 67–89.

———. *Swift and History: Politics and the English Past* (Cambridge: Cambridge University Press, 2015).

———. 'Thinking about Satire', in Paddy Bullard (ed.), *A Handbook of Eighteenth-Century Satire* (Oxford: Oxford University Press, 2019), pp. 475–91.

Maurer, Shawn Lisa, *Proposing Men: Dialectics of Gender and Class in the Eighteenth-Century English Periodical* (Stanford: Stanford University Press, 1998).

McDowell, Paula, *The Women of Grub Street: Press, Politics, and Gender in the London Literary Marketplace 1678–1730* (Oxford: Clarendon Press, 1998).

McLeod, W. R. and V. B. McLeod, *A Graphical Dictionary of English Newspapers and Periodicals, 1702–1714* (Morgantown: West Virginia School of Journalism, 1982).

Milhous, Judith and Robert D. Hume, 'Charles Killigrew's Petition about the Master of the Revels' Power as Censor (1715)', *Theatre Notebook*, 41 (1987), pp. 74–79.

Milic, Louis T., 'Tone in Steele's "*Tatler*"', in Bond and McLeod (eds.), *Newsletters to Newspapers: Eighteenth-Century Journalism*, pp. 33–45.

Minto, William, *Daniel Defoe* (New York: Harper and Brothers, 1879).

Morison, Stanley, *The English Newspaper: Some Account of the Physical Development of Journals Printed in London between 1622 and the Present Day* (Cambridge: Cambridge University Press, 1932).

Müllenbrock, Heinz-Joachim, 'Swift as a Political Essayist: The Strained Medium', in Richard H. Rodino and Hermann J. Real (eds., with the assistance of Helgard Stöver-Leidig), *Reading Swift: Papers from The Second Münster Symposium on Jonathan Swift* (München: Wilhelm Fink, 1993), pp. 151–58.

Munter, Robert, *The History of the Irish Newspaper, 1685–1760* (Cambridge: Cambridge University Press, 1967).

Newman, Donald J., ed., *The Spectator: Emerging Discourses* (Newark: University of Delaware Press, 2005).

Newton, Theodore F. M., 'William Pittis and Queen Anne Journalism (II)', *Modern Philology*, 33 (1936), pp. 279–302.

Nokes, David, *Jonathan Swift, A Hypocrite Reversed: A Critical Biography* (1985; Rpt. Oxford: Oxford University Press, 1987).

Novak, Maximillian E., 'Daniel Defoe and *Applebee's Original Weekly Journal:* An Attempt at Re-Attribution', *Eighteenth-Century Studies*, 45 (2012), pp. 585–608.

——. *Daniel Defoe, Master of Fictions: His Life and Ideas* (Oxford: Oxford University Press, 2001).

——. 'Defoe's political and religious journalism', in John Richetti (ed.), *The Cambridge Companion to Daniel Defoe* (Cambridge: Cambridge University Press, 2008), pp. 25–44.

Oakleaf, David, *A Political Biography of Jonathan Swift* (London: Pickering & Chatto, 2008).

O'Brien, John, *Literature Incorporated: The Cultural Unconscious of the Business Corporation, 1650–1850* (Chicago: University of Chicago Press, 2016).

O'Malley, Thomas, 'Religion and the Newspaper Press, 1660–1685: A Study of the *London Gazette*', in Harris and Lee (eds.), *The Press in English Society*, pp. 25–46.

Osell, Tedra, 'Tatling Women in the Public Sphere: Rhetorical Femininity and the English Essay Periodical', *Eighteenth-Century Studies*, 38 (2005), pp. 283–300.

Parsons, Nicola, *Reading Gossip in Early Eighteenth-Century England* (Basingstoke: Palgrave Macmillan, 2009).

Paulson, Ronald, *The Beautiful, Novel, and Strange: Aesthetics and Heterodoxy* (Baltimore: The Johns Hopkins University Press, 1996).

——. *The Fictions of Satire* (Baltimore: The Johns Hopkins Press, 1967).

——. *Theme and Structure in Swift's* Tale of a Tub (New Haven, CT: Yale University Press, 1960).

Peacey, Jason, *Print and Public Politics in the English Revolution* (Cambridge: Cambridge University Press, 2013).

Pettegree, Andrew, *The Invention of the News: How the World Came to Know about Itself* (New Haven, CT: Yale University Press, 2014).

Phillipson, Nicholas, 'Politeness and Politics in the Reigns of Anne and the Early Hanoverians', in J. G. A. Pocock (ed., with assistance from Gordon J. Schochet and Lois G. Schwoerer), *The Varieties of British Political Thought, 1500–1800* (Cambridge: Cambridge University Press, 1993), pp. 211–45.

Pincus, Steve, *1688: The First Modern Revolution* (New Haven, CT: Yale University Press, 2009).

Pocock, J. G. A., *The Ancient Constitution and the Feudal Law: A Study of English Historical Thought in the Seventeenth Century* (1957; Rpt. Cambridge, MA: Harvard University Press, 1987).

Pollock, Anthony, 'Neutering Addison and Steele: Aesthetic Failure and the Spectatorial Public Sphere', *ELH*, 74 (2007), pp. 707–34.

Polly, Greg, 'A Leviathan of Letters', in Newman (ed.), *The Spectator: Emerging Discourses*, pp. 105–28.

Poston, Lawrence, III, 'Defoe and the Peace Campaign, 1710–1713: A Reconsideration', *Huntington Library Quarterly*, 27 (1963), pp. 1–20.

Powell, Manushag N., *Performing Authorship in Eighteenth-Century English Periodicals* (Lewisburg, PA: Bucknell University Press, 2012).

Price, J. M., 'A Note on the Circulation of the London Press, 1704–1714', *Bulletin of the Institute of Historical Research*, 31 (1958), pp. 215–24.

Ransome, Mary, 'The Press in the General Election of 1710', *The Cambridge Historical Journal*, 6 (1939), pp. 209–21.

Raven, James, *Publishing Business in Eighteenth-Century England* (Woodbridge: The Boydell Press, 2014).

Raymond, Joad, 'The Newspaper, Public Opinion, and the Public Sphere in the Seventeenth Century', in Raymond (ed.), *News, Newspapers, and Society in Early Modern Britain* (London: Frank Cass & Co., 1999), pp. 109–40.

Richards, James O., *Party Propaganda Under Queen Anne: The General Elections of 1702–1713* (Athens: University of Georgia Press, 1972).

Richetti, John, *The Life of Daniel Defoe* (Malden, MA: Blackwell Publishing, 2005).

Rogers, Nicholas, 'Popular Protest in Early Hanoverian London', *Past & Present*, 79 (1978), pp. 70–100.

Schonhorn, Manuel, *Defoe's Politics: Parliament, Power, Kingship, and Robinson Crusoe* (Cambridge: Cambridge University Press, 1991).

Schwoerer, Lois G., 'Liberty of the Press and Public Opinion: 1660–1695', in J. R. Jones (ed.), *Liberty Secured? Britain Before and After 1688* (Stanford: Stanford University Press, 1992), pp. 199–230.

Seager, Nicholas, '"He reviews without Fear, and acts without fainting": Defoe's Review', *Eighteenth-Century Studies*, 46 (2012), pp. 131–54.

——. '"She Will Not Be That Tyrant They Desire": Daniel Defoe and Queen Anne', in Cedric D. Reverand (ed.), *Queen Anne and the Arts* (Lewisburg, PA: Bucknell University Press, 2015), pp. 41–55.

Sherman, Stuart, *Telling Time: Clocks, Diaries, and English Diurnal Form, 1660–1785* (Chicago: University of Chicago Press, 1996).

Shevelow, Kathryn, *Women and Print Culture: The Construction of Femininity in the Early Periodical* (London: Routledge, 1989).

Shugrue, Michael, 'Applebee's Original Weekly Journal: An Index to Eighteenth-Century Taste', *The Newberry Library Bulletin*, 6 (1964), pp. 108–21.

——. 'A Study of *Applebee's Original Weekly Journal*, 1714–1731' (PhD diss.; Duke University, 1960).

Siebert, Frederick Seaton, *Freedom of the Press in England 1476–1776: The Rise and Decline of Government Controls* (Urbana: University of Illinois Press, 1952).

Smithers, Peter, *The Life of Joseph Addison* (1954; 2nd edn. Oxford: Clarendon Press, 1968).

Snyder, Henry L., 'The Circulation of Newspapers in the Reign of Queen Anne', *The Library*, 5th series 23 (1968), pp. 206–35.

———. 'The Contributions of Abel Boyer as Whig Journalist and Writer of the *Protestant Post-Boy*, 1711–1712', in Robert B. White, Jr. (ed.), *The Dress of Words: Essays on Restoration and Eighteenth-Century Literature in Honor of Richmond P. Bond* (Lawrence: University of Kansas Libraries, 1978), pp. 139–49.

———. 'A Further Note on the Circulation of Newspapers in the Reign of Queen Anne', *The Library*, 5th series 31 (1976), pp. 387–89.

———. 'Newsletters in England, 1689–1715 With Special Reference to John Dyer – A Byway in the History of England', in Bond and McLeod (eds.), *Newsletters to Newspapers*, pp. 3–19.

Sommerville, C. John, *The News Revolution in England: Cultural Dynamics of Daily Information* (Oxford: Oxford University Press, 1996).

Speck, W. A., 'The *Examiner* Examined: Swift's Tory Pamphleteering', in C. J. Rawson (ed.), *Focus: Swift* (London: Sphere, 1971), pp. 138–54.

———. 'The *Examiner* Re-Examined', in Downie and Corns (eds.), *Telling People What To Think*, pp. 34–43.

———. 'Political Propaganda in Augustan England', *Transactions of the Royal Historical Society*, 5th series 22 (1972), pp. 17–32.

———. 'Politics and the Press', in Harris and Lee (eds.), *The Press in English Society from the Seventeenth to Nineteenth Centuries*, pp. 47–63.

———. *Reluctant Revolutionaries: Englishmen and the Revolution of 1688* (Oxford: Oxford University Press, 1989).

———. *Stability and Strife: England 1714–1760* (London: Edward Arnold Ltd, 1977).

———. *Tory & Whig: The Struggle in the Constituencies, 1701–1715* (London: Macmillan, 1970).

Stevens, David Harrison, *Party Politics and English Journalism 1702–1742* (1916; Rpt. New York: Russell & Russell, 1967).

Sutherland, James, *The Restoration Newspaper and its Development* (Cambridge: Cambridge University Press, 1986).

Sutherland, James R., 'The Circulation of Newspapers and Literary Periodicals, 1700–1730', *The Library*, 4th series 15 (1934), pp. 110–24.

———. *Defoe* (Philadelphia: J.P. Lippincott Co., 1938).

Thompson, Andrew C., 'Popery, Politics, and Private Judgement in Early Hanoverian Britain', *The Historical Journal*, 45 (2002), pp. 333–56.

Walker, R. B., 'The Newspaper Press in the Reign of William III', *The Historical Journal*, 17 (1974), pp. 691–709.

Warner, Michael, *Publics and Counterpublics* (2002; Rpt. New York: Zone Books, 2010).

Weed, Katherine Kirtley and Richmond Pugh Bond, eds., *Studies of British Newspapers and Periodicals from their Beginning to 1800: A Bibliography* (Chapel Hill, 1946); special issue of *Studies in Philology* 2 (1946).

Williams, Abigail, *Poetry and the Creation of a Whig Literary Culture, 1681–1714* (Oxford: Oxford University Press, 2005).

Williams, Glyn, and John Ramsden, *Ruling Britannia: A Political History of Britain 1688–1988* (New York and London: Longman, 1990).

Wilson, Kathleen, *The Sense of the People: Politics, Culture and Imperialism in England, 1715–1785* (Cambridge: Cambridge University Press, 1995).

Winton, Calhoun, *Captain Steele: The Early Career of Richard Steele* (Baltimore: The Johns Hopkins Press, 1964).

——. *Sir Richard Steele, M.P. The Later Career* (Baltimore: The Johns Hopkins Press, 1970).

——. 'Steele and the Fall of Harley in 1714', *Philological Quarterly*, 37 (1958), pp. 440–47.

Index

Addison, Joseph   16, 46, 57–8, 62, 133, 159–60, 164, 165, 171, 189, 206, 252
   Freeholder   57, 58, 59–61, 190, 229–31, 233, 244, 253
   Old Whig   42, 63–4
   Spectator (with Steele)   22, 35–41, 166–9, 193, 199–200, 204–8, 210, 212, 216–17, 230, 243–5
   Tatler (with Steele)   35–41, 159–65, 179, 186–9, 199–200, 204–9, 216–17, 243, 245, 252
   versus Steele   6, 38, 42, 62–4, 182, 231
   Whig-Examiner (with Mainwaring)   27–8, 127, 151, 212, 235
Anne (Queen)   2–3, 13–17, 21, 26, 33, 74, 78
Applebee's Original Weekly Journal   46, 70–4
Atterbury, Francis   47, 75, 127, 213

Bolingbroke, 1st Viscount *see* St. John, Henry
Boyer, Abel   24, 26, 41, 57, 67, 98, 216, 241
   See also Post Boy

Churchill, John (1st Duke of Marlborough)   17, 22, 24, 33, 40, 123, 143, 153, 160–4, 180n, 188
Cowan, Brian   35–6, 38, 82, 62, 93, 115–16, 117, 157, 159, 166, 171, 195, 199–200, 203, 204–5

Daily Courant   21, 22–3, 40, 41, 57, 105, 160, 236
Defoe, Daniel
   Appeal to Honour and Justice   108, 122
   and Applebee's *Original Weekly Journal*   70–4
   Atalantis Major   121
   Commentator (P)   2, 9, 185, 233, 253, 254
   compared to Swift   112–17
   and *Dyer's Newsletter*   66
   Essay At a Plain Exposition of that Difficult Phrase A Good Peace   103–4
   Essay upon Publick Credit   29, 220
   Family Instructor   65
   and *The Flying-Post and Medley*   65–6, 123
   Jure Divino   72, 86
   Mercator   42, 108n
   Mercurius Politicus   55, 66–9
   and *Mist's Weekly Journal*   66, 68–70
   Old Whig and Modern Whig Revived (P)   66–7
   Reasons why this Nation Ought to put a Speedy End to this Expensive War (P)   98–9, 102–3
   Review   2, 4, 5, 7, 15, 16, 21, 33, 34, 41, 67, 69, 81–124, 139, 147, 152, 156, 158, 160, 161, 163, 186–191, 195, 199, 201, 204, 206, 218, 222–8, 233, 235, 245–6, 249, 250, 251

Robinson Crusoe 222n
Secret History of the White-Staff 120, 121–2
Shortest-Way with the Dissenters 87
and Steele 158–9, 186–91
True-Born Englishman 30
Downie, J. A. 35–6, 75–6, 81, 82, 87, 88, 90, 92, 94–5, 97, 99, 105–7, 125–6, 128, 131, 159, 166, 202–3, 253–4

elections 1, 13, 17, 45, 49, 64, 67, 74, 82–5, 89, 90n, 91, 92–3, 94, 97, 112, 137–8, 156, 214, 219, 223, 229, 249, 253

Flint, George 54, 77, 232–3
Robin's Last Shift 51, 53–4, 56, 77, 232–3
Shift Shifted 54–6, 232–3
Shift's Last Shift 56
Flying Post (Ridpath et al.) 18, 21, 24–5, 27, 30, 41, 53, 57, 65, 152, 250, 252
free press 2–3, 8–9, 45, 75, 76–7, 254
Furbank, P. N. and Owens, W. R. 65, 66, 68–72, 87, 92, 98, 103, 119, 121, 123

George I 17, 45–7, 49–51, 56–63, 65, 70–2, 74, 77–8, 228–30, 252–3
Godolphin, Sidney (1st Earl of Godolphin) 17, 39, 87, 91, 123, 126–7, 153
Gordon, Thomas 42, 51, 168, 251

Habermas, Jürgen 2, 6, 157, 199, 201–5, 212, 216, 246
Harley, Robert (1st Earl of Oxford) 4, 17, 30, 48, 58, 59, 76, 117, 204

and *Examiner* 112, 114, 117, 125–132, 140–2, 144, 146–8, 155, 156
and Defoe 65–6, 81, 82, 87–97, 99, 102, 103–5, 108, 110–14, 117–23, 186
Steele on 22n, 40, 42, 59, 153n, 163, 170, 174–6, 178–80, 186, 192, 205, 231–2, 239
and Swift 145, 149–51
Hoadly, Benjamin 23, 34, 50

Jacobitism 33, 49, 50, 61, 76, 148
criticized in the press 18, 19, 30, 32, 59, 72, 83–4, 119, 181, 228, 231, 232
papers promoting 45, 46, 51–6, 68, 77, 229, 233
See also Pretender

Knight, Charles A. 35, 158, 159, 161–2, 174–5, 194
Knights, Mark 3, 8, 200, 234, 239, 256

Leslie, Charles 7, 27, 208, 220, 223, 228, 244, 245, 249, 251, 256
Rehearsal 30–1, 33–4, 41, 86, 139, 190, 217–19, 221
Licensing Act (1695) 1, 13, 17, 18, 75, 202
London Gazette 19, 21–2, 24, 38, 39, 40, 41, 57, 157, 160, 194, 249

Mainwaring, Arthur 2, 27, 33, 74, 98, 127, 252
Medley 28–9, 42, 136–7, 147, 151, 153, 154, 155, 194, 220, 236–9,
Whig-Examiner (with Addison) 27–8, 127, 151, 212, 235
Manley, Delarivier

and *The Examiner* 125n, 127, 130, 131, 137, 142, 156, 236, 237
Marlborough, 1st Duke of *see* Churchill, John
Mist's Weekly Journal 52, 53, 61–2, 66, 68–70, 71

Observator see Ridpath, George and *see* Tutchin, John
October Club 84, 114, 120, 147–8
Oldisworth, William 30, 148–9, 170
  Annotations on the Tatler 26, 163–4, 240–2
  and *Examiner* 40, 43, 130–2, 135–7, 142–6, 148, 151–2, 155, 156, 192, 211, 213, 214, 235, 236–7, 242
Oldmixon, John 2, 27, 28, 33, 112, 127, 128, 133, 145, 151, 152, 153, 155, 220, 236
  opposition press 4, 74–7, 251–3
  under Anne 75–6, 105, 127, 138, 152, 177
  under George I 45–6, 51–6, 68–9, 252–3
  and Jacobitism 53–6
  and popular unrest 56
  suppression of 45, 51–2, 75, 76–7
Oxford, 1st Earl of *see* Harley, Robert

Paulson, Ronald 36, 37, 165
Peerage Bill (1719) 42, 63–4, 182
Post Boy 18, 21, 22, 24, 26, 29, 38, 40, 41, 52, 57, 131, 152, 164, 205, 251, 252
Post Man 18, 21, 22, 40, 41, 57, 224
Post Man and the Historical Account 24
Pretender 16, 19, 25, 27, 33, 37, 49, 53, 61, 71, 108, 122, 181, 234–5
  See also Jacobitism
Prior, Matthew 17, 47, 104, 127, 144n, 145, 213

public sphere 7, 19, 38, 166–7, 171–4, 177–8, 187, 201–2, 203, 204–13, 216, 220–2, 244–5, 246–7

Read's Weekly Journal 57, 68
Ridpath, George 24–5, 41, 57, 152, 195, 221, 250, 252
  Observator (with Tutchin) 30–4, 74–5, 97, 191, 219, 220–2, 237, 250–1
Riot Act (1715) 48, 59, 61
Roper, Abel 26–7, 131, 152
  See also Post Boy

Sacheverell, Henry 26, 39, 42, 116, 139, 162, 164, 172, 180, 205, 211
satire 36–7, 165, 169, 175, 176, 189, 190, 206
Seager, Nicholas 82, 88, 90, 110, 111, 115, 119–21
Septennial Act (1716) 45, 60, 64, 67, 229, 249
South Sea Bubble 46, 71, 121, 175, 185
Speck, W. A. 1, 14, 49, 63, 125, 128, 140
St. John, Henry (1st Viscount Bolingbroke) 3, 17, 24, 47–8, 49, 59, 104, 110, 120, 147, 149–51, 175, 178, 179, 180, 231
  and *Examiner* 114–15, 125–130, 132, 136, 138, 141–6, 149, 151, 155–6
  Letter to the Examiner 28, 140
  suppression of press 75–6
Stamp Act (1712) 4, 75–6
Steele, Richard 2, 7, 16, 30, 51, 157–60, 157–195, 204–13, 240–3
  attitude toward readers 176–7, 180–1, 189–90, 192, 208, 210–12, 213, 216
  Chit-Chat 181
  Crisis 241

criticized by his contemporaries 162, 163–4, 192, 234, 239–43
and Defoe 158–9, 186–91
Englishman (1713-14) 27, 39, 40, 42, 144, 151–2, 154–5, 171–4, 188, 193, 205, 208–12, 216, 220
Englishman (1715) 57, 59, 175, 178–81, 231–2
epistolary journalism of 187, 192–3, 210–1
vs. *Examiner* 5, 8, 27–8, 33, 42, 145, 151–2, 154–5, 192, 193, 194, 238–9, 244, 252
Guardian 40, 168–70, 188, 193, 239–40
Importance of Dunkirk Consider'd 171, 173
Letter to Sir M[iles] W[harton] Concerning Occasional Peers 171
and *The London Gazette* 22, 39, 157, 160
Lover 42, 174–8, 179
and *Medley* 28, 252
Mr. Steele's Apology for Himself and His Writings 22, 244
Plebeian 42, 63–4
Political Writings 179
on public politics 157, 164, 171–4, 187, 199–200, 206–12, 216–7, 232, 243–5
Reader 174–8, 189, 211
Romish Ecclesiastical History of Late Years 173
Spectator (with Addison) 22, 35–41, 166–8, 177, 193, 204–8, 210, 212–3, 216–17, 230, 243–4
State of the Case Between the Lord-Chamberlain . . . and the Governor of the Royal Company of Comedians 183
Tatler (with Addison) 5, 35–41, 159–65, 172–3, 179, 186–9, 204–8, 212–3, 216–17, 252
Theatre 181–6, 193
Town-Talk 61, 181
versus Addison 36, 38, 42, 62–4, 182, 231
succession (England) 15, 31, 34, 222
Defoe on 81, 84, 91, 94, 108n, 115
Examiner on 133, 134, 193, 194
Steele on 181, 188, 231
See also War of the Spanish Succession
Swift, Jonathan 7, 15, 17–8, 22, 26, 29n, 108–9, 115, 165, 231, 234–9
Argument against Abolishing Christianity 213
Conduct of the Allies 33, 104–7, 130, 143
and Defoe 15, 82, 95, 98, 104–10, 112–17, 123, 152, 226
Examiner 5, 7, 17, 25–30, 33, 35, 43, 52, 82, 83, 95, 108–9, 112–17, 123, 125–56, 161, 169–70, 176–7, 180, 187, 189, 192, 193–4, 205, 208, 213–19, 220, 229, 231, 234–40, 244–5, 251, 252–3
First Ode of the Second Book of Horace Paraphras'd 240
and Harley 145, 149–51
History of the Four Last Years of the Queen 75–6, 120
Importance of the Guardian Considered 162, 174, 213
Journal to Stella 25n, 26, 75, 130, 132, 143, 144, 147, 149, 150, 151, 152
Publick Spirit of the Whigs 131, 240, 241
on regime change 47, 49, 78, 148, 231

and Steele   5, 8, 161–2, 164–5, 7,
    167–70, 171, 173–4, 175, 176–7,
    180, 187, 189, 190, 192, 193–4,
    205, 208, 211, 213, 239, 241,
    244–5, 252–3
  Tale of a Tub   19, 175, 213

Toland, John   67
Treaty of Commerce   42, 108n, 121
Treaty of Utrecht   16, 17, 95, 96, 107,
    108, 111, 142–4, 179
Trenchard, John   42, 51, 168, 251
Tutchin, John   35, 41, 42, 191, 201,
    220–2

Observator (with Ridpath)   30–4,
    74–5, 97, 219, 220–2, 237, 250–1

Walpole, Robert   50, 53, 63, 116, 181, 185
War of the Spanish Succession   14,
    16, 17, 25, 83, 95–112, 142, 160–2
Whig split (*c.*1717)   14, 46, 49, 63–4,
    66–7, 77
William III   14, 15, 18–20, 25, 30, 101,
    103, 112, 188
Wilson, Kathleen   45, 51, 54, 56, 58,
    76, 77, 230
Winton, Calhoun   35, 64, 158, 174,
    176, 179–80, 182

www.ingramcontent.com/pod-product-compliance
Lightning Source LLC
Chambersburg PA
CBHW051600230426
43668CB00013B/1919